PRIVILEGE, ECONOMY AND STATE IN OLD REGIME FRANCE

Privilege, Economy and State in Old Regime France

Marine Insurance, War and the Atlantic Empire under Louis XIV

Lewis Wade

THE BOYDELL PRESS

© Lewis Wade 2023

Some rights reserved. Without limiting the rights under
copyright reserved above, any part of this book may be reproduced,
stored in or introduced into a retrieval system, or transmitted,
in any form or by any means (electronic, mechanical, photocopying,
recording or otherwise)

This title is available under the Open Access licence CC-BY-NC-ND

This volume is published in Open Access thanks to funding
from the European Research Council (ERC) under
the European Union's Horizon 2020 research and Innovation Programme
ERC Grant agreement No. 724544: *AveTransRisk-Average-Transaction
Costs and Risk Management during the First Globalization
(Sixteenth-Eighteenth Centuries)*

The right of Lewis Wade to be identified as
the author of this work has been asserted in accordance with
sections 77 and 78 of the Copyright, Designs and Patents Act 1988

First published 2023

The Boydell Press, Woodbridge

ISBN 978 1 83765 021 7

The Boydell Press is an imprint of Boydell & Brewer Ltd
PO Box 9, Woodbridge, Suffolk IP12 3DF, UK
and of Boydell & Brewer Inc.
668 Mt Hope Avenue, Rochester, NY 14620–2731, USA
website: www.boydellandbrewer.com

A CIP catalogue record for this book is available
from the British Library

The publisher has no responsibility for the continued existence or accuracy of URLs
for external or third-party internet websites referred to in this book, and does not
guarantee that any content on such websites is, or will remain, accurate or
appropriate

For my parents

CONTENTS

List of Illustrations — ix
Acknowledgements — xv
List of Abbreviations — xvii

Introduction — 1

PART 1: INSURANCE, PRIVILEGE AND COMMERCIAL POLICY

1. The Royal Insurance Chamber and Colbertian Commercial Policy, 1664–83 — 29
2. The Royal Insurance Company and Privilege in Post-Colbertian Commercial Policy, 1683–c. 1700 — 59
3. 'Over thirty leagues from the sea': Paris, Information Asymmetries and State Intervention — 89

PART 2: WAR, MARITIME COMMERCE AND EMPIRE

4. Underwriting in War and Peace: Fortune and Failure in the Royal Insurance Chamber, 1668–72 — 131
5. In the Absence of the State: The Royal Insurance Company, the Atlantic Empire and Neutral Shipping, 1686–98 — 167

PART 3: LAW, CONFLICT RESOLUTION AND THE ABSOLUTE MONARCHY

6. 'In the time of the *Ordonnance*': Insurance, Law and Maritime Jurisdiction — 205
7. 'Impavidum ferient': Reputation, Conflict Resolution and State Propaganda in the Royal Insurance Chamber, 1668–86 — 241

Contents

'Nec hostes nec mare terrent': Reputation, Conflict Resolution
and Privilege in the Royal Insurance Company, 1686–1701   283

Conclusion: Privilege at a Premium   309

Bibliography   325

Index   347

ILLUSTRATIONS

IMAGES

1	The Chamber's silver jetton from 1671 (source: CGB.fr, © CGB Numismatique Paris)	247
2	The Company's silver jetton, after 1686 (source: Jetons-Médailles Frédéric Boyer)	285

FIGURES

1	The insurance triangle	16
2	A timeline of the key legal texts and compilations under discussion	210
3	A comparison of the conceptualisation of average in the *Guidon* and the *Ordonnance*	228
4	The procedure for resolving insurance conflicts, as outlined in the 1681 *Ordonnance*	290
5	The Company's procedure for resolving insurance conflicts, following its letters patent from 1686	290

CHARTS

1	The amounts insured by the Chamber in the years 1668–72 in *livres*, alongside recorded and extrapolated losses	141
2	The return on capital at risk in the Chamber in the years 1668–72, in per cent, alongside the total underwritten each year for the same period, in *livres*	142

3	Gilles Mignot's underwriting in the years 1668–72, with his average return on capital at risk alongside the Chamber's average recorded return on capital at risk (in per cent)	153
4	The average premium rate (including war augmentations) of the policies signed by Gilles Mignot in the years 1668–72, alongside the average of all the Chamber's policies	153
5	Elisabeth Hélissant's underwriting in the years 1668–72, with her average return on capital at risk alongside the Chamber's average recorded return on capital at risk (in per cent)	155
6	The Company of General Farmers' mean and median subscription in the policies it signed in *livres*, as compared with the overall mean and median subscription in the Chamber's policies from 1668 to 1672	157
7	The average premium rate (including war augmentations) of the policies signed by the Company of General Farmers in the years 1668–72, alongside the average of all the Chamber's policies	157
8	The Company of General Farmers' underwriting in the years 1668–72, with its average return on capital at risk alongside the Chamber's average recorded return on capital at risk (in per cent)	158
9	Guillaume de Bie's underwriting in the years 1668–72, with his average return on capital at risk alongside the Chamber's average recorded return on capital at risk (in per cent)	159
10	The average premium rate (including war augmentations) of the policies signed by Guillaume de Bie in the years 1668–72, alongside the Chamber average	159
11	Touches in Atlantic France as a percentage of overall touches in the risks which the Company insured and/or to which it gave sea loans and as a percentage of overall touches in voyages that led to claims from the years 1687–92, compared with the raw number of claims in this period	179
12	Touches in the western Atlantic as a percentage of overall touches in the risks which the Company insured and/or to which it gave sea loans and as a percentage of overall touches in voyages that led to claims from the years 1687–92, compared with the raw number of claims in this period	179

Illustrations

13	Touches in the eastern Atlantic, western Atlantic and North Sea as a percentage of overall touches in the risks which the Company insured and/or to which it gave sea loans for the years 1689–92	184
14	Touches in the eastern Atlantic as a percentage of overall touches in the risks which the Company insured and/or to which it gave sea loans and as a percentage of overall touches in voyages that led to claims from the years 1687–92, compared with the raw number of claims in this period	188
15	Touches in the North Sea as a percentage of overall touches in the risks which the Company insured and/or to which it gave sea loans and as a percentage of overall touches in voyages that led to claims from the years 1687–92, compared with the raw number of claims in this period	193
16	Touches in the eastern Atlantic, western Atlantic and North Sea as a percentage of overall touches in voyages that led to claims from the years 1689–92	194
17	The Company's underwriting in the years 1686–93, in *livres*, alongside its claims from the years 1686–92	196

Charts 18–20 can be found in Appendix 2, at boybrew.co/wade-appendices.

TABLES

1	The members of the Chamber on Friday 8 January 1672	51
2	The members of the Company, as per the order of the Council of State of 6 June 1686	65
3	Sea loans for whaling voyages, made in 1688 by Louis and Leon Dulivier on behalf of the Company	85
4	Lagny's merchant correspondents in the seaports, as written in his first letter-book	108
5	Lagny's consular correspondents, as written in his first letter-book	111
6	The frequency of named effects being insured by the Chamber in its policies for the years 1668–72	133

7	The frequency of items being named as insured merchandise/cargo in the Chamber's insurance policies for the years 1668–72	134
8	The named locations of policyholders and intermediaries insuring in the Chamber in its policies for the period 1668–72	137
9	The amounts underwritten by the Chamber in *livres* in the years 1668–79, alongside the premiums garnered and the losses incurred, according to Boiteux	138
10	The number of policies signed by the Chamber in the years 1668–72 and the number of these without marginalia noting the insured vessel/vessels' fate	139
11	The totality of the Chamber's underwriting in the years 1668–72	140
12	The minimum, maximum and mean augmentations on policies with war augmentation clauses in the Chamber in the months November 1671–March 1672, as a percentage of the original premium	146
13	The mean premium rate on the Chamber's policies (calculated both with and without war augmentations factored in) in the years 1668–72	147
14	The Chamber's fourteen largest policies which resulted in total loss in 1672	148
15	The number of policies signed in the Chamber each month in 1672 for voyages touching Newfoundland, Placentia or Cape Chapeau Rouge	150
16	The number of reinsurance policies signed by the Chamber, and the total amounts reinsured, in the years 1668–72	151
17	The tax farmers of the united farms, 1 October 1668–30 September 1674	156
18	The mean, median, minimum and maximum ROCAR rates (as an average of each underwriter's minimum and maximum ROCAR rate) of the three underwriting groups in 1672, and the standard deviation of these rates	161
19	The individuals who signed policies/sea loans with the Company on more than fifty separate risks in the years 1686–98	170

20	The frequency of multiple policies and/or sea loans on a single risk, based on the Company's insurance and sea loans practices from 1686 to 1700	171
21	The frequency of specific types of contract being taken out on a single risk (whether in single or in multiple), based on the Company's insurance and sea loans practices from 1686 to 1700	172
22	The amounts underwritten by the Company and the number of policies it signed, alongside the largest, smallest, median, mode and mean policy in the years 1686–98, in *livres*	173
23	The amounts given by the Company as sea loans and the number of such loans it gave, alongside the largest, smallest, median, mode and mean loan in the years 1686–94, in *livres*	174
24	The frequency of Atlantic ports being touched (or potentially being touched) in the course of risks which the Company insured and/or to which it gave sea loans, for given periods between 1686 and 1689	176
25	The number of policies signed, and the amounts underwritten, by the Company in the years 1686–89, alongside the number of claims in those years	177
26	The frequency of places on the island of Ireland being touched in the course of risks which the Company insured and/or to which it gave sea loans, for the years 1686–93	186
27	The frequency of places on the island of Ireland being touched in the voyages described in the Company's claims, for the years 1690–92	187
28	The number of policies signed, and the amounts underwritten (in *livres*), by the Company in the years 1686–93, alongside the number of claims in the years 1686–92	195
29	Types of statement made about external insurance and/or loans in declarations of abandonment to the Company	234
30	The number of declarations of average and abandonment in the years 1686–92	236
31	The frequency of arbitration cases in the years 1670–72	252
32	The frequency of arbitration cases in the years 1670–74	257

33	Insurance cases brought by policyholders against the Chamber's underwriters before the *table de marbre* of the seat of the admiralty of France in Paris in 1673	259
34	The frequency of arbitration cases in the years 1687–1700	291
35	The amounts underwritten by the Company in the years 1686–92 (in *livres*), the number of policies/loans it offered, the frequency of claims in these years, the frequency of such claims leading to arbitration proceedings, the frequency of such claims leading to admiralty cases, and the frequency of such claims leading to arbitration proceedings and/or admiralty cases	302

Tables 36–42 can be found in Appendix 1 and tables 43–46 can be found in Appendix 2, both online at boybrew.co/wade-appendices.

The author and publisher are grateful to all the institutions and individuals listed for permission to reproduce the materials in which they hold copyright. Every effort has been made to trace the copyright holders; apologies are offered for any omission, and the publisher will be pleased to add any necessary acknowledgement in subsequent editions.

ACKNOWLEDGEMENTS

The research for this book was conducted thanks to funding from the European Research Council: ERC Grant agreement No. 724544: AveTransRisk – Average – Transaction Costs and Risk Management during the First Globalization (Sixteenth–Eighteenth Centuries). This Grant also supplied the funds for the Open Access publication of this book. I finished the book during my tenure as Postan Fellow at the Institute of Historical Research, for which I am most grateful to both the Institute and the Economic History Society.

That this book has materialised at all is due to the truly brilliant people around me who have been so generous to me with their time, energy and thoughts. First, I am grateful to the entire team in the AveTransRisk project, within which I conducted my research. I am grateful to Ian Wellaway for his efforts in designing the project database based on my needs (and those of my colleagues on the team) and working with me to facilitate data analysis for Chapters 4 and 5.

The institutional support I have received has been invaluable to me. I am indebted to the staff at Cambridge University Library, especially to Rose Giles, who have helped me to easily access the literature that has shaped this book at every stage. I am particularly indebted to the staff at the *Archives nationales* in Paris for their consistent help. Their politeness and patience were particularly appreciated during my early days in the archives, where I was finding my feet in a French institution for the first time. I am grateful to David Raymont at the Institute and Faculty of Actuaries for providing me with a copy of the Company policy used in Chapter 6 of this book. I am also grateful to J. Paul Veyssière for his help in locating this policy.

I am grateful to academics who were generous with their time and knowledge in their correspondence with me, including Julie Hardwick, Elisabeth Heijmans, Moritz Isenmann, Anne Mézin, Jacob Soll and Jörg Ulbert. I am also very grateful to Guillaume Calafat, who kindly shared material used in Chapter 3.

I am especially grateful to Cátia Antunes, who, from the moment I met her at Palazzo Datini in Prato in May 2018, encouraged me to follow my instincts on where to take my research. She also was most generous with her time, reading my chapter drafts with great care and consistently daring me to take my findings to their logical conclusions. Similarly, Nandini Chatterjee, Renaud Morieux and James Davey made excellent recommendations that have improved the book immeasurably.

I am most thankful to Maria Fusaro, the PI of AveTransRisk, whose confidence in me and my work never erred, even when my own confidence did. Her extraordinary generosity with her time and thoughts were invaluable throughout the composition of this book.

Gijs Dreijer, Jake Dyble, Antonio Iodice and Mallory Hope have been wonderful colleagues and wonderful friends in equal measure. I thank them from the bottom of my heart for their professional and personal support over the years.

Beyond my professional circle, other friends have also helped me to bear the weight of this book. To Debbie Ashwell, Katie Becher, Gavin Davies, Diarmuid Maguire, Douglas Morton and Robyn Summers, I am very grateful.

That this book has materialised at all is due, first and foremost, to my parents, who have supported me through thick and thin. I dedicate this to them.

ABBREVIATIONS

AN	*Archives nationales*, Paris
ATR	AveTransRisk – Average – Transaction Costs and Risk Management during the First Globalization (Sixteenth–Eighteenth Centuries)
BNF	*Bibliothèque nationale de France*, Paris
CIO	French East India Company (*Compagnie des Indes orientales*)
EIC	English East India Company
ROCAR	return on capital at risk
VOC	Dutch East India Company (*Verenigde Oostindische Compagnie*)

INTRODUCTION

The year 1661 marked the beginning of the personal rule of Louis XIV, king of France. Up to this point, Cardinal Mazarin had served as chief minister, just as he and Cardinal Richelieu had served in the same capacity for Louis XIII in the decades prior. Now though, with Mazarin's death, Louis XIV signalled his intent to rule alone.

The task before him was unenviable. The French Wars of Religion (1562–98), the Thirty Years' War (1618–48) and the *Frondes* (1648–53) – a series of municipal and elite uprisings against Mazarin – had all taken their toll on the kingdom.[1] Now, taking the role of master himself, it was his job to right the French ship of state.

Despite the challenges before him, the young king was no doubt bullish about his chances of making an impression on the European stage. French tracts on political and economic development throughout the seventeenth century were replete with tropes of French exceptionalism. One anonymous sonnet put it thus:

> The fate of France is watched over by Destiny.
> Her happy lot, well founded, is in no danger of reverse.
> Her foreign neighbours find their hands in chains.
> Her abuses are proscribed by a thousand different decrees.
> Already ships in successful trade
> Command the fortune-favoured routes of the two seas.
> They voyage to all lands the sun shines on,
> And the ports of the golden coasts are open to them.
> A hundred times France blesses her guardian angels
> Who give salutary advice to her king,
> By whom we are to see all monsters beaten down.

---

[1] On the French Wars of Religion, see as a starting point R. Briggs, *Early Modern France 1560–1715*, Oxford: Oxford University Press, 1998; on France's place in the Thirty Years' War and the events of the *Frondes*, see D. Parrott, *1652: The Cardinal, the Prince, and the Crisis of the 'Fronde'*, Oxford: Oxford University Press, 2020.

> But whence arises, great Colbert, this happy state?
> I have wished to sketch the good fortune of France,
> And my hand in these verses has outlined your virtues.[2]

The 'great Colbert' to whom this sonnet was addressed was none other than Jean-Baptiste Colbert, Louis XIV's eminent minister. Through his reforming agenda, Colbert sought to wield the power of the state to establish French economic hegemony within Europe, in service to his ambitious master who sought *gloire* in the arena of war.

Certainly, Louis XIV left his mark on European history, but France never emerged as Europe's economic powerhouse under his rule. His reign witnessed a period of economic transformation in the European world-economy, but one which passed France by. Her foreign neighbours to the north, it turns out, did not find their hands in chains: England and the Netherlands continued to develop their commercial and colonial endeavours (the two overlapped in many cases) in the Atlantic and Indian Ocean worlds. This has often been understood within a broader process known as the 'Little Divergence', whereby England and the Netherlands leapt ahead of the rest of Europe in terms of GDP and real wages.[3] At the turn of the century, the centre of gravity in the European world-economy was shifting away from Amsterdam towards London, thanks to the English state's aggressive commercial policy that reduced reliance on Dutch shippers.[4]

Marine insurance serves as a remarkable bellwether for this economic transformation. The logic of this instrument is straightforward: through an insurance policy, the risks of a given voyage are transferred to an insurer in exchange for an agreed sum (known as the premium). The oldest known

---

[2] Quoted in C. Cole, *Colbert and a Century of French Mercantilism*, vol. I, New York: Columbia University Press, 1939, p. 331.

[3] On this argument, see de A. de Pleijt and J. van Zanden, 'Accounting for the "Little Divergence": What Drove Economic Growth in Pre-Industrial Europe, 1300–1800?', *European Review of Economic History* 20 (2016), pp. 387–409, and the literature cited therein. See also L. Prados de la Escosura (ed.), *Exceptionalism and Industrialisation: Britain and Its European Rivals, 1688–1815*, Cambridge: Cambridge University Press, 2004.

[4] This framing owes much to both F. Braudel, *The Mediterranean and the Mediterranean World in the Age of Philip II*, vols I and II, London: Collins, 1990; and F. Braudel, *Civilisation and Capitalism 15th–18th Century*, vol. III, London: Collins, 1988, pp. 21–279. The periodisation of the shift from Amsterdam towards London draws from D. Ormrod, *The Rise of Commercial Empires: England and the Netherlands in the Age of Mercantilism, 1650–1770*, Cambridge: Cambridge University Press, 2003, pp. 334–51.

policy was issued in Genoa on 20 February 1343.[5] From the Italian states, insurance migrated across the Mediterranean and later northwards.[6] After the decline of Antwerp in the latter half of the sixteenth century, Amsterdam took up the mantle of commercial supremacy, becoming Europe's leading insurance centre in the process. In turn, London superseded Amsterdam as Europe's leading insurance centre in the eighteenth century.[7] These shifts have been well documented by historians, as part of a broader renaissance in the history of marine insurance in the last decade, but France has yet to reap the benefits of this renewed interest.

Indeed, Colbert's reforms have been scrutinised for centuries, but his intervention into the Parisian marine insurance market has been largely forgotten. This book centres primarily on two Parisian insurance institutions: the Royal Insurance Chamber (*Chambre générale des assurances et grosses aventures*, 1668–86) and the Royal Insurance Company (*Compagnie générale des assurances et grosses aventures*, 1686–c. 1710), established under the auspices of Colbert and his son, the Marquis de Seignelay. Through these institutions, both men strove to establish the Parisian insurance market as a lasting, legitimate rival to Amsterdam and London. Nevertheless, this never transpired: in the European world-economy, the City of Light waited in vain for its moment in the sun.

Why did the Amsterdam and London markets flourish while that of Paris did not? Answering this question is the core goal of this book. In so doing, it takes a deep dive into the social, economic and political life of Old Regime France – an *histoire totale* of sorts – as understood within broader trends of overseas commerce and empire. Thus, while this book studies marine insurance, it is not strictly a study *of* marine insurance, nor does it presume or require any prior knowledge of (or interest in) this commercial instrument. Put simply, the book posits that marine insurance offers a distinctive and multifaceted vantage point from which to study life in the Old Regime, thereby facilitating new insights into the absolute monarchy

---

5   L. Piccinno, 'Genoa, 1340–1620: Early Development of Marine Insurance', in A. Leonard (ed.), *Marine Insurance: Origins and Institutions, 1300–1850*, Basingstoke: Palgrave Macmillan, 2016, p. 31. On the origins of marine insurance and its development across Europe, see the excellent essays in the rest of the volume. On the forerunners of insurance, see F. Edler de Roover, 'Early Examples of Marine Insurance', *Journal of Economic History* 5 (1945), pp. 172–200.

6   On the early development of marine insurance, see Piccinno, 'Genoa, 1340–1620'; P. Spufford, 'From Genoa to London: The Places of Insurance in Europe', in A. Leonard (ed.), *Marine Insurance: Origins and Institutions, 1300–1850*, Basingstoke: Palgrave Macmillan, 2016, pp. 271–97; G. Ceccarelli, *Risky Markets: Marine Insurance in Renaissance Florence*, Leiden: Brill, 2020.

7   Here, see A. Leonard (ed.), *Marine Insurance: Origins and Institutions, 1300–1850*, Basingstoke: Palgrave Macmillan, 2016. This is discussed in further detail below.

that will interest students and scholars of social, political and economic history alike. Specifically, through studying marine insurance – a powerful tool of commercial risk management – the book proposes a new conceptualisation of absolutism itself as a system of risk management, whereby the absolute monarchy shifted the risks of its policies onto its subjects.

ABSOLUTISM, CREDIBLE COMMITMENT AND ECONOMIC DEVELOPMENT

Absolutism is a truly protean concept, understood by different historiographies and disciplines in multiple ways. This book engages with, and responds to, two very different approaches: that espoused by neo-institutionalism, and the socio-political approach that has arisen amongst historians of early modern France.

Neo-institutionalism has largely endorsed Douglass North's dichotomy between the 'virtuous' institutional development of north-western Europe (i.e. England and the Netherlands) and the 'vicious' institutional development of the so-called 'absolutist' monarchies of southern Europe (including France).[8] The central difference between the two, North suggested in a famous piece co-written with Barry Weingast, was one of 'credible commitment': the so-called Glorious Revolution ostensibly led to a constitutional reform that ensured the English crown was held in check by parliament, protecting property rights by preventing the monarch from 'appropriat[ing] wealth or repudiat[ing] debt' and thus facilitating economic growth.[9] This argument underpins North's broader claims that the 'decentralised' English

---

[8] For discussion and critique of this, see A. Clemente and R. Zaugg, 'Hermes, the Leviathan and the Grand Narrative of New Institutional Economics: The Quest for Development in the Eighteenth-Century Kingdom of Naples', *Journal of Modern European History* 15 (2017), pp. 111–13.

[9] D. North and B. Weingast, 'Constitutions and Commitment: The Evolution of Institutions Governing Public Choice in Seventeenth-Century England', *Journal of Economic History* 49 (1989), p. 829; this argument also underpins D. Acemoglu and J. Robinson, *Why Nations Fail: The Origins of Power, Prosperity, and Poverty*, London: Profile Books, 2012. In response to this line of thought, see, among others, S. Epstein, *Freedom and Growth: The Rise of States and Markets in Europe, 1300–1750*, London: Routledge, 2000, pp. 12–37; A. Irigoin and R. Grafe, 'Bounded Leviathan: Fiscal Constraints and Financial Development in the Early Modern Hispanic World', in D. Coffman, A. Leonard, and L. Neal (eds), *Questioning Credible Commitment: Perspectives on the Rise of Financial Capitalism*, Cambridge: Cambridge University Press, 2013, p. 200. In understanding the transformation of the English/British state in the seventeenth and eighteenth centuries, see the classic J. Brewer, *The Sinews of Power: War, Money and the English State, 1688–1783*, London: Unwin Hyman, 1989; see also Prados de la Escosura (ed.), *Exceptionalism and Industrialisation*.

and Dutch states facilitated the emergence of 'efficient' institutions, such as those for insurance, which significantly reduced transaction costs and supported economic growth.[10] France's fiscal system under Louis XIV, by contrast, is supposed to have not undergone 'fundamental institutional change' in response to the Nine Years' War (1688–97), thus leading to the country falling behind England in the long run.[11] This supports North's broader treatment of the French state as an overbearing and overly bureaucratic creature that 'stifl[ed] initiatives that would have increased productivity', in keeping with liberalist readings of French economic development.[12]

Inspired by the North-Weingast thesis, Ron Harris has recently applied the concept of 'credible commitment' to the study of the European East India Companies in the hopes of understanding why the English and Dutch companies (the EIC and VOC respectively) arose earlier (1600 and 1602 respectively), and with more success, than other European counterparts. A necessary condition for the rise of these companies, he suggests, was the ruler's commitment not to 'expropriate' their assets – a commitment possible only in England and the Netherlands:

> My argument is that the relevant difference between England and the Dutch Republic, on the one hand, and Portugal and France, on the other, was [...] in the political structure. In Portugal and France, the ruler could expropriate the pool of assets created by the investment of private individuals in joint-stock companies. In England, a nascent rule of law allowed the Crown to credibly commit not to expropriate. In the Dutch Republic, a combination of federal political structure and the central role of merchants in the political elite made expropriation impossible.[13]

---

[10] D. North, 'Institutions, Transaction Costs, and the Rise of Merchant Empires', in J. Tracy (ed.), *The Political Economy of Merchant Empires*, Cambridge: Cambridge University Press, 1991, pp. 25–9. 'Efficiency', as Sheilagh Ogilvie notes, is not well defined within works like this; S. Ogilvie, '"Whatever Is, Is Right"? Economic Institutions in Pre-Industrial Europe', *Economic History Review* 60 (2007), pp. 656–7.
[11] North and Weingast, 'Constitutions and Commitment', p. 830.
[12] North, 'Institutions, Transaction Costs', pp. 25–9; on these liberalist readings, and their shortcomings, see in particular P. Minard, *La fortune du colbertisme. État et industrie dans la France des Lumières*, Paris: Éditions Fayard, 1998.
[13] R. Harris, *Going the Distance: Eurasian Trade and the Rise of the Business Corporation, 1400–1700*, Princeton: Princeton University Press, 2020, p. 329; see also pp. 4–5. This echoes the conclusions of G. Dari-Mattiacci, O. Gelderblom, J. Jonker, and E. Perotti, 'The Emergence of the Corporate Form', *The Journal of Law, Economics, and Organization* 33 (2017), pp. 193–236, although these authors nuance the argument by stressing that the risk of expropriation in the English case was decreasing throughout the seventeenth century.

Harris thus invokes the Northian dichotomy between north-western and southern Europe, arguing that 'the [French] Crown was too absolutist and unconstrainable and was not able to credibly commit to private equity investors'.[14] Yet his argument is problematic from both vantage points. Although he qualifies that his argument on English and Dutch credible commitment is a 'relative' one, it is unclear how the English and Dutch states were any less capable of 'expropriation' than France or any other 'absolutist' state.[15] Harris defines expropriation capaciously:

> Expropriation did not have to be outright taking; it could take the form of prioritizing political over business considerations. It could take the form of assessing the Crown's in-kind investment above its market value, or favoring the Crown when it came to dividend distribution. It could take the form of competition by the Crown, restrictions imposed on certain company activities, or new taxation.[16]

By Harris' own definition, the EIC and VOC both suffered from state expropriation in their early decades. Rupali Mishra's recent book documents the 'very complicated relationship between the [English] East India Company and the state' – one that undermines Harris' characterisation of the EIC as existing in 'a space [...] safely beyond the sovereign's ability to breach his commitment'.[17] Most notably, James I used his grant of a competing patent to the short-lived Scottish East India Company (1617–18) as leverage to extract funding for joint ventures between the EIC and Muscovy Company, alongside a loan to the Russian tsar, Michael I; moreover, throughout the 1630s, Charles I supported crown allies in trade that competed with the EIC, culminating in a charter bestowed on the so-called Courten Association which threatened the EIC's existence.[18] Oliver Cromwell supported these

---

[14] Harris, *Going the Distance*, p. 327.
[15] Epstein, *Freedom and Growth*, p. 35.
[16] Harris, *Going the Distance*, p. 326.
[17] R. Mishra, *A Business of State: Commerce, Politics, and the Birth of the East India Company*, Cambridge, MA: Harvard University Press, 2018, p. 3; Harris, *Going the Distance*, p. 315.
[18] Mishra, *A Business of State*, pp. 162–70 and 272–301. Harris discusses the Courten Association in a separate article, but suggests it 'can be interpreted as strategic behaviour by both parties to the agreement' (i.e. the Crown and the EIC), that is, as simply a matter of political negotiation: R. Harris, 'Could the Crown Credibly Commit to Respect Its Charters? England, 1558–1640', in D. Coffman, A. Leonard, and L. Neal (eds), *Questioning Credible Commitment: Perspectives on the Rise of Financial Capitalism*, Cambridge: Cambridge University Press, 2013, pp. 39–40. Yet this same logic could be applied to 'absolutist' France and its chartered companies; here, see K. Banks, 'Financiers, Factors, and French Proprietary Companies in West Africa, 1673–1713', in L. Roper and B. Ruymbeke (eds), *Constructing Early Modern*

efforts too, and even suspended the EIC's monopoly in the period 1654–57. Far from protecting the company, the Glorious Revolution empowered interest groups who sought to undermine or curtail the company's privileges: parliament chartered a 'new', competing East India Company in the 1690s whose principal investor was William III himself. The 'new' and 'old' companies merged only in 1709.[19]

The case of the VOC was more egregious still. Originally, its charter outlined that the company would be liquidated and wound up after a decade (i.e. 1612), giving shareholders the choice of whether they wished to invest in a successor company. Yet this put the VOC in a precarious position: significant long-term military expenditure was necessary to ensure the success of its commercial endeavours, but such expenditure was not possible, since the company itself would not have been able to reap the rewards of such investment before 1612. Faced with the threat of the VOC being liquidated with poor returns – giving little incentive for shareholders to reinvest in a successor company – the Estates General 'formally allowed the company to ignore the statutory liquidation due' in 1612, locking in shareholders' capital against their will.[20] 'Understandably', David Ciepley remarks, 'the investors threw a fit, as there was no hiding that this was a total expropriation'.[21]

Empires: Proprietary Ventures in the Atlantic World, 1500–1750, Leiden: Brill, 2007, pp. 79–116. Harris' argument in this article (which forms the basis for the argument in *Going the Distance*) assumes as its premise that, *without* credible commitment in England, the 'market' for charters would have collapsed – yet it did not, ergo 'there must have been some "credible commitment" devices in operation that kept the market for charters viable'. He provides a list of the companies established in this period, 1550–1630, to substantiate this – yet does not recognise that the same logic would also apply to the 'absolutist' French case and thus imply, following his argument, that credible commitment devices must have existed there too; Harris, 'Could the Crown Credibly Commit?', p. 23. For a long list of France's chartered companies under Louis XIV, see J. Horn, *Economic Development in Early Modern France: The Privilege of Liberty, 1650–1820*, Cambridge: Cambridge University Press, 2015, p. 116.

[19] P. Stern, 'Companies: Monopoly, Sovereignty, and the East Indies', in P. Stern and C. Wennerlind (eds), *Mercantilism Reimagined: Political Economy in Early Modern Britain and Its Empire*, Oxford: Oxford University Press, 2013, pp. 180–91.

[20] O. Gelderblom, A. de Jong, and J. Jonker, 'The Formative Years of the Modern Corporation: The Dutch East India Company VOC, 1602–1623', *Journal of Economic History* 73 (2013), p. 1064.

[21] D. Ciepley, 'The Anglo-American Misconception of Stockholders as "Owners" and "Members": Its Origins and Consequences', *Journal of Institutional Economics* 16 (2020), p. 635. Harris acknowledges in a separate article that 'the commitment to the passive investors to respect the terms of the 1602 charter and allow withdrawal of the investment in 1612 was not credible'; Harris, 'Could the Crown Credibly Commit?', p. 42. Nevertheless, in *Going the Distance*, he only acknowledges the

Thus, the early years of the EIC and VOC do not support Harris' thesis: the EIC was created and operated *despite* an absence of credible commitment both before and after the Glorious Revolution, and the VOC only survived its early years *because of* an absence of credible commitment. Moreover, the charters of the VOC and its counterpart, the Dutch West India Company (WIC), made clear that these were tools of violence and empire-building subordinate to the Estates General; indeed, the Estates General intervened extensively in the WIC's activities in serving these functions.[22] In this light, Harris' premise that credible commitment was a necessary condition for shareholder investment does not hold.[23]

Building on what we might call a political and sociological turn in the literature on corporations, this book argues that the absence of credible commitment was not an inherent impediment to France's chartered companies either. Instead, this absence offered the French state the flexibility necessary to manage these companies in response to changing political and economic circumstances. The fact that these companies were often short-lived is not in and of itself evidence of failure: as Chapter 2 argues, this enduring supposition in the neo-institutional literature relies on a fundamental misunderstanding of how the companies were conceived and deployed.

Although the various historiographical contributions on France's chartered companies are diverse in the ground they cover, two broad, complementary

---

incident, without establishing how this was an archetypal example of the state going against its commitment not to expropriate shareholder assets; he suggests instead that the establishment of a secondary market for shares somehow compensated for this action; Harris, *Going the Distance*, pp. 285–7.

[22] C. Antunes, 'Birthing Empire: The States General and the Chartering of the VOC and the WIC', in R. Koekkoek, A. Richard, and A. Weststeijn (eds), *The Dutch Empire between Ideas and Practice, 1600–2000*, Cham: Springer, 2019, pp. 19–36. This makes clear that Harris' tendency to downplay the role of violence in the success of the VOC and EIC emerges from a misinterpretation of why these companies were established in the first place. Indeed, France's tardiness in entering the Indian Ocean trade can be attributed at least in part to the VOC's aggressive resistance of early French voyages; here, see G. Lelièvre, *La préhistoire de la Compagnie des Indes orientales, 1601–1622. Les Français dans la course aux épices*, Caen: Presses universitaires de Caen, 2021. This is simply one of many instances that demonstrate the VOC and EIC were complex institutions with multiple qualities over space and time; for a valuable articulation of this complexity, framed in terms of the 'corporation's distinctive global sociology', see W. Pettigrew and D. Veevers, 'Introduction', in W. Pettigrew and D. Veevers (eds), *The Corporation as a Protagonist in Global History, c. 1550–1750*, Leiden: Brill, 2019, pp. 1–39. For how this played out in practice, see the essays in the rest of the volume.

[23] Harris, *Going the Distance*, p. 5.

types of analysis can be discerned.²⁴ One focuses on the companies as products of state interests: Glenn Ames offers an episodic study of the French East India Company's (*Compagnie des Indes orientales*, hereafter the CIO) operations under Colbert, while Marie Ménard-Jacob, building on Philippe Haudrère's work, eschews an events-based analysis in arguing that the company served as an exercise in acquiring knowledge and establishing commercial and diplomatic frameworks. France's success in Indian trade in the eighteenth century, she argues, was built on these frameworks, which themselves depended on the efforts of agents operating on the ground in India.²⁵

The other type of analysis builds on Daniel Dessert's work by focusing on how the companies served members' interests.²⁶ Elisabeth Heijmans has recently asked what motivated investors to enter the royal companies when the crown displayed so little respect for shareholders' rights. While membership of the companies was undoubtedly precarious, Heijmans demonstrates that membership of multiple companies could provide competitive advantages, offering access to multiple markets under monopoly in which members could engage on their own account. In this way, members could make private profits even if the companies themselves were unprofitable.²⁷

---

24 My focus in this book is on France's chartered companies under Louis XIV, although I will refer where appropriate to the foundations on which these built; on the earlier companies, see Lelièvre, *La préhistoire de la Compagnie des Indes orientales*; É. Roulet, *La Compagnie des îles de l'Amérique 1635–1651. Une enterprise colonial au XVIIe siècle*, Rennes: Presses universitaires de Rennes, 2017.

25 G. Ames, *Colbert, Mercantilism, and the French Quest for Asian Trade*, DeKalb: Northern Illinois University Press, 1996; M. Ménard-Jacob, *La première compagnie des Indes. Apprentissages, échecs et héritage 1664–1704*, Rennes: Presses universitaires de Rennes, 2016; M. Ménard-Jacob, 'L'apprentissage de l'Inde par les Français de la première compagnie', in G. Le Bouëdec (ed.), *L'Asie, la mer, le monde. Au temps des Compagnies des Indes*, Rennes: Presses universitaires de Rennes, 2014; P. Haudrère, *Les Français dans l'océan Indien XVIIe–XIXe siècle*, Rennes: Presses universitaires de Rennes, 2014. Ménard-Jacob's argument has many parallels with that of Éric Roulet on the *Compagnie des îles de l'Amérique*; Roulet, *La Compagnie des îles de l'Amérique*, pp. 583–9.

26 D. Dessert, *Argent, pouvoir et société au Grand Siècle*, Paris: Fayard, 1984, pp. 379–401; see also D. Dessert, *Le royaume de Monsieur Colbert*, Paris: Perrin, 2007.

27 E. Heijmans, 'Investing in French Overseas Companies: A Bad Deal? The Liquidation Processes of Companies Operating on the West Coast of Africa and in India (1664–1719)', *Itinerario* 43 (2019), pp. 107–21. Heijmans explores the agency of the eighteenth-century overseas directors of the French companies in west Africa and India in E. Heijmans, *The Agency of Empire: Connections and Strategies in French Overseas Expansion (1686–1746)*, Leiden: Brill, 2019. See also Banks, 'Financiers, Factors, and French Proprietary Companies'. NB I also refer to Heijmans' dissertation instead of her book where necessary; E. Heijmans, 'The Agency of Empire:

This book integrates both types of analysis, asking what motivated the monarchy to establish and support its insurance institutions while also asking what motivated their members to join. In this way, I further develop Pierre Boulle's argument that, by being 'plundered from above and from below', France's chartered companies were crucial to the development of overseas trade.[28] This framing helps us to understand why they were so important to commercial policy under Louis XIV.

Nevertheless, this commercial policy was not entirely consistent over time. Jeff Horn has claimed that 'Colbert's approach to reinvigorating French commerce and industry long survived him. His immediate ministerial successors [...] continued Colbert's policies' of using privilege as an economic tool as late as 1750.[29] Perhaps unwittingly, Horn builds on a longstanding line of argument suggesting that, after Colbert's death, French economic policy engaged in *Colbertisme à outrance* – i.e. Colbertianism taken to its extreme.[30] This must be understood within a broader historiographical orthodoxy which has treated royal ministers in the latter decades of Louis XIV's reign as pale imitations of Colbert and the Marquis de Louvois – an orthodoxy that is now being challenged.[31] In this vein, I argue throughout the book that the presumed continuity between Colbertian and post-Colbertian commercial policy can no longer stand: the latter certainly drew on privilege as an economic tool, as Horn suggests, but in very different ways from its Colbertian counterpart. It was thus discrete and cannot simply be dismissed as a poor man's Colbertianism.

While the Northian dichotomy between the 'representative' institutional frameworks of north-western Europe and the 'absolutist' (i.e. unconstrainable) institutional frameworks of southern Europe continues to have wide

---

Personal Connections and Individual Strategies in the Shaping of the French Early Modern Expansion (1686–1746)', PhD thesis, Leiden University (2018).

[28] P. Boulle, 'French Mercantilism, Commercial Companies and Colonial Profitability', in L. Blussé and F. Gaastra (eds), *Companies and Trade: Essays on Overseas Trading Companies during the Ancien Régime*, Leiden: Leiden University Press, 1981, p. 117.

[29] Horn, *Economic Development*, p. 8.

[30] The phrase comes from T. Schaeper, *The French Council of Commerce, 1700–1715: A Study of Mercantilism after Colbert*, Columbus: Ohio State University Press, 1983, p. 65; a key articulation of this argument can be found in C. Cole, *French Mercantilism, 1683–1700*, New York: Columbia University Press, 1943, pp. 3–4 and the remainder of the book.

[31] On how this orthodoxy is being challenged, see the chapters in J. Prest and G. Rowlands (eds), *The Third Reign of Louis XIV, c. 1682–1715*, Abingdon: Routledge, 2017; see also J. Rule and B. Trotter, *A World of Paper: Louis XIV, Colbert de Torcy, and the Rise of the Information State*, Montreal: McGill-Queen's University Press, 2014.

(though not universal) traction amongst economic historians, political historians have long moved beyond it.[32] In the case of France, 'absolutism as social collaboration' has become the mainstream historiographical position in Anglo-American academia in recent decades, increasingly influencing French academia too.[33] This line of argument – first articulated by Perry Anderson and William Beik – has typically stressed the 'common interests between the state and other groups in society' – chiefly, provincial elites.[34] Through these common interests, it is argued, the absolute monarchy was able to exercise its will through mutually beneficial networks of royal patronage, connecting provincial elites to the court.[35]

This socio-political understanding of absolutism is far more useful than the neo-institutional approach, since the latter makes the mistake of taking Louis XIV's theoretically unchecked power for granted. Yet 'collaboration' has perhaps become a victim of its own success. Although Beik's explicitly Marxist framework has been challenged for being too simplistic – the interests of social elites, it is suggested, were far from homogeneous – 'collaboration' has endured as a concept, albeit on theoretical foundations that are no longer clear.[36] So widely deployed is it now that it risks becoming unfalsifiable – not because it is so compelling and supported by such unassailable evidence, but because it is becoming so capaciously defined as to be applicable no matter the circumstances. Indeed, Beik's famous survey on absolutism acknowledges that 'collaboration is not at all a precise concept'; in a nevertheless admirable effort to find common threads in the literature, he uses 'collaboration', 'cooperation' and 'compromise' interchangeably,

---

[32] See D. Coffman and L. Neal, 'Introduction', in D. Coffman, A. Leonard, and L. Neal (eds), *Questioning Credible Commitment: Perspectives on the Rise of Financial Capitalism*, Cambridge: Cambridge University Press, 2013, pp. 1–20, the bibliography therein and the essays in the rest of the volume. See also M. Drelichman and H. Voth, *Lending to the Borrower from Hell: Debt, Taxes and Default in the Age of Philip II*, Princeton: Princeton University Press, 2014; Clemente and Zaugg, 'Hermes'.

[33] For a full survey – and defence – of absolutism as social collaboration, see W. Beik, 'The Absolutism of Louis XIV as Social Collaboration', *Past and Present* 188 (2005), pp. 195–224.

[34] Ibid., p. 197; see also W. Beik, *Absolutism and Society in Seventeenth-Century France*, Cambridge: Cambridge University Press, 1985. For an especially forthright presentation of this position that rejects 'absolutism' entirely, see also R. Mettam, *Power and Faction in Louis XIV's France*, Oxford: Basil Blackwell, 1988.

[35] On clientelism, see especially S. Kettering, *Patrons, Brokers, and Clients in Seventeenth-Century France*, New York: Oxford University Press, 1986.

[36] For these criticisms of Beik, see M. Breen, *Law, City, and King: Legal Culture, Municipal Politics, and State Formation in Early Modern Dijon*, Woodbridge: Boydell & Brewer, 2007; G. Rowlands, *The Dynastic State and the Army under Louis XIV: Royal Service and Private Interest 1661–1701*, Cambridge: Cambridge University Press, 2002, pp. 4–5.

despite these all being 'thick' concepts with very different meanings and implications.[37] The reader will note throughout my analysis that other historians have also muddied the waters through their choice of language.

Responses to 'collaboration' have been broadly structured in synchronic and diachronic terms – or, put another way, historians are now asking if the concept can be applied across France throughout the entirety of Louis XIV's reign. Numerous historians – including James Collins, Darryl Dee and John Hurt – have argued that works espousing 'collaboration' have neglected the latter decades of Louis' reign: the 1680s and early 1690s, they argue, marked a fundamental turning point in the relationship between the state and provincial elites for which 'collaboration' cannot account.[38]

Historians have identified further issues with 'collaboration' through testing its bounds in spaces distant from the court. Michael Breen, in studying the *avocats* of Dijon, finds collaboration

> was the product of a sharp and progressive narrowing of the ranks of those eligible to wield public power and participate in governance. The monarchy may have struck a bargain with those whose cooperation was necessary, but it did not hesitate to ride roughshod over the rest.[39]

In her study of Marseille, Junko Takeda also emphasises the tensions between the French state and provincial elites, arguing there was a consistent 'distrust between royal and local elites', but an adaptation of 'views, behaviours, and speech patterns' amongst these figures allowed the shared goal of commercial expansion to be pursued. She consequently posits that absolutism was underpinned by 'accommodation' rather than collaboration, acknowledging that royal interests and those of the Marseillaises elites were often asymmetrical.[40] Similarly, combining both synchronic and diachronic elements in his critique, Dee stresses that 'obedience' was at the heart of the relationship between Louis

---

[37] Beik, 'The Absolutism of Louis XIV', p. 197.

[38] D. Dee, *Expansion and Crisis in Louis XIV's France: Franche-Comté and Absolute Monarchy, 1674–1715*, Rochester, NY: University of Rochester Press, 2009, p. 10; J. Hurt, *Louis XIV and the Parlements: The Assertion of Royal Authority*, Manchester: Manchester University Press, 2002; M. Potter, *Corps and Clienteles: Public Finance and Political Change in France, 1688–1715*, Aldershot: Ashgate, 2003. See also G. Rowlands and J. Prest, 'Introduction', in J. Prest and G. Rowlands (eds), *The Third Reign of Louis XIV, c. 1682–1715*, Abingdon: Routledge, 2017, pp. 1–23; see also the essays herein. For a conscientious assessment of how Anglo-American historians have approached Louis XIV over time, see G. Rowlands, 'Life After Death in Foreign Lands: Louis XIV and Anglo-American Historians', in S. Externbrink and C. Levillain (eds), *Penser l'après Louis XIV. Histoire, mémoire, representation (1715–2015)*, Paris: Honoré Champion, 2018, pp. 179–209.

[39] Breen, *Law, City, and King*, p. 21.

[40] J. Takeda, *Between Crown and Commerce: Marseille and the Early Modern Mediterranean*, Baltimore: Johns Hopkins University Press, 2011, p. 9.

XIV and provincial elites in Franche-Comté, which came to bear especially after the onset of the Nine Years' War in 1688.[41] Breen, Takeda and Dee thus push the debate in a different direction, acknowledging again the power of the crown while still stressing the agency of provincial powerholders. This turn in the historiography makes clear that stretching 'thick' terms to describe bilateral relationships between the state and a specific (set of) elite group(s) over time will not take the debate any further.

In the face of these choppy waters, one solution might be to jettison the concept of absolutism entirely. Certainly, this is what Collins has advocated: if there is little that is really absolute about absolutism, he suggests, then redefining absolutism as historians of France have tried to do is simply a form of 'linguistic chicanery' that does not address the inextricable link between absolutism and despotism in popular discourse.[42] Nevertheless, so long as historians, economists and academics from other disciplines continue to deploy absolutism in its various guises as an analytical concept, it seems undesirable for historians of Old Regime France – widely perceived to be the archetype of absolutism, however one wishes to define it – to leave the discussion entirely and allow non-specialists to fill the vacuum.[43] To offer new insights on absolutism, I suggest we reconsider a crucial question once posed by Beik: 'what could he [i.e. Louis XIV] really do?'[44] And just as importantly, what could he *not* do?

Answering these questions forces us to confront a premise in the literature on French absolutism, with longstanding roots in Marxist and Annalistes historiography: that it is a concept relevant only to metropolitan France, owing to the fundamentally terrestrial interests of the state and provincial elites alike.[45] This book argues that, like the neo-institutionalists, historians of French absolutism (with Takeda as a crucial exception) have not taken the state's maritime interests seriously enough. From the CIO to the *guerre d'escadre*, French endeavours

---

[41] Dee, *Expansion and Crisis*.
[42] J. Collins, *The State in Early Modern France*, Cambridge: Cambridge University Press, 2009, pp. ix–xxv. For a broader analysis of works pushing back against absolutism as a concept, see F. Cosandey and R. Descimon, *L'absolutisme en France. Histoire et historiographie*, Paris: Éditions du Seuil, 2002, pp. 217–40.
[43] Mettam makes a similar point in Mettam, *Power and Faction*, p. 5. The same challenges apply to the concept of mercantilism; on the rare occasions I refer to this concept throughout the book, this should be understood within the context of the contributions in P. Stern and C. Wennerlind (eds), *Mercantilism Reimagined: Political Economy in Early Modern Britain and Its Empire*, Oxford: Oxford University Press, 2013 – that is to say, by mercantilism, I mean a broad (and not always compatible) set of ideas and measures on commerce and industry conceived and implemented by and for states in response to widespread challenges distinctive to early modern Europe.
[44] Beik, 'The Absolutism of Louis XIV', p. 197.
[45] This is most clearly articulated in Beik, *Absolutism and Society*, pp. 335–9.

at sea and overseas under Louis XIV may not have achieved the same degree of lasting success as their English and Dutch counterparts (although, in some cases, these were themselves failures), but this does not mean they were not important to the monarchy. Indeed, I argue that France's chartered companies should be understood in tandem with metropolitan institutions: these companies are a crucial piece of the broader picture, whereby traditional tools of privilege were being refashioned for novel ends. Put more plainly, chartered companies were tools of absolutism, and thus benefit from comparison with other institutions that sustained the absolute monarchy.

Owing to these prevailing assumptions, the current literature on French absolutism has focused heavily on the provinces of metropolitan France, scarcely acknowledging the global turn, the renaissance of maritime history or developments in the study of legal pluralism.[46] Takeda, Dee and others have demonstrated the value of studying absolutism from the vantage point of France's frontiers, but the French state's claims to authority did not end on France's (sometimes blurred) eastern borders, nor where the kingdom met the Atlantic and the Mediterranean.[47] As we will see throughout this book, the monarchy went to great lengths to exercise power over lands, waters and peoples far beyond metropolitan France. This is consistent with an understanding of the French state as shaped not necessarily by territoriality, but by 'jurisdictional sovereignty'; as Peter Sahlins notes, 'the kingdom was not a coherent territorial entity consistently "bounded" in a linear sense', which invited complex and contested claims to jurisdiction over spaces and peoples often difficult to circumscribe.[48] This, in turn, necessitated the state to mobilise

---

[46] On the traditional divides between global and maritime history, and how these can be overcome, see M. Fusaro, 'Maritime History as Global History? The Methodological Challenges and a Future Research Agenda', in M. Fusaro and A. Polonia (eds), *Maritime History as Global History*, St. John's: IMEHA, 2011, pp. 267–82. On legal pluralism, see as an introduction the excellent essays in L. Benton and R. Ross (eds), *Legal Pluralism and Empires, 1500–1850*, New York: New York University Press, 2013.

[47] On the porosity of France's border with the Holy Roman Empire in Alsace even after the 1697 Treaty of Ryswick, which supposedly granted France sovereignty over the province as a whole, see S. Lazer, *State Formation in Early Modern Alsace, 1648–1789*, Rochester, NY: University of Rochester Press, 2019, p. 7.

[48] P. Sahlins, 'Natural Frontiers Revisited: France's Boundaries since the Seventeenth Century', *The American Historical Review* 95 (1990), p. 1427; P. Steinberg, *The Social Construction of the Ocean*, Cambridge: Cambridge University Press, 2001. See also R. Morieux, *The Channel: England, France and the Construction of a Maritime Border in the Eighteenth Century*, Cambridge: Cambridge University Press, 2016. On the complexities of defining a French subject, and how such complexities could be exploited by the state in pursuit of its policies, see G. Weiss, *Captives and Corsairs: France and Slavery in the Early Modern Mediterranean*, Stanford: Stanford University Press, 2011.

the resources of its subjects in support of its own claims and interests. It is here, this book argues, that the chartered companies were especially valuable.

INSURANCE IN SEVENTEENTH-CENTURY EUROPE: AMSTERDAM, LONDON AND PARIS

The seventeenth-century marine insurance industry sits at the nexus of these crucial debates on absolutism, economic development and the function(s) of corporations. By this point, marine insurance had already become firmly entrenched in commercial centres across Europe. When Louis XIV's personal rule began in 1661, Amsterdam was firmly entrenched as Europe's leading market, although London was already a notable market and would rise to supremacy in the following century.

These markets have been widely studied, benefiting from a recent renaissance in the study of pre-modern insurance that owes a large debt to neo-institutionalism. Neo-institutionalism's focus on property rights reflects a broader emphasis on the importance of transaction costs in economic development. North defines these quite simply as 'all the costs of human beings interacting with each other', but helpfully subdivides these into three different kinds of cost: information (the costs of gathering the information necessary to participate in the market), bargaining (the costs of negotiating contracts) and enforcement (the costs of ensuring contracts are carried out and property rights upheld, e.g. conflict resolution).[49] Here, institutions come into play as crucial determinants of transaction costs. I will use Avner Greif's definition of an institution as 'a system of rules, beliefs, norms, and organisations that together generate a regularity of (social) behaviour' (i.e. 'institutions-as-equilibria') as the basis for my discussion.[50] Given the book's focus on specific organisations (chiefly, but not exclusively, the Royal Insurance Chamber and the Royal Insurance Company),

---

[49] D. North 'Institutions, Transaction Costs, and the Rise of Merchant Empires', in J. Tracy (ed.), *The Political Economy of Merchant Empires*, Cambridge: Cambridge University Press, 1991, p. 24; D. North, 'Institutions', *Journal of Economic Perspectives* 5 (1991), pp. 97–112; D. North, *Institutions, Institutional Change and Economic Performance*, Cambridge: Cambridge University Press, 1990. The concept of transaction costs was pioneered by Oliver Williamson; for a key example of his work, see O. Williamson, 'The Economics of Organization: The Transaction Cost Approach', *American Journal of Sociology* 87 (1981), pp. 548–77. On transaction costs as applied to early chartered companies (including the EIC and VOC), see A. Carlos and S. Nicholas, '"Giants of an Earlier Capitalism": The Chartered Trading Companies as Modern Multinationals', *Business History Review* 62 (1988), pp. 398–419.

[50] A. Greif, *Institutions and the Path to the Modern Economy: Lessons from Medieval Trade*, New York: Cambridge University Press, 2006, p. 30.

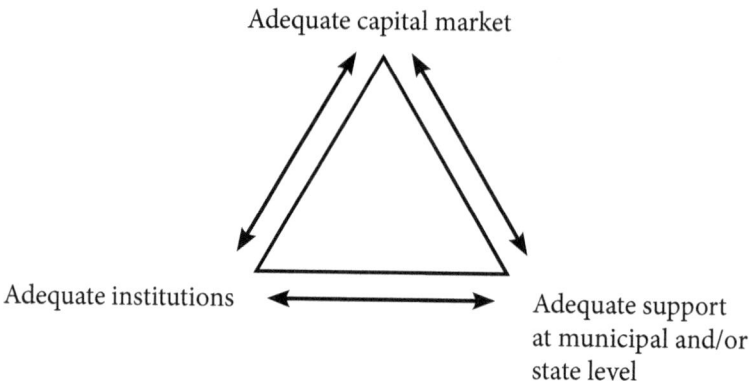

Figure 1 The insurance triangle.

I will primarily use 'institutions' to mean organisations, which are treated and understood as the 'manifestation' of institutional frameworks.[51]

Why did the insurance markets of Amsterdam and London take off – i.e. achieve lasting pre-eminence in Europe? I propose in this book that there were three interrelated elements necessary for an early modern insurance market to take off: an adequate capital market, adequate institutions and adequate support at the municipal and/or state level. This triangle, I will argue, was complete in Amsterdam and London: each had adequate capital markets and institutions, receiving crucial state and/or municipal support.

In the absence of extensive quantitative records on these insurance markets, historians have focused on the heterogeneous institutional frameworks underpinning them. As Guido Rossi puts it, 'the historical development of early markets was typically a product of local circumstances'.[52] Institutions mattered, but they mattered in the context of the social, economic and political environment in which they were established.

Amsterdam's insurance market began to grow towards the end of the sixteenth century, coinciding with the development of the city's commerce after the sack of Antwerp in 1576.[53] Frank Spooner and Sabine Go have

---

[51] Ibid.
[52] G. Rossi, 'England 1523–1601: The Beginnings of Marine Insurance', in A. Leonard (ed.), *Marine Insurance: Origins and Institutions, 1300–1850*, Basingstoke: Palgrave Macmillan, 2016, p. 143.
[53] For different perspectives on the importance of the fall of Antwerp in the rise of Amsterdam, see J. de Vries and A. van der Woude, *The First Modern Economy: Success, Failure, and Perseverance of the Dutch Economy, 1500–1815*, Cambridge: Cambridge University Press, 1997; J. van Zanden, 'The "Revolt of the Early Modernists" and the

been the leading English-language historians on the city's insurance market in its heyday. Go's recent work has supported prior analyses in finding that an influx of new members who played by different rules could prompt the rise of formal institutions that codified rules and enforced compliance.

The rise of Amsterdam's Baltic trade facilitated the emergence of a large capital market that was able to meet the growing demand for insurance in the city.[54] Prolific and infrequent underwriters alike signed policies for clients based as far away as Copenhagen, Hamburg and London.[55] Municipal support completed the insurance triangle through establishing institutions to facilitate exchange, reduce information asymmetries and resolve conflicts efficiently.

This support began early in the market's development. As Go argues, the market's early growth placed a strain on the *Schepenbank*, i.e. the Eschevins Court, as insurance cases became more numerous and complex. This prompted the Burgomasters to issue the city's first insurance ordinance in 1598; this was largely modelled on Antwerp and Bruges' own ordinances, outlining procedures for the construction and contestation of insurance policies.[56] Yet the ordinance deviated from Antwerp and Bruges in creating the *Kamer van Assurantie en Averij*, a subordinate court for all insurance and general average cases that was accessible to all, irrespective of nationality or religion.[57] The court, the establishment of which meant 'commercial conflicts were taken out of the sphere of particularised courts and were transferred to a generalised court's jurisdiction', oversaw the rise of Amsterdam's insurance market from a mere 'sideline activity' to an industry in and of itself.[58]

The *Kamer* complemented the new Exchange, opened in 1611, which provided a central space for brokerage services and the dissemination of

---

"First Modern Economy": An Assessment', *Economic History Review* 55 (2002), pp. 619–41.

[54] S. Go, *Marine Insurance in the Netherlands 1600–1870: A Comparative Institutional Approach*, Amsterdam: Aksant, 2009, pp. 281–2.

[55] S. Go, 'The Amsterdam Chamber of Insurance and Average: A New Phase in Formal Contract Enforcement (Late Sixteenth and Seventeenth Centuries)', *Enterprise and Society* 14 (2013), pp. 520–1.

[56] On marine insurance law in Amsterdam, see J. van Niekerk, *The Development of the Principles of Insurance Law in the Netherlands from 1500 to 1800*, vols I and II, Kenwyn: Juka & Co, 1998.

[57] S. Go, 'Amsterdam 1585–1790: Emergence, Dominance, and Decline', in A. Leonard (ed.), *Marine Insurance: Origins and Institutions, 1300–1850*, Basingstoke: Palgrave Macmillan, 2016, pp. 113–14.

[58] Go, 'The Amsterdam Chamber', pp. 515–16; Go, 'Amsterdam 1585–1790', p. 118.

information. This allowed market players to exploit Amsterdam's status as 'a staple market of information'.[59]

With this institutional support, underwriting flourished: 'the Amsterdam insurance market acquired a reputation as the only market where all risks could be insured, every possible route and risk could be covered, and any asset or merchandise was insurable'.[60] Moreover, Amsterdam insurers 'were said to pay insurance claims promptly and without hassle'.[61] Building on an argument originally made by Violet Barbour, Go argues that 'the reputation of the Amsterdam underwriters, rather than the presence of capital, seems to have been crucial to the city's status'.[62]

The support of a specialist court that met the needs of native and foreign merchants alike (by being affordable and offering speedy justice) was key. Early on in its existence, the *Kamer* agreed to adjudicate cases involving both official and unofficial brokers (the latter known as *bijloopers* or *beunhazen*), recognising the need for legal oversight of policies outside of the Brokers' Guild monopoly.[63] Thus, the wide jurisdiction of the court precluded the need for, and prevented the rise of, merchant or guild courts that would have complicated the legal landscape by dividing jurisdiction on national, religious and/or professional lines.[64]

Nevertheless, the *Kamer*'s tacit acceptance of unofficial brokers – who were not bound by municipal ordinances – weakened the market in the long run. As the line between official and unofficial brokers became increasingly blurred, both groups were accused more and more frequently of price manipulation and unethical practice, including trading on their own account and brokering deals involving parties they knew had no intention of following through on their commitments.[65] This led to a decline in the market's reputation relative to that of London, compounded by frequent wars in the course of the eighteenth century. Spooner argues that 'upheavals of such magnitudes required an arbiter but it seemed that neither the federal system of The Netherlands nor the market of the Dam could at once provide enough control to ensure equilibrium'.[66]

---

[59] Go, *Marine Insurance in the Netherlands*, p. 63.
[60] Go, 'Amsterdam 1585–1790', pp. 118–19.
[61] Go, *Marine Insurance in the Netherlands*, p. 275.
[62] Ibid., p. 149; V. Barbour, 'Marine Risks and Insurance in the Seventeenth Century', *Journal of Economic and Business History* 1 (1929), pp. 561–96.
[63] Go, 'Amsterdam 1585–1790', pp. 109–10; Go, 'The Amsterdam Chamber', p. 519.
[64] Go, 'The Amsterdam Chamber', pp. 537–8.
[65] Go, *Marine Insurance in the Netherlands*, pp. 89–92.
[66] F. Spooner, *Risks at Sea: Amsterdam Insurance and Maritime Europe, 1766–1780*, Cambridge: Cambridge University Press, 1983, pp. 31 and 77–115.

As Amsterdam declined, London rose to prominence in the eighteenth century.[67] Yet this was far from inevitable. Rossi's work on its early market stresses it had achieved 'limited success'.[68] The establishment of the Royal Exchange in 1567 proved a decisive turning point. The 'rules of the game' were challenged as more merchants from different communities entered into underwriting activities, undermining the prior dominance of Florentine and Antwerpian practice. An external institution was needed to settle increasingly numerous and complex disputes.

Unlike in Amsterdam, there was no clear-cut solution in London – reflecting, perhaps, the inability of the English crown to impose its will on the influential commercial groups of the city.[69] A code of insurance, which Rossi has explored extensively, was written in the late 1570s and early 1580s through the impetus of the Aldermen's Court of London and the Queen's Privy Council. The code drew on other customary legal compilations, such as the 1484 Ordinances of Barcelona and compilations from Antwerp. Yet the legal status of the code was ambiguous; it was unclear whether it was binding or merely a guide that described customs at a given point in time.[70]

Alongside this code, an insurance court (to become the Court of Assurance in 1601) and an insurance registry (the Office of Assurances at the Royal Exchange) were created. While the registry seems to have achieved some success, the court did not have exclusive jurisdiction over insurance cases: the Admiralty, Chancery, and King's Bench continued to hear cases and apply either Roman law (in the case of the Admiralty) or common law principles to their judgments, thereby undermining the efficacy of the code further.[71] What emerged was a system where underwriters could drag their feet in paying out on insurance policies by bringing cases before the Admiralty, where cases often took years to resolve, to pressure the insured party into accepting reduced pay-outs.

Unfortunately, very little evidence on the market has survived from the seventeenth century. The underwriting community seems to have remained modest, with merchants continuing to rely generally on familiar colleagues to underwrite their voyages.[72] Nevertheless, London was grad-

---

[67] Here, see in particular A. Leonard, *London Marine Insurance 1438–1824: Risk, Trade, and the Early Modern State*, Woodbridge: Boydell & Brewer, 2022, pp. 107–211.
[68] Rossi, 'England 1523–1601', p. 141.
[69] Ibid., p. 144.
[70] G. Rossi, *Insurance in Elizabethan England: The London Code*, Cambridge: Cambridge University Press, 2016, pp. 146–8.
[71] Rossi, 'England 1523–1601', pp. 144–5; A. Leonard, 'London 1462–1601: Marine Insurance and the Law Merchant', in A. Leonard (ed.), *Marine Insurance: Origins and Institutions, 1300–1850*, Basingstoke: Palgrave Macmillan, 2016, p. 168.
[72] A. Leonard, 'Contingent Commitment: The Development of English Marine Insurance in the Context of New Institutional Economics, 1577–1720', in D. Coffman, A.

ually emerging as a leading market, insuring foreign and colonial expeditions with growing frequency.[73]

In addition to the Royal Exchange, new spaces emerged later in the century that supported insurance activity. The coffeehouse was brought to Europe by migrants from the Ottoman Empire: the first in London was established in 1652 by a Greek servant to a Levant Company merchant. Coffeehouses soon flourished as valuable spaces of mercantile sociability, where a proliferating print culture facilitated commercial discussion.[74] One such coffeehouse, established by Edward Lloyd, became a central space by the end of the century for the circulation of shipping and commercial information.[75] Lloyd's would later become the world's leading insurance market. It remains so to this day.

The rise of Lloyd's was facilitated by extensive state support. Through the 1720 Bubble Act, two chartered companies, Royal Exchange Assurance and London Assurance, were given a duopoly on the insurance market in London in exchange for loans to the crown. With close ties to the South Sea Company, both companies chose to invest heavily in the former's securities. Thus, while the interests of the crown and of speculative investors were being met through the act, it would be legitimate to question whether it served the interests of London's insurance market.[76]

A crucial exception was outlined in the act, however, through which private underwriters remained free to conduct business.[77] As Charles Wright and C. Ernest Fayle suggest, the establishment of the two companies forced private underwriters to come together and pool their resources: while underwriters had been split between several spaces before 1720 – chiefly the Royal Exchange, Lloyd's and other coffeehouses – it was after the Bubble Act that Lloyd's finally cemented its place as London's key insurance

---

Leonard, and L. Neal (eds), *Questioning Credible Commitment: Perspectives on the Rise of Financial Capitalism*, Cambridge: Cambridge University Press, 2013, p. 51.

[73] A. Leonard, 'From Local to Transatlantic: Insuring Trade in the Caribbean', in A. Leonard and D. Pretel (eds), *The Caribbean and the Atlantic World Economy: Circuits of Trade, Money and Knowledge, 1650–1914*, Basingstoke: Palgrave Macmillan, 2015, pp. 137–60.

[74] A. Bevilacqua and H. Pfeifer, 'Turquerie: Culture in Motion, 1650–1750', *Past and Present* 221 (2013), p. 96; P. Lake and S. Pincus, 'Rethinking the Public Sphere in Early Modern England', *Journal of British Studies* 45 (2006), p. 283.

[75] Here, see C. Wright and C. Fayle, *A History of Lloyd's from the Founding of Lloyd's Coffee House to the Present Day*, London: Macmillan and Company, 1928, pp. 11–33.

[76] Leonard, 'Contingent Commitment'; Leonard, *London Marine Insurance*, pp. 136–52.

[77] For a full discussion of this, see A. Bogatyreva, 'England 1660–1720: Corporate or Private?', in A. Leonard (ed.), *Marine Insurance: Origins and Institutions, 1300–1850*, Basingstoke: Palgrave Macmillan, 2016, pp. 179–204.

space.⁷⁸ Thus, while the act may not have had the wellbeing of London's insurance market as its primary goal, the effect of the act, as Christopher Kingston puts it, was to bring about 'path-dependent institutional change': it ensured Lloyd's competition was limited until the nineteenth century, creating a 'stable equilibrium' that remains unchanged to this day.⁷⁹

Lloyd's received further support after the Bubble Act. Wright and Fayle have argued that Lloyd's special arrangement with the Post Office, allowing correspondents to send information at no cost to them, gave Lloyd's 'a practical monopoly of complete and up-to-date shipping intelligence' that ensured it became 'not merely *a* centre, but *the* centre, of London underwriting'.⁸⁰ Kingston goes so far as to hypothesise Lloyd's had an information advantage over the two companies, thereby creating a 'lemons' problem that ensured the success of Lloyd's over its corporate rivals, although Adrian Leonard fairly questions the historical reality of this hypothesis.⁸¹ Nevertheless, Lloyd's relationship with the state helped to ensure its competitiveness in the European and North American marketplaces.

This relationship only deepened as time progressed, with Lloyd's becoming 'partners of the state in promoting their commercial interests and the security of the realm' through effective lobbying.⁸² The Royal Navy came to play a crucial role in protecting wartime commerce: in particular, naval convoys inhibited the ability of enemy privateers to make captures, thus supporting the activity of Lloyd's by reducing losses and helping to keep premium rates competitive.⁸³ In turn, Lloyd's helped to coordinate

---

78 Wright and Fayle, *A History of Lloyd's*, pp. 64–87.
79 C. Kingston, 'Governance and Institutional Change in Marine Insurance, 1350–1850', *European Review of Economic History* 18 (2013), pp. 16–17. On the dubious intentions behind the act, see Leonard, *London Marine Insurance*, pp. 136–56.
80 Wright and Fayle, *A History of Lloyd's*, pp. 74–5 and 78. This will be discussed further in Chapter 3.
81 In saying there was a 'lemons' problem, Kingston means that, by virtue of the supposedly superior resources of the private underwriters, they could attract and secure the 'best' risks, leaving only the 'worst' for the corporate underwriters who would have to raise their premiums as a result. 'Thus', Kingston suggests, 'an equilibrium might develop in which the better risks are insured by private underwriters at low premiums, while the corporations charge high premiums and receive business only from the worst risks'; C. Kingston, 'Marine Insurance in Britain and America, 1720–1844: A Comparative Institutional Analysis', *Journal of Economic History* 67 (2007), p. 399; Leonard, 'Contingent Commitment', p. 53. On the 'lemons' problem, see G. Akerlof, 'The Market for "Lemons": Quality Uncertainty and the Market Mechanism', *The Quarterly Journal of Economics* 84 (1970), pp. 488–500.
82 L. Lobo-Guerrero, *Insuring War: Sovereignty, Security and Risk*, London: Routledge, 2012, p. 41.
83 On convoying and other measures to protect commerce in the eighteenth century – including the Western Squadron – see D. Baugh, 'Naval Power: What Gave the British

these convoys and required insured ships to join them, thereby facilitating the Royal Navy's activities.[84] Moreover, during the French Revolutionary Wars (1792–1802), Lloyd's transmitted signal messages to merchant ships at the Board of Admiralty's request and maintained a Patriotic Fund to reward 'acts of gallantry and valour in protecting British maritime trade'.[85] In this way, a symbiotic relationship formed between Lloyd's and the British state, with the two working in tandem to protect wartime commerce.

In addition, legal reforms instituted by Lord Justice Mansfield helped to overcome longstanding issues in reconciling insurance practice with common law. By appointing merchant juries to advise on prevailing norms in the conduct of insurance, Mansfield was able to establish the court system as a viable method of conflict resolution in London where it had previously proven inadequate.[86]

Thus, while the path had not been as smooth as in Amsterdam, London was able to complete the insurance triangle through the support of the state. Although the motivations underpinning it were dubious, the Bubble Act proved crucial in stimulating the extraordinary rise of the London insurance market.

It was London, and not Paris, which usurped Amsterdam as Europe's leading insurance market. While London's market has been amply treated, those of Paris and other French cities have received little scholarly attention. John Clark and J.F. Bosher have made valuable contributions on marine insurance in eighteenth-century France, but the century prior remains almost entirely unexplored.[87] Even Francesca Trivellato's recent ground-breaking study of anti-Semitic tropes in French literature on commerce, banking and insurance draws primarily from Barbour's 1929 article on 'Marine Risks and Insurance in the Seventeenth Century' to

---

Naval Superiority?', in L. Prados de la Escosura (ed.), *Exceptionalism and Industrialisation: Britain and Its European Rivals, 1688–1815*, Cambridge: Cambridge University Press, 2004, pp. 235–57.

[84] H. Farber, *Underwriters of the United States: How Insurance Shaped the American Founding*, Williamsburg, VA and Chapel Hill, NC: Omohundro Institute of Early American History and Culture and the University of North Carolina Press, 2021, p. 63; Leonard, *London Marine Insurance*, p. 17; R. Knight, *Convoys: The British Struggle Against Napoleonic Europe and America*, New Haven: Yale University Press, 2022, pp. 16 and 32–4.

[85] Lobo-Guerrero, *Insuring War*, pp. 47 and 50–1.

[86] Leonard, *London Marine Insurance*, pp. 187–90.

[87] J. Clark, 'Marine Insurance in Eighteenth-Century La Rochelle', *French Historical Studies* 10 (1978), pp. 572–98; J. Bosher, 'The Paris Business World and the Seaports under Louis XV: Speculators in Marine Insurance, Naval Finances and Trade', *Histoire Sociale* 12 (1979), pp. 281–9.

contextualise insurance practices in the kingdom before 1700.[88] Recent contributions have made only small steps forward.[89]

Louis-Augustin Boiteux is the only historian to have treated extensively on the insurance industry in seventeenth-century France. His 1945 monograph *L'assurance maritime à Paris sous le règne de Louis XIV* discusses the two institutions I will focus on in this book: the Royal Insurance Chamber and Company. Boiteux hails the Chamber as Lloyd's of London *avant la lettre*, but does not explain convincingly why this supposed precursor to Lloyd's did not share the latter's enduring success.[90] Moreover, his brief and negative assessment of the Company draws from a limited and problematic source base.

I do agree with Boiteux, however, that these interventions into the Parisian market should be understood as 'missed opportunities'.[91] This book makes a straightforward argument: while the insurance markets of Amsterdam and London benefited from state and/or municipal support – essential to their long-term success – Paris lacked consistent state support over time. Mistakes in the execution of royal policy, alongside oscillations in French high politics, ensured neither the Chamber nor the Company could overcome the perils of the Dutch War (1672–78) and Nine Years' War respectively. Amsterdam and London did not emerge unscathed from these wars – indeed, some of London's underwriters fell into bankruptcy in the 1690s – but these markets were better placed overall to absorb the shocks of war thanks to extant institutions supported by state/municipal authorities.[92] In short, Paris was never able to complete the insurance triangle whereas its

---

[88] F. Trivellato, *The Promise and Peril of Credit: What a Forgotten Legend about Jews and Finance Tells Us about the Making of European Commercial Society*, Princeton: Princeton University Press, 2019, pp. 22–4.

[89] Here, see the essays on seventeenth-century France in C. Borde and É. Roulet (eds), *L'assurance maritime XIVe–XXIe siècle*, Aachen: Shaker Verlag, 2017. Renewed interest is on the horizon, however; besides my own work, Mallory Hope at Yale University has undertaken research on insurance in eighteenth-century Marseille; M. Hope, 'Underwriting Risk: Trade, War, Insurance, and Legal Institutions in Eighteenth-Century France and Its Empire', PhD thesis, Yale University (2023).

[90] L. Boiteux, *L'assurance maritime à Paris sous le règne de Louis XIV*, Paris: Éditions Roche d'Estrez, 1945, especially pp. 40–1.

[91] Ibid., pp. 40–1. There are clear parallels here between Boiteux, Braudel and, to an extent, myself: as Steven Kaplan puts it, 'of all the qualities that constitute Frenchness for Braudel across the long run, most striking are a genius for *missed opportunities* [emphasis my own] and a gift for (relative) failure'; S. Kaplan, 'Long Run Lamentations: Braudel on France', *The Journal of Modern History* 63 (1991), p. 344. I am grateful to Renaud Morieux, who pointed out these parallels and encouraged me to embrace the Braudelian framing of my argument. This said, my argument does not share the same intensity of lamentation espoused in the works of Boiteux and Braudel.

[92] The difficulties faced in the Amsterdam and London markets in the 1690s are discussed in Chapter 8.

rivals were. Nevertheless, it anticipated developments in marine insurance elsewhere in the eighteenth century: Lloyd's trod ground Parisian insurers had walked decades before; American insurance corporations were established based on logics that had already been articulated in Paris. In short, the market made crucial innovations in the practice of marine insurance, but enjoyed none of the rewards, nor, until now, any of the credit amongst historians. This book brings the market back into the light and treats it with the seriousness it deserves.

SOURCES AND STRUCTURE

These, then, are the key strands of the book's argument: state formation, economic development and marine insurance. In bringing these together, the book revolves primarily – but not exclusively – around two institutions: the Chamber and the Company. The extant registers of these institutions are kept in series Z/1d of the *Archives nationales* in Paris. These are a diverse collection of sources, ranging from policy registers to arbitration registers, inviting both a quantitative and qualitative study of the institutions' activities. Given the widespread paucity of sources on early modern insurance, this source base is especially valuable.[93] Using the institutions' policy registers, I have created two quantitative datasets, which are studied in Chapters 4 and 5.

I have delved into further archival series in the *Archives nationales*, such as the papers of the secretariat of state for maritime affairs, led by Colbert and Seignelay from 1669 to 1690;[94] the letter-books of France's overseas consulates; and the records of the Parisian admiralty court.[95] I have also drawn on valuable material in the *Bibliothèque nationale de France*, The National Archives and the Institute and Faculty of Actuaries library. Finally, I make use of print – most notably, Étienne Cleirac's *Us et coutumes de la mer* and Jacques Savary's *Le parfait négociant* – and material culture.

In focusing so much on state and institutional papers, some readers may conclude that my analysis is top-down. To an extent, this is true: the story I tell is one where the state (in this case, instantiated primarily by the secretariat of state for maritime affairs) is front and centre. Chapters 1, 2 and 3 focus in part on how the state understood marine insurance and its role in shaping insurance practice across France. In the subsequent chapters, we will see that this perception, and its shift over time, was crucial in the

---

[93] This is discussed in greater depth in Chapter 4.
[94] Strictly, this should be translated as 'secretariat of state for the navy'. However, I eschew this translation throughout the book, as the secretariat's remit was far broader than naval affairs.
[95] Formally, the *table de marbre* of the seat of the admiralty of France; on this court, see Chapters 7 and 8.

ultimate fate of the Parisian insurance market under Louis XIV. Yet far from taking state papers at face value, the book brings them into discussion with other sources in order to identify and critically assess the observations of the various individuals who worked in the secretariat over time.

Indeed, these sources document the agency of multiple actors beyond the state: underwriters, *financiers* and other notables are analysed and understood with reference to the concepts of neo-institutionalism, namely the constituent elements of transaction costs. This may surprise the reader, given my intention to challenge the historical narrative neo-institutionalism has constructed around property rights. Let me be clear on this point: institutional analysis is a valuable weapon in the historian's arsenal; to quote North, 'incorporating institutions into history allows us to tell a much better story than we otherwise could'.[96] Yet while understanding institutions as equilibria (as Greif advocates) can be helpful, social history and sociology come into their own in those instances where such equilibria are 'ruptured'.[97] Thus, the book reflects broader trends in the study of absolutism discussed above: as the opening two chapters make clear, understanding privilege as a social, legal and economic construction of its time is crucial to understanding the Parisian insurance market at large. Moreover, Chapter 3 draws extensively on studies of information networks, while Chapters 7 and 8 reflect the sociological turn in the study of legal practice, making clear the limitations of institutions-as-equilibria in understanding contemporary conceptualisations of creditworthiness and legal decision making in Paris. Thus, while the book is in many ways a study of state institutions, it is underpinned by individuals in France and beyond whose interests (and the strategies they deployed in service to them) are captured by the records, even if one must read against the grain at times to find them.

The volume is split into three parts. Part 1 explores the foundations for the Chamber and the Company's activities, situating them within a new interpretation of Colbertian and post-Colbertian commercial policy. Chapters 1 and 2 seek to understand what motivated ministers to establish the Chamber and the Company and, in turn, what motivated members to join them. In the process, they argue that marine insurance was understood as a powerful (albeit volatile) tool for commercial development that the secretariat of state for maritime affairs sought to utilise in France's commercial war with

---

[96] North, *Institutions, Institutional Change and Economic Performance*, p. 131.
[97] The phrase 'ruptured equilibria' paraphrases Fabrice Mauclair, as quoted in M. Breen, 'Law, Society, and the State in Early Modern France', *The Journal of Modern History* 83 (2011), p. 380.

England and the Netherlands. Chapter 3 studies the extent of the institutions' capacity to overcome the natural information disadvantages faced by the landlocked Parisian market, challenging longstanding narratives on the institutional advantages of the Amsterdam and London markets.

Part 2 moves on to the institutions' underwriting activities themselves, drawing on extensive quantitative datasets. The Chamber and Company responded in remarkably different ways to the onset of the Dutch War and Nine Years' War respectively, in keeping with fundamental differences in the economic logics their patrons were espousing.

Finally, Part 3 studies the impact of the institutions' activities on French legal development. Chapter 6 considers the institutions within the broader legal reforms of the period, namely the 1681 *Ordonnance de la marine*, and establishes their significance in furthering state claims to maritime power. Chapters 7 and 8 analyse the institutions' approaches to conflict resolution and how they fashioned their reputations. In the process, the chapters stress the agency of French subjects in legitimating state formation through their legal decision making.

The conclusion evaluates the insurance market of Paris through comparison with the markets of Amsterdam and London. Moreover, it offers broader reflections on absolutism as a system of risk management, through which the absolute monarchy leveraged private resources to act on land, at sea and overseas where it could not itself. Thus, the book's focus on the commercial and maritime realms yields new insights into the ongoing debate on absolutism in Old Regime France.

Part 1

INSURANCE, PRIVILEGE
AND COMMERCIAL POLICY

1

THE ROYAL INSURANCE CHAMBER AND COLBERTIAN COMMERCIAL POLICY, 1664–83

> Of what use is blood that does not circulate?
> Fernand Braudel[1]

In order to understand the activities of the Chamber and the Company, it is necessary to first consider why they were established. This chapter explores how the Chamber fitted into Colbert's commercial policy. Colbert sought to establish Paris as an insurance centre to challenge Amsterdam, thereby transforming insurance into a weapon in France's commercial war with the Dutch. The success of this ambitious endeavour depended upon bringing new insurers into the game, i.e. enticing individuals to participate in new insurance institutions. Following Colbert's unsuccessful attempt at creating a monopoly insurance company in 1664, the Chamber was established in 1668. These were two very different projects enshrining very different institutional structures, yet both were compatible with Colbert's commercial policy. The chapter thus supports the progress made in recent decades in moving past stereotypes of Colbertianism as inherently pro-monopoly. Colbert's commercial policy was flexible; in the case of insurance, he changed tack when alerted to growing endogenous interest in developing the Parisian insurance market.

Yet what was at the heart of this shift? Why did the Chamber come to fruition where the 1664 project did not, and what ultimately motivated individuals to join the Chamber? These questions can only be answered through analysing the culture of venal office holding in Old Regime France. This culture served as a means of social advancement for officeholders and

---

[1] Quoted in Kaplan, 'Long Run Lamentations', p. 350.

as a fiscal expedient for the state. Colbert tried to curb venal office holding and rentier practices as a means of encouraging investment in French commerce. The Chamber incentivised Parisian officeholders and *rentiers* to participate in underwriting through creating a space with flexible access to royal power, namely through its president, Francesco Bellinzani, who was Colbert's right-hand man in commercial affairs.

THE OLD REGIME: A SOCIETY OF PRIVILEGE

The decision to establish these insurance institutions in Paris was the product of the Old Regime itself – or, put differently, the product of France's distinctive regime of privilege. Since Colbert and Seignelay believed mutual underwriting between port merchants could not meet the demand for insurance, their strategies were predicated on the hypothesis that new players needed to be brought into the game to increase capital in the sector as a stimulus to growth.[2] While their strategies shared this premise, the strategies themselves diverged quite significantly.

A key target for the ministers' commercial projects was venal officeholders, *rentiers* and *financiers*. Venal officeholders invested in offices in institutions, such as provincial estates or courts. These bestowed particular privileges and benefits that could support their social and economic rise. Moreover, these offices were considered property that could be used as collateral for loans, and, with the payment of an annual sum called the *paulette*, were heritable.[3] This was significant, as hereditary nobility

---

[2] I draw a crucial distinction between perception and reality here. How far it is true that mutual underwriting in the ports was insufficient is currently impossible to ascertain. My intention here is to look at what *motivated* Colbert to intervene, reserving judgement as to whether such motivations were correctly informed or not.

[3] There is a rich literature surrounding venal office holding: for the most famous piece, see D. Bien, 'Offices, Corps, and a System of State Credit: The Uses of Privilege under the Ancien Régime', in K. Baker (ed.), *The French Revolution and the Creation of Modern Political Culture*, vol. I, Oxford: Pergamon Press, 1987, pp. 89–114. For a detailed description of the origins and legal underpinnings of offices and the practices of *financiers*, see R. Mousnier, *The Institutions of France under the Absolute Monarchy 1598–1789*, vol. II, Chicago: University of Chicago Press, 1984, pp. 27–59, 65–73 and 423–40. For some recent examples, see the excellent essays in V. Meyzie (ed.), *Crédit public, crédit privé et institutions intermédiaires. Monarchie française, monarchie hispanique, XVIe–XVIIIe siècles*, Limoges: Presses universitaires de Limoges, 2012; G. Rowlands, 'Royal Finances in the Third Reign of Louis XIV', in J. Prest and G. Rowlands (eds), *The Third Reign of Louis XIV, c. 1682–1715*, Abingdon: Routledge, 2017, pp. 38–52.

often came in the third generation of office holding.⁴ By contrast, *rentiers* invested directly in the debt of the *Hôtel de Ville de Paris* (essentially, the state debt), receiving annuity payments (*arrérages*) at set intervals until the state reimbursed the principal (*rente perpétuelle* – hereafter *rente(s)*) in full.⁵ Daniel Voysin, the *prévôt des marchands* of Paris, wrote in 1664 that *rentes* on the *Hôtel de Ville* were the 'most handy of all property', as they were recognised as proof of one's credit and could be used as collateral for loans.⁶ Moreover, like offices, *rentes* could be sold on the open market and, upon one's death, were heritable.

Financiers occupied a peculiar position. In Old Regime France, a *financier* 'was any person who handled the king's money'.⁷ The general farmers (*fermiers généraux*) oversaw the collection and management of the crown's indirect taxes, i.e. the salt tax (*gabelles*), food and drink taxes (*aides*) and customs duties (*traites*).⁸ Meanwhile, the receivers general (*receveurs généraux*) and receivers (*receveurs*) were officeholders who collected and managed the direct taxes such as the *taille*.⁹ Finally, contractors (*traitants*) 'administered the extraordinary revenues (*affaires extraordinaires*)', such as the sale of offices.¹⁰ Each group therefore acted as financial intermediaries. At the same time, they were able to support state finances by securing loans with more favourable interest rates than the state itself could secure from banking institutions or other sources of private credit. This was because the state was a riskier debtor: it could not easily be held to keep its commitments, owing chiefly to its capacity to debase the *livre tournois* when it suited its own interests. In return for this support, *financiers* were exempted from paying taxes themselves and could be bestowed other privileges and

---

4   Potter, *Corps and Clienteles*, p. 29. On the distinction between the *noblesse de robe* and the *noblesse d'épée*, see Collins, *The State in Early Modern France*.
5   For a thorough study of *rentes* in the seventeenth century, see K. Béguin, *Financer la guerre au XVIIe siècle. La dette publique et les rentiers de l'absolutisme*, Seyssel: Champ Vallon, 2012.
6   Quoted in ibid., pp. 263–5.
7   Mousnier, *The Institutions of France*, vol. II, p. 66.
8   For a concise discussion of these, see ibid., pp. 423–40.
9   For a full breakdown of the functions of the receivers general, see G. Rowlands, *The Financial Decline of a Great Power: War, Influence, and Money in Louis XIV's France*, Oxford: Oxford University Press, 2012, pp. 5–10 and 58–62. On the complexities of the *taille* (especially in regard to defining who was exempt from it and who was not, and the tensions this created), see R. Blaufarb, *The Politics of Fiscal Privilege in Provence, 1530s–1830s*, Washington, DC: The Catholic University of America Press, 2012.
10 Heijmans, *The Agency of Empire*, p. 27.

benefits through their offices.[11] Moreover, once *financiers* met the terms of their contracts/farms, any further tax revenue was theirs to keep.[12]

Since unexpected liquidity shocks could hinder the state's ability to meet its financial commitments, there was always a risk to these enterprises. This was exacerbated by the state's capacity to act against the interests of their stakeholders.[13] The state extracted forced loans from officeholders, using a mechanism known as *augmentations de gages*. This required the officeholder to increase the investment in their office in exchange for higher *gages*, which occupy an ambiguous middle ground between wages and interest payments attached to the office.[14] Only once this *augmentation* was paid could the officeholder pay the *paulette* – i.e. if they refused to pay their *augmentation*, their office ceased to be heritable. Officeholders were solely liable for any loans they contracted to pay the *augmentation*, meaning they were vulnerable to ruin if the state reneged on payment of *gages* and they were otherwise unable to service their debt.[15] Similarly, the annuity payments of *rentiers* could be suspended at any moment, and return of the principal was not guaranteed. *Financiers* were in an especially tenuous position, as they could fall rapidly from grace if the king decided to call a Chamber of Justice (*chambre de justice*), referred to by J.F. Bosher as 'a royal business institution disguised as a court of law'. Chambers of Justice were used to punish *financiers* for their ostensible malpractice in the handling of royal funds, justifying the cancellation of debts owed to them and the seizure of their venal offices. The 1661 Chamber of Justice sanctioned the fall from grace of Nicolas Fouquet, Louis XIV's *surintendant des finances*, who was the victim of Colbert's rise to power. The *financiers* who had risen

---

[11] Bien, 'Offices, Corps, and a System of State Credit', p. 91.
[12] This paragraph owes much to Heijmans, *The Agency of Empire*. On the public perception of *financiers*, see M. Kwass, 'Court Capitalism, Illicit Markets, and Political Legitimacy in Eighteenth-Century France: The Salt and Tobacco Monopolies', in D. Coffman, A. Leonard, and L. Neal (eds), *Questioning Credible Commitment: Perspectives on the Rise of Financial Capitalism*, Cambridge: Cambridge University Press, 2013, p. 232; J. Shovlin, *The Political Economy of Virtue: Luxury, Patriotism, and the Origins of the French Revolution*, Ithaca, NY: Cornell University Press, 2006, pp. 33–4.
[13] Here, see P. Hoffman, 'Early Modern France, 1450–1700', in P. Hoffman and K. Norberg (eds), *Fiscal Crises, Liberty, and Representative Government, 1450–1789*, Stanford: Stanford University Press, 1994, pp. 229–40.
[14] Whether *gages* were wages or interest payments has been a subject of great debate in recent decades; for an argument against wages, see Collins, *The State in Early Modern France*; for an argument against interest payments, see C. Blanquie, *Une enquête de Colbert en 1665. La généralité de Bordeaux dans l'enquête sur les offices*, Paris: L'Harmattan, 2012.
[15] Hurt, *Louis XIV and the Parlements*, p. 68.

to prominence thanks to Fouquet's patronage were cleared out through this Chamber, making way for the rise of the *lobby Colbert*.[16]

Nevertheless, the riskiness of the state as a debtor ensured higher returns from offices and *rentes* than from other investments. It is partly for this reason that Colbert was strenuously averse to an overreliance on both forms of public finance: they tied the crown into payments of *gages* and *arrérages* that impeded Colbert's efforts to ameliorate the crown's finances as *intendant des finances* from 1661 to 1665, and then as controller general of finances (*contrôleur général des finances*) from 1665.[17] Moreover, the extensive capital invested in offices was, in Colbert's eyes, entirely 'immobilised'.[18] In 1659, Colbert wrote that the king would draw 'an infinitely greater advantage' if those who lived on their *gages* or *arrérages* 'would be obliged to apply themselves to commerce and manufacturing, [or] to agriculture and war, which are the only crafts that make the kingdom flourish'.[19]

The Colbertian strategy up to 1672, therefore, was to reform the culture of venal office holding and *rentes* in order 'to reorient the fortune of [wealthy] families towards investments judged more useful', such as commercial investments.[20] Using templates completed by the intendants – crown-appointed bureaucrats connecting the provinces and the court – Colbert collected information about venal offices across France from 1663 to 1665. The inventory that resulted from this testified to a total of 45,780 venal offices across the kingdom, with an estimated value of 420 million *livres*.[21] This comprehensive endeavour, Christophe Blanquie argues, fulfilled a specific, preconceived aim: to identify the excesses of venal offices, allowing Colbert to persuade the king to pursue reform.[22] Colbert subsequently oversaw the capping of office values, thereby dampening their attractiveness as a form of passive investment.[23] Similarly, Colbert pursued a bold reform of the

---

[16] J. Bosher, '*Chambres de justice* in the French Monarchy', in J. Bosher (ed.), *French Government and Society 1500–1850: Essays in Memory of Alfred Cobban*, London: The Athlone Press of the University of London, 1973, pp. 19–40.

[17] Potter, *Corps and Clienteles*, p. 37. At the end of 1663, Colbert wrote a series of *mémoires* on French finances, condemning the willingness of prior *surintendants de finances* (most particularly, Fouquet) to lean on expedients that enriched their *financier* clients but were ultimately damaging to the state; Dessert, *Le royaume de Monsieur Colbert*, pp. 105–8.

[18] Blanquie, *Une enquête de Colbert*, p. 224.

[19] Quoted in W. Doyle, 'Colbert et les offices', *Histoire, économie et société* 19e année (2000), p. 472.

[20] Blanquie, *Une enquête de Colbert*, p. 9.

[21] Hurt, *Louis XIV and the Parlements*, p. 76.

[22] Blanquie, *Une enquête de Colbert*, p. 225.

[23] J. Dewald, 'Rethinking the 1 Percent: The Failure of the Nobility in Old Regime France', *The American Historical Review* 124 (2019), pp. 925–6; Mousnier, *The*

debt of the *Hôtel de Ville* in 1661 to 1665, reimbursing *rentes* below their face value.[24] While the onset of the Dutch War in 1672 forced Colbert to create offices again as a short-term fiscal expedient, he wrote again after the war that it was essential 'to reduce the number of offices as much as possible [...] the good and the benefit that would come to the people and the state would be difficult to express'.[25]

PARISIAN INSURANCE AND COLBERTIAN COMMERCIAL POLICY

Colbert never composed a treatise outlining his thoughts on marine insurance. It is only by analysing Colbert's insurance projects themselves that we can discern the ways in which they complemented other aspects of his commercial and fiscal policies.

Unravelling a myth: the privileged insurance company project in 1664

The first proposal for a state project for insurance was made in 1664. This project has inadvertently been confused with the Company of 1686 in works published since the turn of the millennium. Let us take the following from a recent essay by Anastasia Bogatyreva:

> A French proposal of 1686 added a mercantilist dimension to the debate [on insurance]. In an ordinance Jean-Baptiste Colbert, finance minister to Louis XIV, encouraged the establishment of a joint-stock marine insurance company. He was concerned over the outflow of insurance premiums, and thus specie, to England and the Dutch Republic, and hoped to remedy the loss by establishing a local insurance corporation. Colbert and the promoters of the scheme expected it would reduce French premium levels and improve the competitiveness of domestic insurance. It was also intended to 'give to the merchants who will use this way to reduce their risks the means to launch their business, and to further it more easily and safely'. However, the conservatively inclined merchants of Rouen, which possessed an entrenched private insurance tradition, saw no need to secure capital by issuing shares, since private underwriters' 'pledge was their word and the trust it inspired'. A corporation was not established because the merchant population deemed it to be unnecessary to meet the needs of trade. They deemed a pool of ready capital unnecessary.[26]

Institutions of France, vol. II, p. 49.
[24] Béguin, *Financer la guerre*, pp. 200–6.
[25] Quoted in Doyle, 'Colbert et les offices', p. 472.
[26] Bogatyreva, 'England 1660–1720', p. 185.

This affair is entirely fictitious. The myth of the stillborn 1686 project – in which Colbert makes an appearance three years after his death – is the culmination of a series of misunderstandings of the primary and secondary source material in French. Unravelling this myth will allow us to correct this mistake in the historiography and identify the ideological roots of the state's intervention into insurance under Colbert and Seignelay.

The beginnings of this misunderstanding can be found in a 2003 article by Michèle Ruffat, upon which Bogatyreva's discussion is based. Ruffat writes that:

> In 1686, the creation of a maritime insurance company was authorised by official ordinance, but to no avail. The merchants of Rouen, visited by a King's emissary to convince them to take advantage of the opportunity and develop the project, showed very limited enthusiasm. Told that the selling of shares would allow the formation of sufficient capital to serve as a guarantee, they argued that 'they saw no need for blocking capital for that purpose, considering that they did not need any funds in advance nor any money in their coffers to write insurance: their pledge was their word and the trust it inspired'.[27]

Here, Ruffat cites Boiteux's discussion of a mission carried out in 1664 by Louis Nicolas de Clerville, a trusted subordinate of Colbert. In discussing how the Rouennais merchants reacted to Clerville's proposal for an insurance company, Boiteux refers to the Company's letters patent from 1686 in order to explore the possible motivations behind the project. Ruffat has simply made a mistake in reading Boiteux.[28] Anglophone literature since 2003 has unfortunately reproduced this mistake, confounding the 1664 project with the 1686 project.[29]

But this still does not clarify the 1664 project entirely. Boiteux's core argument – replicated imprecisely by Ruffat and Bogatyreva – is that the merchants were unconvinced by Clerville's proposal to establish an insurance company, as they were averse to undertaking insurance based on anything other than personal credit and, at heart, were ideologically opposed to anti-competitive royal companies. Boiteux concludes that 'the Rouennais merchants' state of mind is enough to explain the failure' of this and all other insurance projects in the reign of Louis XIV.[30]

---

[27] M. Ruffat, 'French Insurance from the *Ancien Régime* to 1946: Shifting Frontiers between State and Market', Financial History Review 10 (2003), pp. 186–7.
[28] L. Boiteux, *La fortune de mer. Le besoin de sécurité et les débuts de l'assurance maritime*, Paris: École Pratique des Hautes Études, 1968, pp. 171–3.
[29] Besides Bogatyreva, see also Kingston, 'Governance and Institutional Change', p. 14.
[30] Boiteux, *La fortune de mer*, p. 173.

In substantiating these claims, however, Boiteux takes specific quotations from Clerville's report out of context. The chronology documented in the report becomes confused in the process. A full reassessment is needed to understand it.

Clerville's report documented his findings from a mission he undertook in the ports of Picardy and Normandy in 1664 with an eye to 'the re-establishment of commerce'.[31] For Rouen, Clerville's aim was 'to urge them [i.e. the port's merchants] to form the strongest and most powerful companies possible for foreign commerce amongst themselves'.[32] The merchants did not reject this proposal entirely out of hand; they adopted a nuanced position that distinguished between 'companies of the state' and 'private companies'.

The former denoted companies created to explore and establish trade in new territories, 'where the support and authority of the prince are absolutely necessary, as well as the support of several associates' (i.e. investors in a company).[33] The merchants thus recognised the need for crown support in specific markets to establish the diplomatic and/or jurisdictional frameworks necessary for trade. On this front, Clerville wrote, 'they are ready to unite with each other to contribute to these with all their abilities and care'.[34] Indeed, some were especially eager to form a royal company for voyages to China – here, 'the protection of the king would be necessary to surmount the obstacles that Holland has always brought to this design'.[35]

Such 'protection' stemmed from a kingly duty to support the interests of his people: it was a mainstay of early modern political and economic thought that the prince could legitimately bestow monopolies where he thought it would serve the public good (*bien public*).[36] Throughout the seventeenth century, this was developed further, with numerous English writers (such as Charles Davenant) arguing the EIC's monopoly privileges were necessary to ensure private interests would not parasitise the commercial and diplomatic frameworks established through its members' investment.[37]

---

[31] Cinq cents de Colbert 122, fols 1–36, *Bibliothèque nationale de France*, Paris (BNF).
[32] Ibid.
[33] Ibid.
[34] Ibid.
[35] Ibid.
[36] On such thought, see R. Rosolino, 'Vices tyranniques', *Annales. Histoire, Sciences Sociales* 68 année (2013), pp. 793–819. The public good will be discussed further in Chapter 2. On arguments surrounding royal protection of commerce and industry more broadly, see J. Hirsch and P. Minard, '"Laissez-nous faire et protégez-nous beaucoup": pour une histoire des pratiques institutionnelles dans l'industrie française (XVIIIe–XIXe siècle)', in L. Bergeron and P. Bourdelais (eds), *La France n'est-elle pas douée pour l'industrie?*, Paris: Belin, 1998, pp. 135–58.
[37] P. Stern, 'Companies: Monopoly, Sovereignty, and the East Indies', in P. Stern and C. Wennerlind (eds), *Mercantilism Reimagined: Political Economy in Early Modern*

Although not explicitly stating their support for monopolies – which was a pejorative term throughout the early modern period – the merchants of Rouen were hinting at these sorts of argument, acknowledging the king's legitimate power to establish monopolies where private enterprise could not succeed alone.

Money was the only obstacle, the merchants claimed, since the recent collapse of their commerce ostensibly meant they could not fund such a company themselves. The implication was clear: the crown should step in to help. We will return to this shortly.

Private companies, by contrast, were characterised as those that traded with familiar territories – such as Spain, western Africa, the French Caribbean, America, Canada and the Baltic Sea – where neither the wide-scale pooling of capital nor crown support were considered necessary. While royal companies in new markets were, by necessity, led by directors who made decisions on behalf of their members, port merchants ostensibly preferred to conduct trade themselves rather than simply be passive investors in a larger enterprise. Accordingly, the Rouennais suggested that trade in established markets should be undertaken by individuals or small groups of merchants: it was 'the essence of private commerce' that merchants compete with each other and be justly rewarded for their efforts and success.[38]

Having established this distinction, and its implications, the merchants were then asked by Clerville for their thoughts on establishing an insurance company with state support. Clerville had targeted the merchants of Rouen for this plan, most likely because the city was a trendsetter in French insurance practice through the *Guidon de la mer*, a famous collection of norms written in the city in the late sixteenth century that were later published in Étienne Cleirac's bestselling *Us et coutumes de la mer*.[39]

    Britain and Its Empire, Oxford: Oxford University Press, 2013, pp. 177–96. On such ideas being echoed in French thought, see Cole, *Colbert*, vol. I, p. 223.

[38] Cinq cents de Colbert 122, fols 1–36, BNF. Boiteux selectively quotes from this discussion, omitting entirely its nuances. The tension between the value of crown privileges and support to *some* on the one hand, and the desire from *others* for unencumbered commerce on the other hand, is also found in the colonial sphere. The need for state support in colonial endeavours (including commerce) was widely recognised, but precisely what role it should take was widely disputed; J. Pritchard, *In Search of Empire: The French in the Americas, 1670–1730*, Cambridge: Cambridge University Press, 2004, pp. 193–208.

[39] É. Cleirac, *Les us et coutumes de la mer. Divisées en trois parties*, Rouen: Jean Berthelin, 1671. The *Guidon de la mer* will be discussed at length in Chapters 6 and 7.

In response to this proposal, there were no objections: 'on the contrary, [there was] a general approval and a universal confession of the usefulness that would come to the state through this'.[40] Indeed, mutual underwriting in Rouen was proving insufficient to protect larger risks:

> when it [i.e. the insurance needed] has surpassed 20,000 *francs*, recourse to the insurers of London and Amsterdam has been necessary, where a considerable quantity of money is given which could remain in the kingdom if there were well-established insurance companies in some of the key maritime towns.[41]

The merchants agreed that, with the support of partners in Paris or elsewhere, a fund of 400,000 *livres* could be raised. This would be entirely sufficient not only to avoid all need to seek insurance abroad, but even to encourage foreigners to seek their insurance in France.[42] In this way, capital from Paris and elsewhere would make up for the shortfall in the ports.

The logic the merchants had applied to the private companies was not extended to this proposed company. Instead, insurance was treated as a market where the pooling of capital under state supervision was desirable to overcome the challenges of securing coverage without looking abroad.

The merchants even offered their own ideas for the company. They recognised the company's pooled capital would serve as a form of cash fund, ensuring prompt reimbursement of claims.[43] But they noted the typical private insurer, 'who normally provides no other security than their word and their credit',[44] can take the premiums they receive and invest them, while an entirely liquid cash fund would have no such scope for speculative profits.[45] Consequently, they proposed an appropriate portion of the fund should be invested in other ventures to generate a profit, to be distributed with the outstanding premiums to the partners of the company.

As a result, the Rouennais envisioned this company as 'a kind of bank' where any and all from across France could invest, garnering profits from

---

[40] Cinq cents de Colbert 122, fols 1–36, BNF.
[41] Ibid.
[42] Following what I have said above, I make no assessment here as to the representativeness of Rouen vis-à-vis the other ports of France. For Saint-Malo, André Lespagnol notes that, up to the 1680s, 'the possibilities of insurance in the port, undertaken by merchants on a purely individual basis, seem to have been quite limited' and grew only with the rise of insurance companies heading into the eighteenth century; A. Lespagnol, *Messieurs de Saint-Malo. Une élite négociante au temps de Louis XIV*, vol. I, Rennes: Presses universitaires de Rennes, 1997, p. 154.
[43] Cinq cents de Colbert 122, fols 1–36, BNF.
[44] Whence the quotation in Ruffat and Bogatyreva originates, albeit in a context entirely different from what Boiteux suggests.
[45] Cinq cents de Colbert 122, fols 1–36, BNF.

premiums and the portion of the fund earmarked for investment, while policyholders would benefit from the security of the company's liquidity.[46] Such confidence would, Clerville concluded, lead to a blossoming of commerce. Moreover, the company would keep premiums within France and attract prospective policyholders from abroad, 'following the good maxims that we must aim to draw in the greatest quantity [of money] that we can from other [countries] and to allow the smallest amount possible to escape from ours'.[47]

Here, Clerville was playing to Colbert's neo-Aristotelian bullionist tendencies – i.e. his belief that the French economy would benefit from minimising the outflow of specie from the kingdom.[48] These tendencies rested on legitimate concerns: as European countries saw population increases in the sixteenth and seventeenth centuries, specie levels increasingly fell short of demand. This was exacerbated by global economic forces: Dennis Flynn and Arturo Giráldez have demonstrated that demand for America's abundant silver was greater in China than in Europe, owing to the shift under the Ming dynasty to taxation in silver in the 1570s. Asymmetric bimetallic ratios between China and the rest of the world thus ensured the former became the world's 'silver sink': silver carried to Europe did not remain there in its entirety, with a significant proportion of it flowing to China via the Baltic, the Ottoman Empire and the Cape of Good Hope.[49]

These silver flows had significant consequences for daily life in Europe. The scarcity of silver hindered everyday transactions and, where payment was in specie, taxation as well; the system of barter that emerged in England in the sixteenth and seventeenth centuries was sophisticated, but it remained an *ad hoc* solution to the bullion crisis.[50] The situation was no less precarious in France: there was less specie circulating in France in the seventeenth century than in the sixteenth century, which did not, in

---

[46] Ibid.
[47] Ibid.
[48] C. Wennerlind, *Casualties of Credit: The English Financial Revolution, 1620–1720*, London: Harvard University Press, 2011, pp. 20, 32, 34, 36; C. Wennerlind, 'Money: Hartlibian Political Economy and the New Culture of Credit', in P. Stern and C. Wennerlind (eds), *Mercantilism Reimagined: Political Economy in Early Modern Britain and Its Empire*, Oxford: Oxford University Press, 2013, pp. 74–93.
[49] D. Flynn and A. Giráldez, 'Born with a "Silver Spoon": The Origins of World Trade in 1571', *Journal of World History* 6 (1995), pp. 201–21; see also P. de Zwart and J. van Zanden, *The Origins of Globalization: World Trade in the Making of the Global Economy, 1500–1800*, Cambridge: Cambridge University Press, 2018, pp. 37–40.
[50] C. Muldrew, '"Hard Food for Midas": Cash and Its Social Value in Early Modern England', *Past and Present* 170 (2001), pp. 78–120; C. Muldrew, *The Economy of Obligation: The Culture of Credit and Social Relations in Early Modern England*, Basingstoke: Macmillan, 1998.

Colbert's words, make it 'easy for the people to pay higher taxes'.[51] Thus, Colbert's reasonable concern for the state of bullion was rooted in fiscal, economic and social challenges within the kingdom.

This concern shaped Clerville's argument. In his *Testament politique*, Colbert argued that, 'if it is necessary for foreigners to have our specie, this must only be [given] for that [i.e. goods] which cannot [otherwise] be found in the kingdom'.[52] Clerville extended this logic to services, arguing an insurance company would allow France to manage maritime risks itself rather than relying on foreign insurers. Moreover, he argued that enticing merchants to insure in France would create a virtuous circle, strengthening the French economy at the expense of the Dutch economy by turning the outflow of specie to Amsterdam's insurers into an inflow of foreign specie.

This bullionist logic was not isolated to France: indeed, it would have a long history in insurance practice. In 1798, the *consulado* of Cádiz wrote to Francisco de Saavedra, the Spanish minister of finance, stressing the value of the port's insurance industry as a means of preventing outflows of specie.[53] This logic had also made its way across the Atlantic: months before the *consulado* of Cádiz sent its letter, seventy-three merchants of Alexandria, Virginia, petitioned the state legislature to establish a chartered marine insurance company. The need for this company, they argued, stemmed from the town's growing export trade and the growing need for insurance coverage, which private provision in the town alone could not meet. Securing coverage elsewhere, they claimed, 'drains a large Sum of money' from Virginia and 'is attended with [...] additional Expence [sic] and many and great Inconveniences', including the costs of securing a commission agent.[54] As A. Glenn Crothers puts it:

> The creation of a chartered marine insurance company would solve these problems. Instead of draining wealth, the business would attract capital to Virginia from European and northern merchants who traded in the

---

[51] Quoted in Cole, *Colbert*, vol. I, p. 337; M. Vergé-Franceschi, *Colbert: La politique du bon sens*, Paris: Éditions Payot & Rivages, 2003, p. 357.

[52] J. Colbert, *Testament politique de messire Jean Baptiste Colbert, Ministre et Secretaire d'Etat*, The Hague: Henry van Bulderen, 1694, p. 366.

[53] The *consulado* calculated that 1.5 million *pesos* had been exported per year in insurance premiums before Cádiz's rise as an insurance centre – 'a real drain on Spain's capital', as Jeremy Baskes puts it; J. Baskes, *Staying Afloat: Risk and Uncertainty in Spanish Atlantic World Trade, 1760–1820*, Stanford: Stanford University Press, 2013, pp. 189–90.

[54] A. Glenn Crothers, 'Commercial Risk and Capital Formation in Early America: Virginia Merchants and the Rise of American Marine Insurance, 1750–1815', *Business History Review* 78 (2004), p. 621.

town, and would make writing policies and filing claims more efficient and less expensive.[55]

Although the merchants of Alexandria surely did not realise it, their line of argument bore an uncanny resemblance to that of Clerville over a century earlier.[56]

Clerville clearly viewed his exchange with the merchants of Rouen positively. Throughout his report, he wrote summaries documenting the steps that needed to be taken in each port following the report to facilitate commerce. For Rouen, his summary was short and related only to insurance:

> what has been proposed regarding an insurance company is very significant for preventing us from having recourse to foreigners for the safety of our cargoes and for keeping our money in the kingdom. To form this company, it would be necessary to secure four or five notable *bourgeois* of Rouen, and to join their company in providing them with fairly considerable sums.[57]

Despite Boiteux's suggestion to the contrary, the Rouennais remained open to the proposal – and it became Clerville's top priority for the city.

Clerville was not alone in regarding the company as a viable proposition. On 9 May 1664, Willem Boreel, the Dutch ambassador to France, wrote to the Estates General to inform them of two ongoing projects that took square aim at the Dutch: first, he described the efforts 'to create a French company for the East Indies' – the project that would very soon become the CIO.[58] He then wrote of the desire to establish 'a privileged insurance company' in Paris, with offices and staff in 'all the ports of France'.[59] He warned this company would have a monopoly over all insurance in France: nobody, including underwriters in the United Provinces, would be permitted to insure French ships or merchandise besides 'the said French company'.[60] This potent protectionism was a threat to Amsterdam that Boreel took seriously.

Why was Colbert targeting the Dutch? At this point, it would be easy to suggest Colbert espoused a zero-sum approach to economics, and therefore

---

[55] Ibid.
[56] Similar arguments were also presented in Philadelphia when the Insurance Company of North America submitted its charter petition in 1792; H. Farber, 'The Political Economy of Marine Insurance and the Making of the United States', *The William and Mary Quarterly* 77 (2020), pp. 596–7.
[57] Cinq cents de Colbert 122, fols 1–36, BNF.
[58] SP/84/170/58, fol. 141, The National Archives (TNA). Violet Barbour's suggestion that Boreel's 'garbled' account is written in 'bad French' is not unjust; Barbour, 'Marine Risks', p. 578n. Whether this letter was written before or after Clerville's mission is unclear. For more on the CIO, see the Introduction.
[59] SP/84/170/58, fol. 141, TNA.
[60] Ibid.

targeted them as the greatest rival to France in the maritime sphere. This is, after all, the man who famously said that 'commerce is a perpetual war of spirit and industry between nations': for the French to win, the Dutch – and every other European power – had to lose.[61] But the logic is more subtle than this. Moritz Isenmann suggests Colbert's approach to the Dutch drew from a rich genealogy of French works on divine order, most notably Jean Eon's 1646 tract *Le commerce honorable*.[62] Eon emphasised the abundance of resources and goods possessed by the French that other countries needed. Divine will had ordained, Eon argued, that good commercial relations should hold between France and other countries because of its natural gifts: exchange was, after all, a key principle of the *ius gentium*.[63] Thus, for Colbert, 'there was a "natural share" of world commerce belonging to each country according to its economic potential', and this commerce should be governed by the *ius gentium* – i.e. key principles of exchange should apply to all countries equally. In other words, he believed that if the *ius gentium* were followed, France would rule supreme in European commerce thanks to its bountiful natural resources – and, by extension, all efforts to prevent this supremacy were premised on an unjust contravention of the *ius gentium*. In this way, Colbert also drew on French discourses of universal monarchy, which held that divine providence had bestowed upon Louis XIV the legitimate right and duty to serve as arbitrator of European affairs, ensuring peace amongst the Christian monarchs in defence against the infidel.[64]

Colbert thus believed the Dutch had achieved commercial supremacy in Europe through illegitimate means. First, he perceived that the non-tariff barriers and bans routinely imposed on French goods contravened the *ius gentium*.[65] Secondly, he estimated in a famous *mémoire* from 1669 that the Dutch had 15,000–16,000 commercial vessels in operation, compared to

[61] Quoted in C. Levillain, *Vaincre Louis XIV. Angleterre, Hollande, France: Histoire d'une relation triangulaire 1665–1688*, Seyssel: Champ Vallon, 2010, p. 157.
[62] On earlier works, such as those of Laffemas and Montchrétien, see also Cole, *Colbert*, vol. I, pp. 8–9, 28–9 and 86. On how Richelieu drew on such ideas, see Cole, *Colbert*, vol. I, pp. 140–1.
[63] M. Isenmann, 'Égalité, réciprocité, souveraineté: The Role of Commercial Treaties in Colbert's Economic Policy', in A. Alimento and K. Stapelbroek (eds), *The Politics of Commercial Treaties in the Eighteenth Century: Balance of Power, Balance of Trade*, Basingstoke: Palgrave Macmillan, 2017, p. 82.
[64] F. Bosbach, 'The European Debate on Universal Monarchy', in D. Armitage (ed.), *Theories of Empire, 1450–1800*, Aldershot: Ashgate, 1998, pp. 92–8.
[65] M. Isenmann, '(Non-)Knowledge, Political Economy and Trade Policy in Seventeenth-Century France: The Problem of Trade Balances', in C. Zwierlein (ed.), *The Dark Side of Knowledge: Histories of Ignorance, 1400 to 1800*, Leiden: Brill, 2016, pp. 149–51. Isenmann explains Colbert's approach to the *ius gentium* fully in the chapters cited in this discussion.

the 500–600 commercial vessels in use by the French. Colbert suggested this wide disparity was entirely unnatural, emerging only from the 'tyrannical' way in which the Dutch conducted commerce.[66] The French routinely argued in treaty negotiations from the 1650s onwards that illegitimate Dutch violence, and the illegitimate exclusion of foreigners, in the East Indies allowed the VOC to trade without competition, creating the import-export economy on which the Dutch thrived and allowing Dutch shipping to blossom at the expense of the French.[67] Ironically, this argument was similar to that which had been made against the Portuguese some decades earlier by Hugo Grotius in *Mare Liberum*.[68]

With this in mind, we can put the myth of the privileged insurance company to rest. The merchants of Rouen to whom Clerville spoke objected to *some* commercial companies in 1664, but were enthusiastic about the idea of an insurance company in France, and made several recommendations with an eye to ensuring its competitiveness against private underwriters. Far from being a tone-deaf attempt by the state to impose an ill-fitting corporate structure on an industry that would never accept innovation, Boreel felt the project had legs. Indeed, by discussing the proposed company alongside the proposed CIO, he argued to the Estates General that both projects were part of a conscious economic strategy to challenge Dutch commercial supremacy.

As Clerville recognised, the real obstacle to the insurance project was money. The crown needed to find 400,000 *livres*, or a similarly large sum, to get the project rolling.

This never came to pass. Based on current evidence, it is impossible to ascertain precisely why. We are not privileged with a record of what went on behind closed doors: in trying to tempt investors to get on board with the project, Colbert may simply have been unsuccessful. With these qualifications in mind, it is worthwhile to look to the other company discussed in Boreel's letter: the CIO.

Throughout 1664, Colbert went to great lengths to encourage investment in the new CIO. With the Dutch VOC firmly in mind, he envisioned the CIO would have a capital of 15 million *livres* invested across France and the social spectrum.[69]

---

[66] Quoted in Levillain, *Vaincre Louis XIV*, pp. 158–9.
[67] Isenmann, 'Égalité', pp. 86–7.
[68] H. Grotius and R. van Deman Magoffin (trans.), *The Freedom of the Seas – or the Right Which Belongs to the Dutch to Take Part in the East Indian Trade*, New York: Oxford University Press, 1916.
[69] Haudrère, *Les Français dans l'océan Indien*, pp. 32–3.

Shares were acquired through three payments: one in 1664, one in 1665 and one in 1666. Yet interest in the project was low from the outset, with just over 2.2 million *livres* being raised in 1664. Suspicion was rife in the provinces: as one official put it in a letter to Colbert:

> The officeholders among others complain that they are being forced into it. They bruit it about that it's a trap to subject the nobles and other tax-exempt people to the *taille*; that everyone is going to be forced into it – church, nobles, and third estate; next, that they will be taxed every year and that new demands will be made on them, all under the pretext that some loss has been incurred or some seemingly useful enterprise needs to be undertaken; finally, that the King will take hold of everything when it's least expected, just like the revenues at city hall, the domains etc. This kind of talk has a chilling effect on everyone; even those who are persuaded that the enterprise is a good one and would like to participate don't dare to let on as much. The officeholders view as enemies anyone who even talks positively about the enterprise, and as you well know, Sir, the officeholders are feared and dreaded in France. They have the highest credit, both in property and in authority. They set things in motion; everything depends on them …[70]

In Henry Clark's words, 'the first thoughts of the officials who formed such a significant part of the would-be investing class thus concerned not economics, but politics, not profit but privilege'.[71] The CIO was apparently perceived by many powerholders as a Trojan horse: once off the ground, the state would use it to undermine the regime of privilege and levy the *taille* on the nobility on the basis that, traditionally, nobles who engaged in commerce renounced their status and its accompanying privileges. Colbert addressed this concern in an edict of August 1669, allowing noblemen to engage in overseas trade without losing their privileges.[72] Even for those below the nobility, it was feared the state would exploit the CIO's investors long after they acquired their shares. Thus, investment was deemed most risky indeed, albeit for reasons far beyond the CIO's prospective balance sheet.

That the 1669 edict was needed at all suggests the official's account rings true, although we should be wary of grouping diverse groups like officeholders and the nobility together so neatly. In any case, it is easy to imagine that Colbert felt his fiscal reforms were vindicated every time he read letters like this.

Nevertheless, the tardy edict did not help in the short term: even in the ports, interest in investing was lukewarm. Despite the crown's best efforts to

---

[70] Quoted in H. Clark, *Compass of Society: Commerce and Absolutism in Old-Regime France*, Lanham: Lexington Books, 2007, p. 37.
[71] Ibid.
[72] Trivellato, *The Promise and Peril of Credit*, p. 90.

coerce investment in Rouen – an indeterminate number of Rouennais *bourgeois* were condemned to a fine of 300 *livres* in August 1664, ostensibly for the illegitimate use of noble titles – investment from the city amounted to only 300,000 *livres* by January 1665, with the majority of merchant investors begrudgingly buying shares totalling between 1,000 and 3,000 *livres*, the former being the minimum possible investment.[73] If we follow the logic presented to Clerville, the Rouennais ostensibly had neither the money to invest more extensively nor the will to become passive investors in a commercial venture. The pressure apparently exerted by officeholders – which many merchants aspired to become – may also have played a role.

Challenges continued in the years after 1664. The difficulties encountered in establishing a stopover for CIO ships at Port-Dauphin in Madagascar in 1665, followed by the capture of one of the CIO's first ships in 1666, meant that many refused to make the payments required in subsequent years to acquire their shares, so the CIO's capital stood at just over 4.5 million *livres* by the end of 1666 – not even a third of what had been anticipated. Merchant investment from across France accounted for only 26 per cent of this.[74] The French West India Company (*Compagnie des Indes occidentales*), also established in 1664, encountered similar problems and both companies required significant investment from the king himself.[75] Meanwhile, in 1669, the crown forced venal officeholders to make any outstanding payments on their shares in the CIO before they could make their payment on the *paulette*, directly tying the heritability of offices to the state's commercial projects. This laid the groundwork for the state's exploitation of *augmentations de gages* in the following years.[76] In this way, concerns that the CIO was a Trojan horse were vindicated.

With this in mind, Colbert likely recognised that raising the necessary capital for the monopoly insurance company would have been very difficult.[77] With merchant investment not likely to be forthcoming, the onus for investment was shifted onto the king, but the challenges encountered by both Indies companies in their early years were unlikely to have disposed him to invest the requisite capital for the insurance company himself.

---

[73] J. Hoock, 'Le monde marchand face au défi colbertien. Le cas des marchands de Rouen', in M. Isenmann (ed.), *Merkantilsmus: Wiedeaufnahme einer Debatte*, Stuttgart: Franz Steiner Verlag, 2014, pp. 228–30. Strikingly, despite referring frequently to Clerville's report on Rouen, Hoock does not mention the proposed insurance company in his analysis.

[74] Haudrère, *Les Français dans l'océan Indien*, pp. 32–3.

[75] Heijmans, 'Investing in French Overseas Companies', pp. 108–9.

[76] Hurt, *Louis XIV and the Parlements*, p. 68.

[77] Strangely, Boiteux acknowledges this in his earlier work but not in *La fortune de mer*; Boiteux, *L'assurance maritime à Paris*, pp. 19–20.

In short, the company envisaged by Clerville was not inhibited by the merchants of Rouen alone: the crown itself ensured the company never came to fruition.

The 1664 project may never have materialised, but it reveals key principles the French state would espouse until the turn of the eighteenth century for developing the insurance industry. First, the proposed company intended to support the CIO in a broader attack on Dutch commerce: Colbert argued that, across the globe, the Dutch acted in contravention of the *ius gentium*. Using a bullionist logic that would appeal to Colbert, Clerville argued the French had the resources to support an insurance industry of its own, thereby preventing the outflow of specie to Amsterdam and London and encouraging the inflow of specie into Paris. The corporate model would support the accumulation of a significant liquid capital that, when combined with state support, would instil confidence in the institution and encourage merchants to seek coverage there. Moreover, the investment of a portion of the raised capital would produce the sorts of profits that would encourage those looking to make prudent investments – officeholders and *rentiers*, among others – to put their money here rather than in the state debt. The end goal was clear: not only would the Dutch insurance industry suffer, but French commerce more broadly would benefit from merchants' access to competitive coverage – coverage that mutual underwriting in the ports alone could not provide.

'Continual signs of his kindness': the shift to private underwriting in 1668

With the failure of the 1664 project, the establishment of an insurance chamber in Paris in 1668 may seem surprising. Yet the Chamber was an entirely different type of insurance institution emerging in different circumstances.

While Colbert was the driving force behind the 1664 project, using Clerville to try to bring the Rouennais on board, the impetus for the Chamber came from Parisian merchants themselves. In the years running up to 1668, Parisian merchants began to hold modest insurance meetings (*assemblées d'assurance*), where prospective underwriters and policyholders could meet to agree policies. Yet these lacked the scale, resources and legitimacy of a crown-sponsored insurance chamber.[78] Through an order of the Council of State (*arrêt du conseil d'état*) – the central royal council, with decision-making powers on key affairs of state – the Chamber was established on 5 June 1668. The order noted that Henri Desanteul, André Petit, Jacques Rey, Antoine Desmartins, Charles Lhuillier de Creabé and others had entreated the

[78] J. Peuchet, *Dictionnaire universel de la géographie commerçante*, vol. IV, Paris: Blanchon, 1798–99, p. 341.

king to 'accord them his protection' in allowing them to meet in a fixed location to conduct business.[79] They had also sought the king's support in appointing a registrar 'of probity and ability' to oversee a central insurance registry in the Chamber, requesting in so doing that the king continue and extend 'the graces that he bestows on merchants every day'.[80] The proposal had Colbert's explicit support, but the order only granted the Chamber the provisional right to appoint a registrar (Jean Le Roux) and begin business: once the institution's by-laws (*règlement général*) were composed, the king would then give the Chamber his full approval.

This approval did not come until 1671, when the by-laws were finally written. Nevertheless, from the outset, Colbert put his full weight behind the Chamber. As we will see, Colbert intervened to support the Chamber in gathering information from ports across France, pushing through an order of the Council of State on 31 October 1669 for this purpose that was justified by the king's desire to 'give them [i.e. the underwriters] continual signs of his kindness' and to pursue 'all the [possible] means that could augment insurance' in Paris.[81]

Yet Colbert's gaze extended beyond Paris. On 30 June 1670, Colbert wrote to M. d'Oppède, the first president (*premier président*) of the *parlement* of Aix-en-Provence, noting the Chamber's success and 'the advantages that commerce and merchants are enjoying as a result of its establishment'.[82] Consequently, he instructed d'Oppède to support the directors of the Levant Company in establishing an insurance chamber in Marseille 'like that of Paris' to support Levantine trade.[83] Far from seeking to create a central insurance institution, as Colbert had envisaged in 1664, he now sought to use the Parisian chamber as a model for other chambers across France. Like the Parisian chamber, Colbert's push for a chamber in Marseille was justified as another manifestation of the king's desire to 'give signs of [his] kindness' to the mercantile community.[84]

The interest in a Marseillaise chamber was not an indication that Colbert was losing faith or interest in the Parisian chamber.[85] No doubt

---

[79] D. Pouilloux, *Mémoires d'assurances. Recueil de sources françaises sur l'histoire des assurances du XVIème au XIXème siècle*, Paris: Seddita, 2011, p. 419; Z/1d/73, fols 10r–13v, AN.
[80] Pouilloux, *Mémoires d'assurance*, p. 419.
[81] Ibid., p. 420. See Chapter 3.
[82] J. Colbert and P. Clément (ed.), *Lettres, instructions, et mémoires de Colbert*, vol. II, book II, Paris: Imprimerie impériale, 1863, pp. 532–3.
[83] Ibid.
[84] Ibid.
[85] I have been unable to find out what came of the proposal for a Marseillaise chamber. If the track record of Marseille's mercantile community is anything to go by, the

with Colbert's intervention, Francesco Bellinzani became the Chamber's president in 1670. Bellinzani had been appointed as Colbert's first inspector general of manufactures (*inspecteur général des manufactures*) in 1669, and also served as Colbert's *intendant du commerce*.[86] This appointment thus signalled Colbert's strong interest in the institution's success. Bellinzani oversaw the writing of the by-laws that were finally approved by the Chamber on 4 December 1671.[87] An order of the Council of State followed on 10 December, approving the by-laws and bestowing the king's unreserved support for the institution.[88]

The by-laws outlined precisely how the Chamber would function thereafter. Article I confirmed the institution would not restrict underwriting practices in the city or beyond: membership of the Chamber 'is, and will be, permitted to all the merchants, insurers and [prospective] policyholders of this city of Paris and to all other people of the required and necessary quality'.[89] In short, the Chamber sought to facilitate insurance practice through key institutional advantages: it offered a space for the gathering and circulation of information[90] and for the amicable settling of disputes.[91] Rather than restricting membership or creating privileges that excluded outsiders, the Chamber sought to incentivise all interested parties to do their business under one roof.

Only months later, the institution faltered with the onset of the Dutch War.[92] Following this *annus horribilis*, Colbert continued to support the Chamber – albeit following an economic logic that may seem entirely anti-Colbertian at first glance. On 16 December 1673, an order of the Council of State was issued warning that 'the Chamber's entire destruction' was being threatened by Parisian merchants who were signing insurance policies amongst themselves or before notaries rather than in the registry of the Chamber.[93] The order consequently forbade all merchants of Paris from signing insurance policies without registering them with the registrar of the Chamber (and paying the associated fees) and forbade all notaries,

---

proposal was likely rejected as an attempt by Colbert to encroach on the city's commercial activities.
[86] More will be said on Bellinzani later in the chapter.
[87] Z/1d/73, fols 10r–13v, AN.
[88] Pouilloux, *Mémoires d'assurances*, pp. 425–6.
[89] Z/1d/73, fols 10r–13v, AN.
[90] See Chapter 3.
[91] See Chapters 6 and 7. Whether or not these institutional advantages motivated members to join is addressed below.
[92] This will be discussed at length in Chapter 4.
[93] Pouilloux, *Mémoires d'assurances*, pp. 429–30.

admiralty judges and consuls from registering policies themselves, with a fine of 3,000 *livres* put in place for all who contravened this ban.[94]

Besides granting the Chamber a registration monopoly in Paris, which guaranteed a consistent stream of revenue, the measure doubtless sought to bolster underwriting in the institution at this low ebb. Nevertheless, while it perhaps created an impediment to Parisian insurers operating outside the Chamber, it did not restrict insurance practices to the Chamber itself. Colbert still respected the liberty of all Parisians to underwrite as they wished.

This prompts us to reflect on precisely *why* Colbert was willing to support an institution with a private underwriting model. This model stood in complete contrast to the corporate model he had pursued in 1664 – and in complete contrast to every stereotype of Colbertian commercial policy.

Yet, when we look beyond these stereotypes, the two models are not mutually exclusive in Colbertian thought. Far from being an ardent supporter of privileged monopoly companies, Colbert was entirely in favour of private commercial initiatives in France.[95] Yet he was pragmatic and recognised that monopoly companies could be a powerful tool for developing commerce in high-risk markets. In such cases, as the Rouennais merchants recognised, 'the support and authority of the prince are absolutely necessary', and the pooling of capital through companies was a way of mitigating the risks entailed in entering these markets. Monopoly privileges were bestowed only to ensure the investors in these risky ventures would not be immediately undercut by private enterprise once the large costs of creating commercial and diplomatic infrastructures in distant markets were incurred.

Insurance falls into an intriguingly ambiguous position here. Although not a distant market, it was – as Clerville's report emphasises – an instrument which could help to open up markets and increase capital flows through de-risking commercial enterprises. Just like the other chartered companies, the 1664 monopoly company had been conceived with the goal of introducing new players and new capital as a means of beating the Dutch at their own game. The impetus for this project needed to come from the crown, because – so it appeared at the time – the industry could not develop itself without state support. In short, Colbert looked to the corporate model where private endeavours in insurance – namely, mutual underwriting in the ports – had proven insufficient to meet market demand.[96]

---

[94] Ibid.
[95] Horn, *Economic Development in Early Modern France*, p. 115. Moritz Isenmann makes the stimulating argument that Colbert's approach to commercial treaties reflected this belief in open trade alongside his belief in a prince's sovereign right to impose tariffs in order to defend native industry; Isenmann, 'Égalité', pp. 77–103.
[96] Hirsch and Minard, '"Laissez-nous faire"', p. 141.

By 1668, however, the situation was very different. Parisian merchants themselves provided the impetus for the Chamber, and this demonstrated to Colbert that the corporate model was not needed: Parisians were willing to enter the game of their own volition as private underwriters, without the need for monopoly privileges. Colbert's support was needed only to complete the triangle.[97] We will see how he intervened to help the Chamber overcome the challenges posed by being situated in Paris and how crown support bestowed legitimacy upon the Chamber, helping to develop its reputation as a trustworthy institution.[98] Yet the market was left unencumbered: the Chamber's underwriters competed amongst themselves and with other underwriters across France. Furthermore, the private model proved attractive because it required neither upfront capital nor great oversight from Colbert: Bellinzani could be trusted to lead the institution, and no investment from the crown was necessary.

Colbert's approach was therefore pragmatic rather than ideological. When it appeared new players would not enter the insurance market of their own volition in 1664, he looked to the corporate model as a solution; when Parisians proposed to develop the city's insurance market in 1668, he enthusiastically embraced the idea that Paris could stimulate the insurance industry across France through free and open competition. Far from an aberration, the Chamber was entirely compatible with Colbert's nuanced and pragmatic commercial policy.

Flexible access to power:
the appeals of Colbertian private underwriting

Desanteul, Petit, Rey, Desmartins and Lhuillier de Creabé came to Colbert in 1668 to seek his support in establishing the Chamber. But what encouraged others to join the institution? What could be gained from underwriting in a landlocked city?

Advocates of neo-institutionalism may be tempted to focus on the appeal of the Chamber as an archetypal 'inclusive, open access institution' for underwriting, where all underwriters, commission agents (*commissionaires*)[99] and prospective policyholders alike could meet to conduct their business and benefit from institutional perks. We will see that a central insurance chamber and registry benefited players in three ways: first, by creating a single space for the circulation of information about the reputation of other players and about events in the maritime sphere; secondly, by ensuring

---

[97] See p. 16.
[98] See Chapters 3 and 6.
[99] *Commissionaires* signed policies in their own name but on behalf of one or multiple principals.

policies were transparently recorded and were accessible to all interested parties; and finally, by providing set procedures for conflict resolution.[100]

Nevertheless, we should not naïvely believe that all members were drawn to the Chamber by these features. I follow Heijmans' recent work here in suggesting that, to understand the Chamber's appeal, we have to look beyond underwriting itself. For some, the most attractive quality was not *open access*, but simply *access*: membership offered competitive advantages to those in Paris seeking to tap into the tightly knit networks of commerce and royal patronage in the city. The Chamber emerged as a unique space for Parisians seeking to rub shoulders with influential figures, especially the institution's president, Bellinzani, who had considerable influence in French commercial policy.

Table 1   The members of the Chamber on Friday 8 January 1672.[101]

President: Francesco Bellinzani	
First rung	Second rung
Henri Desanteul	Denis Day
Robert Sanson	Simon Boirat
André Petit	Guillaume de la Marre
Jacques Rey	Nicolas Maillet
Gilles Mignot	Jacques Petit
Robert Pocquelin	M. Crouzet
Antoine Desmartins	M. Herinx
Charles Lhuillier de Creabé	Robert Boietet
M. Maillet et M. Pocquelin	Jean-Baptiste Forne
Antoine Sadoc	Étienne Suplegeau
Guillaume de Bie	Nicolas Courtesia et Georges Benson
Pierre Desanteul	Denis Dusault
Alexandre Vinx	Guillaume Bar
Jacques Richard	M. Deresne et M. Dorigny
M. Moret	M. Bernier
Antoine de Gomont	Pierre Denison
Nicolas Chanlatte	M. Regnault
François Lefebvre	Philippe Morisse

[100] The phrase 'inclusive, open access institution' comes from O. Gelderblom, *Cities of Commerce: The Institutional Foundations of International Trade in the Low Countries, 1250–1650*, Princeton: Princeton University Press, 2013.

[101] For more on the two rungs, see Chapter 7.

President: Francesco Bellinzani	
First rung	Second rung
Oudard Thomas de Lisle	Étienne Margas
Pierre Formont	Jean Dumont
François Launay Moreau	Jacques Dekessel et Compagnie
Louis Froment	Mme Vankessel et M. Couvorden
Gaspart Vangangelt	Guillaume Hallé et Bonnaventure Rebillé
Étienne Lenfant et Henri de Vaux	M. Le Couteux
Denis Rousseau	Romul Valenty
Jean Roussel	M. Marchand
Jean-Anthoine Vanopstal	M. van Vayemberg
Pierre Cadelan	M. Desvieux
	Charles Beguin
	Guillaume Aubry

Source: Z/1d/73, fols 16r–17r, AN.

In a discussion of the Chamber in his bestselling *Le parfait négociant*, Savary claimed the institution had thrived because 'there are an infinite number of merchants, and all sorts of officers and *bourgeois* living from their *rentes* [who are] intelligent in maritime commerce [and] who find [it to] their advantage to offer insurance'.[102] Putting aside the hyperbolic implication about the Chamber's size, Savary makes a helpful point about the diversity of its membership more broadly.

Table 1 documents the Chamber's membership list following the approval of its by-laws in December 1671.[103] We can see that some members were very influential figures in the city: Henri Desanteul, the Chamber's leading member on paper,[104] served as *premier échevin* of Paris in 1671, marking him as a leading mercantile figure.[105] Pierre Formont, meanwhile, was a banker and a member of Colbert's Northern Company (*Compagnie*

---

[102] J. Savary, *Le parfait négociant, ou Instruction générale pour ce qui regarde le commerce des marchandises de France et des pays étrangers*, vol. I, book II, Paris: Frères Estienne, 1757, pp. 112–13. Savary's discussion of the Chamber will be explored at greater length in Chapter 7.
[103] This list is not authoritative across the period of the Chamber's existence – members joined and left before and after this point – but is a valuable point of reference.
[104] In practice, the Chamber's leading underwriter up to the end of 1672 was Gilles Mignot; on him, see Chapter 4.
[105] Desanteul referred to himself as 'former *échevin*' in submissions to Paris' admiralty court on 22 July 1689; Z/1d/109, n.p., AN. Coins were minted to commemorate his appointment as *premier échevin* in 1671: see iNumis, 'PARIS (VILLE DE), HENRY DE SANTEUL, PREMIER ÉCHEVIN, 1671' [https://www.inumis.com/shop/paris-ville-de-henry-de-santeul-premier-echevin-1671-1003786/, accessed 12 February 2020].

du Nord); Guillaume de Bie served as an inspector of manufactures; and the Pocquelin family were closely connected to Colbert.[106] Moreover, the Aubry, Launay, Moret, Frémont, Vaux and Regnault families were all represented in the Chamber; each family had strong ties to the *lobby Colbert* and to finance and tax farming across France.[107]

Less is known about other members, who presumably came mostly from the commercial and financial sectors, although Savary's remark that venal office-holders and *rentiers* also participated should not be ignored. Some came as individuals; others underwrote in partnership; even women emerged as leading underwriters, making clear this was far from being a homosocial space.[108]

What drew such a diverse group to this space? For many, the prospect of having access to the Chamber's president, Francesco Bellinzani, must have been attractive. Bellinzani came into Colbert's orbit during the latter's formative years in the entourage of Cardinal Mazarin, the chief minister of Louis XIII and Louis XIV from the death of Cardinal Richelieu in 1642 to his own death in 1661.[109] Colbert later adopted Bellinzani as one of his 'creatures': Bellinzani served as Colbert's *intendant du commerce* in the secretariat of state for maritime affairs.[110] As part of this role, Bellinzani served as 'the eyes and ears of Colbert' in the Levant and Northern Companies and as the liquidator of the West India Company.[111]

With his fingers in so many pies, Bellinzani was truly the archetypal 'man of projects' – and a man whose wide-reaching influence was a valuable asset to the Chamber's members.[112] Records survive of a few instances where Bellinzani interceded on their behalf. We will see the Chamber was consulted on numerous occasions by Colbert during the compilation of the

---

[106] Dessert, *Argent, pouvoir et société*, p. 504; Cole, *Colbert*, vol. I, pp. 325–6.
[107] Dessert, *Argent, pouvoir et société*.
[108] In Chapter 4, we will encounter Elisabeth Hélissant, a leading underwriter in the Chamber in its early years. See also L. Wade, 'Underwriting Empire: Marine Insurance and Female Agency in the French Atlantic World', *Enterprise & Society* (2022), pp. 1–29. doi:10.1017/eso.2022.33
[109] Dessert, *Argent, pouvoir et société*, p. 327. A detailed account of Colbert and Bellinzani's activities together in the 1650s is provided in G. Martin, *La grande industrie sous le regne de Louis XIV (plus particulierement de 1660–1715)*, Paris: Librairie nouvelle de droit et de jurisprudence, 1898, pp. 34–56.
[110] Dessert, *Argent, pouvoir et société*, p. 337.
[111] D. Dessert and J. Journet, 'Le lobby Colbert: un royaume ou une affaire de famille?', *Annales. Economies, sociétés, civilisations* 30e année (1975), pp. 1319–20. Bellinzani was a dummy shareholder of the Levant Company and the Northern Company for the king, allowing him to oversee the affairs of these companies on Colbert's behalf. At the same time, as noted above, he served as Colbert's first inspector general of manufactures from 1669, overseeing the minister's famous inspection system for the production of French cloth, before becoming president of the Chamber in 1670; on this inspection system, see Minard, *La fortune du colbertisme*.
[112] I am grateful to Guillaume Calafat for this wonderful turn of phrase.

1681 *Ordonnance de la marine*, with Bellinzani as his intermediary.[113] But the Chamber became an influential institution in commercial and financial affairs even beyond insurance. When Étienne Rouxelin[114] fell foul of brokering regulations outlined in the 1673 *Ordonnance sur le commerce*, Bellinzani tried to persuade Colbert to change these regulations by rallying the Chamber behind the cause. Savary's lesser-known second volume of *Le parfait négociant* from 1688 records in dramatic language his resistance to, and success in scuppering, Bellinzani's plans through heated discussions in the Chamber's general assembly.[115] Nevertheless, Savary's account makes clear the Chamber had become a hub for the city's commercial and financial communities to engage with the state, with Bellinzani as a powerful (albeit not entirely disinterested) intermediary. Access to such a well-connected figure of state could therefore be worth the time and money needed for a modest underwriting portfolio.

A modest underwriting portfolio could be an attractive proposition in any case. Philip Hoffman, Gilles Postel-Vinay and Jean-Laurent Rosenthal have argued the private credit market in seventeenth-century Paris was limited, in part, by the absence of suitable institutions to facilitate the exchange of information about prospective debtors. Without specialised brokers or a centralised registry for mortgages, there was no way for a creditor to know whether a debtor had already pledged their collateral – be it their house, *rentes* or other property – against a prior loan. This forced creditors to rely on personal connections to gather such information themselves.[116] Insurance could prove a valuable way of diversifying one's commercial activities, as it did not rest on the solvency of the policyholder: indeed, insurance did not even require the upfront provision of capital. While policyholders could still attempt to defraud underwriters, the latter at least had the power to withhold payment until they (or conflict managers) were satisfied a claim was legitimate.[117]

---

[113] See Chapter 6.
[114] Rouxelin conducted underwriting in 1672, and he is recorded as being in attendance for the Chamber's general assemblies on 26 August and 2 October 1673; Z/1d/78, Z/1d/73, fols 27–28r, AN. See also his entry in the AveTransRisk database (ATR).
[115] J. Savary, *Le parfait négociant, ou Instruction générale pour ce qui regarde le commerce des marchandises de France et des pays étrangers*, vol. II, Paris: La Veuve Estienne, 1742, pp. 81–102.
[116] P. Hoffman, G. Postel-Vinay, and J. Rosenthal, *Priceless Markets: The Political Economy of Credit in Paris, 1660–1870*, Chicago: University of Chicago Press, 2000, pp. 64–8.
[117] On conflict managers, see Chapters 7 and 8.

Moreover, the Chamber's private model gave full control to its members to underwrite based on their own appetite for risk.[118] Since membership did not compel one to underwrite, members could withdraw from the market when the risks entailed became more than they could stomach.

Finally, involvement in the Chamber could be a valuable means of developing one's credit.[119] This is difficult to prove directly, but is pointed to through the manner in which those associated with the Chamber presented themselves in legal submissions. Let us take one of the Chamber's cashiers, Pierre Robelot, as an example. In the records of the *Châtelet de Paris*, the city's 'main royal trial court', Robelot was recorded in 1670 – before becoming cashier of the Chamber – as a '*bourgeois* of Paris'.[120] This was a prestigious social status in the city that carried an array of privileges, including exemption from paying property taxes for country residences.[121] Yet, upon becoming cashier, Robelot chose thereafter to adopt a different title in legal documents. In the same records from 1680, for example, he gave 'clerk in the insurance registry in Paris' as his title.[122] Even after the Chamber's dissolution in 1686, Robelot still chose to refer to himself as the 'former cashier of the [Royal] Insurance Chamber' in legal submissions to Paris' admiralty court as late as 30 August 1700.[123] In the same manner, Christophe Lalive – who, having previously served as Bellinzani's personal clerk, became the Chamber's registrar in 1671[124] – styled himself as 'former registrar of the [Royal] Insurance Chamber' in submissions to the admiralty court on 2 December 1686.[125] This was similarly the case for Henri Desanteul, nominally the leading member of the Chamber: in submissions to the admiralty court on 22 July 1689, he referred not only to his status as a former *échevin*, but also to his status as 'former insurer in the [Royal]

---

[118] We will see in Chapter 4 that individual underwriters in the Chamber developed quite contrasting underwriting strategies.

[119] On credit as a construct imbued with both social and economic meaning, see Muldrew, '"Hard Food for Midas"'; Muldrew, *The Economy of Obligation*.

[120] Y//218, fol. 412, AN; A. Kessler, *A Revolution in Commerce: The Parisian Merchant Court and the Rise of Commercial Society in Eighteenth-Century France*, New Haven: Yale University Press, 2007, p. 18.

[121] Bien, 'Offices, Corps, and a System of State Credit', p. 91. Parisians were exempted from paying taxes for properties within the city through an ordinance issued by Charles VII in 1449; L. Bernard, *The Emerging City: Paris in the Age of Louis XIV*, Durham, NC: Duke University Press, 1970, p. 48.

[122] Y//239, fol. 47v, AN.

[123] Z/1d/112, n.p., AN.

[124] Lalive is noted as Bellinzani's 'clerk' in a policy of 26 April 1670, signing the policy on Bellinzani's behalf; Z/1d/75, fol. 159v, AN.

[125] Z/1d/108, n.p., AN.

Insurance Chamber of Paris'.[126] While the Chamber's reputation was gravely damaged in 1673,[127] the self-fashioning of these individuals in legal documents suggests nevertheless that association with it carried a degree of social prestige long after it had closed its doors, no doubt because of the royal patronage it had enjoyed. In an era where credit and reputation were so tightly linked, such social cachet was likely a strong incentive for individuals to join.

Overall, when compared to the CIO and other Colbertian companies – where investment was frequently coerced, and one was left at the mercy of the state to protect this investment[128] – underwriting in the Chamber emerged as a prudent commercial option for Parisians. The access the Chamber provided to influential figures came at little cost to its members, who could choose for themselves how far they wanted to get involved in its affairs.

CONCLUSION

This chapter has contextualised insurance within Colbert's broader economic strategy, which revolved around a staunch refusal to accept what he deemed to be the unnatural and unjust supremacy of the Dutch in global commerce. To encourage economic growth, he strove to reform the state debt by shifting investment from venal offices and the *Hôtel de Ville* to commercial endeavours. Insurance had a large role to play in this strategy: by reducing mercantile transaction costs, commerce could become a more attractive investment. Moreover, developing an indigenous insurance industry could reverse the flows of specie Colbert perceived to be so important in the commercial supremacy of the United Provinces.

He sought to achieve these overlapping ambitions by bringing in new players and capital from Paris. The failed 1664 project stemmed from Colbert's belief that monopoly companies could be justified when they centred on a risky market in which investors could not, or would not, otherwise participate. By 1668, however, it became clear the corporate structure was not needed: Parisian merchants and *financiers* were willing to insure of their own volition. The myth of Colbertianism as a zero-sum protectionist economic system defined – and smothered – by endless monopolisation and regulation has been debunked in recent decades.[129] Building on

---

[126] Z/1d/109, n.p., AN.
[127] See Chapter 7.
[128] On this, see Haudrère, *Les Français dans l'océan Indien*; Heijmans, 'Investing in French Overseas Companies'; and Ames, *Colbert*.
[129] On how this myth was constructed and perpetuated, see K. Malettke, 'Colbert devant les historiens (1683–1983)', in R. Mousnier (ed.), *Un nouveau Colbert: actes du Colloque pour le tricentenaire de la mort de Colbert*, Paris: Editions SEDES/CDU,

these works, this chapter has found that, far from being an aberration in Colbertian policy, the Chamber was *the* archetypal Colbertian institution, marrying open access with the support of the state.

Colbert viewed the Chamber as a model that could be implemented elsewhere in France: besides his efforts in Marseille, Colbert also discussed a proposal to establish an analogous chamber in Bordeaux.[130] I have found no evidence either of these chambers ever came into existence. This did not diminish the Chamber's importance in France, however: as we will see, it was the first major institutionalisation of the Parisian capital market, with significant consequences for French shipping.[131]

The Chamber was so attractive to those who ultimately joined because it offered flexible access to state influence through Bellinzani. Members could join and withdraw from the market at will; while the threat existed of Colbert intervening in the Chamber's activities, members conducted their business as legal individuals, allowing a level of freedom of practice comparable to that later enjoyed by the underwriters of Lloyd's.

The institution that succeeded the Chamber was the product of an ardent rejection of this approach to stimulating the French economy, with Seignelay choosing instead to double down on the state's monopoly of privilege. The role of insurance in post-Colbertian commercial policy will be the focus of the next chapter.

1985, pp. 13–28. Despite the revisionist push, traditional arguments on Colbert continue to have currency in literature today; here, see M. Koskenniemi, *To the Uttermost Parts of the Earth: Legal Imagination and International Power 1300–1870*, Cambridge: Cambridge University Press, 2021, pp. 349–416.

[130] Colbert and Clément, *Lettres, instructions, et mémoires de Colbert*, vol. II, book II, p. 675.

[131] See Chapter 4.

2

THE ROYAL INSURANCE COMPANY AND PRIVILEGE IN POST-COLBERTIAN COMMERCIAL POLICY, 1683–c. 1700

How are we to understand the Company? Charles Woolsey Cole suggests the Company was simply a renewal of the Chamber, consistent with his broader argument on the continuity of commercial policy after Colbert's death.[1] Yet while Seignelay's motivations for intervening in the insurance industry were mostly consistent with those of his father, the strategies he pursued were very different indeed.

This chapter argues that post-Colbertian commercial policy needs to be treated on its own terms rather than as an extreme or poorly executed offshoot of Colbertian commercial policy. In establishing this position, it explores Seignelay's interest in insurance between 1686 and 1690, alongside the motivations of those who joined the Company. The change in international climate in the 1680s fuelled a strategic shift from private underwriting with state lubrication to privileged corporate underwriting with strong state control. Seignelay bestowed privileges that made the Company especially attractive to *financiers* and venal officeholders – privileges that made membership of the Company itself seem like a venal office. However, while the Company may have been a legal person, Seignelay refused to recognise that it had any legitimate interests of its own. Consequently, he treated it as a tool of his commercial policy, circumventing the institution's letters patent in order to extract what were, in all but name, forced loans to fund the state's maritime projects. This vindicates prior analyses that have stressed the political functions of Louis XIV's chartered companies and brings into focus the inherent pitfalls of studying them as profit-making endeavours.

---

[1] Cole, *French Mercantilism*, p. 7. Cole erroneously understands the Chamber as a form of company.

THE SHIFT IN FISCAL POLICY IN THE 1680s

We saw in the last chapter that Colbert strove to bring France's culture of venal office holding in line with state interests. This complemented his broader fiscal reforms: favouring indirect taxation over raising the rates of the most commonplace direct tax, the *taille*, Colbert consolidated the five key tax farms (the *cinq grosses fermes*) into a single auction, ensuring control over finance was kept in the hands of the smallest number of *financiers* possible. This proved broadly successful: 'in 1681 he had reunited most of the farms into a single lease for six years for roughly 56 million *livres*, a much larger sum than for the *taille*'. Guy Rowlands concludes very fairly that, by Colbert's death in 1683, 'the royal finances were [...] in a reasonably healthy condition and the currency was stable'.[2]

Yet, by the death of Louis XIV, the situation had changed dramatically. To quote Rowlands:

> The total state debt (including capital in venal offices attracting *gages*) was probably around 500–600 million *livres* in 1683, and the revenue system was capable of servicing this liability. The French fiscal-military system was certainly no weaker than that of England, even up to 1697. But by 1715 state debt had reached somewhere in the region of 1.8 to 2.3 billion *livres*, serviced by a revenue base that, even with restored economic vitality in the 1720s and 1730s, remained far too weak to cope with major bouts of warfare. The geopolitical and financial world of Colbert's era had passed by 1692, and in the century that followed the monarchy would prove unable to evolve a new fiscal-military constitution to cope sufficiently with the new international environment.[3]

While a shift away from venal office holding and *rentes* had been possible under Colbert, owing to an almost unprecedented period of peace and an auspicious international landscape, this good fortune did not last. Throughout his personal rule up to 1683, Louis XIV had managed to capitalise on the disunity of the powers of Western Europe: the Ottoman Empire posed a serious threat to the eastern frontier of the Holy Roman Empire, creating a power vacuum to the west that the *gloire*-seeking king of France was only too happy to fill.

---

[2] Rowlands, 'Royal Finances', pp. 38 and 43–4. On Colbert's preference for indirect taxation, and the model for this shift in fiscal strategy, see J. Collins, 'Les finances bretonnes du XVIIe siècle: un modèle pour la France?', in *L'administration des finances sous l'Ancien Régime*, Paris: Comité pour l'histoire économique et financière, 1997, pp. 307–15. For more on the *cinq grosses fermes*, see N. Johnson, 'Banking on the King: The Evolution of the Royal Revenue Farms in Old Regime France', *Journal of Economic History* 66 (2006), pp. 963–91.

[3] Rowlands, 'Royal Finances', p. 51.

The War of Devolution (1667–68) and the Dutch War (1672–78) centred on Louis' territorial ambitions in the Low Countries. Charles-Édouard Levillain has argued the 1660s and 1670s 'were marked by the domination of France in European affairs, as much on the diplomatic map as the political', with Louis exploiting the wars between England and the United Provinces and the political challenges each faced in order to assert French power on the European stage.[4] This culminated in the Anglo-French alliance against the United Provinces following the Treaty of Dover in 1670, where Louis offered financial support to Charles II in exchange for a naval invasion. As we will see, the ultimate failure of the Dutch War seemed almost unimaginable as the French army swarmed into the United Provinces in early 1672, and the War of the Réunions (1683–84) saw France continue to make incursions beyond its eastern frontier.[5]

Yet 1683 marked the beginning of a major transformation in European geopolitics. Less than a week after Colbert's death on 6 September 1683, the Second Ottoman Siege of Vienna was broken. Buda fell to imperial forces in 1686, and the 1699 Treaty of Karlowitz cemented the sudden and unexpected end to Ottoman pretensions in central Europe. The 1686 Grand Alliance, uniting Sweden, Spain, the Holy Roman Empire and German princes against France, would be compounded in 1688 by Louis' worst nightmare: the so-called Glorious Revolution saw James II deposed by William of Orange, who took the throne of England alongside his wife, Mary. As king of England and stadtholder of the United Provinces, William was now uniquely equipped to hold French territorial pretensions on its eastern frontier in check. The balance of power had shifted dramatically and Louis would not live to see it shift back in France's favour. France now stood alone in Europe, and it struggled to withstand the assaults of the Nine Years' War (1688–97) and the War of the Spanish Succession (1701–14), both of which saw the country attacked on all sides.[6]

This dramatic shift in European affairs against the French forced Colbert's successors as controller general of finances – Claude Le Peletier, Louis Phélypeaux and Nicolas Desmaretz – to turn again to *rentes* and venal offices

---

4   Levillain, *Vaincre Louis XIV*, p. 339.
5   See Chapter 4.
6   The Dutch War and the Nine Years' War will be discussed further in Chapters 4 and 5. For a full analysis of Louis XIV's wars, see J. Lynn, *The Wars of Louis XIV 1667–1714*, London: Longman, 1999. For a full evaluation of the importance of the geopolitical shift in the 1680s, see Prest and Rowlands (eds), *The Third Reign of Louis XIV*. See also I. Parvev, 'The War of 1683–1699 and the Beginning of the Eastern Question', in C. Heywood and I. Parvev (eds), *The Treaties of Carlowitz (1699)*, Leiden: Brill, 2020, pp. 73–87.

as fiscal expedients.[7] Interest rates on *rentes* reached 12.5 per cent during the Nine Years' War, offering investors an excellent return on investment, so long as they were comfortable with the risk of the state defaulting – as it ultimately did in 1709.[8] Meanwhile, the system of venal offices was taken to new levels in the late 1680s. The crown increasingly resorted to creating new institutional offices that threatened to dilute the privileges, powers and market values of existing offices, putting pressure on those who held these offices to purchase the new offices themselves. This was compounded by the crown's growing tendency to seek capital through *augmentation de gages*, forcing officeholders to find further capital to keep their offices. These pressures prompted officeholders within particular bodies – for example, provincial estates and courts – to come together to contract debts as an individual legal entity, pooling their credit as a means of securing the capital to preserve their offices at better interest rates. The resulting *gages* could then be used to service the debts the bodies contracted.[9] A world away from Colbert's efforts to ease away from a fiscal system that was underpinned by privilege, post-Colbertian fiscal policy saw 'a deeper entrenchment of privilege on the French political landscape'.[10]

French fiscal policy after 1683 therefore diverged from the Colbertian norm. Seignelay lived with the consequences during his tenure as secretary of state for maritime affairs (*secrétaire d'état de la marine*). He could not incentivise officeholders, *rentiers* or *financiers* to engage in commercial practices in the same ways his father had, as the French state was forced to lean into the elaborate infrastructure of privilege as a means of financing its crippling wars.

---

[7] Rowlands, 'Royal Finances', p. 38.
[8] Béguin, *Financer la guerre*, p. 347; Rowlands, 'Royal Finances', p. 46.
[9] M. Legay, 'État, corps intermédiaires et crédit public: un modèle de gestion des finances à l'époque moderne?', in V. Meyzie (ed.), *Crédit public, crédit privé et institutions intermédiaires. Monarchie française, monarchie hispanique, XVIe–XVIIIe siècles*, Limoges: Presses universitaires de Limoges, 2012, pp. 33–4; D. Le Page, 'Les augmentations de gages à la Chambre des comptes de Bretagne sous le règne de Louis XIV', in V. Meyzie (ed.), *Crédit public, crédit privé et institutions intermédiaires. Monarchie française, monarchie hispanique, XVIe–XVIIIe siècles*, Limoges: Presses universitaires de Limoges, 2012, p. 64; Potter, *Corps and Clienteles*, p. 14. Le Page finds that the officeholders of the *Chambre des comptes* of Brittany began to contract debts collectively following the *augmentation de gages* of 1689.
[10] Potter, *Corps and Clienteles*, p. 22.

A VENAL OFFICE BY ANOTHER NAME: CORPORATE INSURANCE, PRIVILEGE AND POST-COLBERTIAN COMMERCIAL POLICY

The 1670s had not been kind to any of Colbert's commercial institutions. The outbreak of war in 1672 had crippled the CIO, the West India Company and the Northern Company.[11] By Colbert's death in 1683, the CIO was alive only in name, the West India Company had been dissolved and replaced by the Senegal Company (*Compagnie du Sénégal*), and the Northern Company had been forced to sell its assets.[12]

A new approach was needed. Seignelay, succeeding his father as secretary of state for maritime affairs, oversaw a complete restructuring of the CIO in 1685. By the end of the process, twelve investors – who had each invested at least 30,000 *livres* – became the key shareholders. In limiting access to shares in this way, Seignelay moved away dramatically from the original Colbertian model. Similarly, the privileges of the Senegal Company were promptly withdrawn in 1685 to make way for the new Guinea Company (*Compagnie du Guinée*), with only a small number of shareholders.[13] As we will see later, these shareholders primarily comprised *financiers*, major officeholders and other close allies to the state.

The 1670s had also been unkind to the Chamber, and by Colbert's death in 1683, it had not recovered. Soon after Colbert's death, Bellinzani was accused of having accepted a bribe of 135,000 *livres* in exchange for granting a minting contract to a group – amongst whom was Christophe Lalive, the Chamber's registrar – who would go on to produce a larger quantity of *quatre sols* coins than had been agreed with the crown. Bellinzani would later die in prison at Vincennes in 1684, while Lalive was subjected to fines as late as 1699. For Lalive, this was a mild inconvenience that did not stop his family from becoming 'one of the most famous in the world of finance' thanks to his activities.[14] Although the Chamber continued its business, with Étienne Jagault as its new registrar (but, seemingly, with no new president), the institution certainly did not benefit from being caught up in this affair.

Once again, new players and new capital were needed in the French insurance industry. While the restructuring of the CIO and the establishment

---

[11] Dessert and Journet, 'Le lobby Colbert', p. 1317.
[12] P. Boissonnade and P. Charliat, 'Colbert et la Compagnie de Commerce du Nord', *Revue d'histoire économique et sociale* 17 (1929), p. 194.
[13] Heijmans, 'Investing in French Overseas Companies', p. 110; Heijmans, *The Agency of Empire*, pp. 33–4.
[14] Dessert, *Argent, pouvoir et société*, pp. 223–4 and 616; Martin, *La grande industrie*, pp. 54–5.

of the Guinea Company were politically delicate – requiring Seignelay to impinge on shareholders' rights – the dismantling of the Chamber entailed no such challenges. As the Chamber was a (now small) group of private underwriters rather than a company, there were no shareholders to alienate.

As with the CIO and the Guinea Company, Seignelay looked to a privileged corporate model to resurrect the Parisian insurance market. Betraying the shift in agency since 1668, the Company's letters patent from May 1686 observed the benefits French merchants had enjoyed since the 1681 *Ordonnance de la marine* – Colbert's famous reform of maritime law[15] – 'having avoided great losses in return for the modest sums they have paid to insure their vessels and merchandise'. The desire to deepen the *Ordonnance*'s impact on French insurance

> has brought us to encourage several merchants and other knowledgeable people in commerce to come together for the establishment of an insurance chamber, in the form of a Company [with] common funds and signatures, on condition they contribute a significant fund in order that merchants who would like to use this means of reducing the risks they run in their daily commerce [can] undertake it and continue it with greater ease and security.[16]

While the Chamber had been merchant-driven, the establishment of the Company was decidedly driven by the state.

The Company had all the hallmarks of Seignelay's restructured companies, with a fixed membership of only thirty members. These members bought a total of seventy-five shares of 4,000 *livres*, creating a fund of 300,000 *livres*. Insurance policies and sea loans (*prêts à la grosse aventure*) were agreed and signed by five directors, who were selected from among the members and replaced in a fixed pattern every six months. (In a sea loan, the creditor gives a lump sum upfront for a voyage, which is only repaid, with very high interest, in the event the ship completes its journey.) The directors met every Monday, Wednesday and Friday from 2:00pm to 5:00pm in the Company's offices at 16 *rue Quincampoix* to conduct the institution's business, with the support of the registry. Jagault continued as registrar for the Company after the dissolution of the Chamber. Members met collectively every Tuesday at 3:00pm to discuss the Company's business with the directors.

The Company was an explicitly unlimited liability institution. If the fund of 300,000 *livres* was depleted, members were liable for losses *pro rata* as

---

[15] See Chapter 6.
[16] P. Bornier, *Conférences des ordonnances de Louis XIV. Roy de France et de Navarre: avec les anciennes ordonnances du Royaume, le droit écrit & les arrêts*, vol. II, Paris: Unknown, 1719, p. 513.

private individuals, while directors were accorded no further liability in their capacity as directors. Where profits were made, these were distributed each year *pro rata*: 10 per cent of any profits from the previous year were distributed every 5 January, while the remaining 90 per cent was paid two years later, allowing and accounting for any further losses reported for policies from said previous year in the meantime.[17]

This liability regime was entirely in keeping with Seignelay's desire to offer merchants 'greater ease and security' in buying insurance. Harris has recently argued that shareholder liability was not expressly delineated by corporations before the period 1780–1830 because the circumstances did not exist for shareholder liability to become an issue.[18] Yet shareholder liability was a central feature of the Company's structure: for Seignelay, a clear demarcation of shareholder liability was essential in ensuring its creditworthiness. Through such a demarcation, policyholders-as-creditors were assured indemnification by the Company's members even if the Company itself became insolvent.[19]

Table 2   The members of the Company, as per the order of the Council of State of 6 June 1686.

Jean-Baptiste de Lagny	Claude Lebrun
M. Soullet	Jean Pasquier
Louis Desvieux	Gilbert Paignon
Phillippes Lefebvre	Antoine Pelletier
Denis Rousseau	Gerard Mollien
Mathurin Le Jariel	Mathurin Baroy
Hugues Mathé de Vitry-la-Ville	Hierôme Cousinet
Oudard Thomas de Lisle	Nicolas Soullet
Charles Lebrun	Nicolas Gaillard
Guillaume Bar	Louis de Lubert
M. Chauvin	François Tranchepain

[17] The past two paragraphs are drawn from the Company's letters patent and its articles of association in Bornier, *Conférences des ordonnances de Louis XIV*, vol. II, pp. 513–25.
[18] R. Harris, 'A New Understanding of the History of Limited Liability: An Invitation for Theoretical Reframing', *Journal of Institutional Economics* 16 (2020), pp. 643–64.
[19] Bornier, *Conférences des ordonnances de Louis XIV*, vol. II, pp. 513–25; Harris also overlooks the case of the French East and West India Companies, where (at least on paper) directors' personal property and bodies were protected from any claims of the companies' creditors; Heijmans, 'Investing in French Overseas Companies'; Heijmans, *The Agency of Empire*. The last two paragraphs draw on L. Wade, 'Royal Companies, Risk Management and Sovereignty in Old Regime France', *English Historical Review*, (2023), pp. 1–32. doi:10.1093/ehr/cead107.

Thomas Tardif	Pierre Héron
Pierre Pocquelin	Henry de la Rivoire
Guillaume André Hébert	Étienne Demeuves
Pierre Chauvin	Claude Céberet du Boullay

Source: Bornier, *Conférences des ordonnances de Louis XIV*, vol. II, p. 524.

Leading the members was Jean-Baptiste de Lagny, Seignelay's director general of commerce (*directeur général du commerce*). Remarkably little has been written about him. He initially made his mark in the realm of finance; having 'started as controller of the *fermes de traites* in Dunkirk [...] he] was then promoted to a general farmer in 1680'.[20] His ties to the royal commercial companies and farms began long before this, however, having been appointed as a director of the Northern Company at La Rochelle in 1669.[21] Lagny found his way into the good graces of both Madame de Montespan and the future Madame de Maintenon – mistress and second wife of Louis XIV respectively – and, through their influence, secured himself and five others a monopoly for the sale of tobacco across France from 1674 to 1680.[22] Lagny was also one of the investors in the leases of the *sous-ferme du Canada* from 1675 onwards.[23] Following Maintenon's marriage to Louis in 1684, Lagny was appointed as a royal secretary (*secrétaire du roi*) in 1685.[24]

Lagny's career peaked when he was appointed as director general in 1686. Since 'one of the principal roles' of this position was 'the administration of the companies of maritime commerce', his appointment was quickly followed by various orders of the Council of State granting him directorship positions in the CIO, the Guinea Company and the Mediterranean Company (*Compagnie de la mer Méditerranée*), alongside management duties of the *Compagnie et domaine d'Occident*.[25] To acquire the necessary

---

[20] Heijmans, 'The Agency of Empire', p. 51.
[21] Boissonnade and Charliat, 'Colbert et la Compagnie de Commerce du Nord'; J. Price, *France and the Chesapeake: A History of the French Tobacco Monopoly, 1684–1791, and of Its Relationship to the British and American Tobacco Trades*, vol. I, Ann Arbor: Michigan University Press, 1973, p. 24. Lagny was also in frequent contact with Colbert during the early 1670s; here, see MAR/B/7/55, fols 1v–2r and 10v–11r, AN.
[22] On the intricate court machinations involved in establishing this monopoly, see Price, *France and the Chesapeake*, pp. 17–23.
[23] Dessert, *Argent, pouvoir et société*, p. 512.
[24] Price, *France and the Chesapeake*, p. 24.
[25] MAR/C/7/159, n.p., AN; Price, *France and the Chesapeake*, p. 24. On the *Compagnie de la mer Méditerranée*, see J. Takeda, 'Silk, Calico and Immigration in Marseille. French Mercantilism and the Early Modern Mediterranean', in M. Isenmann (ed.), *Merkantilsmus: Wiedeaufnahme einer Debatte*, Stuttgart: Franz Steiner Verlag, 2014,

share to hold the directorship in the Mediterranean Company, the king himself made an order on 26 May to Louis de Lubert – general treasurer of the navy (*trésorier général de la marine*) and, conveniently, a member of the Royal Insurance Company – to give Lagny 20,000 *livres*.[26] This royal gesture was disputed after Lagny's death in 1700, as his opponents claimed this was a loan his beneficiaries needed to reimburse.[27]

Other members of the Company were equally active in the financial sphere. Mathurin Lejariel was the general receiver of the duchy of Nevers, and Étienne Demeuves and Guillaume André Hébert were both Parisian bankers.[28] In addition, Hugues Mathé de Vitry-la-Ville began as a receiver in Champagne, before taking a chancellery office.[29] He joined Lagny as one of the investors in the *sous-ferme du Canada* from 1675, and was part of the Mediterranean-oriented *Compagnie du Bastion de France* from at least 1678.[30] Alongside Claude Céberet du Boullay, he would become a director of both the CIO and the Guinea Company in 1685.

In analysing Vitry-la-Ville's investments, Heijmans notes that his inventory upon declaring bankruptcy in 1687 lists 35,000 *livres* of corals, which were likely obtained through his involvement in the *Bastion de France* for sale in the East Indies. For Vitry-la-Ville, 'it made sense [...] to be simultaneously an important shareholder of the *Compagnie du Bastion de France* – he owned one-fourth of the company – and a director of the East India Company, since commodity chains connected the two markets through corals, among other things'.[31] Indeed, membership of so many companies gave Vitry-la-Ville access to numerous markets under monopoly – markets in which he could

---

pp. 254–6. I am in the process of studying the *Compagnie de la mer Méditerranée* in my postdoctoral work on the Languedocian cloth industry between 1686 and 1715.

[26] MAR/B/7/59, fol. 71, AN.

[27] MAR/C/7/159, n.p., AN; Lagny's death 'at the start of this month' (i.e. December 1700) was recorded in the January 1701 edition of *Mercure Galant*; *Mercure Galant dedié à Monsieur le Dauphin. Janvier 1701*, Paris: Michel Brunet, 1701, pp. 143–4.

[28] Hébert would later become an influential figure in the CIO and served as director in Pondicherry in 1708–13 and 1715–17; Lespagnol, *Messieurs de Saint-Malo*, vol. I, p. 485; Heijmans, *The Agency of Empire*, p. 70; Dessert, *Argent, pouvoir et société*, p. 628; J. Félix, *Économie et finances sous l'ancien régime. Guide du chercheur, 1523–1789*, Vincennes: Institut de la gestion publique et du développement économique, Comité pour l'histoire économique et financière de la France, 1994, pp. 49–211.

[29] Heijmans, 'The Agency of Empire', p. 51.

[30] Dessert, *Argent, pouvoir et société*, pp. 506 and 512.

[31] Heijmans, 'Investing in French Overseas Companies', pp. 107–21.

engage for his own account, thereby making private profits even if the companies themselves were unprofitable.[32]

Lagny, Vitry-la-Ville and Céberet were not the only CIO directors to join the Company: Oudard Thomas de Lisle, Louis Desvieux, Lebrun,[33] Soullet[34] and Thomas Tardif also served as directors of the CIO following the restructuring of 1685. Desvieux began his career as a lawyer before becoming a royal secretary – a prestigious position held also by Lagny and de Lisle.[35] Philippes Lefebvre was, like Lubert, a member of the administration for maritime affairs, serving as a treasurer of the navy.[36] Most members therefore had strong ties to the crown before joining the Company.

There were also prominent ties to the prior Chamber: Guillaume Bar, Desvieux, Hébert, Denis Rousseau, de Lisle, Pierre Pocquelin and Lefebvre had all been members. It seems likely Lagny and Seignelay brought these gentlemen on board in order to put their underwriting experience to work as directors. Most of the other members probably had no underwriting experience. Nevertheless, none was required. Since only five directors were needed at any one time, five-sixths of the membership had no obligatory administrative duties: they could attend meetings as they wished, but otherwise could choose to be passive investors, entrusting the daily running of the Company to the directors. For those who were perhaps pressured into investment by Seignelay and/or Lagny, this was likely a redeeming feature: while membership of the Chamber required an active engagement with the institution on a regular basis, members of the Company did not need to be in Paris, or even in France, while underwriting took place.[37] In this way, Seignelay was able to pool the capital of those with no underwriting experience and put it to use in the insurance market by allowing those with prior experience to direct the institution's activities.

In exchange for this investment, the rewards could be lucrative – and not simply through share dividends. To incentivise investment, Seignelay was able to offer a number of enticing privileges. Like the CIO and the Guinea Company, the Company was granted monopoly privileges. These

---

[32] Ibid.
[33] Which of the Lebruns is unclear.
[34] Which of the Soullets is unclear.
[35] Heijmans, *The Agency of Empire*, p. 28; Y//221, fol. 331v, AN.
[36] H. Buffet, 'Lorient sous Louis XIV', *Annales de Bretagne* 44 (1937), p. 76.
[37] Indeed, Céberet was part of the embassy to Siam that left France in March 1687 and only returned in July 1688; G. Riello, 'With Great Pomp and Magnificence: Royal Gifts and the Embassies between Siam and France in the Late Seventeenth Century', in Z. Biedermann, A. Gerritsen, and G. Riello (eds), *Global Gifts: The Material Culture of Diplomacy in Early Modern Eurasia*, New York: Cambridge University Press, 2008, pp. 249–50.

had a very specific geographical scope: within the confines of Paris, all bar the Company were forbidden from offering insurance or sea loans. Parisians were allowed to offer additional coverage/capital for policies/contracts already signed by the Company, but only at the Company's discretion.[38] Beyond the city confines, underwriting remained open to all.

The freedom for all Parisians to underwrite – a freedom Colbert had painstakingly protected throughout the years of the Chamber – abruptly gave way to Seignelay's privileged system, where there was no pretence of open access. After all, privilege is exclusionary by its nature, and this was an institution that exploited this in order to encourage wealthy and influential *financiers*, merchants and other venal officeholders to place their capital here rather than elsewhere.

Indeed, it was surely not the Company's monopoly that was most attractive to prospective members: it was the plethora of social, commercial and legal privileges Seignelay was able to bring to the table for the members themselves. First, the 1686 letters patent ordered that, 'when directorship positions open up in the East India Company, they will be filled by one of the [Royal Insurance Company's] thirty members'.[39] For those members who had not already served as a CIO director, the chance to become one was a great boon.[40] After the Company's establishment in 1686, Bar, Lefebvre, Rousseau, Hébert, Pelletier and Jean-Baptiste Goualt (who joined the Company later, most likely buying Vitry-la-Ville's shares after the latter's bankruptcy in 1687) all served stints as directors of the CIO.[41] This meant twelve of the Company's original thirty members would serve as CIO directors at some point in their lives, with five of those members taking up directorships as a result of their membership in the Company. In this way, Seignelay was able to leverage positions in the royal chartered companies at large, which generated social capital through their manifest ties to royal networks of patronage.[42] Thus, far from being a footnote in Seignelay's commercial agenda, the Company was an integral element of it, incentivising membership by providing a direct path to a directorship role in the CIO.

This was not the only privilege that was likely to have caught the eye of prospective investors. The letters patent also prescribed that 'one of the merchant members will be chosen and elected every two years by a majority

---

[38] Bornier, *Conférences des ordonnances de Louis XIV*, vol. II, pp. 513–25.
[39] Ibid.
[40] Heijmans, *The Agency of Empire*, pp. 33–4.
[41] Heijmans, 'The Agency of Empire', p. 66; Buffet, 'Lorient sous Louis XIV', p. 76.
[42] L. Andriani and A. Christoforou, 'Social Capital: A Roadmap of Theoretical and Empirical Contributions and Limitations', *Journal of Economic Issues* 50 (2016), pp. 11–12. On clientelism in Old Regime France, and the ways in which sociology can illuminate our understanding of it, see Kettering, *Patrons*.

vote to enter – and be received into – the merchant court of the city of Paris'.[43] The merchant court of Paris was comprised of a leading judge and four other judges, known as consuls, who were elected on a yearly basis. As Amalia Kessler argues, the court was essentially an extension of the guild system in the city, intending to facilitate and police commercial practice. Up to 1686, it had been dominated by the six key merchants' guilds – the mercers, drapers, grocer-apothecaries, furriers, hatters and goldsmiths – and a small group of others, such as the wine sellers' and printers' guilds.[44] Serving as a consul on the court was a significant social accolade: consuls 'had tremendous power to shape the development of commercial doctrine and practice' in Paris and beyond.[45] Furthermore, once their tenure ended, consuls joined the *anciens*, a group who

> advised the court on important and undecided questions of law, on how to proceed in jurisdictional conflicts with other courts, on whether and how to petition the king or *parlement*, on matters concerning court property, and on issues related to the employment of staff. Moreover, whenever a current judge or consul was absent, it was one of the *anciens* who would replace him.[46]

A guaranteed seat on the court therefore gave Company members the opportunity to exercise significant power in civic life.

Sure enough, the court's registers record that Charles Lebrun, in his capacity as a member of the Company, was selected to be a consul in 1687; Gilbert Paignon was also selected in 1689; Denis Rousseau in 1691; Pierre Héron in 1693; and Pierre Chauvin in 1695.[47] The importance of this privilege was widely recognised: on 25 June 1687, Lagny wrote to Seignelay that Lebrun had asked 'to stand down from the directorship' of the Company because of the attention that 'he is obliged to give for the functions of consul'.[48] Guillaume Bar was elected for the remainder of Lebrun's tenure to allow the latter to perform his consular duties.[49] The priority for Lebrun was clear: for him, and those who followed, membership of the Company served first and foremost as a stepping stone to the prestigious merchant court.

---

[43] Bornier, *Conférences des ordonnances de Louis XIV*, vol. II, pp. 513–25.
[44] Kessler, *A Revolution in Commerce*; Bernard, *The Emerging City*, pp. 117–18.
[45] Kessler, *A Revolution in Commerce*, p. 9.
[46] Ibid., p. 29.
[47] M. Denière, *La juridiction consulaire de Paris, 1563–1792. Sa création, ses luttes, son administration intérieure, ses usages et ses mœurs*, Paris: Henri Plon, 1872, pp. 413, 415, 417, 419, 421–2.
[48] MAR/B/7/492, fol. 389, AN.
[49] Ibid.

The Company fiercely guarded this privilege, even when its underwriting portfolio was tenuous. Even though all underwriting had ceased in 1695, Chauvin was elected as consul that year without dispute. A fierce disagreement emerged in the elections of 29 January 1697, however, when Antoine Niceron, Adrien Revellois, Florentin Maillard and Pierre Bellavoine were elected as consuls – none of whom were members of the Company. The Company's directors immediately contested the election, asserting its privilege to seat one of its members. Jean-François Chalmette, Charles Charon, Siméon Marcadé, Jean Hallé and Pierre Le Noir – the judge and consuls elected respectively in 1696 – handled the dispute. An order followed on 31 January that Thomas Tardif would serve as consul in place of Bellavoine.[50]

In asserting its privileges, the Company's directors had stirred up a hornet's nest. The mercers' guild, to which Bellavoine belonged, were especially angered by Tardif's seating, as an order of the Council of State of 16 January 1689 had stipulated a mercer *qua* mercer would be elected to the consulate each year (even if a mercer had already been elected *qua* Company member).[51] They argued a different consul-elect should have been unseated instead. Strongly rejecting this logic – and, it seems, angered by prior years of mercer domination because of its own privileges and those of the Company – the other five merchant corps, alongside the community of wine merchants, met with the king at Versailles on 2 July 1697 to demand the mercers' electoral privileges be struck down. The king obliged, and, M.G. Denière suggests, an order of the Council of State of 30 July restored future election procedures to those that had been in place before 1689, where the mercers were not guaranteed a seat.[52] Whether this, in fact, quashed the Company's electoral privileges too is unclear. In any case, the Company did not assert any privileges in 1699 or thereafter. The *status quo*, whereby the six merchant corps dominated the merchant court by virtue of their influence in the city, was restored.

The directors' decision to pursue the Company's privileges in 1697 demonstrates these were a key motivating factor for members in joining and remaining in the institution. Even though the Company had suspended all activity in 1695, and would only recommence briefly in 1698, members still wanted to maximise the return on their investment by squeezing the Company's privileges for all they were worth in social and economic prestige.[53]

Privileges extended beyond access to further opportunities for social and commercial advancement. The letters patent held that, for those who did

---

50 Denière, *La juridiction consulaire de Paris*, pp. 423–4.
51 Ibid., p. 51.
52 Ibid., pp. 51–2.
53 The Company's underwriting portfolio will be discussed in Chapter 5.

not already have the *droit de Committimus*,⁵⁴ members would be granted legal privileges. This meant they would have the right in the first instance to have their civil and criminal legal disputes tried before the *prévot* of Paris – whether as plaintiff or as defendant – and their commercial conflicts before the judge and consuls of the city's merchant court.⁵⁵

Such legal privileges – alongside the other privileges the members enjoyed – helped to develop one's credit and reputation. Just as Robelot had benefited from serving as the Chamber's cashier, Jagault enjoyed the social benefits from serving as the Company's registrar. While Jagault was listed as a '*bourgeois* of Paris' in a parish document from 4 December 1680, his probate inventory from 15 July 1720 – two decades after the Company had ceased all meaningful activity – described him as 'registrar' of the Company.⁵⁶

The members themselves also drew attention to their participation in the institution. In a statement he submitted to Paris' admiralty court⁵⁷ on 23 June 1690, Guillaume Bar referred to himself as 'director of the *Compagnies des Indes et assurances de France*'.⁵⁸ Bar chose here to refer to compan*ies* in the plural, bringing together his directorships in the CIO and the Company as a means of presenting his wide-reaching commercial influence. This is evidence the Company remained a prestigious institution in its own right.

For those members based in Paris, membership could also provide a consistent income from commissions. The Company issued an advertisement across France in June 1687 to try to generate business. It offered to help merchants without suitable contacts in Paris by providing the services of a commission agent 'in return for retainers[?] and a commission of half a per cent'.⁵⁹ Bar, Baroy, Demeuves, Desvieux, Hébert, Héron, Lejariel, Pasquier, Pelletier, Pocquelin, Rousseau, Soullet,⁶⁰ Tardif and Tranchepain all capitalised on this by serving as commission agents on insurance policies signed with the Company's directors on behalf of provincial merchants.⁶¹ This allowed them to double dip: they received commission fees while negotiating policies for a company in which they themselves were shareholders,

---

⁵⁴ This was a legal privilege granted by the king. Depending on whether the letters of *committimus* had a *grand sceau* or a *petit sceau*, the holder was allowed to take legal proceedings to particular jurisdictions in the first instance; G. Cabourdin and G. Viard, *Lexique historique de la France d'Ancien Régime*, Paris: Armand Colin, 1978, p. 71.
⁵⁵ Bornier, *Conférences des ordonnances de Louis XIV*, vol. II, pp. 513–25.
⁵⁶ Y//239, fol. 230v; MC/ET/I/295, n.p., AN.
⁵⁷ On this court, see Chapters 7 and 8.
⁵⁸ Z/1d/109, n.p., AN.
⁵⁹ Pouilloux, *Mémoires d'assurances*, p. 441.
⁶⁰ Which of the Soullets is unclear.
⁶¹ Z/1d/85, AN.

thereby standing to profit twice from the same transaction. The ability to offer such services no doubt allowed these members to broaden and deepen their own personal networks, thereby giving scope for commercial transactions and opportunities beyond the realm of insurance.

This array of privileges betrays a commercial policy very different from that which Colbert espoused. Like his father, Seignelay wished to promote the French insurance industry as a means of developing commerce. To do this, he pursued a strategy that was familiar to prospective members. Membership of the Company was, essentially, a venal office: members bought these offices in exchange for the array of social, legal and economic privileges bestowed by the state. This explains why membership was limited to thirty: diluting privileges by offering them to larger numbers of people would have made them less appealing to investors.

When compared to venal offices, Company membership could be a sound option. Shares were sold at 4,000 *livres* each – not a significant investment compared to those needed for prominent venal offices in Paris. For example, the office of a *président à mortier* in the *parlement* of Paris was fixed at a value of 350,000 *livres* after Colbert's 1665 enquiry – down from 500,000 *livres* before – while councillors' offices were reduced in value from 120,000 to 100,000 *livres*. These valuations remained in place until 1709.[62] Each *président à mortier* paid a total of 20,000 *livres* in *augmentations de gages* across the years 1683, 1692 and 1701, while councillors each paid a total of 7,200 *livres*.[63] Granted, these were the most prestigious offices in Paris, but there was no such thing as an 'affordable' office in any court or institution in the city. For an extreme but instructive point of comparison, even a position as lieutenant general in the rural bailiwick (*baillage*) of Cany in Normandy would set one back 15,000 *livres*.[64] Simply put, Colbert's reforms in 1665 notwithstanding, offices with social clout never came cheaply, and they were not in plentiful supply. Buying shares in the Company offered investors a rare opportunity to secure valuable privileges at an affordable price. In exchange, the capital they invested was 'locked in' to the institution: while members of the Chamber could leave at any time, depleting the institution's underwriting capacity, the Company's fund ensured it could continue operating even in a time of crisis.[65]

---

[62] Doyle, 'Colbert et les offices', p. 476.
[63] Hurt, *Louis XIV and the Parlements*, p. 73.
[64] Z. Schneider, *The King's Bench: Bailiwick Magistrates and Local Governance in Normandy, 1670–1740*, Woodbridge: Boydell & Brewer, 2008, p. 134.
[65] D. Gindis, 'Conceptualizing the Business Corporation: Insights from History', *Journal of Institutional Economics* (2020), pp. 3–4. On the locking in of capital, see also Dari-Mattiacci, Gelderblom, Jonker, and Perotti, 'The Emergence of the Corporate Form'.

While capital invested into the institution was locked in, members themselves were not. Shares were not heritable – a major difference from most venal offices – but they were certainly treated as transferable property.[66] When profits were distributed (or members were forced to replenish the fund) each year on 5 January, members decided whether to elevate or diminish the value of their shares. Vitry-la-Ville declared shares in the Company worth 9,000 *livres* upon his bankruptcy on 24 March 1687. This suggests he originally invested 8,000 *livres* for two shares in 1686, but the shares were reassessed on 5 January 1687 at 4,500 each – or 12.5 per cent above the principal.[67] A year later, on 5 January 1688, it was agreed share values would be raised to '20 per cent beyond the principal of each share', i.e. 4,800 *livres* each.[68] These shifts were important, as they fixed the rate at which shares could be sold. If a member wished to sell their share(s) – as Vitry-la-Ville surely did upon declaring bankruptcy – current members of the Company had right of first refusal, but shares could otherwise be sold on the open market.[69] This was all the more important as, while not heritable, shares did not revert to the crown on one's death, as venal offices did when the *paulette* was not paid. Sharing no part in the profits accrued or the debts incurred after a member's death, his heirs were obliged to sell his share(s) at market value within a year. This preserved the members' investments. When Charles Lebrun died in 1698, his widow, Marguerite Maurice, sought the support of the Parisian admiralty court in receiving detailed accounts from the Company so that she and her children could either collect the profits Lebrun's share(s) had accrued that year up to his death or make the necessary contribution to replenish the fund.[70]

Membership may not have been strictly heritable, but it had one ostensible benefit over other, more traditional types of office holding. Mark Potter notes 'any privileged corps could [theoretically] act as a financial intermediary for the crown' by being tied into contracting loans on its behalf.[71] However, the Company – and its members *qua* members – was exempted on paper from

---

[66] This is not self-evident: the English EIC only introduced transferrable shares in the 1650s, several decades after it was established; Gelderblom, de Jong, and Jonker, 'The Formative Years of the Modern Corporation', pp. 1050–1.
[67] MC/ET/CV/915, n.p., AN.
[68] Z/1d/85, fol. 19r, AN.
[69] Bornier, *Conférences des ordonnances de Louis XIV*, vol. II, pp. 513–25.
[70] Z/1d/111, n.p., AN. The need for the court's action likely arose, as Julie Hardwick puts it, from the fact that 'guardians of minor children were expected to account scrupulously for the money they handled [...] and families calculated equal shares of inheritance down to the last penny'; J. Hardwick, *Family Business: Litigation and the Political Economies of Daily Life in Early Modern France*, Oxford: Oxford University Press, 2009, p. 167.
[71] Potter, *Corps and Clienteles*, p. 13n.

such a function: its letters patent established that its fund 'will remain specifically allocated to the insurance policies made by the Company, without it possibly being seized for, nor diverted to, any other debts, nor even the royal funds'.[72] The prospective members solidified this further in their subsequent articles of association (*acte de société*) from 1686, stating that 'the Company will not be able to give any loans – whether by itself or through its directors – for any cause or under any pretext whatsoever'.[73]

An order of the Council of State was subsequently issued on 6 June, confirming the terms of the articles of association.[74] This meant the crown committed on paper twice to not seek loans from the Company. As Heijmans has found, however, the crown could not credibly commit to this. The CIO's letters patent stipulated that its shareholders would not be forced to invest any further capital beyond their original investment, and they also enshrined the shareholders' limited liability for all debts. These articles were contravened by the crown in the latter decades of the seventeenth century.[75] As we will see, Seignelay went to creative lengths to circumvent the state's commitments to the Company's members and force them to support his pet projects.

Above all else, many members strove to become noblemen and put their families on the path to hereditary noble status. The social cachet of nobility is obvious, but it also carried lucrative tax privileges, such as exemption from the *taille* and other direct taxes.[76] Hereditary nobility typically came with the third generation of office holding. Membership of the Company – and the access to royal patronage it provided – was a stepping stone towards achieving this. Colbert had overseen the issuing of an edict in August 1669 declaring that 'overseas (though not overland) commerce was compatible with the status of nobility', suspending the *loi de*

---

[72] Bornier, *Conférences des ordonnances de Louis XIV*, vol. II, p. 515.
[73] Ibid., p. 519. This guaranteed the Company would not use its fund for investment purposes, putting it at odds with fire and life insurance companies in London, such as the Sun Fire, which would play a leading role in that city's capital market in the eighteenth century; A. John, 'Insurance Investment and the London Money Market of the 18th Century', *Economica* 20 (1953), pp. 137–58. The pooling of capital for investment purposes was also a key draw of the corporate model in eighteenth-century America: here, see R. Wright and C. Kingston, 'Corporate Insurers in Antebellum America', *Business History Review* 86 (2012), pp. 447–76; Glenn Crothers, 'Commercial Risk', pp. 607–33.
[74] Bornier, *Conférences des ordonnances de Louis XIV*, vol. II, pp. 524–5.
[75] Heijmans, 'Investing in French Overseas Companies', pp. 110–11.
[76] The *capitation* was introduced in 1695, following by the *dixième* in 1710; these were direct taxes even on the nobility; Beik, 'The Absolutism of Louis XIV', pp. 209–10; G. McCollim, *Louis XIV's Assault on Privilege: Nicolas Desmaretz and the Tax on Wealth*, Rochester, NY: University of Rochester Press, 2012; Rowlands, *The Financial Decline of a Great Power*, pp. 57–71.

dérogeance that had prevented noblemen from engaging in trade without losing their privileges.[77] Insurance was defined as a 'maritime contract' in the 1681 *Ordonnance*, no doubt with this edict in mind.[78] Even so, the Company's letters patent explicitly exempted its members – including the directors who directly engaged in the conduct of insurance – from the *loi de dérogeance*.[79] Reiterating that the practice of insurance was compatible with nobility reassured prospective members that their involvement in the institution would not undermine their social ambitions.[80]

This was therefore an insurance institution entirely unlike the Chamber, or even the proposed monopoly company of 1664. While the Chamber followed Colbert's commercial policy, allowing merchants to lead the way with Colbert's support, the Company was entirely typical of Seignelay's preference for the privileged corporate model. While the Chamber was a private underwriting institution, meaning every underwriter had to participate actively and of their own accord, the Company structure allowed Seignelay to tap into the capital of wealthy *financiers* and officeholders. Underwriting experience was not necessary: members could be silent partners, relying on more knowledgeable underwriters to serve as the directors and make the underwriting decisions on their behalf. In opting for this corporate structure, Seignelay was clearly seeking a very particular kind of capital: while the merchants of Rouen had suggested the 1664 monopoly company should be 'like a bank', in which any and all could invest, Seignelay's Company had a fixed membership. In this way, he created a corporate structure that exploited the tools of privilege to which Colbert was so averse, thereby bridging the gap between the spheres of commerce and venal office holding.

'CONTRARY TO THE PUBLIC GOOD': SEIGNELAY AND THE *DE FACTO* MONOPOLY OF 1687

What remains unclear is precisely what motivated Seignelay to establish the Company. Certainly, a few ideas can be discerned from the Company's foundational documents. First, the Company's letters patent expressed the desire to support the mercantile community by allowing them to seek insurance with 'greater ease and security'. Their emphasis on the Company's liquidity, and the sense of 'security' this engendered, echoes the arguments

---

[77] Trivellato, *The Promise and Peril of Credit*, p. 90.
[78] R. Valin, *Nouveau commentaire sur l'Ordonnance de la marine du mois d'août 1681*, vol. I, La Rochelle: Jerôme Legier, 1766, p. XXI, and vol. II, p. I.
[79] Bornier, *Conférences des ordonnances de Louis XIV*, vol. II, pp. 513–25
[80] The social ambitions of *financiers* are discussed further in G. Rowlands, *Dangerous and Dishonest Men: The International Bankers of Louis XIV's France*, Basingstoke: Palgrave Macmillan, 2015, pp. 166–73.

made by the Rouennais merchants in 1664. More concrete still was the desire to cement the impact of the 1681 *Ordonnance*.[81] It is only by looking at documents from after 1686, however, that the role of insurance in Seignelay's commercial policy comes into full focus.

With his full support for the Company, Seignelay no doubt hoped the institution would hit the ground running in its underwriting. In reality, the Company's early months were challenging. Although Seignelay and Lagny had both written to allies in ports across Europe to ask them to encourage merchants to insure in Paris, these efforts did not initially bear fruit.[82]

In September 1687, persuasion gave way to coercion. In a series of letters, Seignelay employed every weapon in his rhetorical arsenal to convey to the mercantile communities in the Atlantic ports that the king took umbrage at their behaviour. Dunkirk was the first to feel Seignelay's wrath. In a letter of 16 September to M. Patoulet, intendant in Dunkirk, Seignelay wrote that:

> The partners of the [Royal] Insurance Company – comprised of the most considerable and honest merchants of Paris, established by declaration of the King in the month of May 1686 to help his subjects in their enterprises for maritime commerce and, through the safety of the conditions that His Majesty inserted into the declaration, to protect them from the difficulties that they [have] found with foreigners in collecting payment when losses [have] occurred – have informed me that, since its establishment, the merchants of Dunkirk have had recourse to the Company for all their insurance needs, but, as I have learned that some of the merchants have begun in the past months to undertake their insurance in foreign countries again, it is necessary that you assemble the leading merchants at your house, and that you tell them that the intention of the king is that they will continue to undertake their insurance with the Company of Paris, and that His Majesty will intervene to obtain reasonable conditions from them [i.e. the Company], [henceforth] prohibiting them [i.e. the merchants] from undertaking insurance abroad, and, although there is no appearance that they will contravene this after having known the will of His Majesty, you will be sure to tell them that if they are found to go elsewhere, thereby making an outrage of the great and extraordinary privileges with which His Majesty has favoured them, he will be obliged to treat them less favourably than he has done up to now.[83]

Dunkirk was joined by Saint-Malo. The tone of the letter on the same day to Sieur Leval Le Fer, the syndic of Saint-Malo, is broadly the same, but the contents are different enough to warrant quoting separately:

---

[81] This aim will be discussed further in Chapter 6.
[82] The early years of the Company's underwriting will be discussed in Chapters 3 and 5.
[83] MAR/B/7/58, fols 618–19, AN.

When it pleased the king to form a [Royal] Insurance Company in Paris, His Majesty chose the most significant merchants with the most recognised integrity, and, by the declaration made for its establishment, he perceived all the necessary conditions for the safety of the public, with the intention of protecting French merchants who undertake their insurance outside of the Kingdom from the difficulties that they find with foreigners in collecting payment when losses arrive, and to keep within the state the considerable sums that pass to foreigners in the undertaking of insurance. As I have been given accounts from time to time of the business the insurance chamber[84] [i.e. the Company] has done and the sums it has loaned, I was extremely surprised to see that the merchants of Saint-Malo have given almost no business. What surprises me more is that I have learned they are undertaking part of their insurance with foreigners, which is directly contrary to the public good, and to the same intention of His Majesty. It is [therefore] necessary that, as soon as the present [letter] is received, you assemble the merchants to tell them that His Majesty has prohibited them from continuing to undertake insurance in foreign countries and that he wants them to have recourse to the Company for their [insurance] needs. When they cannot [fully] insure amongst themselves, I want [it] to be well believed that [...] I will intervene to oblige the [Royal] Insurance Company to receive all reasonable propositions. But if the merchants of Saint-Malo contravene what I am giving you the responsibility to tell them on behalf of His Majesty, you must declare to them that [if they choose to] go elsewhere, thereby making an outrage of the continual protection that he has had the kindness to give to them without fail on all occasions, he would be obliged to withdraw it.[85]

Duplicates of the Saint-Malo letter were sent to the admiralty officers of Rouen, Bordeaux and Bayonne, alongside M. Arnoul, the intendant in La Rochelle, and the *sénéchal* of Nantes. Only one modification was made for these letters: Seignelay informed his recipients that the merchants would earn the king's 'indignation' if they continued to insure abroad.[86]

This was an extraordinary intervention on Seignelay's part. Each of the letters points not only to the asymmetrical nature of privilege in early modern French ports, but also to Seignelay's willingness to exploit this in the pursuit of state interests. In particular, his letter to Patoulet demonstrates a willingness to use Dunkirk's privileges as a weapon against its merchants. When Louis XIV bought Dunkirk from England in 1662, he

---

[84] NB the Company was frequently – and confusingly – referred to as a chamber in various documents.
[85] MAR/B/7/58, fols 619–21, AN.
[86] Ibid., fols 621–2.

allowed it to retain its free port status.[87] This meant, following Louis' own statement on the matter, that merchandise could still 'be brought, manipulated, and transformed without any interference from customs on the condition that the goods are re-exported'.[88] This was no small concession: a very unconventional free port status would only be granted to Marseille and Rouen in 1669 for Levantine commerce, a privilege the latter lost again in 1685. Thanks to these privileges – and the capacity these gave for the port to become a hub for smuggling – Dunkirk became a centre for commercial and naval competition with the English and the Dutch during the 1680s.[89] It retained this position until the end of the Old Regime.[90] Yet this story could have been very different. Seignelay made clear the merchants of Dunkirk were obliged to seek insurance in Paris if local coverage was insufficient. He concluded with the ultimate threat: 'if they are found to go elsewhere, thereby making an outrage of the great and extraordinary privileges with which His Majesty has favoured them, he will be obliged to treat them less favourably than he has done up to now'. Dunkirk's free port status was at risk if Seignelay's orders were not followed.

Of course, this was a threat on which Seignelay most likely had no intention of following through. After all, he wrote similar letters to Saint-Malo, Rouen, Bordeaux, Bayonne, La Rochelle and Nantes, none of which had any such privileges he could threaten to withdraw. The language here was no less charged, however, with Seignelay threatening the king's 'indignation' and the withdrawal of his 'continual protection' of the merchants if they continued to insure abroad.[91]

In any case, Patoulet and the merchants of Dunkirk did not wish to play chicken with Seignelay. As we will see, Dunkirk emerged as one of the Company's key sources of business.[92] The French state's power over

---

[87] The declaration extended the privileges theretofore held by the inhabitants of Dunkirk to all foreign merchants who chose to base themselves in the port thereafter; P. Henrat, *Répertoire général des Archives de la Marine, XVIe–XVIIIe siècles*, Paris: SPM, 2018, p. 42.

[88] Quoted in Horn, *Economic Development in Early Modern France*, p. 109.

[89] Christian Pfister-Langanay has reconstructed port traffic in Dunkirk in the period 1683–86, based on the *Rolle général des bastimens*, a document that will be discussed further in Chapter 3. Pfister-Langanay finds that voyages to the rest of France and to the Low Countries comprised 73.5 per cent of all voyages by Dunkerquois vessels in this period; C. Pfister-Langanay, *Ports, navires et négociants à Dunkerque (1662–1792)*, Dunkirk: Société dunkerquoise, 1985, p. 188.

[90] Ibid., pp. 109–10. Here, see also Morieux, *The Channel*, pp. 248–82.

[91] There is no clear sense of why the Mediterranean ports were spared this treatment. With the renowned recalcitrance of the Marseillais, it was vital for Seignelay to pick his battles carefully; this perhaps was one battle he simply preferred not to fight.

[92] See Chapter 5.

commercial privileges was so potent because, just as it could grant these privileges, it could also take them away at will.

What was Seignelay's justification for this intervention? In conceiving of the Company as a vessel of royal 'protection', Seignelay drew on a discourse at the heart of kingship itself. We have seen that Louis XIV's establishment of the Company was presented as a means of helping merchants to conduct their business with 'greater ease and security'; a year later, Seignelay took this logic further, presenting the Company's establishment – and its new *de facto* monopoly – as a specific manifestation of the king's overarching duty to the public good. This enshrined a very different kind of relationship between the prince and the practice of risk management from that espoused in the fifteenth and sixteenth centuries: the Burgundian and Habsburg dukes who encountered insurance during the golden ages of Bruges and Antwerp viewed it as a suspicious speculative tool that ultimately undermined commerce and brought the courts to a halt when underwriters exercised their power to delay payment on policies and drag out legal proceedings.[93] Colbert and Seignelay shared these suspicions, but they believed the risks insurance posed to commerce were not inherent to the instrument itself: insurance could achieve a social good, and the abuses of the instrument were simply the product of short-sighted mercantile greed.[94] This greed could be tackled through state legislation and intervention – whence came the Chamber, the 1681 *Ordonnance* and the Company.

Most striking is that Seignelay adapted Colbertian logic in order to construct his understanding of the public good. Certainly, Colbert's bullionist justification for intervening in insurance had not died with him: Seignelay still wished, in his own words, 'to keep within the state the considerable sums that pass to foreigners in the undertaking of insurance'. Here, Seignelay was pursuing the same economic warfare against the Dutch initiated by his father, and he considered the choice of merchants to insure abroad as 'directly contrary to the public good' insofar as these merchants were fuelling the economic success of the Dutch at the expense of the French.

He pushed this logic further than his father, however, by stating the king had established the Company 'with the intention of protecting French merchants who undertake their insurance outside of the Kingdom from the difficulties that they find with foreigners in receiving payment when losses arrive'. No doubt, this criticism was aimed at the Dutch in particular, but most likely without any basis in reality. In his early eighteenth-century manual on Amsterdam commerce, Jean-Pierre Ricard hailed the insurers of the city for 'their kindness, their cordiality and their promptness in settling

---

[93] D. De ruysscher, 'Antwerp 1490–1590: Insurance and Speculation', in A. Leonard (ed.), *Marine Insurance: Origins and Institutions, 1300–1850*, Basingstoke: Palgrave Macmillan, 2016, pp. 79–105.

[94] See Chapters 7 and 8.

and paying losses and averages'.⁹⁵ The *Kamer van Assurantie* no doubt helped in establishing this reputation.⁹⁶ The fact merchants in the northern French ports were continuing to insure abroad suggests they encountered no problems in receiving payment from foreign insurers, and the Company's letters patent made no such reference to the deceptiveness of foreign underwriters. Moreover, Seignelay's orders simply forbade merchants from insuring abroad: they did not stop merchants from insuring with foreigners based in French ports. While Seignelay hoped to keep premiums within the bounds of metropolitan France, he did not seem especially concerned that premiums might fall into the hands of ostensibly untrustworthy foreigners within France itself. It seems more likely Seignelay appealed to this inconsistent xenophobic logic as a rationalisation of his intervention.⁹⁷

Seignelay had gone to extraordinary lengths for the Company in writing these letters. While the *de jure* monopoly on insurance and sea loans in Paris was not especially valuable, this new *de facto* monopoly on all insurance beyond mutual underwriting in the Atlantic ports was a potentially lucrative privilege for the Company and its members.⁹⁸

Yet Seignelay's weaponisation of privilege cut both ways. After all, the port merchants were not the only ones being submitted to crown orders in these letters, which uniformly note Seignelay's willingness to 'oblige the [Royal] Insurance Company to receive all reasonable propositions'. These were not mere words: on 20 October 1687, Seignelay informed Leval Le Fer that he had specifically ordered the Company to entertain all 'reasonable propositions' for coverage from Malouin merchants.⁹⁹

This had significant consequences for the Company in 1687 and 1688. From early on in Lagny's tenure as director general of commerce, he worked not only on establishing the Company and securing the resources it needed to succeed, but also on an array of other projects.¹⁰⁰ Amongst these was a push, supported strongly by Seignelay, to boost domestic fishing to reduce France's dependency on Dutch imports. As early as 22 May 1686, Lagny wrote to offer state support for the whaling fisheries of Bayonne and Saint-Jean-de-Luz; a duty followed in 1687 on all whale oils and soaps from abroad, which sought to make Dutch imports uncompetitive and encourage local

---

95 Quoted in Barbour, 'Marine Risks', p. 581.
96 See the Introduction.
97 Most likely, this letter was written at least in part by Lagny, who had used similar logic in prior letters to try to persuade merchants to insure with the Company; see Chapter 3. On the widespread presence of Dutch commission agents in France's ports in the seventeenth century, see Braudel, *Civilisation and Capitalism*, vol. III, pp. 256–7.
98 The extent of the success of Seignelay's intervention will be explored in Chapter 5.
99 MAR/B/7/58, fols 646–9, AN.
100 We will see more on Lagny's efforts in Chapter 3.

production.[101] A similar effort was made in the northern ports of Dieppe, Calais, Fécamp, Saint-Valery-sur-Somme and neighbouring ports to boost herring fishing. An order of the Council of State of 24 March 1687 reissued the 1681 *Ordonnance*'s ban on buying herring from foreign ships and introduced a new, fixed fishing season. The order sought to ensure domestic demand for herring could be met by French fishing ships alone.[102]

Linking these projects in Seignelay's mind was the scope for financial support from the Company. In his letters, Seignelay uniformly informed his recipients that, to help merchants establish these ventures, 'the [Royal] Insurance Company established in Paris will lend them money on very reasonable conditions'.[103] This was not an abstract proposal on Seignelay's part, since he emphasised in a later letter to M. de la Boulaye, the *commissaire général de la marine* in Bayonne, that he would order the Company 'to give sea loans to those in need of them'.[104] Seignelay intended to dictate the Company's commercial activities to support state interests.

Sure enough, Seignelay ordered the Company's directors to write a *mémoire* for him outlining the terms it was willing to offer for a series of sea loans on whaling voyages from Bayonne, Saint-Jean-de-Luz, Ciboure and Hendaye. The directors offered an intentionally uncompetitive interest rate of 25 per cent for each loan.[105] Clearly, they were ill at ease with being ordered to offer sea loans that served the protectionist bent of Seignelay's commercial policy rather than the Company's own commercial interests. Sea loans required the fronting of significant capital that the Company certainly had at its disposal, but its fund risked being rapidly depleted if a large number of voyages failed. Indeed, insuring and/or loaning on a bundle of very similar voyages was especially risky practice, as they would all be subject to the same cluster of natural and anthropogenic hazards. It was in the Company's interests to maintain a diverse portfolio.

This apparently did not concern Seignelay, who was decidedly unimpressed by the Company's tactics. In response, he wrote to the Company on 22 December 1687, leveraging its role in serving the public good as a means of criticising its members. Seignelay condemned its resistance to supporting the whaling expeditions, bemoaning its 'preposterous' demand for 25 per cent in interest on each sea loan.[106] This level of interest, Seignelay argued,

---

[101] MAR/B/7/58, fols 110–12 and 690–3, AN.
[102] Valin, *Nouveau commentaire*, vol. II, p. 772. For more on how this played out, see Henrat, *Répertoire général des Archives de la Marine*, p. 158; MAR/B/7/58, fols 593–5 and 600–1, AN.
[103] MAR/B/7/58, fols 593–5, AN. This is also seen in ibid., fols 600–1, 627–30 and 665–8.
[104] Ibid., fols 665–8.
[105] Ibid., fols 685–6.
[106] Ibid., fols 685–6.

was entirely excessive during a period of peace. Drawing on his knowledge of the Company's early struggles in getting business – and the power he had exerted in bringing custom from the Atlantic ports – he noted he felt

> obliged to tell you that if your Company continues to make itself so difficult, it will have only little or no business; that it will struggle to win [further business]; and that the public will not take the support that you had made [them] hope [was on offer], and that His Majesty had promised in its establishment.[107]

In essence, Seignelay argued here that, if the members did not obey his wishes, the king's own desire that French merchants benefit from better access to maritime protection would not be met. Even if Seignelay did not explicitly threaten the Company's privileges as he had done for Dunkirk, he scarcely needed to spell out that these rested on the institution's ability to provide a competitive service, especially when state interests were on the line. Just as the Atlantic ports were acting contrarily to the public good in insuring abroad, the Company was acting contrarily to the public good in putting up obstacles to the state's commercial projects; just as Dunkirk's privileges could be withdrawn, so too could the Company's.

Seignelay also adopted a dubious logic to justify that these sea loans were, in fact, in the Company's commercial interests. Judging the risks the Company would bear, he remarked that 'it seems to me that you will find sufficient safety in the preference the *Ordonnance* gives you on vessels and cargoes [in order] to not demand such [rates of] interest from the Basques'.[108] This assessment refers to article seven of the section *Des Contrats à grosse aventure, ou à retour de voyage* from the 1681 *Ordonnance*, which stipulated that the creditor's claim to the ship, its furniture and freight superseded all other claims, up to the sum of the amount loaned and the interest charged.[109] Doubtless, this limited the scope for the Company to be defrauded, as the ship, furniture, and freight served as collateral that could be seized if debtors refused to make payment after a successful voyage. This did not limit the risks of the voyages themselves, however, which were surely the directors' primary concern. Besides the perennial risks of the sea, whaling was notoriously dangerous. Giving sea loans on a series of whaling ships due to sail within a similar timespan was amongst the riskiest gambles a creditor could make.

Of course, in this instance it was not a gamble at all, as it was not a willing choice. Seignelay concluded his letter by promising the crown's logistical support in arranging the sea loans, 'but on this occasion I also expect, on your side, that you will do everything possible to not alienate

---

[107] Ibid., fols 685–6.
[108] Ibid., fols 685–6.
[109] Valin, *Nouveau commentaire*, vol. I, p. 9.

the merchants'.[110] He ordered the members to liaise with Lagny to discuss reducing the interest rates on the loans.

With Seignelay's letter leaving no room for further stall tactics, the Company had no choice but to offer better rates. Between 12 February and 27 March 1688, the Company empowered Louis and Leon Dulivier of Bayonne to sign thirteen sea loans on its behalf for whaling voyages from Saint-Jean-de-Luz, Bayonne and Socoa (near Ciboure), totalling 51,200 *livres*. This comprised around two-thirds of the total value of the Company's loans for the year and put over a sixth of the original fund at risk.[111] The Company had capitulated to Seignelay's demand, with each loan having an interest rate of only 20 per cent. In a nutshell, these were forced loans in a novel form that circumvented the Company's letters patent.[112]

The Company's early challenges thus paved the way for Seignelay to make bold interventions, revealing a richer commercial policy than is suggested by the letters patent alone. Seignelay weaponised privilege as a means of pushing the state's commercial interests: he threatened the privileges of Dunkirk, and royal support of other Atlantic ports, to coerce merchants into insuring with the Company in Paris; and he threatened the Company's privileges to coerce it into giving sea loans for the state's maritime projects. The state's monopolisation of privilege throughout the seventeenth century proved most valuable here in allowing the royal will to be fulfilled: privileged groups became indebted to the state for their very existence, and Seignelay was not afraid to remind them of this.

Seignelay justified his interventions through an enhanced Colbertian logic that drew on the kingly duty to the public good. Far from being an independent institution that benefited from the resources and legitimation of the state, Seignelay treated the Company – like insurance itself – as a tool of commercial policy serving the interests of French shipping and, by extension, the state.

CONCLUSION

These two chapters have explored the Chamber and the Company from the perspective of those who were engaged in them. In studying the motivations underpinning the establishment of these institutions, we have seen they were

---

[110] MAR/B/7/58, fols 685–6, AN.

[111] Z/1d/81, fols 32v–33; and Z/1d/85, AN. 1688 was the year with the second highest rate of loaning in the Company's history; on this, see Chapter 5.

[112] The interests of a key royal ally were met through these loans. On 27 December 1688, Lagny wrote to Jean Magon de la Lande, a powerful Malouin merchant and a notable figure in the Company's history, as we will see in Chapters 3 and 8. Lagny confirmed that Seignelay had made all the requisite arrangements in Bayonne to ensure that whaling could begin shortly. Magon would oversee the manufacture of whale oil soap in Normandy with Seignelay's blessing; MAR/B/7/58, fols 690–3, AN.

Table 3 Sea loans for whaling voyages, made in 1688 by Louis and Leon Dulivier on behalf of the Company.

Date (1688)	Debtor	Vessel and shipmaster	Sum (*livres*)	Interest rate
12 February, 24 March	Joachin Diturbide	*Saint Thomas*, Joachin Diturbide	2,000	20%
18 February	Dominique de Havane	*Saint Nicolas*, Joannis Dauretche	2,200	20%
21 February	Martin de Courthiau	*Saint Joseph*, Joannis de Sallabery	6,000	20%
21 February	Pierre Maron	*Notre Dame du Rosaire*, Joannis Detcheuercy	6,000	20%
21 February	Gratian de Napias	*Sainte Barbe*, Domingo Damestoy	3,000	20%
22 February	Jean de Lasson	*Saint Michel*, Martin Dareche	750	20%
22 February	Jean de Lasson	*Saint Jean Baptiste*, Jean Perits de Lasson	750	20%
24 February	Michel and Joannis de Gellos	*Notre Dame du Rosaire*, Joannis de Gellos	3,000	20%
7 March	Jean de la Sabielhe l'ainé and Joannis de Mareoch	*Sainte Therese de Jesus*, Joannis de Mareoch	3,000	20%
11 March	Jacques Sopitte and Petrisans d'Olsabide	*Saint Vincent*, Petrisans d'Olsabide	6,000	20%
12 March	Gratian de Napias and Domingo Dameston	*Sainte Barbe*, Domingo Damestoy	3,000	20%
18 March	Jean du Conte	*Saint Michel*, Martin Daureche	1,000	20%
23 March	Jeanne Doriots (widow of Marsans d'Olhobarats), Jean d'Olhobarats and Jean Dihoursen	*Sainte Anne*, Jean Dihoursen	3,500	20%
23 March	Jean de la Sabielhe and Joannis de Lasson	*Inclination*, Joannis de Lasson	3,000	20%
23 March	Michel and Joannis de Gellos père et fils	*Notre Dame du Rosaire*, Joannis de Gellos	1,000	20%
27 March	Joachin Diturbide	*Saint Pierre d'Alcantara*, Marsans Detcheuercy	7,000	20%

Source: Z/1d/81, fols 32v–33, AN.

far from obscure novelties: they were entirely conventional institutions that reflected their patrons' distinct commercial policies.

This chapter has thus offered a significant corrective to prevailing narratives in the historiography. While we saw in Chapter 1 that Colbertianism has been rehabilitated in recent decades, the implications of this have not been widely considered for our understanding of Colbert's immediate successors, who to date have been broadly understood as continuing Colbertianism or even pushing it to its limits. Besides being built on a flawed understanding of Colbert's own policies, this orthodoxy obscures the significant transformations that took place in commercial policy in the 1680s and 1690s in line with similar transformations in fiscal policy.

Marine insurance offers a valuable window into these transformations. Like his father, Seignelay intended to challenge the supremacy of the Dutch. He agreed with Colbert that a strong indigenous insurance industry would prevent the outflow of premiums to the United Provinces and help to challenge the latter's commercial supremacy. Seignelay diverged from his father, however, in suggesting the king's interventions into insurance were the manifestation of his duty towards the public good. By establishing the Company, Seignelay suggested the king was protecting French merchants from the ostensibly untrustworthy conduct of Dutch insurers and 'help[ing] his subjects in their enterprises for maritime commerce'. This logic justified the establishment of the Company's curious monopoly in the Atlantic ports in 1687.

In this way, the state's interest in insurance remained steadfast, but the means of promoting it shifted significantly. By 1686, much had changed: the transformation of the European political stage after 1683 had forced a similar transformation of French fiscal policy. While Colbert had sought to suppress unnecessary offices, Seignelay leaned into the tools of privilege instead when he became secretary of state for maritime affairs. The corporate form was exploited to try to revive the fortunes of the CIO and to create the Guinea and Royal Insurance Companies. Heijmans has argued persuasively that investment in the CIO and Guinea Company gave scope for investors to engage in private trade in markets under monopoly. The Royal Insurance Company – whose membership ultimately overlapped with that of these institutions greatly – did not have this appeal: its monopoly over insurance and sea loans in Paris was not an especially lucrative one *per se*, and its *de facto* Atlantic monopoly only came a year after its members had already committed to the project. By offering social, commercial and legal privileges to prospective members, in lieu of access to an attractive market under monopoly, Seignelay revealed the underlying logic of his commercial strategy: investment in his chartered companies was an investment in a quasi-venal office. The privileges of membership in these companies – in the Company's case, offering a direct path to directorship of the CIO and a seat on the Parisian merchant court – meant, to quote David Bien, that 'the return was a different kind, one measured not in money but in the psychic satisfaction found in enhanced social standing'.[113] Although their motivations for intervening in the insurance industry were similar, Colbert *père et fils* did not share the same strategy for their interventions.

While the Chamber had offered flexible access to power through Bellinzani, membership of the Company offered no such flexibility: whether a member was serving as a director or not, he was liable for all losses in proportion to his investment. Moreover, with the state's capacity to renege on its commitments, those who joined could not be certain their investment – or even more, since the Company was an unlimited liability institution – would not be lost entirely. Seignelay transformed the Company into a tool of commercial policy by circumventing his promise to not draw the institution into loans to the state, forcing it to give sea loans to support the state's pet maritime projects. In short, the Company's privileges came at a premium; rather like underwriting itself, membership was a calculated risk.

When I originally began the research for this book, I hoped to answer the overarching question of why the Chamber and the Company failed. These chapters have suggested that this was, and is, *une question mal posée*. The institutions' aims were not confined to the bottom line: this was only one of several possible measures of success. Certainly, the institutions failed to fulfil their patrons' desires to seriously undermine the insurance markets of Amsterdam and London, but they still served as valuable tools in their patrons' divergent commercial policies. Similarly, the institutions' members had ambitions beyond the almighty *livre*. Like the other royal companies of the period, the Company was created to be 'plundered from above and from below';[114] the Chamber, by contrast, might more subtly be characterised as having been created to be *leveraged* from above and from below.[115] These distinctions aside, both institutions served an array of interests quite divorced from the direct profitability of their underwriting endeavours.

State interests were often incompatible with those of the institutions' members. Nevertheless, interests could occasionally align: for example, the institutions only functioned thanks to state support in accessing maritime information networks. This will be the focus of the next chapter.

---

[113] Bien, 'Offices, Corps, and a System of State Credit', p. 94.
[114] Boulle, 'French Mercantilism', p. 117. For more on this, and its implications for our analysis of the Company in regard to shareholder primacy, see Chapter 5.
[115] On how the Chamber was leveraged from above, see Chapter 6; and Wade, 'Underwriting Empire'.

3

'OVER THIRTY LEAGUES FROM THE SEA': PARIS, INFORMATION ASYMMETRIES AND STATE INTERVENTION

We have seen that state projects for developing the French insurance industry favoured Paris in order to tap into the city's deep well of capital. Yet we must acknowledge the elephant in the room: as Savary observed in *Le parfait négociant*, Paris was 'over thirty leagues from the sea'.[1]

This reality was not lost on the secretariat of state for maritime affairs. At the turn of the eighteenth century, the Company was in dire straits. Jérôme Phélypeaux, comte de Pontchartrain (hereafter Pontchartrain *fils*) – who succeeded his father, Louis Phélypeaux (hereafter Pontchartrain *père*), as secretary of state in 1699 – wrote a letter on 12 January 1701 offering a pre-mortem analysis of the institution.[2] At its core is the argument that

> the distance the Company in Paris is from the ports prevents it from knowing the quality of the vessels and the good faith of those who want to be insured, which has produced two deleterious effects: one [being] that it has often been deceived; the other [being] that, having become mistrustful through its losses, it wants to choose and chooses badly.[3]

This line of argument – rooted in longstanding tropes about the social and cultural divide between Paris and the rest of France – endured even in the later eighteenth century. When a new marine insurance company was established in Paris in 1750, Montesquieu was decidedly pessimistic about its likelihood of success:

---

[1] Savary, *Le parfait négociant*, vol. I, book II, pp. 112–13.
[2] Boiteux, *L'assurance maritime à Paris*, pp. 64–5. On the Phélypeaux family, see S. Chapman, *Private Ambition and Political Alliances: The Phélypeaux de Pontchartrain Family and Louis XIV's Government, 1650–1715*, Rochester, NY: University of Rochester Press, 2004.
[3] Quoted in Boiteux, *L'assurance maritime à Paris*, pp. 64–5.

> In the seaports a company of merchants gathers together to underwrite insurance. They know their work and inform each other; they know whether the ship they are insuring is good or bad, whether the crew is good or bad, whether the captain is experienced and wise or ignorant and confused, whether the shippers are suspect, of good reputation or likely to be dishonest, whether the voyage is to be long, whether the season is beginning well or not; they know everything because everyone makes it his business to find out. In Paris they know nothing and for the Company to know all that, it would lose as much in the cost of postal charges and correspondence as it would earn in premiums.[4]

At first glance, Pontchartrain *fils*' line of argument is attractive. It draws on key concepts that now underpin neo-institutionalism, the influence of which has been especially significant in recent studies of pre-modern insurance.[5] At the heart of his argument is the significance of information. Mutual underwriting amongst merchants was common in European ports precisely because they had the necessary information at their disposal to decide if they wished to underwrite a voyage and, if so, at what cost. Without information, one cannot ascertain risk: as Montesquieu suggests, port merchants could inspect the vessel to gauge its seaworthiness; they could draw on prior experience or that of their colleagues to judge the skill, trustworthiness and sobriety of the shipmaster; and finally – so neo-institutionalism argues – they could rely on their professional ties to the policyholder, who was bound by prudential self-interest to behave righteously.[6]

The success of Amsterdam and London's insurance markets has also been attributed to their ability to address information asymmetries. Amsterdam was, in Sabine Go's words, 'a staple market of information': the circulation of extensive commercial information by mouth in the Exchange and through printed material – such as the *Prijscouranten* – facilitated the competitiveness of the underwriters.[7] Lloyd's coffeehouse emerged in the

---

[4] Quoted in Bosher, 'The Paris Business World', pp. 288–9.
[5] See the Introduction. The various excellent chapters in Adrian Leonard's recent edited volume owe a great debt to New Institutional Economics and frequently refer to the challenges posed by information asymmetries in pre-modern insurance; A. Leonard (ed.), *Marine Insurance: Origins and Institutions, 1300–1850*, Basingstoke: Palgrave Macmillan, 2016. See also Kingston, 'Governance and Institutional Change', pp. 1–18; Ceccarelli, *Risky Markets*, pp. 127–8.
[6] On similar models, inspired by game theory, see Greif, *Institutions and the Path to the Modern Economy*.
[7] Go, *Marine Insurance in the Netherlands*, p. 63; Go, 'Amsterdam 1585–1790', p. 119. See also W. Smith, 'The Function of Commercial Centers in the Modernization of European Capitalism: Amsterdam as an Information Exchange in the Seventeenth Century', *Journal of Economic History* 44 (1984), pp. 985–1005.

latter decades of the seventeenth century as a 'hub for information about ships and their crews, political and economic developments, and the many other factors affecting the risk of a voyage, and also for information about the reputations of market participants'.[8] From 1692, Edward Lloyd published a newssheet – later to become *Lloyd's List*, which informs the marine insurance industry even today – providing a 'significant advantage to marine insurers by creating a market standard for shipping information' at minimal cost.[9] By 1792, Lloyd's had thirty-two correspondents in twenty-eight ports in Britain and Ireland, all of whom sent their information at no cost, thanks to a special arrangement with the Post Office. This gave Lloyd's 'a practical monopoly of complete and up-to-date shipping intelligence' that ensured it became 'not merely *a* centre, but *the* centre, of London underwriting'.[10] In short, new spaces and materials for the circulation of information reduced transaction costs, allowing private underwriters in Amsterdam and London to gain a competitive advantage.[11] Moreover, better information facilitated a more accurate assessment of risk, leading to more competitive premium rates than could be offered elsewhere.

Pontchartrain *fils* suggests the Company had none of the advantages of mutual underwriters nor of the leading markets: being situated in the inland city of Paris, underwriters suffered from significant information asymmetries, leaving them acutely vulnerable to moral hazard on the part of unknown policyholders. Moreover, the ports, alongside Amsterdam and London, had the necessary information at hand to offer competitive premium rates for the least risky voyages and to the most reputable policy seekers. This meant the Company could only 'choose badly', being left with the riskiest voyages and least reputable policy seekers to insure.[12] Implicit to this argument is the apparent absence of strong formal institutions in France that could facilitate the dissemination of information and enforce righteous conduct, allowing informal networks of mutual underwriting in the French ports to remain dominant.

[8] Kingston, 'Marine Insurance in Britain and America', p. 380.
[9] A. Leonard, 'Introduction: The Nature and Study of Marine Insurance', in A. Leonard (ed.), *Marine Insurance: Origins and Institutions, 1300–1850*, Basingstoke: Palgrave Macmillan, 2016, p. 11.
[10] Wright and Fayle, *A History of Lloyd's*, pp. 74–5 and 78.
[11] Kingston argues that the private underwriters of Lloyd's of London had 'superior access to the information needed to assess risks' compared to the corporations that arose after the Bubble Act of 1720; Kingston, 'Marine Insurance in Britain and America', p. 398.
[12] On this 'lemons' problem in insurance, see Kingston, 'Marine Insurance in Britain and America'.

Convincing as it may seem on the surface, Pontchartrain *fils*' argument needs to be reassessed. The Company's members were acutely aware of what I will henceforth call the 'Parisian problem' and – with the support of the state itself – established a global network of information gathering in 1686 to overcome information asymmetries. This network sheds light on the hitherto unknown functions of various state institutions, including the admiralties, consulates and colonial bodies. It took inspiration from the Chamber, which faced the same challenges and attempted in a piecemeal manner to establish its own reliable tools for overcoming these obstacles. Far from being disconnected from the maritime world, the Company – based only streets away from the offices of the secretariat of state for maritime affairs – benefited from insider knowledge and crucial state support. This chapter thus contributes to broader debates on the rise of the 'information state' in the early modern period, articulating how commercial knowledge was collected, processed and used by the absolute monarchy in support of the insurance industry.[13]

AD HOC ORIGINS:
THE CHAMBER AND THE MANAGEMENT OF INFORMATION

The early years of the Chamber's existence were characterised by an *ad hoc* approach to insurance, and this was especially true for information. Not only did the Chamber need to receive information, but it also needed to disseminate information about its existence and activities to attract business. The institution's assemblies, alongside an array of orders of the Council of State, testify to the piecemeal efforts made over time to advertise the Chamber and gather the information necessary to make informed underwriting choices and avoid being defrauded. Domestic and consular correspondents alike were identified as valuable nodes of information transmission.

The Chamber's members recognised the need to establish strong ties to the ports. The minutes of the Chamber's general assembly of 17 April 1671 noted Louis Froment had been asked to write to Morlaix to clarify the fate of the *Anna*, underwritten by Pierre Formont; in addition, M. Lenfant and M. de Vaux had been asked to write to San Sebastián to gather information regarding

---

[13] The literature on the state and information gathering (and surveillance) is extensive. On the 'information state', see as an introduction, E. Higgs, *The Information State in England: The Central Collection of Information on Citizens since 1500*, Basingstoke: Palgrave Macmillan, 2004. For echoes of the themes in this chapter, see Rule and Trotter, *A World of Paper*; J. Soll, *The Information Master: Jean-Baptiste Colbert's Secret State Intelligence System*, Ann Arbor: University of Michigan Press, 2009; L. Müller, *Consuls, Corsairs, and Commerce: The Swedish Consular Service and Long-Distance Shipping, 1720–1815*, Uppsala: Uppsala Universitet, 2004.

a ship insured by M. Regnault and M. Charpentier.[14] Such informal, *ad hoc* attempts to gather information on insurance claims were no doubt common, but relied upon a member of the Chamber having a suitable contact.

This likely prompted the formalisation of information gathering enshrined in the Chamber's by-laws, written on 16 June 1671 and approved on 10 December by an order of the Council of State. This document outlined the Chamber's operational procedures for the future, specifying the registrar's responsibility 'to maintain [the exchange of] news and correspondence with the maritime towns' up to the expense of 800 *livres* per year – a considerable sum.[15] Moreover, the registrar was required on the second and fourth Thursday of each month to attend an informal assembly of the Chamber, where he would share news from the ports.

As time progressed, the Chamber's requests for information become more extensive. In a general assembly of 7 January 1673, it was agreed that, 'in the future, the insured gentlemen [of the Chamber] will make mention in their abandonments of the time and place where the loss occurred, and the ports where captured ships will have been taken'. To this effect, the members of the Chamber who served as commission agents for port merchants were entreated in instances of abandonment 'to write to all their friends and correspondents in the seaports […] to be informed by them exactly of all the circumstances of losses'.[16]

This uniformity in the collection of information intended to assuage the underwriters' fears they were being deceived. The request was no doubt rooted in the challenges of obtaining verified accounts of loss: while insurers' colleagues in the Chamber who served as commission agents may have been trustworthy, this did not mean the principals in the ports were so honourable. Information asymmetries were the bane of the underwriter's existence, and policyholders could exploit such asymmetries to secure lower premium rates, secure policies on ships they knew already to have been lost, or receive payment on fraudulent claims.[17] Since principals did not even need to be named in the policy, those who employed Chamber members as commission agents may have sought to leverage the relationship between the commission agents and the underwriters to facilitate such acts. This tension between the interests of insurers and principals came to a head in a general assembly on 11 January 1675, where it was agreed that those who insured on behalf of others were to be required to sign a separate written declaration

[14] Z/1d/73, fol. 7, AN.
[15] Ibid., fols 10r–13v.
[16] Ibid., fols 25v–26v.
[17] On the most extreme of fraudulent claims, see G. Jackson, 'Marine Insurance Frauds in Scotland 1751–1821: Cases of Deliberate Shipwreck Tried in the Scottish Court of Admiralty', *The Mariner's Mirror* 57 (1971), pp. 307–22.

detailing precisely who was party to the policy. This was to be done in order to facilitate the gathering of information in instances of loss or damage.[18]

While the Chamber took notable measures to gather the information necessary for its underwriting, it was unable to overcome the 'Parisian problem' alone. Here, Colbert was uniquely positioned to help: he was, in Jacob Soll's words, an 'information master' who understood well the power of knowledge. Colbert sought to reform society from the bottom up, but this could only be achieved through a painstaking understanding of society itself and everything that went on in it and beyond it. To quote Soll:

> With the resources of a nation-state at his disposal, Colbert [...] amassed enormous libraries and state, diplomatic, industrial, colonial, and naval archives; hired researchers and archival teams; founded scientific academies and journals; ran a publishing house; and managed an international network of scholars. By Colbert's death in 1683, the Royal Library [...] was one of the largest collections in the world. Aside from scholarly curiosity and the advancement of the cultural prestige of the French monarchy, the focus of this new collection was to defend national interests in the conflicts over the Dutch annexations, the *régale*, and Spanish rights; to compete with Dutch and English trade; and to assert royal prerogative over the *parlements*. Colbert thus set out to create a national, legal, and financial database.[19]

Colbert's zeal for information was reflected in his extraordinary epistolary exchanges. His incoming correspondence from January 1661 to December 1677 alone – now kept in the *Bibliothèque nationale de France* – spans seventy-five archival series.[20] This becomes all the more impressive when we take into account that Colbert implored his correspondents to write concisely, leading quickly to a standardisation of administrative letter writing. Pierre Arnoul, the *commissaire général* in Toulon, was a famous target of Colbert's ire: the minister frequently chastised him for writing messy and verbose letters that lingered on matters unimportant to state interests.[21] Indeed, studies on seventeenth-century France are replete with Colbert's curt but knowledgeable

---

[18] Z/1d/73, fols 28v–29r, AN.
[19] Soll, *The Information Master*, p. 7. For a remarkable and thorough study of how information was handled by the foreign office under Colbert's nephew, Colbert de Torcy, see Rule and Trotter, *A World of Paper*.
[20] *Mélanges de Colbert*, 102–76, BNF.
[21] S. Martin, 'La correspondance ministérielle du secrétariat d'État de la Marine avec les arsenaux: circulation de l'information et pratiques épistolaires des administrateurs de la Marine (XVIIe–XVIIIe siècles)', in J. Ulbert and S. Llinare (eds), *La liasse et la plume. Les bureaux du secrétariat d'État de la Marine (1669–1792)*, Rennes: Presses universitaires de Rennes, 2017, p. 38.

letters on a staggering range of topics, addressed to individuals stationed across the globe.[22]

Colbert's interests extended greatly into the maritime realm, where he sought to understand, develop and harness France's naval capabilities. Information was at the heart of this: for example, addressing the shortage of seamen for the French fleet required intimate knowledge of the supply of merchant seamen across France, which Colbert acquired through a census-like process in the years 1668 to 1673.[23] This formed the basis of the conscription system known as the *classes*, which ensured the needs of the navy were met.[24] Moreover, Colbert oversaw the reclassification of the French ships-of-the-line 'for tactical and administrative convenience', culminating in the *règlement* of 6 October 1674.[25]

The Chamber was incorporated into this broader process of information gathering. From the outset, Colbert pulled strings at court and drew on the state's growing resources to help the Chamber to gather information. Likely in consultation with the Chamber, an order of the Council of State was issued on 31 October 1669. As part of Louis XIV's desire 'to give them [i.e. the Chamber] continual signs of his kindness', the officers of the admiralties were ordered to deliver to Le Roux, the registrar of the Chamber until 1671, 'certificates of all the vessels that leave and make their return to the ports and harbours of their jurisdictions, and on which there have been insurance policies' at their own expense. These certificates were to be registered by Le Roux in the Chamber's registry for the underwriters to be able to

---

[22] The literature on Colbert and the gathering of information is extensive. For a range of examples, see Blanquie, *Une enquête de Colbert*; Minard, *La fortune du colbertisme*; R. Warlomont, 'Les sources néerlandaises de l'Ordonnance maritime de Colbert (1681)', *Revue belge de philologie et d'histoire* 33 (1955), pp. 333–44; J. Chadelat, 'L'élaboration de l'Ordonnance de la marine d'août 1681' I, *Revue historique de droit français et étranger* 31 (1954), pp. 74–98; J. Chadelat, 'L'élaboration de l'Ordonnance de la marine d'août 1681' II, *Revue historique de droit français et étranger* 31 (1954), pp. 228–53; Dessert, *Le royaume de Monsieur Colbert*; Horn, *Economic Development in Early Modern France*; Isenmann, '(Non-)Knowledge', pp. 139–55; Takeda, *Between Crown and Commerce*.

[23] G. Symcox, *The Crisis of French Sea Power 1688–1697: From the* Guerre d'Escadre *to the* Guerre de Course, The Hague: Martinus Nijhoff, 1974, pp. 14–15.

[24] Ibid.; A. Zysberg, 'Entre soumission et résistance: le système des classes et les levées des gens de mer en Provence et Languedoc pendant les guerres de Louis XIV (1672–1712)', in X. Daumalin, D. Faget, and O. Raveux (eds), *La mer en partage. Sociétés littorales et économies maritimes XVIe–XXe siècle*, Aix-en-Provence: Presses universitaires de Provence, 2016, pp. 73–87; P. Villiers, *Marine Royale, corsaires et trafic dans l'Atlantique de Louis XIV à Louis XVI*, Dunkirk: Société Dunkerquoise d'Histoire et d'Archéologie, 1991, pp. 24–30.

[25] Symcox, *The Crisis of French Sea Power*, p. 37. On the success of Colbert's naval reforms, see Chapter 6.

consult.²⁶ Here, Colbert acknowledged the scope for Parisian underwriters to be defrauded by policyholders in the ports, especially in policies made 'per month', where it was otherwise challenging for the underwriters to ascertain whether a maritime event occurred during the insured period.²⁷ Such certificates – sent at the admiralties' expense – substantiated the admiralties' knowledge of a voyage's fate and shifted information costs away from the Chamber, thereby allowing the Chamber to defend itself against fraudulent claims while limiting its transaction costs.²⁸

Domestic correspondents undeniably had value – but voyages beyond France, which often required coverage of more valuable cargoes and/or vessels, could not be fully accounted for within France alone. Here, Colbert drew on the foreign consulates. These were based primarily in the Mediterranean, but extended also into the Atlantic, the North Sea and the Baltic.²⁹ With Colbert's rise to the position of secretary of state for maritime affairs in 1669, the consulates were brought under the direct administration of the secretariat.³⁰ Based at the *Hôtel Colbert* in central Paris – not far from *rue Quincampoix*, where the Chamber was located – specific offices were created over time to administer different regional clusters of consulates. Together, these offices maintained consistent and standardised correspondence with the consulates, whose original role as representatives of French merchants came to be subsumed within the broader remit of defending and furthering the commercial, legal and diplomatic interests of the French state.³¹ By

---

26   Pouilloux, *Mémoires d'assurances*, p. 420.
27   Ibid.
28   Owing to the admiralties' constant struggle for jurisdiction over maritime affairs before the 1680s and 1690s, however, it is unclear whether they were successful in issuing certificates for every relevant voyage. Moreover, since there were no strict regulations across France for the registration of insurance contracts before the *Ordonnance de la marine* of 1681, it is unclear how the admiralties were expected to know if any given voyage was subject to an insurance contract. It is possible that the Chamber informed the admiralties of all the insurance policies it signed pertaining to their geographical remit, but this is not explicitly addressed in the order.
29   J. Ulbert, 'L'origine géographique des consuls français sous Louis XIV', *Cahiers de la Méditerranée* 98 (2019), pp. 18–24.
30   Control of the consulates of the Ottoman Empire was shared with the *chambre de commerce* in Marseille. An order of the Council of State of 31 July 1691 confirmed this shared control arrangement, but made the *chambre* responsible for paying for the maintenance of the Ottoman consulates rather than the crown; in return, the crown granted the *chambre* the right of *tonnelage*. J. Ulbert, 'L'administration des consulats au sein du secrétariat d'État de la Marine (1669-1715)', in J. Ulbert and S. Llinares (eds), *La liasse et la plume. Les bureaux du secrétariat d'État de la Marine (1669-1792)*, Rennes: Presses universitaires de Rennes, 2017, pp. 73–86.
31   J. Ulbert, 'Les bureaux du secrétariat d'État de la Marine sous Louis XIV (1669-1715)', in J. Ulbert and S. Llinares (eds), *La liasse et la plume. Les bureaux du secrétariat*

Louis XIV's death in 1715, there were thirty-five *commis* across the offices (not all of which dealt with consular affairs) administering seventy-one consulates in total.[32]

The Chamber was a beneficiary of these reforms. When its general assembly met on 9 January 1672, Bellinzani informed the members that

> Monsieur Colbert, want[ing] to give new signs of his protection to the Chamber, and desiring that they are informed of all which happens in all [of] Europe touching commerce at sea, has written a circular letter on this subject to all the consuls of the French nation in the name of the king.[33]

This letter, dated 26 December 1671, explicitly outlined the challenges the Chamber faced in gathering the information necessary to conduct its underwriting. In the absence of uniform standards for declaring damages and losses throughout and beyond France, the Chamber could be left in the dark on the fates of particular voyages. Colbert wrote to the consuls that, 'regarding accidents at sea, the majority of disagreements which occur are a product of the difficulty of having certain news about the loss of insured vessels and merchandise'.[34] Colbert's instructions to mitigate this were emphatic:

> be sure to keep an exact correspondence with *sieur* Bellinzani, director of the Chamber, and give him notice of all the vessels entering or leaving the ports in the extent of your consulate, as well as the losses and shipwrecks which occur, and generally all that concerns commerce and shipping.[35]

Colbert intended to draw on the consuls' capacity to gather information on the state's behalf in order to support the Chamber's activities. This was a resource on which Bellinzani fully intended to draw: in the general assembly of 7 January 1673 discussed above, in which it was agreed that

---

d'État de la Marine (1669–1792), Rennes: Presses universitaires de Rennes, 2017, p. 29. On the epistolary conventions of consular correspondence, see J. Sempéré, 'La correspondance du consulat français de Barcelone (1679–1716). Informer comme un consul ou comme un marchand?', in S. Marzagalli (ed.), *Les consuls en Méditerranée, agents d'information: XVIe–XXe siècle*, Paris: Éditions Classiques Garnier, 2015, pp. 121–40; J. Ulbert, 'La dépêche consulaire française et son acheminement en Méditerranée sous Louis XIV (1661–1715)', in S. Marzagalli (ed.), *Les consuls en Méditerranée, agents d'information: XVIe–XXe siècle*, Paris: Éditions Classiques Garnier, 2015, pp. 31–57. For more on the functions of consulates, and their role in economic development, see Müller, *Consuls*.

32 Ulbert, 'Les bureaux du secrétariat', p. 29; Ulbert, 'L'administration des consulats', pp. 74–5.
33 Z/1d/73, fols 16r–17r, AN.
34 Ibid.; this letter is reproduced in Colbert and Clément, *Lettres, instructions, et mémoires de Colbert*, vol. II, book II, p. 640.
35 Z/1d/73, fols 16r–17r, AN.

commission agents in the Chamber would help to facilitate information gathering in cases of loss or damage, it was also agreed that, when losses or captures were reported in places where the Chamber's members had no correspondents, Bellinzani would write to the relevant French consul to gather information on their behalf.[36]

Nevertheless, Colbert's intervention faced some resistance along the way. In a penetrating rhetorical style so typical of his letters, François Cotolendy, the French consul in Livorno, wrote to Colbert on 17 June 1672 confirming he had been following the minister's instructions in keeping Bellinzani informed on ship movements in and out of Livorno, 'even though there were great trouble[s] and costs to bear'. However, he noted that, 'as I have executed your orders so punctually, I am strongly surprised that so many of the letters I have sent him [i.e. Bellinzani] have had no response'.[37]

Whether Cotolendy's frustrations were fair or not is debatable. In his haste to criticise Bellinzani, Cotolendy perhaps underestimated the impact of the outbreak of the Dutch War in April 1672, which proved utterly disastrous for the Chamber.[38] As *intendant du commerce*, Bellinzani likely had his hands full in this tumultuous period.

In any case, Cotolendy's letter points to the value of his correspondence. Although he may have been frustrated by Bellinzani's silence, he nevertheless strove to provide 'all the information necessary for the good of the [Royal] Insurance Chamber', as Colbert had ordered. Cotolendy also noted the 'costs' he bore for this. As with the admiralty certificates, the Chamber's underwriters benefited not only from access to invaluable information, but from the shifting of the burden of information costs onto the state's own infrastructure.

The Chamber had a further plan whose fate is unclear. In the aftermath of the ratification of the Chamber's by-laws by an order of the Council of State on 10 December 1671, members proposed a variety of measures to aid the establishment of a good institutional reputation throughout Europe and to facilitate their underwriting. One stands out: 'a table will be made containing all the names, ports, ages and strengths of all the ships of each port of France and elsewhere, together [with] the names and reputations of their captains'.[39]

---

[36] Ibid., fols 25v–26v.
[37] AE/B/I/695, fol. 31r, AN. I am grateful to Guillaume Calafat for providing me with a transcription of this letter; the register is presently unavailable for consultation, and is awaiting digitisation. For more on Cotolendy, see G. Calafat, 'Livourne et la Chambre de commerce de Marseille au XVIIe siècle. Consuls français, agents et perception du droit de *cottimo*', in X. Daumalin, D. Faget, and O. Raveux (eds), *La mer en partage. Sociétés littorales et économies maritimes XVIe–XXe siècle*, Aix-en-Provence: Presses universitaires de Provence, 2016, pp. 209–26.
[38] See Chapter 4.
[39] Z/1d/73, fols 14r–15v, AN.

A table like this would have offered key benefits in overcoming the 'Parisian problem', as it would have allowed them to evaluate the risks posed by vessels and their shipmasters. Indeed, they would have been able to update the table over time with their own experiences and knowledge of the conduct of particular shipmasters.

I have found no evidence this table was ever constructed, although absence of evidence is not evidence of absence. It is also unclear how such a table would have been compiled, although Colbert's 1664 *Inventaire général des vaisseaux* could perhaps have served as a model.[40] In any case, we will see later that the Chamber's proposal would significantly shape the state's approach to insurance throughout the 1680s.

Advertising the Chamber required a similar combination of ambitious thinking and support from personal correspondents and the state. In the course of his efforts to enlist officials to provide information to the Chamber, Colbert also pushed them to advertise the institution within their respective communities. As we have seen, the order of the Council of State of October 1669 obliged admiralty officers to send certificates to the Chamber for pertinent ships. It went further than this, however, by also tasking the officers of the admiralties, and all other judges, with advertising the Chamber to the kingdom. In order to inform provincial merchants of the 'notices [i.e. advertisements] and deliberations taken in the [Royal] Insurance Chamber, His Majesty wills that they are read, published and attached in all public and accustomed places'.[41] This order likely stemmed from the Chamber's desire to advertise its recent decision to offer sea loans: it issued an advertisement in September 1669 offering sea loans 'for all the places of the world [...] with very reasonable terms'.[42]

Similarly, in his circular letter to the French consuls in December 1671, Colbert solicited the support of French merchants trading in the Mediterranean: he emphasised to the consuls that it is 'important to the success of this establishment [i.e. the Chamber], and also for strengthening it more and more, that you encourage all the merchants trading in the place where you reside to undertake their insurance in Paris'.[43]

This complemented the push made by the Chamber following the ratification of its by-laws in the same month. In a general assembly on 18 December, it was agreed that copies of the 'by-laws will be printed in French and several foreign languages like German, English, Spanish and Italian',

---

[40] G. Buti, 'Flottes de commerce et de pêche en Languedoc au temps de Louis XIV', in P. Louvier (ed.), *Le Languedoc et la mer (XVIe–XXIe siècle)*, Montpellier: Presses universitaires de la Méditerranée, 2012, p. 135.
[41] Pouilloux, *Mémoires d'assurances*, p. 420.
[42] Ibid.
[43] Z/1d/73, fols 16r–17r, AN.

to be 'distributed in all the places of commerce and seaports of Europe'. Similarly, when insurance premiums for given voyages were agreed within the Chamber, these were to be printed and 'sent to all the places of correspondence within and without the kingdom'.[44]

Certainly, the Chamber's efforts did not follow a grand vision: *ad hoc* measures were taken in response to pressing problems, which stemmed precisely from the 'Parisian problem' identified by Pontchartrain *fils*. Despite these challenges, the future appeared promising in December 1671; the Chamber's ambitious efforts to advertise itself across Europe, supported fully by Colbert, gave every impression the institution was on course to scale up its activities and increase its reach across Europe. The reality proved very different indeed, and the Chamber never recovered from the onset of the Dutch War in 1672.[45] The 'Parisian problem' would rear its head again in the following decade.

DÉJÀ VU? THE COMPANY AND THE INFORMATION PROJECT OF 1686

The deaths of Colbert and Bellinzani precipitated a new Parisian insurance project. This was ultimately to be led by Jean-Baptiste de Lagny, who became director general of commerce in early 1686.[46] Before Lagny's appointment, there was already a desire to bring a new lease of life to the Chamber. On 13 and 22 January 1684, having learned of Marius-Basile Morel de Boistiroux's appointment as director general of commerce, the Chamber resolved to send a group of members to meet with Morel and Seignelay, who had now succeeded his late father as secretary of state for maritime affairs.[47]

This was a valuable opportunity to secure support from the new secretary and his right-hand man in commercial matters. Clearly, Seignelay and Morel were receptive to the members' interests, as the duo drew up bold plans in 1685 for a Parisian insurance company with a monopoly over all insurance coverage across France. Unsurprisingly, the *chambre de commerce* of Marseille objected in the strongest terms to this proposal and it did not come to fruition.[48]

In light of this, Morel took stock and planned a new project.[49] On 21 January 1686, Seignelay wrote to Nicolas Soullet – who would soon invest

---

[44] Ibid., fols 14r-15v.
[45] See Chapter 4.
[46] For more on Lagny, see Chapter 2.
[47] Z/1d/73, fol. 30v, AN.
[48] Boiteux, *L'assurance maritime à Paris*, pp. 50-6. The documentation on this is preserved in the *Archives CCI* in Marseille; the COVID-19 pandemic prevented me from consulting it.
[49] MAR/B/7/492, fols 123-4r, AN.

in the Company – to implore him to work closely with Morel on the plans for the new institution.[50]

The documentary trail runs cold until April 1686, after Morel's death. We are not privileged with a detailed record of the events which transpired at this point: after Lagny's appointment as Morel's successor in March, Lagny frequently communicated with Seignelay in person at Versailles rather than through letters. It is clear, however, that Parisian insurance was a key priority for Seignelay upon appointing Lagny: in April and the months that followed, Lagny worked to draft the Company's letters patent and managed to bring the prospective investors on board.[51]

On 16 April, Seignelay impressed on Lagny that 'it is necessary to finish this business promptly' (i.e. the establishment of the Company).[52] In May, Seignelay urgently pushed through the Company's letters patent in the form of a royal edict. This was followed on 20 May by the articles of association written by the thirty members of the new Company.[53] By the end of the month, the Company had opened its offices in 16 *rue Quincampoix* and began underwriting.[54]

This was premature, however, as the first president (*premier président*) of the *parlement* of Paris, Nicolas Potier de Novion, had objected to the letters patent, most likely in the form of a remonstrance.[55] His objection likely revolved around the monopoly powers the letters patent granted.[56]

Seignelay's response was swift and decisive, as was often the case when *parlements* issued remonstrances. Writing to the *parlement*'s attorney general (*procureur général*) on 28 May, Seignelay explained that Louis XIV had rejected the logic of Potier de Novion's objection and ordered that the letters patent be registered 'promptly'.[57]

Conscious that the *parlement*'s resistance could put the Company in a precarious position, Lagny wrote to Seignelay on 6 June to inform him that 'the partners of the [Royal] Insurance Chamber need the registered edict and the homologating order for their company'.[58] An order of the Council of State was issued on the very same day, with Lagny at the top of

---

[50] MAR/B/7/58, fols 38–9, AN.
[51] MAR/B/7/492, fols 297–8r and 300, AN; MAR/C/7/15, n.p., AN; MAR/G/229, n.p., AN.
[52] MAR/G/229, n.p., AN.
[53] Bornier, *Conférences des ordonnances de Louis XIV*, vol. II, pp. 513–24.
[54] Z/1d/85, AN.
[55] On the remonstrances of the *parlement* of Paris – and the way they were transformed by Louis XIV in the course of his reign – see Hurt, *Louis XIV and the Parlements*.
[56] Bornier, *Conférences des ordonnances de Louis XIV*, vol. II, pp. 513–24. On these monopoly privileges, see Chapter 2.
[57] O/1/30, fol. 187, AN.
[58] MAR/B/7/492, fol. 305, AN.

the membership list, and Seignelay wrote again to the attorney general on 12 June to ask that a copy of the registered letters patent be sent to Lagny.[59] On 20 June, Seignelay wrote to Lagny that 'the advertisement the [Royal] Insurance Company proposes to print is good, and you can send it'.[60]

Seignelay's broader urgency in his correspondence speaks to the desire he had for the Company to begin its underwriting quickly – but the 'Parisian problem', which had required a patchwork of *ad hoc* solutions from the Chamber during its existence, still threatened the new Company.

Seignelay recognised this. He was his father's son, and had been trained extensively in 'a decade-long course to prepare his [expected] succession as the great intendant of the state'.[61] At the age of eighteen, for example, Seignelay had been sent to Rochefort by Colbert to complete an apprenticeship in port administration and to learn how to receive, manage and compile information for state purposes. As Soll notes, the correspondence between Colbert and Seignelay during the latter's training gave 'a blueprint of how to create, use, and control a state information system'.[62]

Seignelay put his father's training to use in tackling the 'Parisian problem'. With the Chamber as a conscious model, Seignelay and Lagny began an extensive epistolary project while the plans for the Company were being formulated and formalised in March, April and May. Conceived within the broader remit of Lagny's role as director general of commerce, this project sought to support the Company's underwriting by leveraging the state's infrastructure of information, establishing a global network Lagny could depend on for commercial knowledge of all types.

This network did not go unnoticed within the secretariat of state for maritime affairs. Not even a week had passed since Seignelay's death when Nicolas Clairambault, a clerk in the secretariat, penned a *mémoire* on 9 November 1690 for the new secretary, Pontchartrain *père*, cataloguing the leading figures in the secretariat at the time, alongside their duties and powers.[63] In describing Lagny and his role as director general of commerce in the *bureau du commerce* – established by Seignelay in 1684 – Clairambault identified three of the four poles of this global network: provincial officers, merchants and colonial officers. To this, we can also add the overseas consuls. These poles will be the focus of my analysis.

---

[59] Bornier, *Conférences des ordonnances de Louis XIV*, vol. II, pp. 524–5; MAR/B/7/58, fol. 134, AN.
[60] MAR/B/7/59, fol. 82, AN.
[61] Soll, *The Information Master*, pp. 84–6.
[62] Ibid.
[63] MAR/B/8/18, n.p., AN.

Provincial officers: rethinking the Rolle général des bastimens

Clairambault noted in his analysis of the *bureau du commerce* that Lagny communicated freely with provincial intendants and was responsible for handling Seignelay's correspondence with them, including issuing orders. Moreover, when the consular *bureaux* encountered commercial matters, they worked with Lagny to draw up the responses.[64]

From the outset, then, it is clear Lagny was a significant figure in the secretariat. He was kept entirely abreast of all commercial developments in the provinces and was the central figure in coordinating commercial policy under Seignelay. This not only provided him with the means to gather information on what *had* happened in the maritime and commercial spheres of France and beyond, but also bestowed him with power over what was *going* to happen in the future – a power which could prove invaluable in ascertaining the risks involved in maritime voyages.

With the extant evidence, it is difficult to demonstrate Lagny used this power systematically. Far better documented are the information flows Lagny received from provincial officers. The most remarkable product of these flows was a beloved maritime historical document: the *Rolle général des bastimens de mer*. The *Rolle* – a copy of which is kept in the *Archives de Dunkerque* – was created with the intent of cataloguing every ship in France in 1686, with columns for the following data for each ship:

1. Name
2. Names of their owners, masters or patrons
3. Tonnage
4. Number of cannons with which they were armed
5. Size of their crew
6. When they were built
7. Voyages undertaken in the years 1683 to 1686.[65]

The *Rolle* was first brought to prominent scholarly attention by Michel Morineau, who argues it 'has all the appearances of spontaneity', stemming from a sudden need to gather information on maritime affairs.[66] He suggests through unreferenced and undated correspondence that M. Arnoul, the

---

[64] Ibid. For more on these offices, see Ulbert, 'Les bureaux du secrétariat'.
[65] *Rolle général des bastimens de mer* (uncoded document), *Archives de Dunkerque – Centre de la Mémoire Urbaine d'Agglomération*.
[66] M. Morineau, 'La marine française de commerce de Colbert à Seignelay', in H. Méchoulan and J. Cornette (eds), *L'état classique. Regards sur la pensée politique de la France dans le second XVIIe siècle*, Paris: Librairie Philosophique J. Vrin, 1996, p. 241n; M. Morineau, *Jauges et méthodes de jauge anciennes et modernes*, Paris: Librarie Armand Colin, 1966.

intendant in Rochefort, had 'an overabundance of sailors, a large share [of whom] remained without employment'.[67] By contrast, André Zysberg argues that the revocation of the Edict of Nantes in 1685 had engendered fears of a flight of Protestant sailors which required formal investigation. In any case, both conclude that Seignelay commissioned the *Rolle* to ascertain the number of sailors and marine officers in every port across France.[68] Since Morineau's original publication, the *Rolle* has been used to reconstruct commercial and fishing activities in particular ports in the 1680s.[69] In understanding the origins and contemporary uses of this document, these works have largely relied on Morineau's original analysis.

Undeniably, ascertaining sailor numbers was a potential use of the *Rolle*: indeed, Zysberg identifies documents created in the years after 1686 which relied on its data to discuss sailor numbers. However, the *Rolle* contains so many columns unrelated to sailors that there must have been other uses in mind.

Morineau and Zysberg correctly suggest Seignelay commissioned the document, but it was not at all spontaneous. I argue it was commissioned explicitly for Lagny's sake, and it was Lagny himself who oversaw the process of compiling it. In so doing, Lagny created a document with exceptional value for insurance purposes.

While Seignelay and Lagny forged their plans for the Company in March and April 1686, they implemented several measures to begin gathering commercial information on Lagny's behalf. On 31 March, Seignelay wrote to the eschevins and *députés du commerce* of Marseille, informing them that,

> the king having chosen *sieur* de Lagny to fill the commission of director general of commerce, His Majesty has ordered me to give you notice of this, and to instruct you that his intention is that you inform *sieur* de Lagny of what is happening in all matters of your commerce and the difficulties that occur; that, immediately after the arrival of ships, you

---

[67] Morineau, 'La marine française', p. 240.

[68] Ibid., pp. 240–1; A. Zysberg, 'La flotte de commerce et de pêche des ports normands en 1686 et 1786. Essai de comparaison', in É. Wauters (ed.), *Les ports normands: un modèle?*, Mont-Saint-Aignan: Presses universitaires de Rouen et du Havre, 1999, pp. 97–116. Zysberg suggests that Morineau was arguing that the flight of Protestant sailors triggered the need for investigation, but this seems to be precisely what Morineau argues *against*.

[69] For example, see A. Zysberg, 'De Honfleur à Granville: bâtiments de commerce et de pêche au cours de la seconde moitié du XVIIe siècle', *Cahier des Annales de Normandie* 24 (1992), pp. 201–24; Pfister-Langanay, *Ports, navires et négociants*; C. Pfister-Langanay, 'Dunkerque sous Louis XIV: un port de commerce qui se cherche', in A. Piétri-Lévy, J. Barzman, and É. Barré (eds), *Environnements portuaires. Port environments*, Mont-Saint-Aignan: Presses universitaires de Rouen et du Havre, 2003, pp. 261–71; Buti, 'Flottes de commerce', pp. 133–61.

will also send him copy of the declarations that the captains have made to the *intendants de la santé*.⁷⁰

Seignelay quickly followed this up on 2 April with a circular letter to all the admiralty officers of France:

> The king having chosen *Sieur* de Lagny to fill the commission of director general of commerce, His Majesty has ordered me to write to you that, from time to time, not only will you act to send to *Sieur* de Lagny the state [and] reports of all the ships coming from the sea in the extent of your resort, and of those leaving to go outside the kingdom, but also that you will inform him of the difficulties and all that comes to your knowledge concerning commerce and that you will give him all the clarifications he has occasion to ask of you, in order that he can give an account to me of everything. It is why you will be sure to satisfy [this] punctually as His Majesty intends.⁷¹

In asking the admiralties and the officers of Marseille to send the shipmasters' voyage reports to Lagny, Seignelay drew on the admiralties' new administrative duties as enshrined in the 1681 *Ordonnance*. His request for reports on ships leaving France likely refers to the passports issued for these voyages. In combination, these documents would allow Lagny to develop a timeline of the voyages undertaken by French ships – including those insured by the Company. This echoed Colbert's request to the admiralties to send 'certificates' of all ships with insurance policies to the Chamber's registrar, but went further by granting Lagny access to more extensive shipping information, thereby allowing him to build a macro understanding of the trends affecting French maritime commerce. Moreover, Seignelay's specific order that the admiralties inform Lagny of any 'difficulties and all which comes to your knowledge concerning commerce' points to his desire to assist Lagny in gathering not only *reactive* information (i.e. information which would facilitate the substantiation of insurance claims) but also *proactive* information (i.e. information which would allow the Company to make informed underwriting decisions).⁷² In short, Seignelay drew on both the Chamber's prior experience and the new admiralty duties in the *Ordonnance* to support Lagny's quest for valuable underwriting information.

Lagny used Seignelay's instructions as a platform for collecting information from the admiralties on maritime developments. On 5 July, he wrote to the admiralty officers of La Rochelle to ask for all intelligence on corsair movements: Lagny had been informed of the *Martinique de La Rochelle*'s capture 'off the coast of Senegal', and 'the Newfoundland fishers coming

---

⁷⁰ MAR/B/7/58, fols 61–2, AN.
⁷¹ Ibid., fol. 62.
⁷² NB by 'informed', I do not necessarily mean 'profitable'; to understand what I mean in saying this, see Chapter 5.

from the bank [of Newfoundland] have reported that several pirates [*forbans*] have passed there, which have pillaged various fishing ships'. On Seignelay's behalf, therefore, he wrote requesting any relevant information the admiralty officers had received, and would go on to receive, so that Seignelay 'can give the necessary orders' for the protection of French shipping.[73] As Clairambault's *mémoire* suggests, however, it was likely Lagny himself who would have written these orders.

Similarly, on 16 February 1687, Lagny wrote to seventeen admiralties about implementing convoys in the strait of Gibraltar in response to the ongoing threat posed by corsairs based in Salé. Since Seignelay wanted 'as much as possible to provide for the safety of the navigation of French ships', Lagny asked the admiralties to gather the names and locations of any ships in their purview wishing to sail soon to Spain or Portugal.[74] Lagny sought to bring these ships to a single meeting point so they could sail together through the strait and deter opportunistic corsair attacks. As we will see, this was pursued by Lagny throughout the year.

In his capacity as director general of commerce, Lagny was therefore party to all news reaching the secretariat of state for maritime affairs and oversaw the responses that would influence the extent of risk in voyages.

In asking the admiralties on 2 April to send this wealth of information, Seignelay's slightly ambiguous request for them to evaluate the 'state' of the ships in their purview was possibly overlooked. Recognising the value of such information, Lagny pursued this himself with greater clarity through a series of letters asking the admiralties to assist in this project. On 3 June – just days after the Company had underwritten its first insurance policy – he wrote to the admiralties repeating a request he had previously made (but which seems not to have been recorded in his letter-book) that they 'inform me of all the things that could have relation to commerce' as per Seignelay's orders. Moreover,

> I find myself obliged to renew the request I made to you by my first letter [...] to promptly send to me the state of the ships belonging to subjects of the king in the extent of your resort, following the model attached [to the letter] to which I ask you to conform.[75]

It was Lagny, and not Seignelay, who oversaw the collection of the information needed to compile the *Rolle*.

In gathering information on every ship in France, Lagny was persistent in ensuring the model (i.e. the seven columns listed above) was adhered to as systematically as possible. Lagny wrote separately to various admiralty figures in Brittany to request they adhere to it so that the *Rolle* could

---

[73] MAR/B/7/58, fols 161–2, AN.
[74] Ibid., fols 369–70.
[75] Ibid., fol. 124.

be compiled. He wrote to M. Macé, the attorney general for the admiralty of Saint-Malo, acknowledging receipt of his letters before asking that he 'rectify' the information he had provided and send it back to him 'with the greatest exactitude possible'. He again attached the model, asking that Macé conform to it and add information that would facilitate 'a more perfect clarification, [such as] the owners or captains of the vessels' – the second column of the *Rolle*.[76] He wrote similarly to the seneschal of Nantes, asking for the same information on the state of the ships in the admiralty's purview 'following the model attached'.[77] In a letter to M. Richome, the seneschal of Saint-Malo, Lagny thanked him for his help with the exercise, asking him in closing to keep him abreast of all maritime developments.[78]

Therefore, while the new Company was being discussed, formulated and established, the *Rolle* was being commissioned, pursued and compiled with equal urgency. The product was broadly faithful to the document previously envisaged by the Chamber in 1671: 'a table [...] containing all the names, ports, ages and strengths of all the ships of each port of France [...] together [with] the names and reputations of their captains'.[79] Laurier Turgeon notes the voyages undertaken by the ships of Saintonge before 1686 were described imprecisely in the *Rolle*, stating simply that they undertook 'ocean' voyages, but even such non-conforming entries could be useful: they indicated the capacity for these ships to undertake long-distance voyages, most likely to Newfoundland in the case of Saintonge.[80] In combination with the age of the vessel, such details would therefore help the directors to assess a ship's suitability for a given voyage.

Of course, Turgeon's concerns are entirely appropriate for those ports where whole columns were left blank. Even Lagny's persistence could not induce some admiralties to provide all the information he had requested. Moreover, the *Rolle*'s utility risked deteriorating over time as ships were lost, upgraded and built. Only regular updates would have ensured the document remained useful over time.

We should also acknowledge that there were many possible uses for the *Rolle* besides insurance: Lagny himself noted in a letter of 15 July that

---

[76] Ibid., fols 125–6.
[77] Ibid., fols 127–8.
[78] Ibid., fol. 126.
[79] Of course, the reputations of the shipmasters were not recorded, but this is information the Company itself could have compiled over time through its own experiences.
[80] L. Turgeon, 'Colbert et la pêche française à Terre Neuve', in R. Mousnier (ed.), *Un nouveau Colbert: actes du Colloque pour le tricentenaire de la mort de Colbert*, Paris: Editions SEDES/CDU, 1985, p. 256.

Marseille's admiralty officers had sent him 'an ultra-exact state' of the port's ships that 'will serve a thousand of my needs'.[81]

Nevertheless, we should not understate the *Rolle*'s extraordinary value and historical significance as an insurance tool that supported the Company's underwriting. A society of underwriters at Lloyd's coffeehouse would go on to make a similar document themselves (*Lloyd's Register*), but, based on extant records, this seems to have come to fruition only in 1760.[82]

The *Rolle* must therefore be reinterpreted within a far broader context: Seignelay's original letter makes clear it was only one desired product from a more extensive effort to gather commercial and maritime information for Lagny. Provincial officers were valuable to this effort, but they were only a small piece of the puzzle. Let us now look wider.

Merchants

Besides the provincial officers, Clairambault documented in his *mémoire* that Lagny 'has liberty of correspondence with the merchants within and without [the kingdom]'.[83] Certainly, Lagny had extensive commercial contacts: in the opening pages of his letter-book, he kept the following list of 'merchant correspondents in the seaports':[84]

Table 4 Lagny's merchant correspondents in the seaports, as written in his first letter-book.

Name	Location
Maron	Bayonne
Pontoise	Bordeaux
[Empty]	Dunkerque
Eon Lavellebague	Saint Malo
Lalande Magon	Saint Malo
Grilleau	Nantes
Maillet	Rouen
Legendre	Rouen
Heron	La Rochelle
Magis	Marseille
Fabre	Marseille

Source: MAR/B/7/58, fol. 60, AN.

---

[81] MAR/B/7/58, fols 193–7, AN. True to Lagny's judgement, the pages of the *Rolle* dedicated to the ships of Marseille are especially detailed.
[82] Wright and Fayle, *A History of Lloyd's*, pp. 84–6.
[83] MAR/B/8/18, n.p., AN.
[84] MAR/B/7/58, fol. 60, AN.

These were leading merchants in each of these ports. To take the key examples, Julien Eon de la Villebague belonged to a powerful Malouin family that engaged extensively in global trade. The Magon family, whence came Lagny's other correspondent in the port, had a similar reputation.[85] Thomas Legendre in Rouen had capitalised on the revocation of the Edict of Nantes: while Protestant family members moved to other commercial centres, Legendre converted to Catholicism and leveraged his family network to conduct business. According to Rouen's intendant, Legendre had 'a universal correspondence'.[86] Augustin Magy was a merchant-banker in Marseille and member of the Mediterranean Company.[87] Joseph Fabre was the leading member of this company and his family had ties to naval finance.[88]

These were merchants who had agreed to inform the crown on maritime and commercial developments in exchange for personal advancement. Introducing himself to each of them in a circular letter on 19 April 1676, Lagny wrote that 'he [i.e. Seignelay] has especially recommended to me to undertake an exact correspondence with you', since they were 'well informed' on commerce, and 'sensitive to the public interest'. As such, Lagny asked the merchants to keep him intimately informed of maritime affairs, just as he had asked of the provincial officers.[89]

The merchants obliged; on 25 April, Lagny wrote to Magon in Saint-Malo acknowledging receipt of his letters and thanking him 'with all my heart for the news you have given me; I ask you to continue [sending] it to me'.[90] This began an extensive epistolary exchange between Lagny and the merchants which would extend far beyond 1686.

These maritime connections proved fruitful when Lagny was dealing with the threat posed by Salé corsairs in 1687. We have seen that Lagny sought to introduce a convoy system in the strait of Gibraltar; by 5 June, the crown had armed a fleet of ships to protect French shipping. Yet Lagny wrote to the port merchants after this, using his position to pursue several goals: he warned the ports of the ongoing threat posed by the corsairs; he directed shipmasters to show caution in their voyages, thereby seeking to mitigate the risks of capture;

---

[85] Lespagnol, *Messieurs de Saint-Malo*, vol. II, pp. 849–50. On Jean Magon de la Lande, see also H. Hillmann, *The Corsairs of Saint-Malo: Network Organization of a Merchant Elite under the Ancien Régime*, New York: Columbia University Press, 2021, pp. 149–51.

[86] Quoted in L. Rothkrug, *Opposition to Louis XIV: The Political and Social Origins of the French Enlightenment*, Princeton: Princeton University Press, 1965, p. 396n.

[87] Dessert, *Argent, pouvoir et société*, pp. 504–5.

[88] Ibid. On Fabre, see Takeda, 'Silk, Calico and Immigration in Marseille', pp. 254–6.

[89] MAR/B/7/58, fols 68–71, AN.

[90] Ibid., fols 76–80.

and he sought information on all encounters with corsairs.[91] In short, within his broader remit in the secretariat, Lagny was able to gather information and issue orders in service to the interests of the Company.

Lagny's remit also allowed him to gather information from the royal companies, in which he often had a personal stake. As the crown's representative in the CIO, Lagny was party to the information flows to and from the East Indies: he wrote to the directors in Surat and Pondicherry in India on 29 November 1686, and was in frequent dialogue with its directors in France, such as Claude Céberet du Boullay – also a member of the Company.[92] Céberet was part of the embassy to Siam that left France in March 1687 and returned in July 1688, and Lagny himself was involved in this embassy: he had written to Constance Phaulkon, the first minister of the kingdom, on 13 February 1687 to discuss the luxury French goods that Phaulkon had commissioned on behalf of King Narai.[93] Lagny no doubt kept close tabs on the embassy – and on Asian commercial affairs more broadly – through Céberet in 1687 and 1688.[94]

Lagny was also in frequent contact with Augustin Magy and Joseph Fabre in their capacities as directors of the Mediterranean Company.[95] Besides Magy and Fabre, Lagny often wrote to M. Martin, an officer in Marseille who was appointed to administer the business of the *Compagnie du Bastion de France*, a company specialising in Mediterranean coral fishing in which Lagny was also involved. This intersecting correspondence supports Heijmans' argument that it was prudent for *financiers* to join multiple royal companies: the *Bastion de France* and the CIO were connected through commodity chains, e.g. coral, which was highly valued

---

[91] See ibid., fols 493–5.
[92] For Lagny's letters to the directors in India, see ibid., fols 322–6. Céberet was normally based in Port-Louis; for Lagny's correspondence with him, see for example ibid., fols 154–5.
[93] Riello, 'With Great Pomp and Magnificence', pp. 249–50; D. van der Cruysse, *Louis XIV et le Siam*, Paris: Fayard, 1991, pp. 411–38; MAR/B/7/58, fols 371–82, AN. For a *mémoire* written by Lagny on the preparations for sending the ambassadors to Siam, see MAR/B/7/59, fols 318–20, AN. There are also numerous letters from Lagny regarding the Siam negotiations in the *Archives nationales d'outre-mer*. For letters Seignelay and Lagny received from the leading Siamese ambassador, written from the Cape of Good Hope on 24 June 1687 during the latter's return to Siam after a mission to France in 1686–87, see G. Coedès, 'Siamese Documents of the Seventeenth Century', *Journal of the Siam Society* 14 (1921), pp. 16–21.
[94] We will see in Chapter 5 that the Company almost never insured voyages in the Indian Ocean. Nevertheless, Lagny's information could have been useful in informing this strategic choice, although we will see in that chapter that other factors likely played a larger role.
[95] MAR/B/7/58, AN.

in East Indies commerce.[96] Lagny's extensive correspondence with the companies' directors and delegates within and without France ensured he was kept abreast of mercantile news from across the globe.

Yet these figures could not document all the news that was of interest to the Company. For more extensive support, Seignelay and Lagny turned to a familiar source.

Consuls

Clairambault's *mémoire* did not draw attention to Lagny's relationship with France's consuls. Yet Lagny viewed them as a vital source of information, and kept a list of them in the front of his first letter-book.

Table 5 Lagny's consular correspondents, as written in his first letter-book.[97]

Name	Location
Julien	Alep
Magys	Alexandrie
Francisco Bon'aventure	Alexandrette
Piolle	Alger
Jolivet	Alicant
Pierre Cadix	Almaries
Chabert	Amsterdam
Piquet	Bagdat
Soleil	Barcelone
Noüel	Bilbao
Revola	Cap-Négre
Catalan	Cadix
Maillet	Candie
Sauvan	Chipre
Radedantes	Canaries Illes
Parvis	Caillery
François Dolard	Carthagene
Voiret	Rome

[96] Heijmans, *The Agency of Empire*, pp. 44–5.
[97] For a list of all known consuls and vice-consuls serving during the reign of Louis XIV, alongside an illuminating discussion on the decline of the Marseillais domination of these positions in the second half of the seventeenth century, see Ulbert, 'L'origine géographique des consuls français'.

Name	Location
Valleton	La Corogne
Fabre	Constantinople
[Blank]	Fayal Ille
Jean Baptiste Aubert	Génes
Julien Fournier	Gibraltar
Cotolendy	Ligourne
Desgranges	Lisbon
Barbier	Mayorque
Trouin	Malaga
Francois Biart	Madeira isle
Antoine Guillon	Messine
Zucco	Milo et L'Argentiere
Antoine Chatagner	La Moréé
Maurel	Naple
[Blank]	Palerme
[Illegible]	Porto
Perillié	Sâlé et Terouan
Blancon	Satalie
Jaques Gléze	Salonique
L'empereur	Seyde
Louis Fabre	Smirne
Stellet	Tanger
Negres	Tercéres Illes
Viel	Tino
Lemaire	Tripoli
Michel	Tunis
Jean Baptiste Ducru	Valance
Le Blond	Venise
Jean Tellignant	Zantes

Source: MAR/B/7/58, fols 57–8, AN.

As with the provincial officers, Seignelay initially wrote to the consuls on 25 March 1686 to ask for their assistance. The letters followed the same format as those to the provincial officers and merchant correspondents.[98] Just as he

[98] MAR/B/7/58, fol. 61, AN. A copy of Seignelay's letter to Julien Fournier, consul in Gibraltar, can be found in MAR/B/7/59, fol. 43r, AN.

did with the provincial officers, Lagny followed up these letters with a more detailed request for information on 18 April. Seeking 'to undertake an exact correspondence with you on all which concerns the functions of your consulate, and all which is related to commerce in general and to the subjects of the king and shipping in particular', Lagny emphasised the necessity that 'I am well instructed on the state and details of present affairs and of all that occurs in the future'.[99] Consequently, he asked each consul to send him an extensive *mémoire* detailing the present state of their consulate, the region it served, the merchandise most commonly traded in the region (by the French and by foreigners), its commercial affairs, the challenges it faced, and 'finally [...] your *mémoire* will please contain as well an estimation for a common year of the number of French ships which ordinarily visit [the region of the consulate's purview] and the value of their commerce'. To complete this lengthy request, he asked the consuls to inform him of 'general news of every nature [...] and of all sorts of movements, especially those happening at sea, in [the form of] merchandise, war or *Corso*', alongside 'the difficulties' faced by French ships and merchants.[100]

The parallels with Colbert's letter to the consuls in 1671 are striking.[101] In asking for all information pertaining to French merchants and shipping, Lagny replicated the request that Colbert had made for Bellinzani, but went further in asking for detailed *mémoires* that would allow him to construct a broader understanding of French economic activity across Europe.

Lagny's request seems to have been well received. He received *mémoires* from Pierre Catalan in Cádiz;[102] M. Maillet in Chania (Crete);[103] Jean-Baptiste Aubert in Genoa;[104] and Louis-Marseille Fabre in Izmir.[105] Still consul for the French nation in Livorno, Cotolendy wrote to Seignelay on 17 May confirming receipt of his order 'to keep *Monsieur* Lagny abreast of all that concerns the commerce and shipping of His Majesty's subjects', which Cotolendy assured Seignelay he would begin executing the same day.[106] True to his word, he sent a lengthy *mémoire* to Lagny the same day, congratulating him on his

---

[99] MAR/B/7/58, fols 63–5, AN.
[100] Ibid.
[101] Colbert's letter was recorded in the Chamber's register of assemblies; it would not be surprising if Lagny referred to this register while laying the groundwork for the Company.
[102] AE/B/I/212, fols 450–3r, AN.
[103] AE/B/I/340, n.p., AN.
[104] Referenced in MAR/B/7/58, fols 228–30, AN.
[105] AE/B/I/379, fols 455–60r, AN. COVID-19 prevented me from consulting the *mémoires* from Chania and Izmir, but their existence is catalogued by the AN. For more on the Fabre family, see Takeda, 'Silk, Calico and Immigration in Marseille', pp. 241–63.
[106] AE/B/I/698, fol. 308v, AN.

appointment as director general and informing him on the intricacies of political and commercial affairs in Livorno. Although Lagny had written in his capacity as director general, and maintained a pretence of professional distance from the Company and his other commercial interests in his letters where possible, Cotolendy finished his *mémoire* with the assurance that 'I will be sure to also inform you of [any] news I receive which could satisfy your curiosity and that of your friends'.[107] Cotolendy recognised that the lines between Lagny's extensive interests as director general and as an individual were blurred, and, among others, the Company stood to gain from the information he provided.

The dialogue continued beyond these *mémoires*: in one of many letters to Pierre Chabert in Amsterdam, Lagny asked him 'to not omit to send me the gazettes' of the city, which specialised in commercial news.[108] In another to M. Piolle in Algiers, Lagny requested a report on the port's corsairs, including the number of ships they had put to sea and their prizes in 'the most exact' detail possible, alongside news on all ship movements in the Mediterranean.[109] In another to Aubert in Genoa, he asked for information on the size of Genoa's galley fleet and reiterated his desire to be informed of every ship arriving and leaving the port, be they French or foreign.[110] He similarly reminded M. Nouel in Bilbao, M. Stelle in Tétouan, M. Michel in Tunis and M. Julien in Aleppo of his need for regular updates on the French nations' commerce and ship movements. Lagny also noted Stelle's tardiness in sending the *mémoire* he had requested.[111]

Lagny's consular correspondence was extensive enough for Seignelay to rely on him for information about consular affairs. In a brief letter dated 30 June 1686, Seignelay asked Lagny 'to speak to me about *Sieur* Perillié, consul in Salé, the next time you come here; the merchants are complaining greatly about his conduct'.[112] It transpired that Perillié had been sent 400 *livres* by M. Heron, Lagny's correspondent in La Rochelle, to redeem a captive in Salé but had decided to simply keep the money for himself. This forced Seignelay to seek Lagny's assistance in order to intervene.[113]

---

[107] Ibid., fols 309r-13r.
[108] MAR/B/7/58, fols 93-4, AN. With the outbreak of the Nine Years' War, Chabert returned to Paris. Here, he helped to resolve an explosive dispute between the Company and another royal company by serving as an arbiter; Wade, 'Royal Companies', Z/1d/84, fols 4v-6, AN.
[109] MAR/B/7/58, fols 227-8, AN.
[110] Ibid., fols 228-30.
[111] Ibid., fols 249, 485-6, 486 and 501. Not all required chasing up for news, however: Cotolendy informed Seignelay in a letter on 17 May 1687 that he had forwarded news to Lagny from Cairo's consul; AE/B/I/698, fol. 395, AN.
[112] MAR/B/7/59, fol. 84v, AN.
[113] MAR/B/7/58, fols 218-19, AN.

Such incidents point to the agency problems created by drawing on the consuls' support. The Company had to trust that the consuls were providing accurate and/or complete information in their letters. Consuls occupied an especially ambiguous position, tasked as they were with representing the state and the mercantile community at the same time. The interests of each did not always align, which left consuls in a vulnerable position, since they relied on the community for their upkeep and their support. Sharing information on ship movements was thus an inherently political act, and consuls may have chosen to omit or to fabricate the movements of specific ships in particular situations.[114] We will return later to such agency problems.

Colonial officers

Completing the network were the colonial officers, who were one of many sources of knowledge for the French state about colonial affairs. Paris had already cemented itself as a centre for colonial knowledge and material culture by the middle of the seventeenth century. Besides the patronage of wealthy *financiers* and political notables, the city's printing presses were all too eager to publish texts documenting the exotic and the esoteric when travellers returned from the colonies. The first French atlas – featuring maps of Guadeloupe, Martinique and Saint Kitts – was published to great success in Paris by Nicolas Sanson in 1658. Moreover, with the rise of Colbert, the secretariat of state for maritime affairs became a hub for cartographic and colonial expertise. Colbert also championed the establishment of the *Observatoire de Paris* in 1667, whose astronomers oversaw the annual publication of *Connaissance des temps* after 1679. This periodical reinforced Paris' significance 'as centre of reference for mariners and French cartographers, the tables and longitudes being communicated in reference to the Paris meridian'.[115] The ports often looked to the city for guidance on colonial affairs and navigation, not the other way around.[116]

---

[114] I am grateful to Cátia Antunes for her thoughts on this. On the challenges consuls faced, see L. Sicking and A. Wijffels, 'Flotsam and Jetsam in the Historiography of Maritime Trade and Conflicts', in L. Sicking and A. Wijffels (eds), *Conflict Management in the Mediterranean and the Atlantic, 1000–1800: Actors, Institutions and Strategies of Dispute Settlement*, Leiden: Brill, 2020, p. 12. See also Müller, *Consuls*, pp. 77–9.

[115] F. Regourd, 'Capitale savante, capitale coloniale: sciences et savoirs coloniaux à Paris aux XVIIe et XVIIIe siècles', *Revue d'histoire moderne & contemporaine* 55 (2008), p. 138. For more on Paris as a centre for colonial knowledge, see the full article.

[116] For a recent study of the ways in which the Atlantic world (including the French colonies) influenced French life, see J. Wimmler, *The Sun King's Atlantic: Drugs, Demons and Dyestuffs in the Atlantic World, 1640–1730*, Leiden: Brill, 2017.

Lagny was at the heart of the action, which yielded information supporting the Company's underwriting. According to Clairambault, it was Lagny who handled the secretariat's colonial business: he issued passports for colonial voyages, maintained the secretariat's correspondence with colonial officials, and managed pressing colonial affairs, including, at the time Clairambault was writing, coordinating French efforts to retake Saint Kitts from the English and ensuring the safety of the French against Iroquois incursions in Canada.[117]

Seignelay therefore relied on Lagny to manage these flows of information. Indeed, throughout 1686 and 1687, Lagny kept up semi-regular exchanges with Jean Bochart de Champigny, intendant in Canada; Pierre-Paul Tarin de Cussy, the governor of Tortuga and Saint-Domingue; M. de Ferelles, the royal lieutenant in Cayenne; and Claude de Roux, chevalier de Saint-Laurent, the governor of Saint Kitts.[118] With the onset of the Nine Years' War, Lagny wrote to a variety of Canadian merchants and royal officers to assure them of the crown's continued protection.[119] He was also closely connected to Jean-Baptiste du Casse, and successfully championed the latter's nomination to become governor of Saint-Domingue in 1691, following Seignelay's death.[120] Before then, Seignelay continued to depend on Lagny to handle colonial affairs: in a letter to Lagny on 8 December 1686, Seignelay noted he was forwarding a letter concerning the commerce of Acadia and Québec and, 'this affair being important, I ask you to speak to me about it the next time you come here'.[121]

Most important, perhaps, was Lagny's control over the process for issuing colonial passports. On 8 April 1686, an order of the Council of State was issued granting Lagny control over the affairs of the *Compagnie et domaine d'Occident*, the tax farm for the French Caribbean and Canada that emerged from the collapse of the West India Company.[122] In order to oversee the

---

[117] MAR/B/8/18, n.p., AN.
[118] MAR/B/7/58, AN. For more on these figures, see Pritchard, *In Search of Empire*.
[119] MAR/B/7/60, fols 96–108r, AN.
[120] P. Hroděj, 'L'amiral Du Casse: de la marchandise à la Toison d'Or', *Annales de Bretagne et des pays de l'Ouest* 104 (1997), p. 29. Du Casse became a client of the Pontchartrain family; Chapman, *Private Ambition*, pp. 137–9.
[121] MAR/B/7/59, fol. 135v, AN.
[122] Heijmans, 'The Agency of Empire', p. 61. Here, Lagny replaced the late Morel. This colonial tax farm had been added in 1685 to the contract for the consolidated tax farms signed in 1681 (as discussed in Chapter 1), in which Lagny was a partner; Mousnier, *The Institutions of France*, vol. II, p. 442. Lagny shared control over the affairs of the *Compagnie et Domaine d'Occident* with M. Mesnager. On the value of the *Domaine d'Occident* as a potential means for the *financiers* also involved in the Guinea Company to cook the books to the benefit of their slave trade activities, see Banks, 'Financiers, Factors, and French Proprietary Companies', pp. 79–116.

tax farm's affairs and liquidate the West India Company's debts effectively, Lagny was empowered to undertake 'the necessary correspondence in the seaports of the kingdom, the islands of America, New France and [any] other places' deemed appropriate.[123] Most significantly, 'merchants and masters of French vessels wanting to trade with the islands of America and in New France' were henceforth obliged to obtain passports from Lagny authorising the voyage. Upon the return of the vessel, the shipmaster was required to provide Lagny with 'signed copies of the bills of lading, containing the cargo of the vessels, with certificates from the admiralty officers of the ports of the kingdom where they unload, [in order] to know if the clauses in the passports [...] have been carried out by the merchants'.[124] All maritime officials were forbidden from issuing passports for voyages to the Caribbean or Canada, and all were forbidden from allowing ships to undertake voyages to these places without a passport.[125]

This monopoly over colonial passports gave Lagny access to a rich flow of information. Not only were merchants and shipmasters obliged to provide the requisite information for their voyage to Lagny *before* it took place, but also signed copies of the bills of lading and admiralty certificates *after* the voyage. These powers centred first and foremost on the French state's desire to track the movement of French vessels in the Caribbean – which were forbidden from undertaking trade with islands under foreign possession, as per the 'exclusive system'[126] – but, in the process, they also provided Lagny

---

[123] MAR/C/7/159, n.p., AN.
[124] Ibid.
[125] This privilege was not granted on paper alone, as Seignelay himself relied on Lagny to draw up the passports; on 23 April 1686 (just a few weeks after the order of the Council of State was issued), Seignelay asked Lagny 'to send me promptly a passport for Joseph Barbarin of Marseille, commanding the vessel the St Ignace of around 180 tons, which is expected to leave the said city to go to the islands of America'; MAR/B/7/59, fol. 54r, AN.
[126] Here, see S. Marzagalli, 'Was Warfare Necessary for the Functioning of Eighteenth-Century Colonial Systems? Some Reflections on the Necessity of Cross-Imperial and Foreign Trade in the French Case', in C. Antunes and A. Polónia (eds), *Beyond Empires: Global, Self-Organizing, Cross-Imperial Networks, 1500–1800*, Leiden: Brill, 2016, pp. 253–77; B. Mandelblatt, 'How Feeding Slaves Shaped the French Atlantic: Mercantilism and the Crisis of Food Provisioning in the Franco-Caribbean during the Seventeenth and Eighteenth Centuries', in S. Reinert and P. Røge (eds), *The Political Economy of Empire in the Early Modern World*, Basingstoke: Palgrave Macmillan, 2013, pp. 198–9.

with consistent access to information on all commercial activity between the colonies and metropolitan France.

These unique powers clearly caused friction within the secretariat, as Clairambault warned Pontchartrain *père* that Lagny and Seignelay had been uncooperative with the other *bureaux*, refusing to give them access to the passports. This led, Clairambault suggests, to an 'abuse' of the process.[127] As we will see, Clairambault had ample interest in getting Lagny replaced, so we should be cautious in accepting this judgement fully. This does, however, point to the extent of Lagny's power over these passports, perhaps casting the Company's underwriting in a new light. Voyages to and from the Caribbean and Canada were amongst the most frequent to be insured by the Company;[128] could those seeking a passport have felt pressure to insure with the Company to secure one? This can only be speculated. In any case, Lagny was well placed to ensure the Company's interests were served, with easy access to key documents that could help to substantiate or repudiate claims for colonial voyages. Moreover, policyholders who recognised Lagny's power over colonial passports may have been especially reluctant to try to defraud the Company in light of the information they knew they would have to provide to him at the start and conclusion of the voyage. More broadly, these documents gave Lagny access to the sort of contextual information that served the daily practice of informed underwriting.

In short, Lagny's access to information on colonial commerce was unparalleled in France. Far from being uninformed in this field, the Company had a strong commercial advantage: here, it had the full apparatus of the French state behind it; here, Lagny was perhaps the best informed man in France.

'A WORK OF HIS OWN HAND': LEVERAGING THE NETWORK

Information is essential to good underwriting, and we have seen the four poles of Lagny's network were invaluable to the Company in procuring it. But good underwriting also presupposes voyages to underwrite, and like the Chamber, the Company needed support in finding prospective policyholders. Here, the network was leveraged again, but with far more mixed results. Encountering widespread suspicion towards the Company, the network proved unable to widely persuade merchants to take out their insurance in Paris.

All began well and predictably: Seignelay and Lagny wrote to various figures across the network to ask for their support in advertising the

---

[127] MAR/B/8/18, n.p., AN.
[128] See Chapter 5.

Company. Unfortunately, it seems Lagny's letter-book does not record every letter they wrote for the Company's interests, but enough are documented to build a coherent picture of the process. On 26 August 1686, Seignelay wrote to M. du Gué de Bagnols, the intendant in Lille, enjoining him to persuade merchants there to insure with the Company in Paris rather than abroad to keep insurance premiums within France. To this end, he provided the intendant with a copy of the Company's letters patent, promising that merchants of the city would 'profit' from the institution's 'reliability' and its 'other advantages'.[129] Seignelay thus strove to garner business for the Company even in a city that had only been annexed in 1668.

Meanwhile, Lagny was also writing letters, and saw the consuls as valuable allies in generating business for the Company. Although the relevant letters have not been recorded in his letter-book, it is clear from the content of later letters that Lagny had written to the consuls to introduce the Company, attaching copies of its letters patent to help the consuls promote the institution. A letter to Aubert, dated 23 September 1686, offers an insight into the mixed results of this process. Here, Lagny adopted an almost searing rhetoric to persuade Aubert and the French nation in Genoa that the Company was a valuable resource for their business, and to dispel their concerns about the scope for non-payment of claims. Referring to the letters patent sent to Aubert, Lagny conceded that the Company's liquidity ran only to 300,000 *livres*, but he made clear that policyholders were protected by the institution's unlimited liability regime. He also highlighted that the Company, 'comprised of thirty of the most powerful people of the state', offered 'security' apparently not found with insurers 'elsewhere' – most certainly referring to foreign insurers. 'Besides', Lagny continued, 'these people are too wise and too rich to insure sums [which are] too large on the same ship'.[130] He warned that, if French merchants in Genoa chose not to insure in Paris, the Company 'will not lack for business and they alone will lose out'.[131]

Lagny finished his letter with similar assertiveness, noting that the Company wanted to underwrite foreign voyages based on the advice of correspondents based abroad. It was envisaged that these correspondents would negotiate policies, compiling the necessary details – the merchandise and/or ships to be insured, the condition of each, etc. – to then be sent to Paris for the policy to be signed by a commission agent.[132] Lagny hoped the Company could rely on Aubert as a man of 'integrity' to negotiate policies on its behalf and provide 'truth[ful]' information.[133] Lagny therefore leveraged

---

[129] MAR/B/7/58, fols 242–3, AN.
[130] Ibid., fols 259–61.
[131] Ibid., fols 259–61.
[132] Ibid., fols 259–61.
[133] Ibid., fols 259–61.

Aubert's ties to the crown to facilitate the Company's underwriting, hoping to garner business through Aubert himself. Aubert no longer served the state just as a consul: he had now been co-opted as an insurance broker too.

Lagny equally sought the support of the provincial officers. In the case of M. Patoulet, intendant in Dunkirk, Lagny encountered difficulties. On 9 September 1686, Patoulet wrote to Lagny, informing him that the merchants of Dunkirk were not interested in insuring with the Company because the institution demanded higher premiums than the Dutch. Lagny responded on 15 September: Seignelay, who was said to regard the Company 'as a work of his own hand', had discovered through his discussions with Lagny that the merchants of Dunkirk had not even tried to negotiate policies with the Company up to that point. Lagny thus enjoined Patoulet to ask the merchants to sign their policies with the Company rather than the Dutch, since recourse to the Amsterdam market was being propelled only by 'habit'. Moreover, Lagny claimed, 'there is a large difference [between the Company and the insurers of Amsterdam] in reliability and good faith' owing to the 'chicanery' of the latter.[134] Thus, through letters like this, Lagny hoped to enlist the port intendants to help bring business to the Company and to establish its reputation as a credible option for insurance coverage.

Lagny also sought the support of his merchant correspondents, with varying degrees of success. In June 1686, the Company issued an advertisement distributed throughout the ports of France that stressed its creditworthiness. To facilitate business, the advertisement noted that, 'at the home of M. *[blank]* of this city, prints of the edict, [articles of] association and order [of the Council of State, establishing the Company] will be distributed for free'.[135] The blank name was almost certainly filled with the name of Lagny's correspondent in the given port, who was entrusted with distributing the printed materials, all of which were of royal provenance. The advertisement also offered merchants the capacity 'to receive their money in the provinces' rather than in Paris; this was surely done through bills of exchange, and the Company likely relied on these notable port merchants to remit funds to provincial policyholders.[136]

Lagny hoped his merchant correspondents would go further than being passive receptacles of royal documents. Here, his most fruitful exchange was with Magy, a fellow member of the Mediterranean Company, who helped the Company break into the insurance market of Marseille. 'I beseech you', Lagny wrote in a letter of 23 August 1686,

---

[134] Ibid., fols 250–1.
[135] Pouilloux, *Mémoires d'assurances*, p. 441.
[136] Ibid.

'to get business [in Marseille] for the [Royal] Insurance Chamber by any means', assuring Magy that any success he could achieve 'would bring great pleasure' to Seignelay.[137] Magy obliged and wrote to Lagny detailing his gestures of support on 27 September, prompting a grateful response from Lagny on 7 October, who felt Magy's intervention was all that was needed to kick off the Company's business in Marseille – business that would ultimately prove beneficial, Lagny suggested, to the port itself. He added that 'the [current] directors, to whom I have sent an extract of your letter, will be sure to write to you'.[138]

Marseille, as perhaps the only port in France besides Rouen that already had an entrenched insurance market in 1686, was never likely to be receptive to the Company. Moreover, the Marseillaise *chambre de commerce*'s resistance to the plan for a monopoly insurance company in 1685 reflected a broader civic culture of recalcitrance in the face of crown intervention.[139] Therefore, it is no surprise a crown-sponsored Parisian insurance company was a hard sell in Marseille. Nevertheless, Lagny believed that Magy's intervention would allow the Company to overcome this hurdle.

The reluctance of the Breton ports to insure with the Company, by contrast, revealed potential shortcomings in the Company's model. Lagny pressed M. Grilleau in Nantes to encourage his colleagues to underwrite with the Company rather than abroad. When Grilleau responded that Nantais merchants had already begun to enquire with the Company about coverage, Lagny remained unsatisfied and wrote again on 24 September 1686, imploring him to persuade the merchants to recognise the Company's advantages over its foreign competitors.[140]

Grilleau responded with concerns, which Lagny sought to allay in his response on 2 October. Lagny acknowledged that the Company's insurance rates could be higher than those found elsewhere, but argued that the liquidity of the Company's fund 'merits some difference in the premiums'. It is 'not prudent', he argued, for merchants to simply opt for the insurer offering the lowest rates without considering their reliability and creditworthiness.[141]

The Company's premium rates therefore emerged as a potential problem, albeit one that is impossible to study in depth.[142] As Lagny argued in this letter and in that to Aubert, the Company's liquidity was an asset that came

---

[137] MAR/B/7/58, fols 236–7, AN.
[138] Ibid., fols 280–2.
[139] On this, see Takeda, *Between Crown and Commerce*.
[140] MAR/B/7/58, fol. 266, AN.
[141] Ibid., fols 275–6. On the trustworthiness of underwriters, see Chapter 7.
[142] In the absence of the Company's full insurance registers, it is impossible to compare its insurance rates to those offered elsewhere. In any case, such comparison can be fraught with challenges for the historian: premium rates fluctuated based on – *inter*

at a price. Simply put, premiums alone did not generate great profits in the long run: even today, insurers typically invest premiums in other ventures in order to generate their profits. Ignoring the Rouennais' proposal for the 1664 monopoly company project,[143] the Company's fund of 300,000 *livres* – which sat in its cashier's office – was intentionally left idle, along with all premiums deposited there. This obsession with liquidity gave security to policyholders that their claims would be promptly and fully reimbursed, but it denied a valuable revenue stream to the Company which required higher premiums as a consequence. There was thus the risk the Company would struggle to compete with Amsterdam and London.

Nevertheless, if we look at transaction costs more broadly, rather than premium rates specifically, the Company's model was not necessarily flawed. Indeed, Lagny's argument that the Company's fund was a value-added feature of its services prefigured those made during the corporate boom of the eighteenth century. In America, the establishment of new chartered insurance companies was justified partly on the grounds that 'those seeking insurance would be willing to pay a higher premium for a more secure policy', meaning lucrative profits were possible for investors.[144] Indeed, 'most witnesses reported that by 1810 American insurance premiums were actually higher than those that could be obtained in London through Lloyd's'.[145] Despite these higher costs, chartered insurance companies proliferated, and were widely used by American merchants because of the costs involved in transacting business across the Atlantic and holding insolvent underwriters to account. American merchants who secured coverage with local companies limited their transaction costs at every stage, being able to trust that the companies were solvent and being able to more easily and cheaply hold them to account if they refused to make payment on a policy. We can therefore see that the Company – to the best of my knowledge, the first chartered company in the history of marine insurance – articulated a logic for corporate insurance that outlived the institution itself.

These early challenges help to explain why the Company's business remained modest up to September 1687. As we have already seen, it was at this point that Seignelay abandoned persuasion in favour of coercing merchants in the Atlantic ports into securing their coverage in Paris.[146] Lagny's network, while certainly powerful, was far from omnipotent: where the network could not succeed in supporting the Company's

---

alia – knowledge of the vessel and the shipmaster, meaning that the premium rate was not necessarily fixed for particular routes.
[143] See Chapter 1.
[144] Wright and Kingston, 'Corporate Insurers in Antebellum America', p. 451.
[145] Glenn Crothers, 'Commercial Risk', p. 632.
[146] See Chapter 2.

endeavours, Lagny looked to Seignelay to speak on the king's behalf. This risky strategy, which threatened to alienate merchants in the Atlantic ports entirely, actually paid off.[147]

This did not mean the network became useful only for information, however. Correspondents were even co-opted into handling business on the Company's behalf. On 8 June 1687, Lagny wrote to Eon, one of his correspondents in Saint-Malo, to complain that 'you have rather abandoned our correspondence', emphasising again his need to be kept informed on maritime affairs.[148] Perhaps Eon had not been diligent in keeping Lagny informed of broader commercial affairs, but in the months around this letter, he served the Company extensively as a commercial agent. When the *Saint Leon* encountered strong storms on 2 December 1686 and grounded off the coast of Saint-Jean-des-Monts in western France, the Company was given permission to recover the wine and whale oil it had insured on board.[149] These were salvaged and loaded onto the *Sainte Anne*, which completed the insured voyage to Saint-Malo.[150] Here, Eon took over. Eon wrote to the Company on 3 April 1687 regarding the merchandise, before writing again on 20 April to acknowledge receipt of the merchandise after the *Sainte Anne*'s safe arrival in Saint-Malo. On the directors' request – they had written to him on 7 May – Eon handled the sale of the merchandise, writing to them on 19 July and 13 August to confirm the fees he had incurred from this.[151] Although the Company rarely dealt directly with physical goods by the very nature of its activities, Eon and the other port merchants could be entrusted to handle the Company's commercial affairs in the ports when there was scope for abandoned merchandise to be salvaged.

With the onset of war, the fairly frequent references to the Company in Lagny and Seignelay's letters came to a sudden halt. Protecting commercial shipping and arranging exchanges of captured sailors became Lagny's main priority.[152] This did not stop him from using his position to serve

---

[147] See below and Chapter 5.
[148] MAR/B/7/58, fols 496–8, AN.
[149] The proceeds from the sale of this were then to be distributed *pro rata*; Z/1d/82, fol. 2v, AN.
[150] An account of the fees arising from salvaging the wine and the oil was made in La Rochelle on 10 May 1687, amounting to 2,224 *livres*, 9 *sols* and 6 *deniers*. Richard Massiot in La Rochelle, acting on the directors' behalf, paid these fees and drew two bills of exchange on the Company for reimbursement; Z/1d/84, fols 3–4, AN. For the policy, see Z/1d/85, fol. 44r, AN.
[151] Z/1d/84, fols 3–4, AN. Our knowledge of this dense level of communication and delegation of legal powers arises only because the policy's commission agent sought the support of arbiters in reclaiming profits arising from the sale of the merchandise.
[152] Here, see Chapter 5.

the Company's interests, however; in a letter to M. Alaire du Beignon in La Rochelle on 26 August 1689, he wrote regarding the Company's 'great suspicions that a ship from Dieppe called the *Liberté*' had been taken by the Dutch 'through intelligence from the crew and others'. Lagny asked for help with deposing the crew, who were believed to be in the port, and requested a copy of their testimony.[153] In the meantime, arbitration proceedings were agreed for the policies and sea loans on the vessel, but these were ultimately dropped, suggesting the depositions had provided no evidence that collusion had taken place.[154]

CONCLUSION

Philippe Minard has argued that state support in the French cloth industry helped to overcome inherent market weaknesses in accessing information, ensuring consumers could make informed choices by creating high standards to which wares had to adhere.[155] In a similar vein, this chapter has articulated the great lengths to which Colbert and Seignelay went to address the information asymmetries faced by the Chamber and the Company, thus allowing insurers to make informed underwriting choices. Both tapped into the French state's apparatus of information gathering and dissemination to fashion information networks for Bellinzani and Lagny, shifting information costs away from both institutions' underwriters in the process. To the best of my knowledge, no other insurance institutions gathered maritime information in such a way before the rise of Lloyd's: this was an unprecedented alliance between underwriters and the 'information state'.[156]

As the Chamber's business grew, *ad hoc* measures were instituted to facilitate information gathering for its underwriters. Colbert enlisted the admiralties and the consulates for support, giving Bellinzani direct access to shipping information from across Europe in the years after he became president. Colbert also pressured the admiralties and the consulates to encourage merchants to conduct their underwriting in Paris.

The Company, by contrast, was equipped with a global apparatus for gathering information from the outset. Seignelay helped Lagny to establish an information network with four key poles: provincial officers, merchant correspondents, consuls and colonial officers. This network was established in a systematic manner at the outset of Lagny's tenure as director general of commerce, learning the lessons of the Chamber's

---

[153] MAR/B/7/60, fols 166–7r, AN.
[154] Z/1d/85, fol. 44r, AN; Z/1d/82, fols 26r and 30; Z/1d/83, fol. 6r, AN.
[155] Minard, *La fortune du colbertisme*.
[156] On Lloyd's, see the Introduction.

more piecemeal efforts and desires. The *Rolle général des bastimens* leveraged the state's capacity to gather information to create a document that ostensibly catalogued every vessel in France. This document had great potential for underwriting purposes. Frequent epistolary exchanges with provincial officers, merchant correspondents, consuls and colonial officers equipped the Company with a rich, up-to-date understanding of ship movements and the ebb and flow of natural and anthropogenic risks across the globe. Lagny's monopoly privileges on colonial passports gave him access to a breadth and depth of information on colonial commerce that even the most influential port merchants would have struggled to match. Moreover, Lagny was able to rely on his correspondents not only as transmitters of information, but also as intermediaries: correspondents could serve intermittently as commercial agents, insurance brokers or legal allies when pressed by Lagny and/or by the serving directors.

Far from being entirely disconnected from the maritime world as Pontchartrain *fils* suggested, the Company had the tools at its disposal to respond to commercial and political developments across Europe and the Atlantic. It may have been 'over thirty leagues from the sea', as Savary acknowledged, but *rue Quincampoix* was only fifteen minutes by foot from the secretariat of state for maritime affairs.[157]

This was not a perfect network for maritime information by any stretch of the imagination. Even with agents across the globe, information never moved quickly in the early modern world, which hindered the network's efficacy *a priori*.[158] Moreover, agency problems were inevitably rife, especially beyond metropolitan France. To be sure, the absolute monarchy was able to exercise a degree of power over French mercantile communities abroad, but such power could clash with the interests of these communities. Consuls in particular were ambiguous agents of state, whose allegiances were pulled in multiple directions.[159] Nevertheless, such agency problems were not unique to the Company, since private underwriters across Europe, with correspondents or factors elsewhere, were equally susceptible to misinformation or omission. The same holds true for the

---

[157] Savary, *Le parfait négociant*, vol. I, book II, pp. 112–13.
[158] Indeed, as noted in the Introduction, Marie Ménard-Jacob suggests this is part of why the CIO had so many problems early on; communication was so tenuous between France and India that information included in letters could become out-of-date on arrival, and such information could feed poor decision-making; Ménard-Jacob, 'L'apprentissage de l'Inde'. To some extent, this explains why the Company rarely insured Indian Ocean voyages (see Chapter 5).
[159] Unsurprisingly, no evidence survives to suggest they intentionally omitted or distorted information in their dispatches to Lagny, but we should recognise the scope for such practices over time.

challenges posed by distance and time in the early modern world. My intention in this chapter has been to stress the *relative*, not *absolute*, strength of the Company's network.

How then should we understand Pontchartrain *fils*' letter, introduced at the beginning of this chapter? As we will see, the Company was caught in a political struggle between the Colbert and Phélypeaux clans.[160] These political manoeuvrings underpinned Clairambault's *mémoire*, written so shortly after Seignelay's death. As Jörg Ulbert has argued, Clairambault's observations were motivated by a broader desire to ingratiate himself with Pontchartrain *père*: in suggesting Lagny was implicated in fraud, 'his management of [commercial] affairs was sufficiently called into question to justify his replacement'. After all, Lagny was an ally of Seignelay rather than Pontchartrain, and 'the goal of such a reorganisation of the offices [of the secretariat] was without doubt less to improve the efficacy and integrity of the institution than to oust the allies of the Colbert clan to the benefit of the clients of the Phélypeaux family'.[161] Lagny was ultimately retained as part of Pontchartrain *père*'s pragmatic broader strategy for the secretariat, through which he retained Colbertian clients and tried to bring them into the Pontchartrain patronage network rather than restructuring the entire framework outlined in this chapter with his own clients.[162] Nevertheless, we will see Pontchartrain *père* wished to make his own mark on the secretariat, including in the realm of insurance. The choice to leave Seignelay's insurance project to wither while focusing his attentions elsewhere was one motivated by high politics.

In this light, Pontchartrain *fils*' letter appears to be especially problematic. In reflecting on an institution created by a rival clan and allowed to crumble under his father – who was now the king's chancellor – Pontchartrain *fils* had every reason to present structural reasons for its ostensible failure. Recognising the Company had fallen victim to the oscillations of high politics would have meant acknowledging his father's role in this.

Beyond the realm of court politics, the findings of this chapter complicate our current understanding of insurance in seventeenth-century Europe. Neo-institutionalism has long emphasised the significance of information

---

[160] See Chapter 8.
[161] Ulbert, 'Les bureaux du secrétariat', p. 24. On this clan dispute, see also Cole, *French Mercantilism*, p. 4.
[162] On this strategy, see Chapman, *Private Ambition*, pp. 115–44.

in conducting successful underwriting, and stressed the advantages London and Amsterdam had in collecting and disseminating it. Yet while Edward Lloyd's weekly shipping newssheet was being printed as early as 1692, the Chamber and the Company had already been receiving detailed information on ship movements and political developments through the secretariat of state for maritime affairs long before this point.[163] Moreover, the *Rolle général des bastimens* was drawn up over seventy years before *Lloyd's Register* was (to our knowledge) first published. The Chamber and the Company's information resources thus rivalled, or even surpassed, those of these markets. Such resources were necessary for the take-off of these markets, but they were not sufficient.

How then do we explain London and Amsterdam's continued dominance at the turn of the eighteenth century? The coming chapters will explore the many facets of this question by studying the ways the Chamber and the Company put their information advantages to work. Namely, the chapters will analyse the institutions' underwriting patterns and their approaches to conflict management. What will emerge is the state's profound role in the Parisian insurance market's ultimate failure to take off. Contrary to the presumptions of neo-institutional studies in European economic development to this point, the state did not inhibit the market through smothering and overzealous intervention, but offered inadequate support in critical moments.

---

[163] Leonard, 'Introduction', p. 11; Wright and Fayle, *A History of Lloyd's*, p. 27.

Part 2

WAR, MARITIME COMMERCE AND EMPIRE

4

UNDERWRITING IN WAR AND PEACE: FORTUNE AND FAILURE IN THE ROYAL INSURANCE CHAMBER, 1668–72[1]

The seventeenth century was a crucial period in the development of Europe's insurance markets, yet quantitative analyses on this period are decidedly scarce. This is not for a lack of will on the part of historians: in a fascinating study of Juan Henriquez, a broker and underwriter in Antwerp in the sixteenth century, Jeroen Puttevils and Marc Deloof note the significance of his ledgers:

> substantial sources on the actual operations and organization of marine insurance (either policies or merchant accounts) are scarce. The haphazard survival of documents on insurance has limited the study of marine insurance. Research has focused on either late medieval Italy (Venice, Genoa, Firenze), its dependencies, or the more mature insurance markets of eighteenth-century Northwestern Europe such as Amsterdam, London, La Rochelle, and Cádiz. The two main account ledgers of Henriquez are thus an exceptional source for studying marine insurance between those two periods.[2]

For France, as for elsewhere, records of insurance policies are scarce because the policies themselves were 'generally destroyed' after the insured risk had ceased.[3] Records from eighteenth-century Marseille are well preserved – and

---

[1] This chapter is based primarily on the analysis of one of two datasets, which is accessible online on the AveTransRisk website; AveTransRisk [http://humanities-research.exeter.ac.uk/avetransrisk, accessed 26 April 2020]. I am grateful to Ian Wellaway for his efforts in designing the database based on my needs (and those of my colleagues on the AveTransRisk team) and working with me to facilitate data analysis. I am also grateful to Sabine Go for her valuable recommendations in dealing with the peculiarities of the Chamber data.

[2] J. Puttevils and M. Deloof, 'Marketing and Pricing Risk in Marine Insurance in Sixteenth-Century Antwerp', *Journal of Economic History* 77 (2017), pp. 797–8.

[3] M. Tanguy, 'Un contrat nantais pour un voyage aux Antilles au XVIIe siècle', in C. Borde and É. Roulet (eds), *L'assurance maritime XIVe–XXIe siècle*, Aachen: Shaker

are currently being studied by Mallory Hope – but many of the records from Rouen, the other key underwriting centre in France, have been lost.[4]

The Chamber's records are invaluable in filling the significant gap in our knowledge of marine insurance in early modern France. Henriquez's ledgers document 1,621 policies signed in Antwerp between 1562 and 1563. The Chamber's extant registers document somewhere around 10,000 policies. A sample of 4,154, comprising all the policies from the years 1668 to 1672, is analysed in this chapter.

These policies covered numerous insured effects, often in different combinations, on a wide array of voyages in the western hemisphere. The Chamber was thus the first major institutionalisation of the Parisian capital market, serving as a fixed meeting space for the mobilisation of capital for ventures within and beyond metropolitan France – and even beyond the French empire. Revising Boiteux's figures, I find that stability in commerce and shipping allowed insurers to confidently increase the scale of their underwriting each year.

This progress was abruptly halted with the outbreak of the Dutch War in 1672. Risky underwriting strategies – namely, the extensive insuring of Newfoundland and Greenland fishing voyages – did not pay off, owing to Dutch success in seizing ships throughout the Atlantic. Moreover, attempts by underwriters to diversify their portfolio by underwriting Mediterranean voyages backfired. Using the data of different underwriting entities, I demonstrate that more prolific underwriters generally fared better in 1672 than more infrequent underwriters. Nevertheless, the Chamber's returns for the year were wiped out, and this offered little incentive to continue underwriting when investments outside commerce proved more stable and lucrative.

TAILORED UNDERWRITING:
THE CHAMBER AND THE DIVERSITY OF UNDERWRITING

In marine insurance, the division is commonly made between hull and cargo insurance. Yet there was great flexibility in the Chamber in the underwriting of different effects. The hull could be insured, yes, but so

---

Verlag, 2017, p. 47.

[4] The consular archives of Rouen burned down in the nineteenth century, and various registers documenting the insurance policies signed in the city have been lost; Rossi, *Insurance in Elizabethan England*, pp. 18–20; L. Boiteux, 'Contributions de l'assurance à l'histoire de l'économie maritime en France', in M. Mollat (ed.), *Les sources de l'histoire maritime en Europe, du moyen âge au XVIIIe siècle*, Paris: SEVPEN, 1962, pp. 447–63; Hope, 'Underwriting Risk'. For the study of an exceptional set of sources from an underwriting syndicate in Rouen in the early eighteenth century, see W. Dawson, *Marine Underwriting at Rouen 1727–1742*, London: Lloyd's, 1931.

could other elements of the ship – the keel, cords, tools and ship furniture – in different combinations. This is most likely the by-product of the complex ship-owning arrangements in early modern Europe.[5] Moreover, some policyholders may have been willing to bear the risks of particular elements of the ship.

Table 6 The frequency of named effects being insured by the Chamber in its policies for the years 1668–72.[6]

Insured effect	1668	1669	1670	1671	1672	Total
Hull (*corps*)	145	203	248	359	602	1,557
Keel (*quille*)	88	158	199	291	568	1,304
Cords (*agrès*)	61	49	93	200	430	833
Tools (*ustensiles*)	62	46	70	127	182	487
Food provisions (*victuailles*)	35	29	48	103	184	399
Ship furniture, e.g. anchor, sail (*apparaux*)	49	46	92	198	422	807
Sea loan/respondentia (*argent donné à la grosse*)	45	32	60	105	171	413
Merchandise/cargo (*marchandise/cargaison*)	316	456	605	787	1,310	3,474
Life (*assurance sur la personne de [nom]*)	1	–	8	10	1	20
Advances to the crew (*avances faites aux matelots/à l'équipage*)	–	3	14	12	22	51

Source: The AveTransRisk database (hereafter ATR), based on data from Z/1d/75–8, AN.

Eminently, some policyholders were concerned with the investments they had made in the maintenance of their crews: food provisions were insured with some regularity, while advances to the crew were insured on occasions.

Although various parts of the ship could be covered, cargo was by far the most frequently insured effect in the Chamber. Policies rarely specified the precise cargo that was being insured. In most cases, the

---

[5] For an example of part ownership in ships in action, see G. Buti, 'La "marine de Sète" au XVIIIe siècle: entre trafic de proximité et grand cabotage européen', in L. Dumond, S. Durand, and J. Thomas (eds), *Les ports dans l'Europe méditerranéenne: trafics et circulation: images et représentations*, Montpellier: Presses universitaires de le Méditerranée, 2007, pp. 187–213.

[6] NB various combinations of effects were possible.

underwriters seem to have been content to remain in the dark, so long as the policyholder could demonstrate their interest in the cargo when submitting a claim. Where named, the cargo insured was most likely to comprise wine or eaux de vie, France's great agricultural exports. Other named cargoes, such as silver, sugar, tobacco and cochineal, reflected the Chamber's propensity to insure western Atlantic voyages.[7]

Table 7 The frequency of items being named as insured merchandise/cargo in the Chamber's insurance policies for the years 1668–72.

Item	Frequency
Wine	230
Eaux de vie	142
Wool	71
Silver	65
Salt	59
Oil	51
Gold	48
Wheat	47
Whalebone	45
Cloth	21
Sugar	20
Fish	15
Leather	13
Tobacco	13
Vinegar	12
Whale oil	12
Dried fish	11
Plums	10
Cochineal	9
Cod	9
Herring	7
Lead	7
Tin	7
Copper	6
Rye	6
Fruit	5
Marble	5
Butter	4
Paper	4
Barley	3
Gems	3

[7] See below.

Fortune and Failure in the Royal Insurance Chamber, 1668–72 135

Ham	3
Honey	3
Iron	3
Metal threads	3
Oats	3
Sardines	3
Beef	2
Cannon	2
Clove	2
Enslaved people (*nègres*)[8]	2
Indigo	2
Linen	2
Liquorice	2
Oars	2
Silk	2
Soap	2
Walnut	2
Wood	2
Alum	1
Coal	1
Cotton	1
Fat	1
Grapes	1
Lemons	1
Linseed	1
Metal	1
Olive oil	1
Oranges	1
Pepper	1
Potash	1
Saffron	1
Salmon	1
Tallow	1
Verdigris	1

Source: ATR, based on data from Z/1d/75–8, AN.

The Chamber insured a notable number of sea loans as part of its business. In marine insurance, the underwriter bears a risk in return for an upfront premium from the policyholder, while in a sea loan, the creditor gives a lump sum upfront for a voyage, which is only repaid (with very high

---

[8] For the avoidance of confusion, it is the policies in question that conceive the slaves as merchandise; this is certainly not my own characterisation.

interest) in the event the ship completes its journey. In early modern French juridical practice, a debtor could pledge the ship itself as collateral for the loan (more commonly known as a bottomry), the merchandise with which they were loading it (more commonly known as a *respondentia*) or both.[9]

Up to now, the place of the sea loan in early modern commerce has not been given due attention. The theoretical literature has regarded it as a precursor of insurance that fell afoul of prohibitions on usury and, in any case, proved inadequate in meeting mercantile needs in managing risk.[10] Even the empirical literature has typically treated insurance and sea loans as discrete entities, at best tacitly recognising the interplay between the two.[11]

In fact, sea loans had a long life after the rise of insurance precisely because they were instruments of credit and thus an insurable interest, i.e. they could be insured. By insuring a sea loan, the creditor sacrificed a part of their potential profits, but protected themselves from total loss of the sum they loaned if the voyage failed. By shifting their risks to underwriters, creditors could develop a suitably de-risked portfolio of sea loans with lucrative profit margins on offer. The Chamber's sea loan registers do not seem to have survived, so it is impossible to speak of the scale of the loans it offered. Nevertheless, the Chamber's insurance registers note the frequent insuring of sea loans for voyages to and from the Caribbean, Newfoundland and Greenland.

Besides insuring sea loans, the Chamber also engaged in life insurance on rare occasions, albeit of a very specific kind. In these policies, an individual was named, alongside their age. The policies specified that, if the named individual were to be captured by 'the Turks or corsairs of Barbary' and required to pay a ransom, the underwriters would be obliged to make payment on the policy within three weeks of receiving evidence of the captive's detention. Demonstrating the high stakes involved in such arrangements, the

---

[9] On this juridical practice, see Valin, *Nouveau commentaire*, vol. II, pp. 3–26.
[10] Harris, *Going the Distance*, pp. 110–18; Edler de Roover, 'Early Examples of Marine Insurance'; North, 'Institutions, Transaction Costs', pp. 22–40.
[11] For example, see Baskes, *Staying Afloat*, p. 182. For exceptions to this rule, see O. Cruz Barney, 'The Risk in Hispanic-Indies Trade. Sea Loans and Maritime Insurances (16th–19th century)', in L. Brunori, S. Dauchy, O. Descaps, and X. Prévost (eds), *Le Droit face à l'économie sans travail*, vol. II, Paris: Éditions Classiques Garnier, 2020, pp. 265–95; A. Zanini, 'Financing and Risk in Genoese Maritime Trade during the Eighteenth Century: Strategies and Practices', in M. Fusaro, A. Addobbati, and L. Piccinno (eds), *General Average and Risk Management in Medieval and Early Modern Maritime Business*, Basingstoke: Palgrave Macmillan, 2023, pp. 335–59.

underwriters explicitly offered 'all our present and future movable assets [*biens meubles*] and inheritances' as collateral on the policy.[12]

It therefore seems more appropriate to call this 'ransom insurance' instead. Individuals involved in voyages heading towards the Mediterranean chose to take out ransom insurance with the Chamber to avoid the need to rely on family networks, charitable foundations or the state to secure their release.[13] Louis Sorindho and Pierre Bastere secured coverage for themselves in 1671 for their return voyage on board the *Saint Jean* from Bordeaux to Madeira and the Canary Islands. They were surely glad to have done so, since they were captured by corsairs in the course of their voyage.[14] Based on the findings of Wolfgang Kaiser, it seems likely that the underwriters' payments were remitted to North Africa through a bill of exchange to secure the release of the captives.[15]

The Chamber's underwriters offered this diverse coverage for an equally diverse group across Europe. Amongst its policyholders, the Chamber could count Thomas Hamilton, burgomaster of Ostend; the Papal Treasury; and none other than Charles XI, king of Sweden.[16] As Colbert had intended, the Chamber's underwriting drew business – and specie – from across Europe.

Table 8 The named locations of policyholders and intermediaries insuring in the Chamber in its policies for the period 1668–72.

Abbeville	Genoa	Paris
Alicante	Granville	Plymouth
Amiens	Hamburg	Port-Sainte-Marie
Amsterdam	Honfleur	Rennes
Antwerp	La Rochelle	Rome
Bayonne	La Teste-de-Buch	Rotterdam

[12] Z/1d/75, fol. 290r, AN.
[13] On Mediterranean captivity, and the networks that emerged for the redemption of captives, see W. Kaiser and G. Calafat, 'The Economy of Ransoming in the Early Modern Mediterranean: A Form of Cross-Cultural Trade between Southern Europe and the Maghreb (Sixteenth to Eighteenth Centuries)', in F. Trivellato, L. Halevi, and C. Antunes (eds), *Religion and Trade: Cross-Cultural Exchanges in World History, 1000–1900*, Oxford: Oxford University Press, 2014, pp. 108–30. On how the state treated the rescue of captives as a litmus test for French identity, see Weiss, *Captives and Corsairs*.
[14] Z/1d/75, fol. 290r, AN.
[15] W. Kaiser, 'Les "hommes de crédit" dans les rachats provençaux (XVIe–XVIIe siècles)', in W. Kaiser (ed.), *Le commerce des captifs. Les intermédiaires dans l'échange et le rachat des prisonniers en Méditerranée, XVe–XVIIIe siècle*, Rome: École Française de Rome, 2008, pp. 291–319.
[16] Z/1d/77, fol. 105v; Z/1d/78, fols 52r and 55r, AN.

Bordeaux	Le Havre	Rouen
Boulogne-sur-Mer	Lille	Saint-Chamond
Breda	Lisbon	Saint-Jean-de-Luz
Bruges	London	Saint-Malo
Cádiz	Lyon	Saint-Quentin
Caen	Madeira	Saint-Valery-sur-Somme
Calais	Marenne	Spain
Capbreton	Marseille	St Gallen (Switzerland)
Ciboure	Middelburg	Stockholm
Dieppe	Montségur	Sweden
Dublin	Morlaix	Terceira
Dunkirk	Nantes	Toulon
England	Nice	Tours
Exeter	Norrköping	Vannes
Florence	Olonne-sur-Mer	Venice
Galway	Orléans	
Gdansk	Ostend	

Source: ATR, based on data from Z/1d/75-8, AN.

TRANS-IMPERIAL UNDERWRITING: THE CHAMBER'S TRACK RECORD, 1668–72

Predictably, in serving such a diverse clientele, the Chamber also underwrote a great diversity of voyages – but, in the end, this came at a cost. This section studies the Chamber's track record in the years 1668 to 1672, seeking to understand the types of voyage the underwriters insured and how they developed their portfolios over time.

Before jumping into the analysis, it is important to note I am not the first to have undertaken this exercise. Working with Rémi Mathieu at the *Archives nationales*, Boiteux compiled the table below, documenting the Chamber's overall activities.

Table 9 The amounts underwritten by the Chamber in *livres* in the years 1668–79, alongside the premiums garnered and the losses incurred, according to Boiteux.[17]

Year	Total underwritten	Gross premium income	Total losses
1668	1,030,700	69,500	6,000
1669	1,909,300	103,600	7,500
1670	3,012,400	169,400	146,700
1671	4,334,600	239,600	16,000
1672	6,100,000	427,000	556,800

[17] For full explanation, critique and correction, see the text.

1673	1,633,000	170,000	124,500
1674	2,368,000	240,000	70,000
1675	2,283,000	230,000	90,000
1676	2,896,000	290,000	55,000
1677	2,822,000	245,000	7,000
1678	1,529,000	76,500	10,000
1679	2,405,000	120,000	100,000
Total	32,323,000	2,420,600	1,175,600

Source: Boiteux, *L'assurance maritime à Paris*, p. 43.

This table raises several questions. While the Chamber's underwriting grows annually up to 1672, its losses appear inexplicably random. Following Boiteux's numbers, losses remain low in 1668 and 1669, but then shoot up in 1670, before dropping again dramatically in 1671. With no war in 1670 to explain this aberration, and no explanation forthcoming from Boiteux, I was forced to evaluate his methodology.

In creating this table, Boiteux explains that he used the marginalia in the Chamber's policy registers, which recorded whether a vessel had arrived safely or encountered an incident, to determine the losses. He acknowledged that the resulting data could not account for averages; although he claims averages 'were rare and generally of little cost', this is still a notable omission in the data.[18]

More significantly, he does not acknowledge that the marginalia are not consistent across the registers – in other words, not every policy has a recorded outcome. We cannot assume that these policies without marginalia are subject to the idiom 'no news is good news', since the Parisian admiralty court records[19] reveal policies without marginalia where losses occurred and were pursued in the court.

Table 10   The number of policies signed by the Chamber in the years 1668–72 and the number of these without marginalia noting the insured vessel/vessels' fate.

Year	Number of policies	Number without marginalia	%
1668	364	88	24.2
1669	523	64	12.2
1670	727	35	4.8
1671	977	162	16.6
1672	1,563	373	23.9
Total	4,154	722	17.4

[18]   Boiteux, *L'assurance maritime à Paris*, p. 46. For a counter to Boiteux's perspective, based on the Company's data, see Chapter 6.
[19]   See Chapters 7 and 8.

Table 11 The totality of the Chamber's underwriting in the years 1668–72.

Year	Total underwritten	Number of policies	Gross premium income (range)*	Recorded losses	Extrapolated losses	Recorded gross profit (range)	Extrapolated gross profit (range)	Recorded return on capital at risk (%)	Extrapolated return on capital at risk (%)
1668	998,130	364	67,454	5,600	7,388	61,854	60,066	6.65	6.45
1669	1,824,250	523	98,828	11,400	12,984	87,428	85,844	5.07	4.98
1670	3,023,102	727	174,175	73,500	77,206	100,675	96,969	3.54	3.40
1671	4,726,072	977	≥ 265,000	131,200	157,314	≥ 133,800	≥ 107,686	≥ 3.00	≥ 2.41
			≤ 265,260			≤ 134,060	≤ 107,946	≤ 3.01	≤ 2.42
1672	6,086,089	1,563	≥ 582,950	614,258	807,172	≥ -31,308	≤ -168,964	≥ -0.57	≤ -3.10
			≤ 638,208			≤ 23,950	≥ -224,222	≤ 0.44	≥ -4.07
Total	16,657,643	4,154	≥ 1,188,408	835,958	1,062,064	≥ 352,450	≥ 126,344	≥ 2.28	≥ 0.82
			≤ 1,243,926			≤ 407,968	≤ 181,862	≤ 2.65	≤ 1.18

* This column, alongside others, has a range because the Chamber began signing policies with war augmentation clauses in 1671. For more on these, see below.

Source: ATR, based on data from Z/1d/75-78, AN.

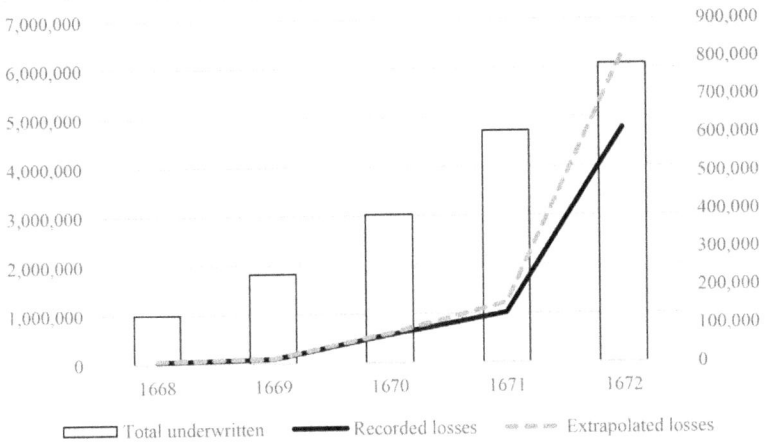

Chart 1 The amounts insured by the Chamber in the years 1668–72 in *livres*, alongside recorded and extrapolated losses.

Source: ATR, based on data from Z/1d/75–78, AN.

Each year has a different percentage of policies without marginalia. My working hypothesis was that this asymmetry was creating year-to-year aberrations (put another way, the registers were significantly understating losses for some years but not for others) that risked making the registers useless for judging losses over time.

In fact, this was not the case. Table 11 is the product of my own data analysis for the years 1668 to 1672. Unexpectedly, the AveTransRisk data diverge quite extraordinarily from Boiteux's in three key respects:

1. In 1670, I find recorded losses totalled 73,500 *livres*, while Boiteux records losses almost double this figure.

2. In 1671, I find the Chamber's underwriting was 400,000 *livres* greater in volume than Boiteux notes. Moreover, I note losses of 131,200 *livres*, as opposed to the 16,000 *livres* recorded by Boiteux.

3. In 1672, I find the Chamber's gross premium income was at least 160,000 *livres* greater than Boiteux suggests.

My corrections help us to make greater sense of the Chamber's underwriting: 1670 is no longer an aberration that needs to be accounted for; now it fits comfortably into the 1668–72 trend whereby, as time progressed, the Chamber's underwriting increased in volume, as did its losses.

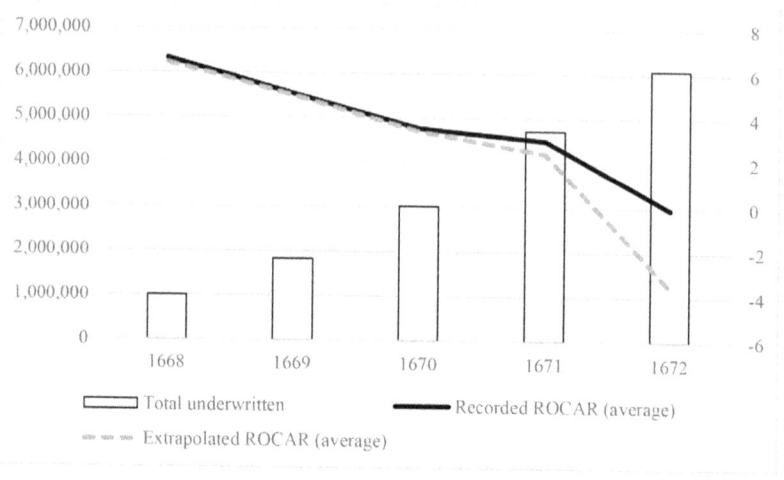

Chart 2 The return on capital at risk in the Chamber in the years 1668–72, in per cent, alongside the total underwritten each year for the same period, in *livres*.*

*For full explanation, see the text and Table 11.
Source: ATR, based on data from Z/1d/75–78, AN.

Table 11 and Chart 1 provide both the recorded losses and an 'extrapolated' set of losses. By adjusting the recorded losses based on the percentage of policies without marginalia in each year, these data would, I hypothesised, reveal any notable abnormalities in the recorded data.

There are no such abnormalities: the extrapolated loss data follow the same trends as the recorded loss data. Chart 2 documents the rates of return on capital at risk in the Chamber (hereafter ROCAR rate) using both sets of data. This is calculated as follows:[20]

$$\frac{\textit{Gross premium income – recorded or extrapolated losses}}{\textit{Total underwritten – gross premium income}}$$

The recorded data do not create any unexpected surprises: the extrapolated losses only suggest that the recorded losses are unduly optimistic in 1672. So long as we keep this in mind, we can make good use of the recorded data.

---

[20] This calculation is applied to similar effect in the analysis of Puttevils and Deloof, 'Marketing and Pricing Risk'.

The calm before the storm: 1668 to 1671

On 2 May 1668, the treaty of Aix-la-Chapelle brought an end to France's war with Spain over territory in the Spanish Netherlands.[21] On the exact same day, the first policies were signed in the Chamber.[22] The period 1668 to 1671, during which France was at peace, gave the Chamber's underwriters a window to underwrite without the risks of war.

To study the nature of these voyages, I have categorised ports/countries/regions by different sea and ocean spaces. This is not simply the unconscious reflex of an avowed Braudelian: it is a conscious analytical decision, acknowledging the different economic arenas in play and the diversity of risks pertaining to each over time. The results are displayed in Table 36 of Appendix 1.[23]

The table is based on the concept of 'touches'. Put simply, a port or place is considered 'touched' if it serves as a port of origin, a port of destination and/or a waypoint in an insured voyage. In the Chamber's policies, voyages described could include 'or' constructions, meaning places could be 'potentially' touched; to avoid confusion, these are included in the table without being distinguished. In the hypothetical voyage below, La Rochelle would be recorded twice in Table 36, while Guadeloupe and Nantes would each be recorded once. Of course, only one option could obtain in reality – La Rochelle *or* Nantes – but without further information, we cannot ascertain either way. Moreover, insurance is taken out precisely because the vessel might not have reached either port in the first place. Thus, rather than being representative of concrete economic activity, we must treat these data as hypothetical voyages that indicate *planned* economic activity and connections. Touches are dated based on the date of the policy.

La Rochelle → Guadeloupe → La Rochelle or Nantes

The Chamber insured voyages touching a total of 258 different named places up to 1672. Its underwriting was overwhelmingly Atlantic in scope: of the 11,009 touches recorded in Table 36, Atlantic France, the eastern Atlantic and the western Atlantic accounted for 9,232 (almost 84 per cent) of them. Atlantic France alone accounted for 6,167 (56 per cent) of touches, with Nantes, Bayonne, Bordeaux, Le Havre, La Rochelle and Rouen being the most touched ports.

Cádiz, Lisbon, Bilbao, San Sebastián and Pasaia were the most commonly touched ports in the eastern Atlantic.[24] These touches often, but not always,

---

[21] On the conclusion of the War of Devolution, see P. Sonnino, *Louis XIV and the Origins of the Dutch War*, Cambridge: Cambridge University Press, 1988, pp. 9–28.
[22] ATR.
[23] Appendix 1 can be found online at boybrew.co/wade-appendices.
[24] Voyages to Greenland for whaling were also commonly insured, as we will see below.

came in voyages that connected France to Spanish- and Portuguese-American commercial networks.

In the case of Cádiz, commerce revolved around the Spanish silver fleet – and so did the Chamber's policies. This was very much in keeping with Colbert's interest in the Cádiz trade as a significant source of specie. Goods – in particular, French linen – were regularly smuggled on board ships bound for the Americas, and French merchants were reimbursed when the silver fleet returned. 'Frequently', Cole notes, 'this payment was made directly and illegally, without landing or registration of the silver'.[25]

The Chamber seemed to directly support this illicit trade. On 19 April 1669, the underwriters signed four policies worth 33,800 *livres* on 'the admiral' and the 'vice-admiral' of 'the fleet of New Spain', i.e. the Spanish silver fleet.[26] Here, the underwriters bore the risks on the silver and cochineal loaded on the vessels for their voyages from Veracruz to Spain, in which the Malouin merchant Jean Magon de la Lande[27] or any unnamed parties had a stake. The Chamber continued to insure voyages like this in later years; in this way, the Chamber supported the Colbertian goal of bringing New World silver into France by any means necessary.[28] Yet the Chamber did not only underwrite French interests in the silver fleet: in 1671, they also insured a total of 48,000 *livres* of interest that policyholders from Cádiz and Genoa had in the fleet.[29]

Besides Veracruz, common fixtures in the Chamber's underwriting included Buenos Aires, Cartagena, Havana and Honduras. Outside the Spanish empire, voyages touching Portuguese Brazil were infrequently insured, as were those touching English imperial territories such as Virginia, New England, Jamaica and Barbados. Strikingly, the voyages of the *Hoope of England* and the *Anne of London* from Barbados to England and Vlissingen were insured in Paris in 1669 rather than (exclusively) in London. Moreover, in 1671, the Chamber insured return voyages from France to Jamaica – voyages that would, on the surface, have breached France's 'exclusive system', which prohibited French vessels from trading with non-French Caribbean territories.[30] Such activities reflect the simple

---

[25] Cole, *Colbert*, vol. I, p. 405; Hillmann, *The Corsairs of Saint-Malo*, pp. 32–4.
[26] Z/1d/75, fol. 87v, AN.
[27] We will encounter Magon again in Chapter 8.
[28] A year later, the Chamber underwrote 6,000 *livres* for Julien Magon, another Malouin merchant, for his share in the silver and cochineal on these vessels for the same journey to Spain. In 1671, the Chamber underwrote 16,000 for an anonymous policyholder's share in the silver and gold loaded on the vessels of the admiral and captain of the silver fleet; ATR.
[29] ATR.
[30] Ibid.

reality that, despite the French state's desire to restrict access to colonial commerce (echoed in England through the Navigation Acts), Atlantic empires were inherently trans-imperial spaces. It is therefore no surprise that trans-imperial underwriting was at the core of the Chamber's activity.

Nevertheless, the French colonies figured far more prominently in the Chamber's underwriting. As we will see below, the Chamber frequently insured Newfoundland fishing voyages. When vessels were insured for voyages to the French Caribbean, many policies did not specify precisely where they were going – the generic phrase *les îles de l'Amérique* seemed sufficient, perhaps to give ample freedom for smuggling – but some were more specific: Guadeloupe, Saint-Domingue (modern-day Haiti), Saint Kitts and Martinique were the most common destinations.

As we saw in Chart 1 above, the Chamber's underwriting grew consistently from year to year up to 1672. Touches in each sea/ocean space grew accordingly over time. The Chamber's ROCAR rate fell steadily with each passing year, but even in 1671, the recorded rate of 3.00–3.01 per cent and extrapolated rate of 2.41–2.42 per cent remained higher than the average ROCAR rate of Antwerp's underwriters in peacetime in 1562–63 (2.30 per cent).[31] With the issuing of the institution's by-laws in December 1671, the Chamber looked set to truly take off in 1672.

Riding out the storm? The Chamber's underwriting in 1672

This was not to be. In 1672, everything fell apart with the onset of the Dutch War.

This war was a long time coming. By June 1669, Colbert was aware that Louis XIV sought war with the Dutch. Colbert's attempts to shift treaty negotiations with England away from a continental invasion towards a triple alliance with Portugal against the VOC in the East Indies were in vain, as were his efforts to encourage Louis to postpone the continental war indefinitely while Colbert's commercial projects bore fruit.[32] The 1670 Secret Treaty of Dover, which tied England into a military alliance with France against the Dutch, made war almost inevitable.

Within this volatile state of affairs, the Chamber was well placed. Bellinzani had Colbert's ear and was abreast of all war developments as *intendant du commerce* in the secretariat of state for maritime affairs. On 19 February 1672 – almost two whole months before war was declared on 7 April

---

[31] Puttevils and Deloof, 'Marketing and Pricing Risk', p. 826. The comparison cannot be exact, of course, because averages are not included in the Chamber data.

[32] P. Sonnino, 'Jean-Baptiste Colbert and the Origins of the Dutch War', *European Studies Review* 13 (1983), pp. 4–6; Ames, *Colbert*, pp. 66–88.

– Bellinzani announced to the Chamber that war was imminent.[33] Yet this only confirmed what the Chamber had already presumed: already on 28 November 1671, it had issued the first of many insurance policies including a war augmentation clause, requiring the policyholder to pay a stipulated increase in the premium in the event of the outbreak of war.[34] Nevertheless, through Bellinzani, the Chamber's underwriters were being kept informed of the shifting climate in the early part of the year.

In the face of war, it was entirely commonplace for early modern underwriters to withdraw immediately from the market in order to mitigate the risk of losses.[35] Yet many underwriters chose to commit to their portfolios: as we will see below, forty-five underwriting entities signed twenty-five or more policies in the course of the year. By the time Bellinzani made his announcement on 19 February, the Chamber had already issued thirty-two policies that month, with an average premium augmentation of just over 100 per cent of the original premium; for the rest of the month, the institution continued with this practice. In March, the final full month before war was declared, augmentations continued to increase in size, with some augmentations hitting over 266 per cent.[36] With these clauses, the underwriters hoped they would be able to withstand the imminent outbreak of war. By the time war was declared on 7 April, the underwriters had already underwritten over 1.6 million *livres* for the year.

Table 12   The minimum, maximum and mean augmentations on policies with war augmentation clauses in the Chamber in the months November 1671–March 1672, as a percentage of the original premium.

Month	Policies with augmentation clauses	Min	Max	Mean
November 1671	1	20	20	20
December 1671	2	16.67	16.67	16.67
January 1672	3	63.64	100	81.21
February 1672	61	40	125	101.58
March 1672	117	25	266.67	154.74

Source: ATR, based on data from Z/1d/75–78, AN.

[33] Z/1d/73, fols 18v–20v, AN; Colbert wrote to the ports on the same day to share the same information; Cole, *Colbert*, vol. I, p. 386.
[34] For policies with these clauses, see ATR. Such clauses were widely used in Cádiz in the late eighteenth century; Baskes, *Staying Afloat*, p. 227.
[35] A. Addobbati, 'L'assurance à Livourne au XVIIIe siècle, entre mutualisme et marché concurrentiel', in C. Nuñez (ed.), *Insurance in Industrial Societies: Economic Role, Agents and Market from the Eighteenth Century to Today*, Seville: Universidad de Sevilla, 1998, p. 17.
[36] See Table 12.

Fortune and Failure in the Royal Insurance Chamber, 1668–72   147

The insurers did not scale back their underwriting with the outbreak of war. By the time the year was out, they had signed over a thousand further policies, totalling more than 4.4 million *livres*. They clearly hoped higher premium rates would make up for the inevitable increase in losses. The mean premium rate had dropped to a remarkably consistent rate in the years 1669 to 1671 after a tentative opening year. This rate more than doubled in 1672, factoring in war augmentations. Although this is a crude measurement that does not factor in shifts in insured routes or insured effects over time, the effect of the war is evident in any case.

Table 13   The mean premium rate on the Chamber's policies (calculated both with and without war augmentations factored in) in the years 1668–72.

Year	Mean premium rate (without war augmentations)	Mean premium rate (with war augmentations)
1668	6.57	–
1669	5.30	–
1670	5.22	–
1671	5.26	5.26
1672	10.23	11.15

Source: ATR, based on data from Z/1d/75–78, AN.

This strategy failed overall, with the Chamber's recorded ROCAR rate hovering around zero.[37] Once we factor in averages and non-recorded losses, the Chamber was surely in the red for the year overall.

Certainly, the early months of the war had taken their toll on the French maritime world. Dutch privateers targeted the Atlantic coastline of France as well as the colonies in the Caribbean and Canada.[38] Meanwhile, the Anglo-French fleet failed to defeat the Dutch navy at Solebay in early June. The stalemate at Solebay prevented the landing of English troops which could have precipitated the rapid capitulation of the United Provinces in place of the long, protracted retreat of the French which followed.[39] The impact on French commerce was predictable: according to the extant records of the Dutch admiralties, Dutch privateers were able to make 640 captures

---

[37] See Chart 2.
[38] On this, see R. Barazzutti, 'Les Néerlandais du Centre-Ouest français au Canada: des relations particulières au XVIIe siècle', in M. Augeron, J. Péret, and T. Sauzeau (eds), *Le golfe du Saint-Laurent et le Centre-Ouest français. Histoire d'une relation singulière (XVIIe–XIXe siècle)*, Rennes: Presses universitaires de Rennes, 2010, pp. 123–37.
[39] Levillain, *Vaincre Louis XIV*, pp. 174–5.

and ransoms in the years 1672 to 1674.[40] Granted, this does not distinguish between French and English losses, but it is clear the French were routinely harassed on the coasts. Indeed, the duc de Chaulnes claimed in a letter of 13 August 1672 that 'the entire kingdom suffers and cries because of the frequent captures that the Dutch and Zeelander privateers are making'.[41] It was inevitable the Chamber's underwriting would suffer as a result of this ubiquitous elevation of anthropogenic risk.

Indeed, the Chamber's losses came from varied sources. A total of 1563 policies were signed in 1672. Losses were recorded on 189 of these, totalling 614,258 *livres*; 184,450 *livres* (30 per cent) came from just fourteen policies, each worth 10,000 *livres* or more.

Table 14   The Chamber's fourteen largest policies which resulted in total loss in 1672.

Date of policy	Amount underwritten	Insured voyage
28 January 1672	21,500	La Rochelle to Malta
19 March 1672	20,000	Lisbon to Marseille and La Rochelle
19 August 1672	15,200	Bayonne to Lisbon, return
9 August 1672	14,650	Venice to Cádiz
14 June 1672	14,100	Venice to London
15 January 1672	14,000	Rouen to Bayonne
11 January 1672	12,000	Villefranche to Rotterdam
26 March 1672	12,000	Le Havre to Livorno, return
26 April 1672	11,000	Pasaia to Greenland and France
15 June 1672	10,000	Bayonne to Rouen
18 June 1672	10,000	Cape Chapeau Rouge to Bilbao
1 October 1672	10,000	Bordeaux to Lisbon
17 October 1672	10,000	French Caribbean to Normandy
17 October 1672	10,000	Greenland to France

Source: ATR, based on data from Z/1d/75–78, AN.

Although losses came from all over, three niches in the Chamber's underwriting in 1672 drew especially frequent losses: Newfoundland, Greenland and the Mediterranean.

Newfoundland was a unique space: the island was inhabited by the French, whose capital was Placentia; the English, whose major settlement was St

---

[40] R. Barazzutti, 'La guerre de course hollandaise sous Louis XIV: essai de quantification', *Revue historique de Dunkerque et du littoral* 37 (2004), pp. 269–80.
[41] Quoted in ibid.

John's; and the indigenous Beothuk and Mi'kmaq peoples.[42] Centuries before it was colonised, Newfoundland had already been a major fishing space for Europeans. By the end of the seventeenth century, French colonists typically specialised in coastal fishing – producing dried cod – while metropolitan French fishing ships came to the Grand Bank each year, typically bringing 'green' cod (which was salted but not dried) back to Europe.[43] Some ships came back to France directly, while others – especially those from Saint-Malo – sailed into the western Mediterranean to sell cod there and then load goods for a return voyage to France or Amsterdam.[44]

The Chamber had already insured these voyages in their various configurations before 1672, but the outbreak of war saw them take centre stage in its underwriting. Fishing ships usually left France between February and June; after fishing off the coast of Newfoundland, they then typically left to return to France between August and October.[45] On cue, the Chamber started signing policies for Newfoundland on 11 February, and by the end of June the underwriters had signed fifty-eight policies, almost all of which were on return voyages. A lull followed until August, when, like clockwork, a new flurry of policies were signed. By this point, war was in full force, and the Newfoundland fleets were out of position: they needed to return home, but the threat from Dutch privateers was great. By the end of October, a further 126 policies had been signed. From the 205 policies signed for the year, sixty-one (29.8 per cent) included coverage of sea loans on the voyages, reflecting the significant capital resources that had been devoted to these voyages.[46]

[42] On the Beothuk and Mi'kmaq peoples in Newfoundland, see S. Manning, 'Contrasting Colonisations: (Re)storying Newfoundland/Ktaqmkuk as Place', *Settler Colonial Studies* 8 (2017), pp. 314–31.

[43] Here, see N. Landry, 'Échanges entre une colonie et un port métropolitain: Plaisance (Terre-Neuve) et La Rochelle, 1688–1713', in M. Augeron, J. Péret, and T. Sauzeau (eds), *Le golfe du Saint-Laurent et le Centre-Ouest français. Histoire d'une relation singulière (XVIIe–XIXe siècle)*, Rennes: Presses universitaires de Rennes, 2010, pp. 107–21. Malouin expeditions were the key exception to the rule, typically opting for coastal fishing in order to prepare dried cod for the Mediterranean market; Hillmann, *The Corsairs of Saint-Malo*, pp. 29–30.

[44] A. Lespagnol, 'Saint-Malo, les Malouins et Marseille. Une relation particulière', in X. Daumalin, D. Faget, and O. Raveux (eds), *La mer en partage. Sociétés littorales et économies maritimes XVIe–XXe siècle*, Aix-en-Provence: Presses universitaires de Provence, 2016, pp. 181–93; J. Delumeau, 'Méthode mécanographique et trafic maritime: les terre-neuviers malouins à la fin du XVIIe siècle', *Annales. Economies, sociétés, civilisation* 16 année (1961), p. 671.

[45] Landry, 'Échanges entre une colonie et un port métropolitain', p. 117; A. Zysberg, 'Les terre-neuvas honfleurs au temps du Roi-Soleil (1665–1685)', *Annales de Normandie* 68 année (2018), pp. 107–8.

[46] On the costs of Newfoundland fishing voyages (and comparison of these costs with those of other types of voyage), see Hillmann, *The Corsairs of Saint-Malo*, pp. 85–90.

Table 15 The number of policies signed in the Chamber each month in 1672 for voyages touching Newfoundland, Placentia or Cape Chapeau Rouge.

Month	Number of policies signed
January	–
February	12
March	19
April	5
May	4
June	18
July	4
August	20
September	59
October	47
November	14
December	3

Source: ATR, based on data from Z/1d/75–78, AN.

These policies left their mark on the Chamber's underwriting in 1672: only Bordeaux, Bayonne, Nantes, La Rochelle and Le Havre were touched more often than Newfoundland that year.

The losses mounted. Colbert acknowledged in October 1672 that the fleets of Saint-Jean-de-Luz and Ciboure had been captured on their return from Newfoundland. The fleets of Nantes, La Rochelle and the Channel ports, however, had apparently emerged unscathed.[47] The Chamber certainly did not: from the 205 Newfoundland policies, seventy-six losses were recorded totalling 154,651 *livres*, vastly outstripping the 56,608–63,938 *livres* garnered in premiums. These losses singlehandedly accounted for a quarter (25.2 per cent) of the total recorded in 1672.

The Chamber also chose to insure risky whaling voyages off the coast of Greenland. Whales were a source of multiple materials, including whale oil (used to make soap) and whalebone. Even with war looming, vessels continued to be equipped for the voyages and sent on their way. From March until the end of May, policyholders sought coverage for return voyages to Greenland. From June onwards, with the onset of war and the need for vessels to come back to France or Spain, policyholders sought coverage for these one-way voyages, ensuring flexibility in their policies by securing terms that allowed insured ships to return to one of many named ports. The Chamber's underwriters signed

---

[47] As Charles Woolsey Cole puts it: 'contrary winds and the pressure of other duties had prevented naval vessels from being on hand to protect them', i.e. the Newfoundland fleets: Cole, *Colbert*, vol. I, p. 387.

a total of 100 policies touching Greenland in 1672. Of these, seventy covered sea loans on the insured voyages. Eminently, creditors were willing to sacrifice some of the potential profits from their sea loans if it ensured all or part of the principal was protected.

The underwriters paid the price for underwriting these voyages: losses were recorded on eighteen of them, totalling 80,200 *livres*, while premiums from all the voyages totalled only 61,801–69,621 *livres*. Together, Newfoundland and Greenland voyages accounted for almost two-fifths (38.2 per cent) of the Chamber's losses in 1672.

The Mediterranean emerged as the Chamber's final niche in 1672, as well as its final source of major losses. Recognising that they were playing a risky game in insuring so many Newfoundland and Greenland voyages, some of the underwriters tried to diversify their portfolios by reinsuring Mediterranean voyages, where the risk profiles were different. Accordingly, touches in the Mediterranean jumped from 5.7 per cent of overall touches in 1671 to 9.9 per cent in 1672.[48] Yet these efforts backfired. The principal source of this business was Pierre de la Roche, a French merchant based in Venice who reinsured policies he signed there through Philippe Pocquelin in Paris. In total, Pocquelin secured 115 reinsurance policies for Roche in 1672, amounting to 451,205 *livres*. Premiums totalled 23,921 *livres*, but North African corsairs succeeded in a series of captures, resulting in 50,510 *livres* of recorded losses on the policies – comprising just under one-twelfth of overall losses recorded in 1672.[49] The Chamber also signed a series of standard insurance policies with Venetian policyholders, totalling 124,325 *livres*, but 22,500 *livres* of recorded losses outweighed the 11,183 *livres* garnered in premiums.[50] In the end, the Mediterranean was not the best choice in diversifying one's portfolio.

Table 16   The number of reinsurance policies signed by the Chamber, and the total amounts reinsured, in the years 1668–72.

Year	Number of reinsurance policies	Amount reinsured
1668	4	1,800
1669	3	900
1670	–	–
1671	33	101,600
1672	186	545,540
Total	226	649,840

Source: ATR, based on data from Z/1d/75–78, AN.

[48] ATR.
[49] Ibid.
[50] Ibid.

THE POWER OF THE PORTFOLIO: INDIVIDUALS, PARTNERSHIPS AND COMPANIES

It has been useful to treat the underwriters as a collective body in order to establish the broader trends that underpinned the Chamber's activity and its troubles in 1672. Yet it is only by shifting to the perspective of individual underwriters that we can understand why so many underwriters committed to their portfolios in 1672 rather than withdrawing from the market entirely. Underwriters were legal individuals, which allowed for the development of quite diverse portfolios. Thus, 1672 proved a disastrous year for the Chamber, but it was not disastrous for all its underwriters. The most prolific underwriters fared better than infrequent underwriters when war struck.

Fifty-three underwriting entities – forty-seven individuals and six partnerships/companies – signed more than fifty policies in the years 1668 to 1672 (i.e. an average of ten policies per year). The underwriting of these entities totalled 16,027,938 *livres*, just over 96 per cent of all underwriting in the Chamber in these years.[51] Tables 37, 38, 39, 40, 41 and 42 in Appendix 1 document this underwriting. What follows are a series of case studies, looking at underwriting entities with diverse track records.

The leading underwriter: Gilles Mignot

In early 1672, the Chamber created a table, listing its members in order of seniority. Henri Desanteul, Robert Sanson, André Petit and Jacques Rey topped the list.[52] Yet the Chamber's leading underwriter up to the end of 1672, both in capital underwritten and in the number of policies signed, was Gilles Mignot, the fifth underwriter in the table. In the years 1668 to 1672, a total of 4,154 policies were drawn up in the Chamber's registry; Mignot's signature could be found on 1,604 (38.6 per cent) of them.

It has been difficult to find information on Mignot outside the Chamber. One Gilles Mignot became a minter in the Paris Mint in 1653, and continued in this role until at least 1674; it would certainly make sense if this was the same man who underwrote in the Chamber.[53]

Mignot kept a diverse portfolio in the early years, although domestic French voyages, Newfoundland fishing voyages, Iberian voyages and French Caribbean voyages featured especially prominently. In 1672, Mignot followed (or, perhaps, set) the trend in the Chamber that year by heavily insuring Newfoundland fishing voyages, Greenland whaling voyages and

---

[51] Ibid.
[52] Z/1d/73, fols 16–17r, AN. See Chapter 1.
[53] Archives Monétaires.org [http://www.archivesmonetaires.org/inventaires/mp/F45.htm, accessed 1 October 2020]; T//1491/45, n.p., AN.

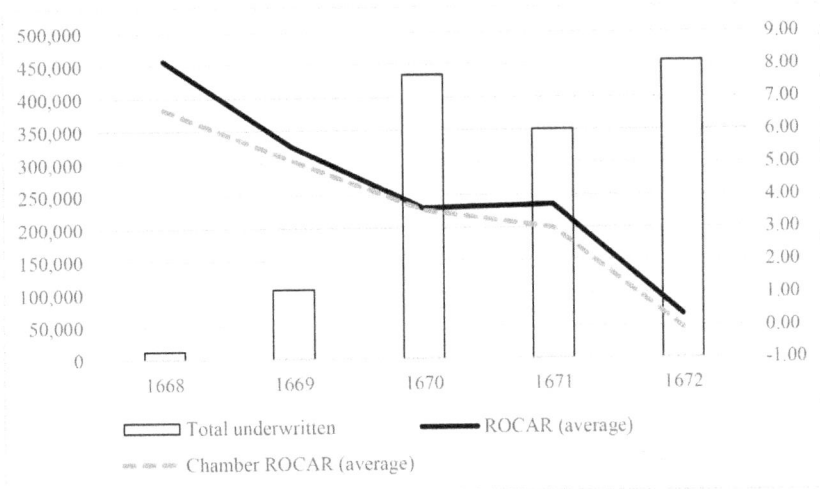

Chart 3 Gilles Mignot's underwriting in the years 1668–72, with his average return on capital at risk alongside the Chamber's average recorded return on capital at risk (in per cent).

Source: ATR, based on data from Z/1d/75–78, AN.

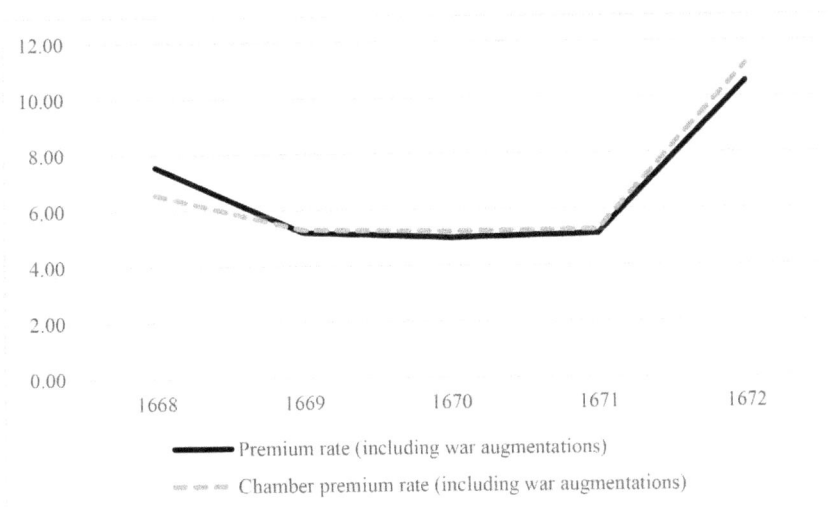

Chart 4 The average premium rate (including war augmentations) of the policies signed by Gilles Mignot in the years 1668–72, alongside the average of all the Chamber's policies.

Source: ATR, based on data from Z/1d/75–78, AN.

Mediterranean voyages touching Venice. Unsurprisingly, his losses for the year spiked, amounting to a recorded 41,583 *livres*.

Mignot's portfolio thus reflected broader trends in the Chamber. Indeed, Mignot's ROCAR rate and average premium rate (including and excluding war augmentations) tracked remarkably closely with that of the Chamber overall. Mignot's ROCAR rate consistently fell from year to year, except for a modest rise from 1670 to 1671, which corresponded with a dip in Mignot's underwriting where the Chamber's overall underwriting increased. Meanwhile, his average premium rate remained consistent throughout 1669, 1670 and 1671, before jumping (like the Chamber average) in 1672.

A widow's portfolio: Elisabeth Hélissant[54]

The first insurance policies were signed in the Chamber on 2 May 1668. Amongst those who began underwriting that day was Hugues Desanteul. But he signed his last policy only ten days later; his brother, Henri Desanteul, signed a policy on his behalf on 16 May, but before the end of the month, Hugues Desanteul had died. On 30 May, his widow, Elisabeth Hélissant, began underwriting as 'the widow of Hugues Desanteul'.[55]

A rich historiography has documented the indispensability of women in early modern credit networks.[56] Hélissant was one of many women in Paris who developed a commercial portfolio, and she was one of a handful who chose to diversify through insurance. In both 1668 and 1669, she was the sixth most prolific underwriter in the Chamber by amount underwritten, although her ROCAR rate sat below the Chamber's overall ROCAR rate in these years. Like Mignot, Newfoundland fishing voyages and Iberian voyages figured especially prominently in her portfolio.

For reasons unknown, she scaled her underwriting back in 1670. She re-emerged in the Chamber briefly in August 1671, before entrusting her brother-in-law, Henri, with her portfolio from October until the end of the year. Since her portfolio was smaller in these years, Hélissant was able to escape with no losses, leaving her a ROCAR rate higher than she had achieved in preceding years.

When she took back control of her portfolio in early 1672, she followed Mignot and the other leading underwriters in ambitiously scaling it up. The touches in her portfolio that year centred, unsurprisingly, on some of the leading Atlantic ports – namely, Le Havre, La Rochelle, Bordeaux and Bayonne – but she also underwrote Newfoundland fishing voyages heavily,

---

[54] This draws from (and is developed further in) Wade, 'Underwriting Empire'.
[55] ATR.
[56] For our purposes, on the role of women in credit networks in seventeenth-century France, see Hardwick, *Family Business*, pp. 128–82.

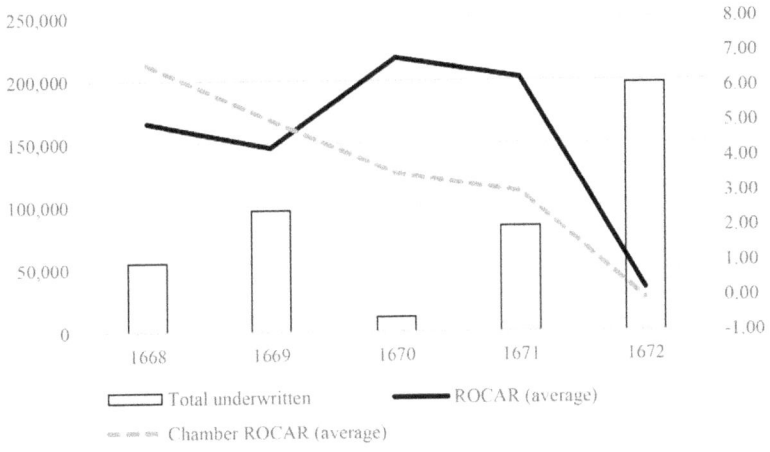

Chart 5 Elisabeth Hélissant's underwriting in the years 1668–72, with her average return on capital at risk alongside the Chamber's average recorded return on capital at risk (in per cent).

Source: ATR, based on data from Z/1d/75–78, AN.

and joined Mignot and others in insuring and reinsuring Mediterranean policies. Her losses from the year totalled 19,360 *livres*, leaving her with a ROCAR rate hovering perilously close to 0 per cent, in line with the Chamber's overall rate that year. We will see she joined her brother-in-law in trying to push her ROCAR rate back up through litigation and arbitration in 1673.[57]

When tax farmers become underwriters: the Company of General Farmers

The general farmers in the state's tax farming contract from 1668 to 1674 conducted underwriting together in the Chamber. Jacques Pollart, François Berthelot, Nicolas de Frémont and Jean-Baptiste Brunet are named throughout the Chamber's policy registers, each underwriting policies on behalf of a company comprising the general farmers.[58] There can be little doubt Colbert had a hand in this underwriting: following the 1661 Chamber of Justice, he had helped Berthelot to keep his creditors at bay in exchange for

---

[57] See Chapter 7.
[58] Z/1d/75, AN; Dessert, *Argent, pouvoir et société*. In an arbitration case from 2 September 1670, Jacques Pollart was said to have been present on behalf of 'the farmers of the united farms', where the original policy listed Pollart alone as the policyholder: Z/1d/74, fol 10v; Z/1d/75, fol 125v, AN. On tax farming, see Chapter 1.

investment in his commercial projects, including the West India Company and the *Compagnie du Bastion de France*.[59] In keeping with this, Colbert most likely pushed Berthelot and the other general farmers to maintain an underwriting portfolio in the Chamber in exchange for continued royal favour.

Table 17   The tax farmers of the united farms, 1 October 1668–30 September 1674.

André Bauyn	Étienne Landais
Antoine de Benoist	Yves Malet
François Berthelot	Daniel Morel
Jean-Baptiste Brunet	Louis Moret
Jacques Chevalier	Étienne Moulle
Claude Coquille	Antoine Pellissier
Jean Coquille	Jacques Pollart
Bernard de Cotteblanche	Pierre de Saint-André
Christophe Dalmas	Aimé Solu
Philippe Jacques	

Source: Dessert, *Argent, pouvoir et société*, p. 458.

The company started out by specialising in triangular France–Newfoundland–Mediterranean voyages, before shifting towards Cádiz voyages in 1671. Although Greenland was not a major focus of its portfolio, the loss of the *Saint Jean de Bayonne* that year to a boiler fire while whaling accounted for half of its overall losses for the year, pulling its ROCAR rate down below the Chamber's average.[60]

Up to this point, the company had stood out from the crowd in consistently making large subscriptions to the policies it signed: the company's median subscription sat at 3,000 *livres* in 1670 and 1671, amounting to six and three times the median subscription in the Chamber's policies respectively. The company was able to underwrite such large figures because it had so many members to spread losses between: the corporate form thus served as a form of risk management. This logic informed the later establishment of the Company, and would underpin the explosion of insurance companies in Europe and America in the eighteenth century.[61] Moreover, the company's average premium rate (including and excluding war augmentations) sat consistently and comfortably above the

---

[59] Dessert, *Le royaume de Monsieur Colbert*, pp. 204–11.
[60] ATR.
[61] On this, see Wright and Kingston, 'Corporate Insurers in Antebellum America', pp. 447–76; Glenn Crothers, 'Commercial Risk', pp. 607–33; Baskes, *Staying Afloat*.

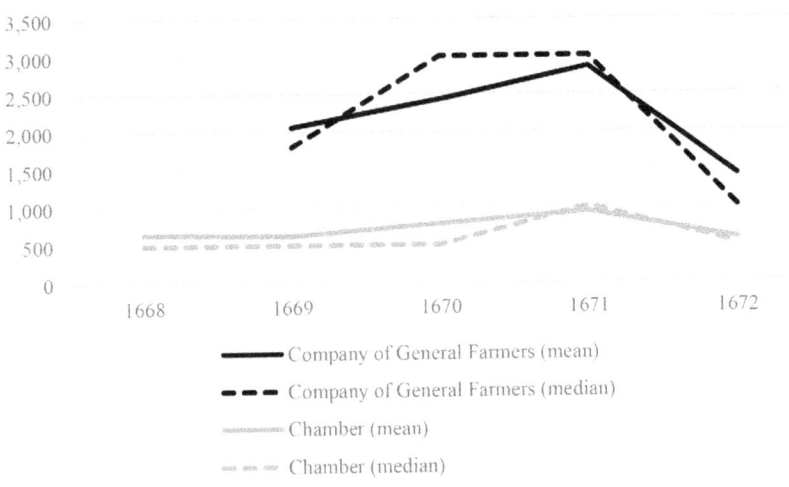

Chart 6 The Company of General Farmers' mean and median subscription in the policies it signed in *livres*, as compared with the overall mean and median subscription in the Chamber's policies from 1668 to 1672.

Source: ATR, based on data from Z/1d/75–78, AN.

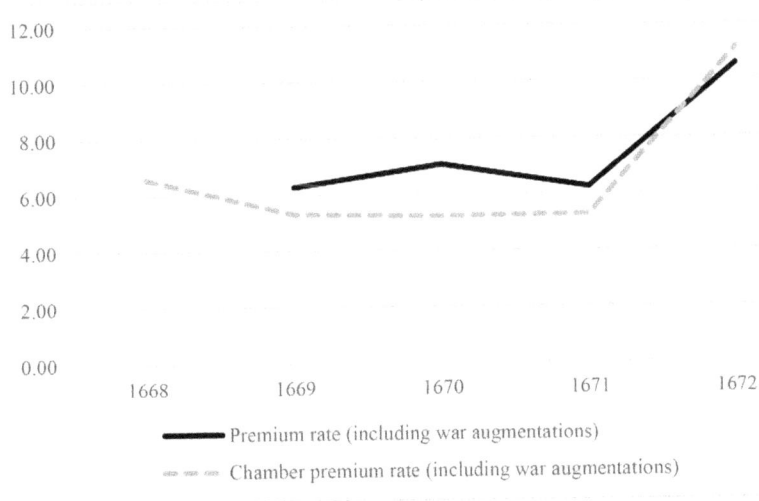

Chart 7 The average premium rate (including war augmentations) of the policies signed by the Company of General Farmers in the years 1668–72, alongside the average of all the Chamber's policies.

Source: ATR, based on data from Z/1d/75–78, AN.

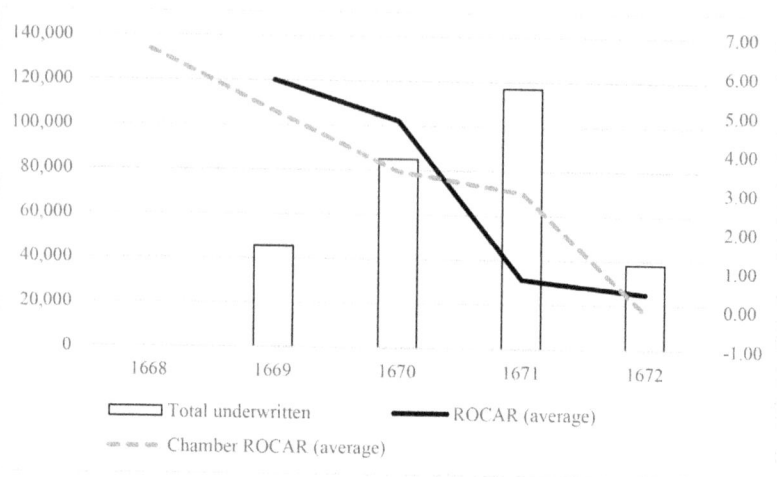

Chart 8   The Company of General Farmers' underwriting in the years 1668–72, with its average return on capital at risk alongside the Chamber's average recorded return on capital at risk (in per cent).

Source: ATR, based on data from Z/1d/75–78, AN.

Chamber average until 1672. In short, the company had consciously put together a riskier portfolio, with ample resources to absorb any losses that resulted.

Nevertheless, the company was not willing to continue this strategy into 1672. Its median subscription dropped to 1,000 *livres*, its portfolio for the year dropped from 117,000 *livres* to 38,300 *livres*, and its average premium rate fell below the Chamber average for the first time, inclusive and exclusive of war augmentations. This can almost certainly be explained by the threat, and eventual outbreak, of war. The company's average premium rate rises a remarkable 1.7 per cent when war augmentations are included. This points to its disproportionate reliance on policies with such clauses in the run up to the outbreak of war; these clauses helped to mitigate war risks for which the general farmers had little appetite. Once war was declared, they had little interest in extending their portfolio further: foreseeing the further deterioration of commerce throughout the remainder of the year, they signed their last policy on 27 June. In the policies they had signed up to this point, the general farmers had avoided Newfoundland voyages, although they had still insured a handful of Greenland whaling voyages. Despite their caution, the company's recorded losses wiped out any meaningful profits. Nevertheless, it is unlikely the general farmers were too concerned with this: with their responsibility for tax farms worth tens of millions of *livres*, the company's underwriting portfolio was very much a lesser priority.

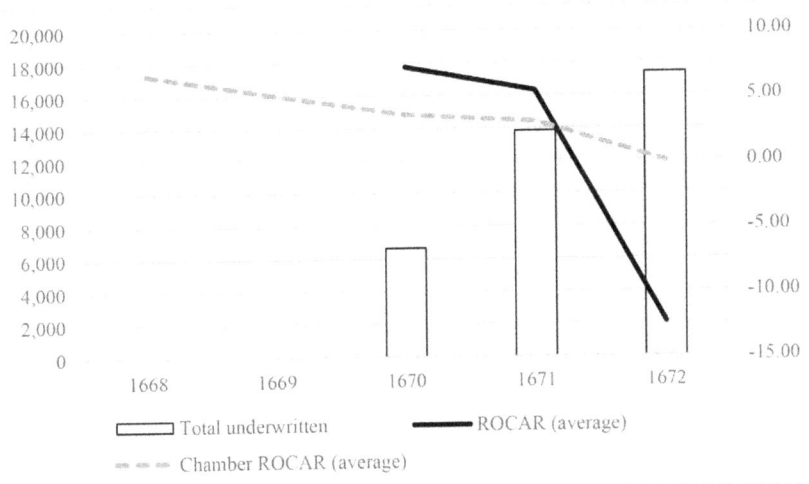

Chart 9 Guillaume de Bie's underwriting in the years 1668–72, with his average return on capital at risk alongside the Chamber's average recorded return on capital at risk (in per cent).

Source: ATR, based on data from Z/1d/75–78, AN.

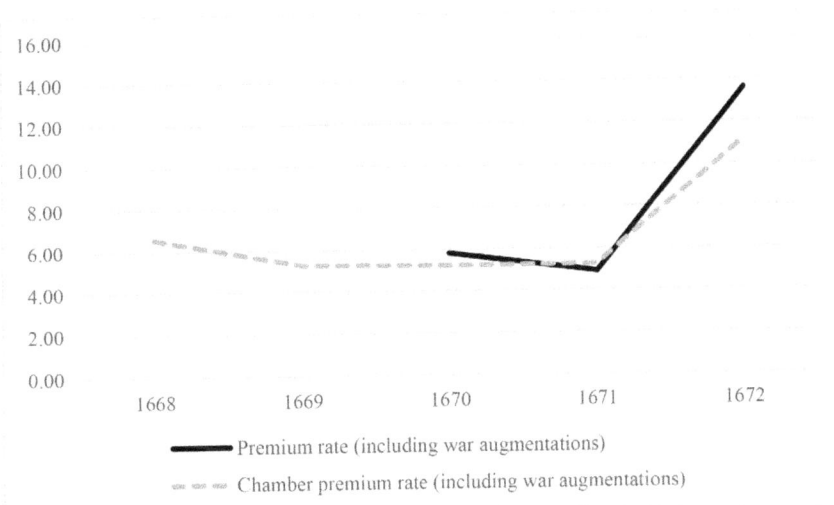

Chart 10 The average premium rate (including war augmentations) of the policies signed by Guillaume de Bie in the years 1668–72, alongside the Chamber average.

Source: ATR, based on data from Z/1d/75–78, AN.

A minor player who gets it wrong: Guillaume de Bie

Not all were as clairvoyant as the general farmers. Guillaume de Bie established a modest underwriting portfolio in 1670 and 1671, in which he specialised in voyages touching Spain (especially Cádiz) and its American colonies (Buenos Aires most prominently). This was perhaps in line with his own business interests and, therefore, his own information resources. Whatever the reason, this portfolio served him well, with no recorded losses for either year.

In 1672, however, he signed fifty-eight policies, increasing his portfolio to 17,361 *livres*. He followed Mignot and others in underwriting voyages to and from Newfoundland, Greenland and the French Caribbean. Accordingly, the average premium rate on the policies he signed shot up to 13.22 per cent (exclusive of war augmentations) and 13.59 per cent (inclusive) – over 2 cent above the average for all the Chamber's policies that year by each measure. Recognising he was taking on riskier voyages, he made smaller subscriptions to the policies he signed: his mean and median subscription dropped from 986 and 1,000 *livres* respectively in 1671 to 299 and 300 *livres* in 1672. Nevertheless, this did not shield him from losses. Having enjoyed a ROCAR rate over 2 per cent above the Chamber's average in 1670 and 1671, Bie was one of the unfortunate underwriters who suffered heavy losses in 1672, with an average ROCAR rate of −12.41 per cent.

'Enticed by gain'? Underwriting strategies in war

Bie was not alone in expanding his portfolio in 1672, nor was he alone in suffering big losses. Colbert did not hesitate to lay the blame for the year's losses at the feet of the underwriters themselves. In a letter of 3 March 1673 to M. de Sève, the intendant in Bordeaux, Colbert suggested that the underwriters, 'enticed by the gains they made in the first three or four years [of the Chamber's existence], have thoughtlessly insured everything in the past year, and as they lost [so] much, they have almost all stopped' underwriting entirely. Colbert concluded unsympathetically that 'perhaps […] those who will get involved [in insurance] in the future will have a bit more circumspection'.[62]

In justifying his assessment, Colbert would surely have pointed to Bie as a case in point. Yet while Bie's underwriting was greater in 1672 than in prior years, and the riskiness of the voyages he insured had shot up, he remained a small player in the Chamber. In fact, counter to Colbert's suggestion, those who underwrote infrequently were at the greatest risk of big losses with the outbreak of war. We can see this in Table 18 below. In 1672, forty-five underwriting entities signed twenty-five or more policies in the Chamber.

---

[62] Colbert and Clément, *Lettres, instructions, et mémoires de Colbert*, vol. II, book II, p. 675.

The table analyses the ROCAR rates of the fifteen most prolific underwriters (group 1), the fifteen least prolific (group 3) and the middle fifteen (group 2), by number of policies signed. Bie – who is in group 3 – did not fare the worst: Jean-Baptiste Forne and Isaac Pierre Jouan, who signed thirty-one policies, recorded an average ROCAR rate of −26.18 per cent. Yet M. Crommelin, who signed only twenty-five policies, was far more fortunate, with an average ROCAR rate of 13.60 per cent.

Table 18 The mean, median, minimum and maximum ROCAR rates (as an average of each underwriter's minimum and maximum ROCAR rate) of the three underwriting groups in 1672, and the standard deviation of these rates.

	Group 1[63]	Group 2[64]	Group 3[65]
Mean	0.08	−0.55	−4.17
Median	0.34	0.36	−2.94
Standard deviation	1.36	2.20	8.79
Minimum	−3.06	−4.67	−26.18
Maximum	2.97	2.38	13.60
Number of underwriters	15	15	15

Source: ATR, based on data from Z/1d/75–78, AN.

None of the most prolific underwriters in group 1 recorded such highs – but they did not record such lows either, and this was key. The standard deviation for the average ROCAR rates of group 1 is fairly small, while that of group 2 is somewhat larger and that of group 3 is significantly larger.

This vindicates the strategy of the most prolific underwriters and challenges Colbert's logic. The underwriters' ROCAR rates in 1672 suggest that three courses of action were possible: underwriters could insure widely,

---

[63] This comprises André Petit, Gilles Mignot, Henri Desanteul, Anne Jousse and Jean-Anthoine Vanopstal, Denis Rousseau, M. Marchand, Charles Lhuillier de Creabé, François Lefebvre, Antoine Lachasse, Alexandre Vinx, Pierre Desanteul, Jacques Rey, Elisabeth Hélissant, Jean Roussel and Louis Froment.

[64] This comprises Nicolas Formont, Simon Boirat, Nicolas Maillet, Robert Sanson, M. Herlau, Pierre Formont, Guillaume Hallé and Bonnaventure Rebillé, Étienne Rouxelin, Jacques Petit, Jacques Richard, Henri de Vaux, Jean Dumont, Étienne Suplegeau, Guillaume de la Marre and Elisabeth Lefebvre.

[65] This comprises Étienne and Simon Lenfant and Henri de Vaux, M. Maillet and company, Guillaume de Voulges, Oudard Thomas de Lisle, Claude Gueston, Étienne Margas, Guillaume de Bie, Guillaume André Hébert, Jean Bellot, Jean Marlot, Pierre Cadelan, Jean-Baptiste Forne and Isaac Pierre Jouan, the Company of General Farmers, Jean Proust and M. Crommelin.

and accept limited returns; they could insure infrequently, and accept the risks this entailed; or they could withdraw from the market entirely.[66] Far from underwriting 'thoughtlessly', as Colbert suggested, the most prolific underwriters were following a common logic in pre-modern insurance. Benedetto Cotrugli recommended in 1458 that insurers should underwrite 'continuously and upon every ship, since they [i.e. the policies] balance each other and through many policies [the insurer] makes a profit for sure'. Similarly, Daniel Defoe would write in 1697 that 'it is not the smallness of a premium [that] ruins the insurer, but it is the smallness of the quantity he insures'.[67] While it was not a fruitful year for the leading underwriters, most had avoided disaster by swapping the chance of higher returns for more predictable ones.

CONCLUSION

The Chamber was established in auspicious times: the period from 1668 to 1671 provided its underwriters with the ideal conditions to conduct profitable underwriting. The scale of the Chamber's underwriting increased consistently year on year, reflecting this growing confidence in the institution and the value of underwriting as part of a diversified commercial portfolio. In this period, the underwriters gave coverage to a diverse clientele across Europe for voyages spanning the western hemisphere. Eschewing imperial boundaries, Parisian insurers underwrote commercial interests in Spanish-, Portuguese- and English-American ventures alongside those in the French Atlantic colonies.

The Chamber's reach, and the diversity of its activities, forces us to nuance prior analyses of the Parisian capital market. In their ground-breaking work, Hoffman, Postel-Vinay and Rosenthal have argued that the capital market 'stagnated' in the seventeenth century, owing to the state's 'vicious' conduct, chiefly through manipulating the currency to suit its short-term needs. Moreover, they suggest that the decentralised nature of the capital market gave rise to significant information asymmetries, discouraging impersonal exchange.[68] It is only in the eighteenth century that credit truly took off in the city: notaries brokered long-term credit agreements that were increasingly impersonal and, as Kessler has found, the city's merchant court handled disputes over negotiable bills of exchange in a speedy manner.[69]

---

[66] Of course, this does not factor in portfolio diversity: I am not in a position to speak to this.
[67] Quoted in Puttevils and Deloof, 'Marketing and Pricing Risk', pp. 827–8.
[68] Hoffman, Postel-Vinay, and Rosenthal, *Priceless Markets*, pp. 50–68.
[69] Ibid., pp. 96–113; Kessler, *A Revolution in Commerce*.

This chapter has demonstrated that the Chamber was, in fact, Colbert's forgotten attempt at institutionalising the Parisian capital market.[70] The institution brought together the complementary insurance and credit markets, thereby offering Parisians of means the opportunity to rebalance their investment portfolio to the benefit of policyholders and creditors in the capital-starved ports of France.[71] Creditors were able to sell all, or a portion of, the risks in their sea loan portfolios to underwriters. By virtue of being a fixed space for flows of commercial information, the Chamber facilitated the mobilisation of capital for commercial endeavours far beyond the confines of Paris. Commission agents served a key role in this process: in signing a policy, commission agents offered a form of credit check on the principal, as they were accepting responsibility for the policy's outcome and execution. In this way, Parisian insurers and creditors entered into contracts with individuals across Europe whose names they did not even necessarily know, with a significant number of the Chamber's policies being signed for unnamed parties (*pour compte de qui que se puisse être* or *pour tel compte que se puisse être*).[72] Moreover, the Chamber's registrar, Lalive, acted as a financial intermediary, allowing policyholders to secure insurance policies on credit.[73] The Chamber was therefore a key institution in the execution of Colbert's commercial policy.

Yet Colbert's strategy to mobilise Parisian capital in service to the needs of commerce and industry could only work if these offered a better or comparable return – and I do not mean this in the strictly financial sense – to the state debt. As an open-access institution, the Chamber was uniquely placed in the array of Colbertian institutions to test the receptiveness of Parisians to this agenda.

Up to 1672, the Chamber fared quite well. True, its overall ROCAR rate fell year on year up to 1672, suggesting that, as they scaled up their underwriting, insurers were bearing more and more 'lower quality' risks. Nevertheless, the Chamber's ROCAR rate up to 1672 seems to have compared favourably with that of the insurers of Antwerp in 1562–63, one of Europe's great insurance centres in the sixteenth century.[74] It is not that the Chamber performed especially poorly in the early years: underwriting on any great scale simply did not generate big profits. Even for Amsterdam, Frank

---

[70] I am grateful to Cátia Antunes for drawing me towards this line of analysis.
[71] Much of what is said here applies to the Company too, although to a lesser extent as a monopoly institution.
[72] ATR.
[73] See Chapter 7.
[74] The comparison cannot be exact, because averages are not accounted for in the Chamber's dataset.

Spooner has noted that 'the margins of profits in the eighteenth century were often astonishingly narrow'.[75]

This was not an inherent flaw in the Chamber's model or in Colbert's strategy. Underwriting in the Chamber did not need to beat the financial returns on the state debt: they were very different types of investment. Capital invested in the state debt had to be provided up front, while the capital at risk in an underwriting portfolio was only relinquished as and when losses were incurred. The flexibility of underwriting, combined with the modest returns it offered, ensured it was only ever going to be a supplementary activity, i.e. one of many that Colbert hoped capital-rich Parisians would engage in in developing their commercial portfolios. The 'soft' benefits of membership – namely, flexible access to royal power[76] – gave non-financial 'returns' that further incentivised underwriters to keep up their portfolios.

This logic fell apart in 1672 with the onset of war. While individual performances varied, the ROCAR rate in the Chamber overall plummeted. For infrequent underwriters, underwriting became a true gamble, albeit one where large losses were far more likely than large profits. By contrast, the most prolific underwriters were protected by the size of their portfolios, but this came at the expense of good returns. Although 1672 did not inflict the sort of crippling damage previously suggested by Boiteux, who greatly understated the Chamber's gross premium income for the year, there remained little incentive for many underwriters to continue throughout the rest of the war. The 'soft' benefits of membership alone could not make up for negative or meagre returns, and there was little sense the underwriters would fare better in 1673 or thereafter, with the end of war coming only in 1678. Moreover, the Chamber's underwriters were subjected to a glut of court cases in 1673, which surely disincentivised underwriting further.[77]

Predictably, the war took its toll on Colbert's companies too. While the *Heeren XVII* of the VOC sent supplies to reinforce Batavia even as the French army poured into the Republic, Colbert proved unable to persuade Louis to send reinforcements to support the CIO in India. With no support in sight, M. de la Haye was forced to surrender San Thomé – a recent and promising acquisition on the Coromandel Coast – to the Qutb Shahi-Dutch alliance in September 1674. The CIO struggled to recover from this

---

[75] Spooner, *Risks at Sea*, p. 5; see also A. Addobbati, 'Italy 1500–1800: Cooperation and Competition', in A. Leonard (ed.), *Marine Insurance: Origins and Institutions, 1300–1850*, Basingstoke: Palgrave Macmillan, 2016, pp. 60–1.
[76] See Chapter 1.
[77] See Chapter 7.

dramatic setback.[78] The Northern Company had also suffered from the Dutch War and was ultimately forced to sell its assets.[79]

Meanwhile, just as commerce was becoming a precarious investment, the state debt became very lucrative indeed. Colbert had reduced the interest rate on *rentes* in 1665, arguing that profits for annuitants were 'excessive' and deterred investment in commerce and manufacturing.[80] Yet with the onset of war in 1672, and the need to tap into private capital to cover war expenses, Colbert was forced to issue new *rentes* on the *Hôtel de Ville* with an interest rate of 5.5 per cent.[81]

The outbreak of war had thus proven a disaster for French commerce, and Colbertianism more broadly. Even so, it need not have been a fatal blow to the Chamber: the history of early modern insurance is replete with tales of capital shocks that damaged key insurance markets.[82] Put simply, capital shocks are an occupational hazard of underwriting, and while the war was damaging, that is only part of the story. There were still underwriters who wanted to continue underwriting, and more could have been encouraged back over time, especially with the end of war in 1678. With only fifty-three regular underwriting entities in the years up to 1672, the Chamber had barely penetrated the surface of Paris' deep well of capital. What the underwriters lacked after 1672 was business, thanks to key institutional weaknesses. Understanding these weaknesses will be the focus of Chapter 7.

Now, however, we will turn to the Company, which faced some familiar challenges – and some unfamiliar ones indeed.

[78] Ames, *Colbert*, pp. 165–85.
[79] Boissonnade and Charliat, 'Colbert et la Compagnie de Commerce du Nord', p. 194.
[80] Quoted in M. Moulin, 'Les rentes sur l'Hôtel de Ville de Paris sous Louis XIV', *Histoire, économie et société* 17 (1998), p. 627.
[81] Sonnino, *Louis XIV and the Origins of the Dutch War*, p. 184.
[82] For example, on the 1693 Smyna disaster and its impact on the Amsterdam and London markets, see Go, 'Amsterdam 1585–1790', p. 121.

5

IN THE ABSENCE OF THE STATE: THE ROYAL INSURANCE COMPANY, THE ATLANTIC EMPIRE AND NEUTRAL SHIPPING, 1686–98[1]

The historian wishing to understand the Company's portfolio faces numerous challenges. In the first place, its policy registers do not seem to have survived. However, article XVIII from the Company's articles of association obliged the registrar to keep an alphabetical register with 'the names of the ships, people, sums and dates' of the institution's insurance policies and sea loans.[2] In this way, the registrar would be able to warn the directors if they had already insured, or loaned money for, a particular risk[3] before signing further contracts on it.

This register has survived. Each risk is listed on a single line: all insurance policies and sea loans pertaining to it are listed, with their dates and the sums involved conventionally given.[4]

This register is the basis for a dataset quite different from the Chamber's: while I used the policy as the central unit of analysis for the Chamber, the Company's register requires using the risk itself as the central unit. Unfortunately, the

---

[1] Like Chapter 4, this chapter is based primarily on the analysis of one of two datasets, which is accessible online on the AveTransRisk website; AveTransRisk [http://humanities-research.exeter.ac.uk/avetransrisk, accessed 26 April 2020]. I am once again grateful to Ian Wellaway for his efforts in designing the database based on my needs (and those of my colleagues on the AveTransRisk team) and working with me to facilitate data analysis.

[2] Bornier, *Conférences des ordonnances de Louis XIV*, vol. II, pp. 513–25.

[3] Here, I define a 'risk' as any particular combination of vessel, voyage and policyholder/debtor.

[4] There are rare omissions of some details throughout the register. Boiteux mistakenly attributes this alphabetical register to the Chamber rather than the Company in his chapter on the Chamber, but then correctly attributes it to the Company later; Boiteux, *L'assurance maritime à Paris*, pp. 39 and 61.

register does not record the premium/interest rate for each insurance policy and sea loan, nor the insured effects. This chapter therefore cannot offer any insights on the Company's overall returns. Nevertheless, the dataset is invaluable for studying the strategies the Company pursued in its business. Indeed, when used in conjunction with the Company's surviving records for claims,[5] it is possible to develop a rich analysis of its losses over time.

This chapter builds on Chapter 2 in finding that the Company was treated as a tool of commercial policy. Thanks in large part to the *de facto* Atlantic monopoly the Company was granted in 1687, its insurance portfolio grew from less than half a million *livres* in 1686 to over three million in 1691. However, the outbreak of the Nine Years' War in 1688 saw it taking on risky voyages in sea and ocean spaces where the state was unable to offer support itself. Claims rose rapidly after 1689, which sealed the Company's fate.

THE COMPANY'S PORTFOLIO AND THE MECHANICS OF MERCANTILE RISK MANAGEMENT

This chapter uses the same 'touches' methodology as the last chapter to study the Company's portfolio. In the course of its existence, the Company's portfolio touched 178 different named places across the world.[6]

The Company was, at least on the surface, an Atlantic creature like the Chamber. In the course of its existence, French Mediterranean ports were touched eighteen times less frequently in its risks than French Atlantic ports – and less frequently than any other Atlantic space beyond France. In part, this can be explained by Marseille's indifference towards the institution: while the port was the most touched port in the Company's portfolio in 1687 – most likely a result of Augustin Magy's intervention[7] – it never figured significantly thereafter. Perhaps Marseille's insurance market was able to cater sufficiently to demand in the port; perhaps Marseillais merchants found it inconvenient arranging coverage so far away; perhaps, renowned as they were for their deep-seated suspicion of the crown, they simply distrusted the Company as a product of state intervention; most likely, all played a role. It certainly did not help that French Mediterranean and Mediterranean touches figured disproportionately in claims in the

---

[5] Strictly, these are declarations of average and/or abandonment; for more on these, see Chapter 6. For brevity and the avoidance of unnecessary confusion, I am using 'claim' here to mean both insurance claims and declarations made to justify non-payment of sea loans.
[6] See Table 43 of Appendix 2 online at boybrew.co/wade-appendices.
[7] See Chapter 3.

early years, which explains the increasingly marginal role of these spaces in the Company's portfolio at the turn of the decade.[8]

Atlantic France was the Company's bread and butter: La Rochelle, Dunkirk, Nantes, Saint-Malo, Rouen, Bordeaux, Le Havre and Dieppe were the eight most touched ports in the Company's entire portfolio. We will see below that Seignelay helped to secure business from these ports. Nevertheless, the directors felt comfortable underwriting commercial activity in even the smallest ports.

Lisbon, Cádiz, Bilbao, Dublin and Limerick were frequent destinations in the eastern Atlantic. Voyages touching Cape Verde and Guinea were triangular voyages, suggesting the Company, like the Chamber, insured the Atlantic slave trade.[9]

Nevertheless, ports in the western Atlantic (i.e. the Americas) were touched over twice as often as eastern Atlantic ports in the Company's portfolio. This is all the more striking when we acknowledge that the western Atlantic data is systematically understated, owing to the tendency for policies to simply state a voyage's destination as the French Caribbean (the *îles de l'Amérique*) rather than specify the numerous Caribbean ports which vessels typically touched in such voyages.

Thus, the Company was a major underwriter of France's Atlantic empire. Where voyages to the French Caribbean were specified, Martinique and Saint-Domingue figured prominently, as did voyages to French Guiana (and specifically to Cayenne). Looking north, Québec was a common destination and, following in the Chamber's footsteps, the Company underwrote Newfoundland fishing voyages, with a notable peak with the outbreak of war in 1688 (see below).

Strikingly, besides a voyage from Nzwani in the modern-day Comoros and two voyages from Lisbon to Goa, the Indian Ocean did not figure at all in the Company's portfolio. This can surely be attributed to the close ties between the Company and the CIO, which held a monopoly on all French trade east of the Cape of Good Hope. The CIO's monopoly limited the number of French ships entering the Indian Ocean; moreover, there was a significant overlap between the memberships of the two companies.[10] It would therefore have made no sense for the CIO to insure with the Company on any regular basis.

---

8   See below, and Charts 18 and 19 in Appendix 2.
9   ATR. On the Chamber's underwriting of the Atlantic slave trade, see Wade, 'Underwriting Empire'.
10 See Chapter 2.

Table 19 The individuals who signed policies/sea loans with the Company on more than fifty separate risks in the years 1686–98.

Individual	Number of risks
Guillaume Bar	247
Guillaume André Hébert	201
Alexandre Lallier	180
Antoine Pelletier	167
Jean Gellée	143
Nicolas Desanteul	87
Thomas Tardif	71
Gerard Mollien	59
Jacques and Antoine Lescouteux	56
Jean Ducamp	56
Louis Michel Hazon	51

Source: ATR, based on data from Z/1d/85, AN.

Commercial networks across France facilitated the Company's underwriting. Indeed, many provincial policyholders relied on the services of a core group of commission agents in Paris, who had diverse ties to the ports of France and beyond. The policies and sea loans on 1,318 separate risks – just over half of the total, 2,453 – were signed by the individuals in Table 19 above. The alphabetical register does not tell us whether each of these was signed for their own account or for the account of others, but in the 304 claims these gentlemen made in the years 1686 to 1692,[11] they were noted as making these in their own name alone in only fourteen cases.[12] We can therefore conclude with confidence that, in the vast majority of cases, they were serving as commission agents, negotiating and signing policies on behalf of principals outside of Paris. Five of these eleven commission agents – Bar, Hébert, Pelletier, Tardif and Mollien – were themselves members of the Company, thereby double dipping in the institution's activities by adding commission fees to any share dividends. While Lallier was a professional financial broker in the city and controller general of the *rentes* of the *Hôtel de Ville de Paris*, Gellée, Desanteul, Ducamp, Hazon and the Lescouteux were merchants who made use of their commercial ties to the provinces to offer their services.[13] Some had deep connections to specific ports, while others had looser ties to several ports: Ducamp made all his claims on behalf

---

[11] For more on these claims, see Chapters 6 and 8.
[12] Z/1d/82 and Z/1d/88, AN.
[13] Z/1d/82, fols 1v–2r, 18r, 27v, 40r and 54r; Z/1d/110, n.p., AN.

of principals in Saint-Malo, Gellée on behalf of principals in Rouen, Abbeville, Marseille, Brest, Roscoff, Honfleur and Dieppe.[14]

These commission agents could negotiate one or multiple insurance policies and/or sea loans with the Company on the same risk. While 1,770 of the 2,453 risks had only a single insurance policy or sea loan attached to them, 683 – just over a quarter – received multiple policies and/or sea loans. In two cases, policyholders held nine insurance policies with the Company on the same risk. Without the full policies, it is hard to ascertain precisely what motivated such behaviour, especially since the policies do not seem to follow any patterns. The absence of such patterns suggests the desire to receive further coverage was the result of exogenous factors: policyholders possibly received new information over time that prompted them to secure more coverage, perhaps with different premium rates for each policy to reflect the changing circumstances. What is striking is that the Company was willing to indulge these requests, bearing greater liabilities on the same risk with each policy signed.

Table 20 The frequency of multiple policies and/or sea loans on a single risk, based on the Company's insurance and sea loans practices from 1686 to 1700.

Number of policies/loans	Frequency
1	1,770
2	443
3	142
4	52
5	29
6	10
7	4
8	1
9	2
Total	2,453

Source: ATR, based on data from Z/1d/85, AN.

Nevertheless, these groups of policies totalled only 17,840 and 36,100 *livres* respectively. The Company signed individual policies worth more than this, albeit not on a frequent basis. In evaluating the scale of the Company's activities, Boiteux claims the Company's maximum risk appetite was only 50,000 *livres*, compared with the Chamber's appetite of 100,000 *livres*.[15] In fact, the Company signed a policy worth 102,200 *livres* on 14

---

[14] Z/1d/82 and Z/1d/88, AN.
[15] Boiteux, *L'assurance maritime à Paris*, p. 64.

January 1688.[16] This aside, we should not assume the size of an insurance institution's risk appetite corresponded to the significance of its activities. Signing large policies on a frequent basis could go horribly wrong, especially in periods of war. Even in the eighteenth century, several insurance companies in France limited their maximum risk appetite: Clark finds that one of the Parisian companies limited its policies to 30,000 *livres* on either the vessel or its cargo, despite a capital far larger than that of the Company.[17] Rather than being an indictment on the Company's activities, its tendency towards smaller policies reflects prudent portfolio management.

Indeed, the directors only rarely engaged in the especially risky practice of underwriting and giving sea loans on the same risk. Where this happened, it was typically for voyages to the French colonies – namely, the Caribbean and Canada, including Newfoundland fishing – which involved significant upfront investments. In these instances, the Company was mobilised to support colonial commerce where capital markets in the ports fell short. Nevertheless, only sixty-nine of the 2,453 risks in which the Company had an interest received both insurance and sea loans, so this was not a regular occurrence.

Table 21 The frequency of specific types of contract being taken out on a single risk (whether in single or in multiple), based on the Company's insurance and sea loans practices from 1686 to 1700.

Type of contract	Frequency
Insurance alone	2,320
Sea loan alone	64
Insurance and sea loan	69
Total	2,453

Source: ATR, based on data from Z/1d/85, AN.

WAR, EXPOSURE AND STATE INTERESTS, 1686–1700

Tables 22 and 23 summarise the key figures from the Company's register. In total, it attests to 3,549 insurance policies and sea loans on 2,453 separate risks.

These tables are essential to understanding the Company's underwriting. The outbreak of war saw French commerce face threats on all fronts, with

---

[16] Z/1d/85, fol. 47v, AN.
[17] Clark, 'Marine Insurance in Eighteenth-Century La Rochelle', pp. 576–7. One Rochelais company, Clark finds, limited its policies to 40,000 *livres* per vessel. On the same practice in eighteenth-century Cádiz, see Baskes, *Staying Afloat*, pp. 179–255.

Table 22 The amounts underwritten by the Company and the number of policies it signed, alongside the largest, smallest, median, mode and mean policy in the years 1686–98, in *livres*.*

Year	Total underwritten	Number of policies	Largest	Smallest	Median	Mode	Mean**
1686	478,166	117	23,500	300	2,100	1,500	4,158
1687	1,491,356	286	40,000	300	3,000	3,000	5,251
1688	1,901,135	426	102,200	100	1,800	200	4,473
1689	1,392,734	427	45,000	200	2,000	2,000	3,269
1690	2,801,588	610	46,800	150	3,000	3,000	4,631
1691	3,420,920	673	35,000	200	3,000	2,000	5,207
1692	2,369,080	549	60,000	270	3,000	2,000	4,420
1693	852,302	226	26,000	300	3,000	3,000	3,983
1694	148,500	52	10,200	300	2,000	2,000	2,912
1695	10,400	4	4,700	700	2,500	N/A	2,600
1698	170,000	39	10,600	800	3,000	3,000	4,359
Total/overall	15,036,181	3,409	102,200	100	2,900	2,000	4,480

* NB policies where the amount insured was not stated have been removed in calculating the largest, smallest, median, mode and mean policy.

** This has been rounded to the nearest whole number.

Source: ATR, based on data from Z/1d/85, AN.

Table 23 The amounts given by the Company as sea loans and the number of such loans it gave, alongside the largest, smallest, median, mode and mean loan in the years 1686–94, in *livres*.*

Year	Total loaned	Number of loans	Largest	Smallest	Median	Mode	Mean**
1686	45,800	16	10,000	500	2,000	2,000	2,863
1687	90,475	35	12,000	450	2,000	3,000	2,585
1688	81,500	31	7,000	750	2,100	1,500	2,911
1689	20,040	10	6,000	300	1,100	1,000	2,004
1690	55,600	19	6,000	500	3,000	3,000	2,926
1691	34,340	15	6,000	800	1,900	1,500	2,453
1692	21,350	6	8,350	1,500	2,750	2,000	3,558
1693	4,700	4	1,600	600	1,250	N/A	1,175
1694	6,700	4	4,000	600	1,050	600	1,675
Total/overall	360,505	140	12,000	300	2,000	2,000	2,651

* NB loans where the amount loaned was not stated have been removed in calculating the largest, smallest, median, mode and mean loan.

** This has been rounded to the nearest whole number.

Source: ATR, based on data from Z/1d/85, AN.

significant implications for underwriting. Yet, at least on paper, the Company was uniquely qualified to respond to these changing circumstances. As Kingston has observed: 'to assess risks in wartime [...] what mattered most was information about systematic risks, such as the activities of enemy privateers, the disposition of the prize courts, and other political and military developments that could increase the risks to all ships simultaneously'.[18] In every single respect, the Company had an unprecedented advantage over other underwriters in France: Lagny had access to all information flows in the secretariat of state for maritime affairs and wielded considerable power in commercial decision making.[19] Through his information network, he received updates on the activities of enemy privateers and warships, and he had full knowledge of the secretariat's naval decision making.

By 1695, however, the Company had stopped underwriting, owing to the losses it had sustained. How are we to understand this? This section offers some answers by analysing the development of the Company's underwriting portfolio over time. The Company's portfolio was not fuelled by commercial prudence, but by the state's desire to protect especially vulnerable areas of commerce in this precarious period.

The early years: putting the state to the test

The Company got off to a slow but steady start in its opening year. We saw in Chapter 3 that, initially, port merchants were reluctant to insure in Paris. Seignelay and Lagny wrote to leading merchants to encourage them to promote the Company. Besides Marseille, which figured strongly in the Company's underwriting portfolio in 1687, these efforts seem to have made little impact. By the end of 1686, the Company had underwritten only 478,166 *livres*. At the end of August 1687, the figure for the year stood at 721,750 *livres* – already a marked improvement on the year prior, to be sure, but still modest.

Decidedly unimpressed with this tepid response from France's merchants, Seignelay responded on 16 September 1687 by writing to Dunkirk, Saint-Malo, Rouen, Bordeaux, Bayonne, La Rochelle and Nantes to issue a ban on all foreign insurance: merchants who could not find local coverage were henceforth compelled to seek the Company's support.[20]

Was this intervention successful? The Company's register does not detail the location of policyholders, so a direct assessment is not possible. Nevertheless, we can indirectly trace the Company's coverage of maritime

---

[18] C. Kingston, 'America 1720–1820: War and Organisation', in A. Leonard (ed.), *Marine Insurance: Origins and Institutions, 1300–1850*, Basingstoke: Palgrave Macmillan, 2016, p. 220.
[19] See Chapter 3.
[20] See Chapter 2.

activity in these ports by analysing the number of times each port was touched in the year before Seignelay's intervention and in the three subsequent years.

Table 24 The frequency of Atlantic ports being touched (or potentially being touched) in the course of risks which the Company insured and/or to which it gave sea loans, for given periods between 1686 and 1689.*

Place	Touches, 17 September 1686–16 September 1687	Touches, 17 September 1687–16 September 1688	Touches, 17 September 1688–16 September 1689	Touches, 17 September 1689–16 September 1690
Dunkirk	47	21	31	78
Saint-Malo	7	19	44	37
Rouen	50	57	49	28
Bordeaux	12	22	53	43
Bayonne	5	9	7	4
La Rochelle	44	37	72	98
Nantes	18	24	58	108
Total	183	189	314	396

* NB the 'touches' are categorised per year based on when the risk was first insured or when a sea loan was first given.

Source: ATR, based on data from Z/1d/85, AN.

Originally, Seignelay's intervention had little effect. In the first year, Dunkirk touches plummeted, while Saint-Malo, Rouen, Bordeaux and Nantes recorded modest increases, leaving only a slight increase on the year prior.

The following year was the turning point. With the outbreak of war in September 1688, it is likely that, while the demand for insurance coverage grew, mutual underwriting in the ports began to dry up.[21] In normal circumstances, merchants might have looked to Amsterdam as an alternative source of coverage, since its market was well equipped to withstand war losses. Indeed, some merchants likely circumvented Seignelay's ban and took their business there in any case. For those who did not want to risk royal condemnation, however, the Amsterdam market was no longer an option.

This left the Company in Paris as the main alternative, as Seignelay had intended all along. In the two years following the outbreak of war, the Company underwrote, or gave loans to, voyages which touched the Atlantic

[21] Addobbati, 'L'assurance à Livourne', p. 17.

ports with far greater frequency. Seignelay's attempt to funnel business to Paris ultimately proved successful.

1688–89: war and the Atlantic

As the Company's coverage of interests in these ports grew, so did its underwriting more broadly. In 1688, with the outbreak of war, the Company's portfolio grew by almost 27.5 per cent from the year before, while the number of policies it signed increased by 49 per cent. Its mode policy dropped from 3,000 *livres* in 1687 to 200 *livres* in 1688, alongside a drop of almost 800 *livres* in its mean policy.[22]

The Company therefore adjusted its strategy, spreading risks across many smaller policies. Despite this, it suffered its first great set of losses in 1689. Claims jumped over 300 per cent to 113 and continued to climb thereafter.

Table 25 The number of policies signed, and the amounts underwritten, by the Company in the years 1686–89, alongside the number of claims in those years.

Year	Total underwritten	Number of policies	Claims*
1686	478,166	117	6
1687	1,491,356	286	27
1688	1,901,135	426	28
1689	1,392,734	427	113

* For a full discussion of this column, see Chapters 6 and 8.

Source: Z/1d/82, Z/1d/85 and Z/1d/88, AN.

From the outset, the war took its toll on French trade. Despite Seignelay's ambitions, the navy was simply not ready at the outbreak of war, with shipyards in disarray for lack of vital resources and the Colbertian system of inscription proving unable to meet the minister's demands.[23] Moreover, the naval fleet which *could* be mobilised had been stationed in the Mediterranean in the summer of 1688, leaving the Atlantic coastline exposed with the outbreak of war.[24] Even when there was a naval presence in the Atlantic, losses to privateers and warships were common. Based on extant records from the Dutch admiralties, 47 per cent of all French ships the Dutch

---

[22] While 1688 saw the Company sign its largest policy in its history – 102,200 *livres* – this came on 14 January, several months before war broke out; ATR.

[23] D. Pilgrim, 'The Colbert-Seignelay Naval Reforms and the Beginnings of the War of the League of Augsburg', *French Historical Studies* 9 (1975), pp. 242–3.

[24] Levillain, *Vaincre Louis XIV*, p. 355; Symcox, *The Crisis of French Sea Power*, pp. 74–5.

captured during the war were seized in the Bay of Biscay itself, despite efforts to establish modest naval convoys between the Atlantic ports.[25] Seignelay had masterfully funnelled business towards the Company from these ports, but war losses inescapably followed.

Atlantic France is only part of the story, however. I have created a series of charts displaying the presence of each sea/ocean space in the Company's risks and its claims. These once again draw on the 'touches' methodology, but in slightly different ways. While we have seen that the 'risks' data draw from the touches in every voyage the Company insured and/or to which it gave a sea loan, the 'claims' data draw from the touches in the voyages described in every claim. For example, if a hypothetical vessel was described in a claim as having been insured for 'a return voyage from La Rochelle to Newfoundland', La Rochelle would be recorded twice in the 'claims' data and Newfoundland once.[26]

We can see in Chart 11 below that touches from Atlantic France always figured pre-eminently in the Company's risks, but touches in its claims always tracked closely in percentage terms.[27] Moreover, the Company's tendency to insure return voyages (like the hypothetical voyage above) means Atlantic France's significance in both datasets is exaggerated to an extent. Undeniably, Atlantic France played a large role in losses throughout the war – it was the commerce of Atlantic France that was overwhelmingly being insured – but it is shifts in other parts of the Company's portfolio that help us to fully understand why claims spiked in 1689 and continued to climb thereafter.

The Company's portfolio shifted dramatically towards the western Atlantic in 1688, with touches in that space jumping from 10 per cent in 1687 to almost 20 per cent the following year.[28] Western Atlantic touches in the Company's claims spiked the year after – reflecting the length of

---

[25] Barazzutti, 'Les Néerlandais', p. 114; É. Delobette, 'Les mutations du commerce maritime du Havre, 1680–1730. Première partie', *Annales de Normandie* 51 année (2001), p. 12. For more on English and Dutch privateering during the war, see G. Clark, *The Dutch Alliance and the War Against French Trade 1688–1697*, New York: Russell & Russell, 1971, pp. 44–62.

[26] This would not change even if the vessel was described as having been seized on the outward leg. Thus, for the purposes of this exercise, the location of any incident is immaterial (not least since it is rarely stated). To see this in action, see Table 44 in Appendix 2.

[27] For Atlantic France, 1689 and 1690 are the exceptions that prove the rule: touches in the portfolio spiked in 1689, and touches in the claims followed suit in the following year.

[28] In the coming pages, I provide charts tracking the presences of the western Atlantic, the eastern Atlantic and the North Sea in the Company's risks and claims. For charts from the remaining sea spaces (excluding the Indian Ocean), see Appendix 2.

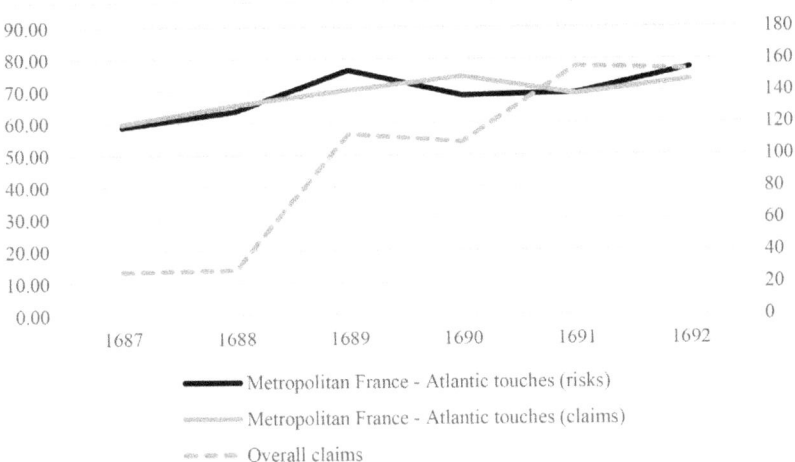

Chart 11 Touches in Atlantic France as a percentage of overall touches in the risks which the Company insured and/or to which it gave sea loans and as a percentage of overall touches in voyages that led to claims from the years 1687–92, compared with the raw number of claims in this period.

Source: Z/1d/82, Z/1d/88 and ATR, based on data from Z/1d/85, AN.

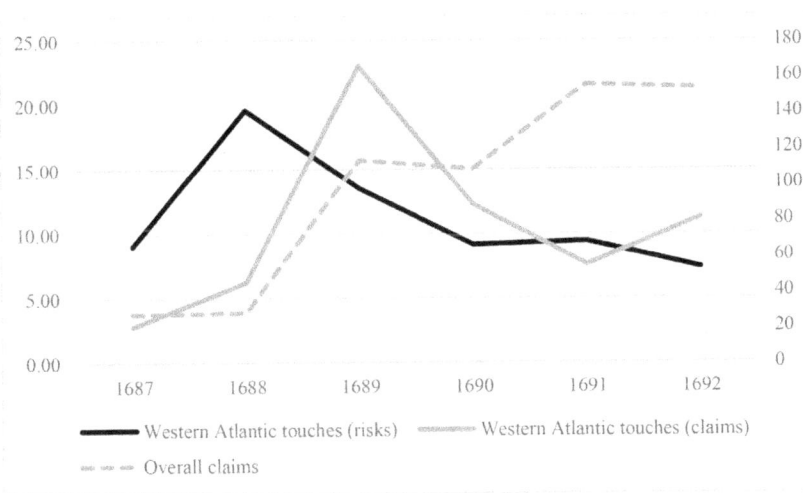

Chart 12 Touches in the western Atlantic as a percentage of overall touches in the risks which the Company insured and/or to which it gave sea loans and as a percentage of overall touches in voyages that led to claims from the years 1687–92, compared with the raw number of claims in this period.

Source: Z/1d/82, Z/1d/88 and ATR, based on data from Z/1d/85, AN.

transatlantic voyages and the time lag in the movement of information across such a distance – and now comprised almost a quarter of all touches.

Three locations in the western Atlantic stood out in the Company's portfolio in 1688: the French Caribbean,[29] Newfoundland and French Guiana. French Guiana (including Cayenne) was touched forty times in the Company's portfolio that year (out of a total of 122 touches in the western Atlantic). Despite this, Cayenne specifically was only touched in two claims in 1689, and French Guiana not at all.

Instead, touches in the claims came overwhelmingly from the Caribbean and Newfoundland. The state regarded its West Indian colonies as crucial to its economic and geopolitical interests, since these colonies were situated on the doorstep of Spanish America.[30] Nevertheless, by the start of the war, colonial society was being forged through sugar cultivation rather than trade with Spanish America. In the case of Saint-Domingue, this cultivation was being sustained by a 400 per cent increase in the number of enslaved people in the colony in the years 1684 to 1700. This cultivation would make the colony's fortunes in the eighteenth century.[31] None of this would have been possible if France had failed to maintain control over Saint-Domingue throughout the war and secure Spain's recognition of French sovereignty over the colony in 1697. The challenging waters of Newfoundland, by contrast, were crucial for training sailors capable of sustaining French commerce and serving in the French navy.[32] Sustained disruption to Newfoundland fishing voyages throughout the war would thus have risked economic damage to the Atlantic ports, the exacerbation of harvest failures during the 1690s and long-term

---

[29] My discussion here includes the Caribbean colonies named in the Company's portfolio (Guadeloupe, Martinique, etc.).

[30] D. Chaunu, 'Route des Indes ou îles esclavagistes? La "pénétration commerce de l'Amérique espagnole" à l'épreuve de la diplomatie des îles sous Louis XIV', in É. Schnakenbourg and F. Ternat (eds), *Une diplomatie des lointains. La France face à la mondialisation des rivalités internationales, XVIIe–XVIIIe siècles*, Rennes: Presses universitaires de Rennes, 2020, pp. 115–34.

[31] G. Venegoni, 'Creating a Caribbean Colony in the Long Seventeenth Century: Saint-Domingue and the Pirates', in L. Roper (ed.), *The Torrid Zone: Caribbean Colonization and Cultural Interaction in the Long Seventeenth Century*, Columbia: University of South Carolina Press, 2018, pp. 136–7; P. Hrodĕj, 'L'établissement laborieux du pouvoir royal à Saint-Domingue au temps des premiers gouveneurs', in G. Le Bouëdec, F. Chappé, and C. Cérino (eds), *Pouvoirs et littoraux du XVe au XXe siècle*, Rennes: Presses universitaires de Rennes, 2000, pp. 168–9. For more on French West Indian trade in the eighteenth century, see Pritchard, *In Search of Empire*.

[32] Hillmann, *The Corsairs of Saint-Malo*, p. 31.

challenges in meeting the needs of the navy at a time when the *classes* system was already being stretched beyond its limits.³³

Nevertheless, the secretariat of state for maritime affairs was slow to send support to both regions following the outbreak of war. By the end of 1688, news had already reached Seignelay that privateers were pillaging France's Caribbean colonies, but only in March and April 1689 did he dispatch warships to protect the colonies and their trade. With the French fleet needed back at home in 1690 to face off against the Anglo-Dutch fleet – culminating in the French victory at Beachy Head in July – colonial leaders were widely left to defend the islands with their own resources.³⁴ In response, Pierre-Paul Tarin de Cussy, governor of Tortuga and Saint-Domingue, had to turn to the Company for support in provisioning the islands, securing Gabriel Apoil as a commission agent in Paris to insure the merchandise on at least two ships that were ultimately lost: the *Constance*, having set sail from La Rochelle, was seized off the coast of Saint-Domingue by the English in late March 1690; the *Françoise*, on its return to La Rochelle after completing the outward leg of its journey to Saint-Domingue, was seized on 19 July by a Vlissinger frigate, fifteen leagues from the Île-d'Yeu.³⁵ Both vessels were thus lost agonisingly close to the conclusion of their journeys; to cap off his woeful fortune, Cussy died in an engagement with the Spanish in early 1691.³⁶ Naval convoys to the Caribbean were introduced only later in the war.³⁷

Newfoundland fared no better: shortly after the outbreak of war, Louis XIV appointed Jacques-François de Monbeton de Brouillon as the new governor of Placentia and recalled the incumbent governor, Antoine Parat. Brouillon arrived in Newfoundland only in June 1691, after Parat had already abandoned his post in September 1690. The first French naval squadron to sail to Newfoundland reached Placentia only in 1692.³⁸ In the meantime, cod fishers were left vulnerable during their voyages. On 7 March 1689, Pierre Levier came to 16 *rue Quincampoix* to submit claims on three Newfoundland fishing vessels which suffered the same fate: on their return journeys to Le Havre, the *Saint Sauveur*, the *Saint Louis* and the

---

33   D. Degroot *et al.*, 'Towards a Rigorous Understanding of Societal Responses to Climate Change', *Nature* 591 (2021), p. 546; Pilgrim, 'The Colbert-Seignelay Naval Reforms', p. 247.
34   Pritchard, *In Search of Empire*, pp. 306–15.
35   Z Z/1d/82, fols 63r and 68r, AN. For how colonies relied on metropolitan France for food provisions for both planters and enslaved people, and the problems that arose from this, see Mandelblatt, 'How Feeding Slaves Shaped the French Atlantic'.
36   Pritchard, *In Search of Empire*, p. 315.
37   Delobette, 'Les mutations du commerce maritime', p. 12.
38   Pritchard, *In Search of Empire*, p. 347.

Saint Nicolas de Grace were all seized between November 1688 and January 1689. The latter two were seized by the Dutch and taken to Plymouth, with the *Saint Nicolas de Grace* then being taken on to Vlissingen.[39] Despite the losses faced on these return journeys, vessels continued to venture out towards Newfoundland: the *Oranger*, leaving Honfleur in a convoy of fishing ships, was seized by two English warships on 22 May 1689, destined to join the *Saint Louis* in Plymouth while the crew were sent to Guernsey as prisoners of war.[40]

While France's colonies were being left to fend for themselves, the English were establishing the roots for a rather different approach, instituting convoys for North Sea voyages alongside some – although certainly not all – of the most lucrative overseas trade routes.[41] More than eighty-five warships were committed to guarding tobacco convoys to and from the Chesapeake Bay in the years 1690 to 1715. London's underwriters supported the Royal Navy's efforts here by requiring vessels to sail in these convoys, with lower premiums offered to policyholders in compensation for the mitigated risk. While the Company was making up for the absence of the French navy in the western Atlantic, the London insurance market and the Royal Navy were beginning to work hand in hand during the war in pursuit of their mutual interests.[42]

Unsurprisingly, insuring Caribbean and Newfoundland voyages did not serve the Company well. Touches in the French Caribbean in the Company's claims in 1689 reached thirty-seven, while Newfoundland accounted for another sixteen. Together, these comprised over 20 per cent of touches that year. This is all the more extraordinary when we acknowledge the unintended inflation of French Atlantic touches, which accounted for 70 per cent of overall touches in claims that year. Put simply, the Caribbean and Newfoundland were a disproportionate source of losses.

This underwriting strategy was not executed out of ignorance. Lagny was entirely aware of what was happening in the colonies: this was within his remit as director general of commerce. Lagny and Seignelay seemed to disagree on the extent of naval support needed for the Caribbean: after Seignelay's death in November 1690, Lagny promptly briefed Seignelay's successor, Louis Phélypeaux, comte de Pontchartrain, on the immediate need

---

[39] Z/1d/82, fols 18v–19r, AN.
[40] Ibid., fol. 26v. On trends in Newfoundland fishing voyages from Saint-Malo – with ship departures plummeting around 1689 – see Hillmann, *The Corsairs of Saint-Malo*, p. 28; Delumeau, 'Méthode mécanographique', p. 668.
[41] On the North Sea convoys, see J. Bromley, *Corsairs and Navies 1660–1760*, London: The Hambledon Press, 1987, pp. 60–2.
[42] Farber, 'Political Economy', p. 590.

for defensive reinforcement in the Caribbean.[43] Pontchartrain responded by sending a squadron from Le Havre to Saint-Domingue at the end of the year.[44] With Cussy's death in early 1691, Lagny persuaded Pontchartrain to appoint Jean-Baptiste du Casse (a former director of the Senegal Company) in his place as governor of Tortuga and Saint-Domingue.[45]

Nor was this strategy executed out of incompetence. In response to their losses in 1689, the directors made three sensible decisions: they scaled down their underwriting that year by almost 40 per cent; they decreased the share of French Mediterranean and Mediterranean touches in their portfolio;[46] and, in turn, they increased the share of French Atlantic touches,[47] thereby tailoring the Company's portfolio to a familiar ocean space where the Company could more easily and quickly gather information. Eminently, the directors recognised that their losses required a change in tack, or else the Company would follow the Chamber's lead in succumbing to war.

On paper, the directors also seemed to scale down their western Atlantic interests: touches there in their portfolio dropped considerably in 1689, and never returned to the peak witnessed in 1688. Nevertheless, this drop consisted mostly of a reduction in touches in Newfoundland (from 54 in 1688 to 18 in 1689) and French Guiana (from 37 to 0). Touches in the French Caribbean (including the individual islands named in the Company's portfolio) increased from 24 in 1688 to 67 in 1689, and remained consistently at this elevated level up to 1692. This did not seem to cause the Company notable harm: after the peak in 1689, western Atlantic touches dropped in the Company's claims relative to other sea/ocean spaces until 1692.[48] This notwithstanding, increasing the Company's exposure to Caribbean risks stands out as an aberration within an otherwise coherent set of responses to the losses sustained in 1689.

1690–92: Ireland, the North Sea and neutral shipping

The foundations of the Company had been weakened with the outbreak of war, but the years 1690 to 1692 brought it to the ground entirely. The shift in strategy that took place is displayed with remarkable clarity in Chart 13: while western Atlantic touches were trending downwards in the Company's portfolio in 1690, eastern Atlantic touches peaked, and North Sea touches were on the rise.

---

[43] See discussions of Pontchartrain in Chapters 3 and 8.
[44] Pritchard, *In Search of Empire*, p. 306.
[45] Ibid., p. 315; Chapman, *Private Ambition*, p. 137.
[46] These spaces continued to figure disproportionately in the Company's claims up to 1689; see Charts 18 and 19 in Appendix 2.
[47] See Chart 11 above.
[48] See Chart 12.

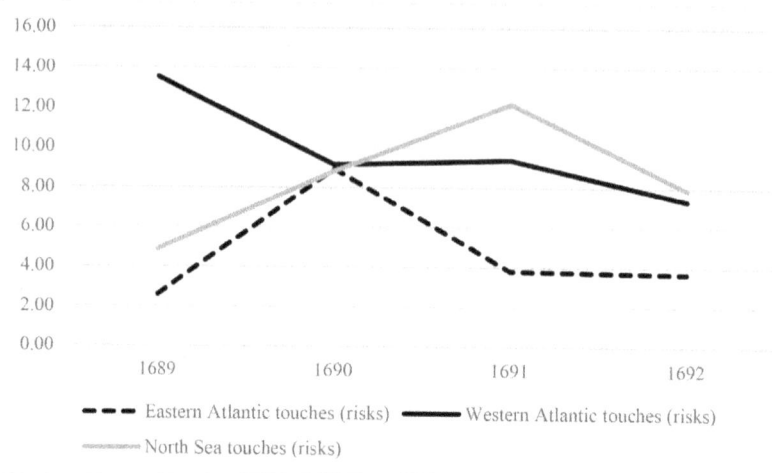

Chart 13 Touches in the eastern Atlantic, western Atlantic and North Sea as a percentage of overall touches in the risks which the Company insured and/or to which it gave sea loans for the years 1689-92.

Source: ATR, based on data from Z/1d/85, AN.

The rise in eastern Atlantic touches came almost exclusively from Ireland. With William of Orange seizing the throne of England with the so-called Glorious Revolution in November 1688, the Catholic James II was forced to flee to France in December. Here, he became a pawn in Louis XIV's war strategy: French naval policy henceforth centred on restoring James' territories on the island of Britain, and Ireland – where James still commanded significant support – became the arena for this dispute.[49]

This was not simply to be a war of weapons, but also of commerce. The comte d'Avaux – Louis XIV's ambassador extraordinary to James II – observed that one of the best ways to weaken England and to reinforce Ireland was to redirect Irish trade towards France.[50] The state thus sought to further develop Ireland's long-established ties to French commerce, hoping to draw on the connections of communities of Irish *émigrés* in ports like Saint-Malo to facilitate mutually beneficial commerce between France and Ireland.[51]

[49] B. Darnell, 'Reconsidering the *Guerre de Course* under Louis XIV: Naval Policy and Strategic Downsizing in an Era of Fiscal Overextension', in N. Rodger, J. Dancy, B. Darnell, and E. Wilson (eds), *Strategy and the Sea: Essays in Honour of John B. Hattendorf*, Woodbridge: Boydell Press, 2016, pp. 47–8.

[50] F. Boulaire, 'L'Irlande, la France et l'Europe en 1689–1690: les négociations de M. le Comte d'Avaux en Irlande', *Études irlandaises* 26 (2001), pp. 77–8.

[51] A. Lespagnol, 'Les relations commerciales entre l'Irlande et la Bretagne aux temps modernes (XVe–XVIIIe siècles). Complémentarité ou concurrence?', in C. Laurent

True to form, Lagny wrote to his commercial correspondents[52] on 9 February 1689, positing that 'the wool of Ireland is […] better than that of England', with the consequence that French trade in this would be 'strongly advantageous to the Irish and our [cloth] manufactures'.[53] He also announced that Irish butter and beef would be exempted from standard duties.[54] With these incentives, Lagny implored his correspondents to encourage merchants 'to profit from the[se] circumstances' by undertaking trade in Ireland, and demanded a list of merchants who would be willing to engage in this trade.[55] Here, commercial policy and foreign policy converged.

Lagny pursued the Irish cause throughout the year. On 22 March 1689, James II disembarked at Kinsale, and while his subsequent siege of Londonderry failed – not helped by France's meagre naval support – he held control of most of Ireland for the remainder of the year.[56] Lagny wrote to his port correspondents on 10 June that, before he had left France in February, James had given orders to allow the French to export wool from Ireland unencumbered; as a consequence, Lagny implored his correspondents to push merchants to capitalise on the opportunity.[57] He later sweetened the pot on 31 July, allowing French vessels to carry Irish beef directly to the Caribbean.[58]

---

and H. Davis (eds), *Irlande et Bretagne. Vingt siècles d'histoire*, Rennes: Terre de Brume Éditions, 1994, p. 173. On the Irish community in France, see also S. Talbott, '"Such unjustifiable practices"? Irish Trade, Settlement, and Society in France, 1688–1715', *Economic History Review* 67 (2014), pp. 556–77; Hillmann, *The Corsairs of Saint-Malo*, pp. 71–2; Bromley, *Corsairs and Navies*, pp. 144–5; É. Ó Ciosain, 'Les Irlandais en Bretagne 1603–1780: "invasion", accueil, intégration', in C. Laurent and H. Davis (eds), *Irlande et Bretagne. Vingt siècles d'histoire*, Rennes: Terre de Brume Éditions, 1994, pp. 153–66.

[52] On these, see Chapter 3.
[53] MAR/B/7/60, fols 37–8r, AN.
[54] The duties would henceforth be levied per the 1664 tariff schedule instead; ibid.
[55] MAR/B/7/60, fols 37–8r, AN.
[56] G. Clark, 'The Nine Years' War, 1688–1697', in J. Bromley (ed.), *The New Cambridge Modern History*, vol. VI, Cambridge: Cambridge University Press, 1970, pp. 235–7; Symcox, *The Crisis of French Sea Power*, pp. 85–6.
[57] MAR/B/7/60, fols 95v–6r, AN.
[58] Ibid., fol. 139r. Irish salted beef – of a higher quality than French beef, and cheaper too – became a colonial staple, in normal times imported to France and then re-exported to the French Caribbean; J. Meyer, 'La France et l'Irlande pendant le règne de Louis XIV', in C. Laurent and H. Davis (eds), *Irlande et Bretagne. Vingt siècles d'histoire*, Rennes: Terre de Brume Éditions, 1994, pp. 144–5; Lespagnol, 'Les relations commerciales entre l'Irlande et la Bretagne', p. 176; B. Mandelblatt, 'A Transatlantic Commodity: Irish Salt Beef in the French Atlantic World', *History Workshop Journal* 63 (2007), pp. 18–47.

The response was a delayed one, but merchants eventually responded with enthusiasm in 1690. In a letter to Seignelay in January, Jean Magon de la Lande noted that Irish merchants in Saint-Malo had bought ships seized by Malouin privateers and loaded them with salt, Spanish wine, eaux de vie and an array of colonial and East Indian commodities to send to Ireland. Predictably, Malouin voyages to Ireland peaked in this year, with forty-six vessels participating.[59] In keeping with this broader trend, the Company underwrote significant numbers of Irish voyages. Before 1690, there had only been a total of five touches in Ireland in the Company's portfolio; in 1690 alone, there were forty-nine.[60]

Table 26 The frequency of places on the island of Ireland being touched in the course of risks which the Company insured and/or to which it gave sea loans, for the years 1686–93.

Place	1686	1687	1688	1689	1690	1691	1692	1693	Total
Cork	–	–	–	–	11	–	–	2	13
Drogheda	–	–	–	–	1	–	–	–	1
Dublin	–	–	–	2	13	–	6	4	25
Galway	–	1	–	–	6	1	2	–	10
Ireland (generic)	–	–	–	1	3	2	–	–	6
Kinsale	–	–	–	–	1	–	–	–	1
Limerick	–	1	–	–	12	4	1	–	18
Londonderry	–	–	–	–	–	1	1	–	2
Waterford	–	–	–	–	2	–	–	–	2

Source: ATR, based on data from Z/1d/85, AN.

Lagny was heartened by this response, and his correspondence makes clear that the secretariat of state for maritime affairs was preparing for this trade to become a mainstay of French commerce thereafter. On 1 July, Lagny even agreed with an unnamed correspondent in Saint-Malo that France should appoint and maintain a consul in Dublin.[61]

This was premature, as this 'exceptional' boom in Franco-Irish trade (as André Lespagnol puts it) was not to last.[62] France had landed 6,000

---

[59] Lespagnol, 'Les relations commerciales entre l'Irlande et la Bretagne', pp. 172–3. For more on Magon, see Chapters 3 and 8.
[60] This coincided with a coordinated privateering cruise in the Irish Sea in the same year, although the results of this were 'poor'; Bromley, *Corsairs and Navies*, p. 141.
[61] MAR/B/7/62, fols 95–98r, AN.
[62] Lespagnol, 'Les relations commerciales entre l'Irlande et la Bretagne', p. 173.

troops in Ireland in June, but, by the end of the month, William of Orange had landed too. Seignelay had ordered a squadron of frigates to forestall English efforts in the Irish Sea, but it arrived only in July.[63] The French navy's victory at Beachy Head on 10 July was counterbalanced by William's victory at the battle of the Boyne the next day, which forced James to return to France once again. By the end of the year, William was able to secure the ports on the eastern coast of Ireland from Dublin to Kinsale.[64] This caused inevitable disruption to Franco-Irish trade: the *Anne et Marie*, insured by the Company, was sailing from Bordeaux to Dublin alongside a French naval squadron in 1690 when it was seized off the coast of Ireland by order of Sir Edward Scott, the governor of the Jacobite stronghold at Kinsale that would fall in October.[65] Unaware of Kinsale's fate, and faced with high winds, Richard Cheevers, the ship-master of another insured vessel named the *Richard*, chose to stop at the port, where William's officers duly seized the vessel.[66]

In response to these military losses, the French landed new troops in Limerick in 1691, but this did not stop Williamite forces from seizing the port, alongside Galway.[67] One insured vessel to fall victim to these turbulent circumstances was the *Jeanneton*, which was captured on the River Shannon on its entry to or departure from Limerick.[68]

Table 27 The frequency of places on the island of Ireland being touched in the voyages described in the Company's claims, for the years 1690–92.

Place	1690	1691	1692	Total
Cork	–	2	–	2
Dublin	3	2	–	5
Galway	3	1	–	4
Ireland (generic)	2	–	–	2
Limerick	1	4	–	5
Londonderry	–	–	1	1
Waterford	–	1	–	1

Source: Z/1d/82 and Z/1d/88, AN.

[63] Clark, 'The Nine Years' War', pp. 238–40; Symcox, *The Crisis of French Sea Power*, pp. 96–7.
[64] Clark, 'The Nine Years' War', pp. 240–1.
[65] Z/1d/82, fol. 87v, AN.
[66] Ibid., fol. 85.
[67] Clark, 'The Nine Years' War', pp. 240–1.
[68] Z/1d/88, fols 17v–18r, AN.

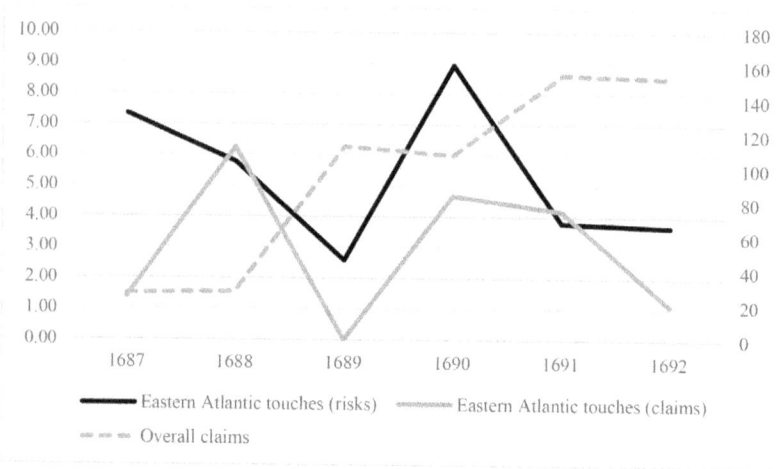

Chart 14 Touches in the eastern Atlantic as a percentage of overall touches in the risks which the Company insured and/or to which it gave sea loans and as a percentage of overall touches in voyages that led to claims from the years 1687–92, compared with the raw number of claims in this period.

Source: Z/1d/82, Z/1d/88 and ATR, based on data from Z/1d/85, AN.

Despite these failures for the French in Ireland – and the constant threat of the Anglo-Dutch navy and privateers in the English Channel and Irish Sea – the eastern Atlantic accounted for a relatively modest percentage of touches in the Company's claims between 1690 and 1692. Without premium rate data, we cannot draw decisive conclusions on Ireland's impact on the Company's returns; nevertheless, the seventy-eight touches in Ireland in the Company's risks up to 1693 produced at least twenty such touches in its claims, so we can safely assume Ireland was not a source of profits. Regardless, it could have been much worse.

The Company was not so fortunate in the North Sea. Following Colbert's death, French ministers increasingly pushed neutral powers to carry French goods during wartime to support the French economy and ensure that shipbuilding materials, colonial goods and raw materials for manufacturing could be procured.[69] Yet neutral shipping and legitimate prizes were 'a thorny juridico-diplomatic problem', revolving around 'regimes of

---

[69] A. Alimento, 'Commercial Treaties and the Harmonisation of National Interests: The Anglo-French Case (1667–1713)', in A. Alimento (ed.), *War, Trade and Neutrality: Europe and the Mediterranean in the Seventeenth and Eighteenth Centuries*, Milan: FrancoAngeli, 2011, pp. 107–28.

property rights concomitant to regimes of subjection'.[70] For our purposes, we can narrow the debate to two seemingly simple questions: does the flag cover merchandise? Or should a distinction be made between the flag and the cargo – i.e. can a privateer seize enemy cargo laden on an allied or neutral ship? As with many juridical problems in this period, a consensus was not reached, although Denis Dusault suggested in 1680 that Christian corsairs in the Mediterranean generally differentiated between flag and cargo to maximise their gains.[71] This oblique distinction between legitimate and illegitimate prizes often precipitated fraught diplomatic stalemates.[72]

With no consensus, France was in a precarious position. On 22 August 1689, William of Orange and the Estates General of the United Provinces issued a proclamation, announcing an 'audacious' fictive blockade of France's ports.[73] Through this, any neutral or allied ship stopped 'under the apparent suspicion' of going to a French port or carrying French merchandise would be deemed a legitimate prize by the Maritime Powers (England and the United Provinces).[74] This was, as William put it, '*le droit du canon*'.[75]

This might not have posed a problem if Seignelay's naval ambitions for 1690 had been achieved. He had planned to have seventy-five ships-of-the-line in the North Sea by mid-April, before the Anglo-Dutch fleet could even put to sea for the spring campaign, to try to cut off London's vital trade with the Baltic and beyond. If this naval mobilisation had been accomplished, the situation could have looked very different for at least some time, although Donald Pilgrim rightly questions how long such a large fleet could have been sustained so far from home. Yet delays owing to logistical problems and unfavourable winds ensured the French fleet left two months later than scheduled. The French success at Beachy Head in July belies the reality that

---

[70] G. Calafat and W. Kaiser, 'Le laboratoire méditerranéen. Course et piraterie aux XVIe et XVIIe siècles', in G. Buti and P. Hroděj (eds), *Histoire des pirates et corsaires. De l'antiquité à nos jours*, Paris: CNRS Éditions, 2016, p. 245; C. Antunes and K. Ekama, 'Mediterranean and Atlantic Maritime Conflict Resolution: Critical Insights into Geographies of Conflict in the Early Modern Period', in L. Sicking and A. Wijffels (eds), *Conflict Management in the Mediterranean and the Atlantic, 1000–1800: Actors, Institutions and Strategies of Dispute Settlement*, Leiden: Brill, 2020, p. 279.

[71] Calafat and Kaiser, 'Le laboratoire méditerranéen', p. 245.

[72] P. Pourchasse, 'Les conflits permanents entre corsaires et neutres: L'exemple de la France et du Danemark au XVIIIe siècle', in L. Sicking and A. Wijffels (eds), *Conflict Management in the Mediterranean and the Atlantic, 1000–1800: Actors, Institutions and Strategies of Dispute Settlement*, Leiden: Brill, 2020, pp. 325–53.

[73] Bromley, *Corsairs and Navies*, p. 44.

[74] Quoted in É. Schnakenbourg, *Entre la guerre et la paix. Neutralité et relations internationales, XVIIe–XVIIIe siècles*, Rennes: Presses universitaires de Rennes, 2013, pp. 131–80.

[75] Quoted in Clark, 'The Nine Years' War', pp. 234–5. On how the French approached prizes after the *Ordonnance de la marine*, see Clark, *The Dutch Alliance*, p. 121.

this engagement was never intended to happen, nor was the navy able to disrupt English and Dutch activities in the North Sea as planned.[76] Moreover, as Patrick Villiers observes, investing the resources necessary for 'a naval victory makes sense only if it is exploited'; the French navy proved unable to do this, managing only to land in Teignmouth and burn down part of the town.[77] In short, difficulties in manning and supplying the French navy inhibited its ability to make the impact necessary to justify the significant resources required to sustain it.

In this fraught environment, Lagny was tasked with managing neutral shipping. As he explained in a letter from 2 August 1690, 'I am charged with the discussion of requests from merchants for passports for foreign vessels, be they from enemy or neutral nations'.[78] His letter-books from around this time are replete with correspondence on such requests, where Lagny gathered information on the merchandise to be traded. Assuming he was satisfied that French needs were being met, the passport was then drawn up, with specific conditions laid out, ready to be signed by Louis XIV. This signature was simply the formal conclusion of a process Lagny controlled.[79]

Neutral shipping – especially from Denmark and Sweden – was a valuable lifeline to France, and it also offered the scope for merchants to capitalise on wartime market imbalances in supply and demand. Nevertheless, it was not without challenges. Lagny noted candidly in the same letter from August 1690 that

> I had hoped the events of this campaign would give us openings for greater commerce in the future, but I do not [fore]see this happening yet: the English and the Dutch [still] have the same resolve to prevent the commerce of neutral nations in France and to take their vessels.[80]

In the face of Anglo-Dutch seizures of neutral ships, the state could offer little support. Jean Mathieu Leers, a representative of the king of Denmark in Nantes, had expressed concerns to Lagny that the Danish were afraid to use French passports, as these left their ships open to seizure. Lagny responded on 27 January 1690, suggesting that 'it would be for the king of Denmark to make

---

[76] Pilgrim, 'The Colbert-Seignelay Naval Reforms', pp. 250–1; Villiers, *Marine Royale*, pp. 75–7.
[77] Villiers, *Marine Royale*, pp. 75–7.
[78] MAR/B/7/62, fol. 158r, AN.
[79] Ibid. It seems passports could be secured through local admiralties too, although Lagny's letters make clear merchants were often eager to leapfrog the admiralties and contact Lagny directly; S. Talbott, *Conflict, Commerce and Franco-Scottish Relations, 1560–1713*, London: Pickering & Chatto, 2014, p. 125; D. Smith, 'Structuring Politics in Early Eighteenth-Century France: The Political Innovations of the French Council of Commerce', *Journal of Modern History* 74 (2002), p. 508.
[80] MAR/B/7/62, fol. 158r, AN.

the English and the Dutch stop the vexation that they are exercising against his subjects at the expense of the law of nations and public freedom'.[81] As far as Lagny was concerned, France could only restrain the activity of French privateers, who were not permitted to seize neutral ships bearing French passports.[82] In any case, Lagny's recommendation pre-empted later events: in December 1690, Christian V demanded compensation from the United Provinces for the ostensibly unjust damages inflicted on Danish ships. As we will see, this was just the first effort from Christian to protect Danish interests.[83]

Faced with these risks, Leers secured policies with the Company for the goods he loaded on neutral vessels.[84] He was far from alone. On 16 June 1690, Pierre Héron and Étienne Demeuves – two of the Company's directors at the time – presented themselves in the registry of the Parisian admiralty court[85] to submit a list of every foreign ship the Company had insured since the start of 1689. Four vessels are listed for 1689, one of which was a Hamburger vessel and another an Ostender; the list for 1690 (up to 15 June) runs to around three full pages, including vessels from Bruges, Nieuwpoort, Glückstadt, Altona,[86] Copenhagen, Gdansk and even London and Hull.[87]

This is a reflection of the growing role of the North Sea (and, to a much lesser extent, the Baltic) in the Company's portfolio at the turn of the decade: having comprised 2.89 per cent of touches in the Company's risks in 1688, North Sea touches peaked at 12.19 per cent in 1691 – a growth of over 300 per cent. This was fuelled by the Company's growing portfolio in neutral and enemy ships with French passports.[88] Hamburg offered neutral shipping until 6 June 1690, when the city was forced to finally acknowledge its formal state of war with France.[89] This shifted the focus for neutral shipping onto the Scandinavian monarchies: on 10 March 1691, Denmark and Sweden agreed a mutual protection pact with the aim of advancing each other's right to pursue neutral shipping without hindrance. The two kingdoms agreed to acts of reprisals where these rights were infringed and received no satisfaction within four months. As part of this agreement, joint convoys were instituted to protect both countries' vessels, to sail each year from Flekkerøy in southern Norway. A secret

---

[81] Ibid., fol. 22.
[82] Clark, *The Dutch Alliance*, pp. 121–2.
[83] Schnakenbourg, *Entre la guerre et la paix*, pp. 131–80.
[84] Evidence of this can be found in the claims registers: Z/1d/88, fols 68r and 86r, AN.
[85] For more on this, see Chapters 7 and 8.
[86] Altona is now a neighbourhood in Hamburg, but at this point it was a key Danish port.
[87] Z/1d/109, n.p., AN.
[88] On the ways in which English and Scottish vessels continued to conduct trade with France during the war, see Talbott, *Conflict, Commerce and Franco-Scottish Relations*, pp. 113–34.
[89] Schnakenbourg, *Entre la guerre et la paix*, pp. 131–80.

treaty between France and Denmark was concluded shortly after on 27 March, limiting the scope for the latter to provide troops for enemy expeditions in exchange for subsidies from France. The treaty also acknowledged Denmark's right to engage in commerce with both France *and* its enemies, provided it did not supply contraband merchandise to the latter. This 'expensive neutrality' reflected France's desperate need to secure neutral shipping for the duration of the war. Accordingly, Hamburger merchants were able to shift their operations clandestinely to Altona and Glückstadt, which were under Danish control.[90]

Insuring neutral shipping soon caught up with the Company. North Sea touches in the Company's claims rose year on year after the outbreak of war, until they figured disproportionately in 1691 and 1692, hitting 13.58 and 12.04 per cent respectively. Predictably, these claims frequently pertained to neutral and enemy vessels. This was largely the consequence of the Maritime Powers' decision, in spite of the 1691 Scandinavian pact, to allow the continued seizure of Scandinavian ships: thirty-four Danish ships passed before the English prize court in 1692 alone, and almost all were condemned.[91] Even ships in convoy remained vulnerable: Dutch ships intercepted the Scandinavian convoy in 1691 and discovered ships with false papers and contraband merchandise.[92] The voyage of Jean Bart, the famous Dunkirker privateer, to Flekkerøy in the winter of 1693–94 to help escort the Scandinavian merchant fleet reflects the crucial role of neutral shipping in the health of the French economy, while encapsulating how difficult it was to protect: its success depended on the actions of an array of third parties over whom France had little, if any, control.[93]

Securing a passport for a neutral vessel required excellent communication across the North Sea. With this in mind, it is no surprise the Company's claims from 1690 to 1692 are replete with the names of notable merchants from Calais, Le Havre, Rouen, Nantes and La Rochelle who had the necessary connections.[94] Thomas Legendre, Rouen's leading merchant, stands out: one

---

[90] Ibid.; Bromley, *Corsairs and Navies*, p. 54. On the scope for fraud in neutral shipping more broadly, see Clark, *The Dutch Alliance*, pp. 74–5. Neutral vessels were also offered passports to undertake voyages to the Caribbean, thereby suspending the 'exclusive' system to ensure the provision of the colonies; MAR/B/7/62, fols 277v–8r, AN. For the frequency with which Swedish, Danish, German, English and Scottish vessels with passports entered Le Havre during the war, see Delobette, 'Les mutations du commerce maritime', pp. 14–15.

[91] Schnakenbourg, *Entre la guerre et la paix*, pp. 131–80.

[92] Ibid., pp. 75–125. For more on the Swedish convoy system, see Müller, *Consuls*, pp. 65–9.

[93] Bromley, *Corsairs and Navies*, p. 47.

[94] Key examples include Jean Bouchel and Dominique Morel (Calais); Claude and Claude Houssaye (Le Havre); Thomas Legendre, Nicolas Menage and Jean Porter (Rouen); Jean Robinet, Jacques Souchay and François Bouchand (Nantes); and Charles de Caux, Abraham Duport and Edmond and Jean Gould (La Rochelle).

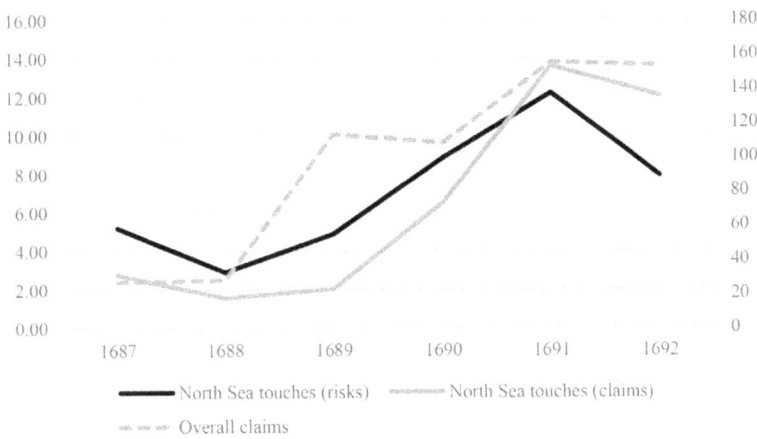

Chart 15 Touches in the North Sea as a percentage of overall touches in the risks which the Company insured and/or to which it gave sea loans and as a percentage of overall touches in voyages that led to claims from the years 1687–92, compared with the raw number of claims in this period.

Source: Z/1d/82, Z/1d/88 and ATR, based on data from Z/1d/85, AN.

of Lagny's correspondents, he was in direct contact with the director general to secure passports for these voyages.[95] The *Sainte Catherine de Stockholm* was captured in the course of its voyage from London to Rouen in 1691, and with it Legendre's merchandise on board; the *Saint Jean de Frederickstat* [sic] was also captured during its journey from Le Havre to Altona, ultimately to be taken to Ostend. In the process, Legendre lost the molasses he had loaded on the ship – a valuable reminder that the war impacted not only France's direct colonial trade, but its re-export trade with the rest of the continent as well.[96]

We can see in Chart 16 how neutral shipping figured into the broader shift in the Company's portfolio after 1690. While eastern Atlantic touches in the Company's claims figured only modestly – Ireland, we have seen, proved a lucky escape – North Sea touches took off. Together, the North Sea and the western Atlantic comprised 21.15 and 23.24 per cent of all touches in claims from 1691 and 1692.

Bouchel, Legendre, Menage, Caux and the Houssayes were all correspondents of Lagny. For more on Duport and Gould, see Talbott, *Conflict, Commerce and Franco-Scottish Relations*, p. 125.

[95] MAR/B/7/62, fols 75v–6r, AN; see also Chapter 3.
[96] Z/1d/88, fols 6v–7r and 34v–35r, AN.

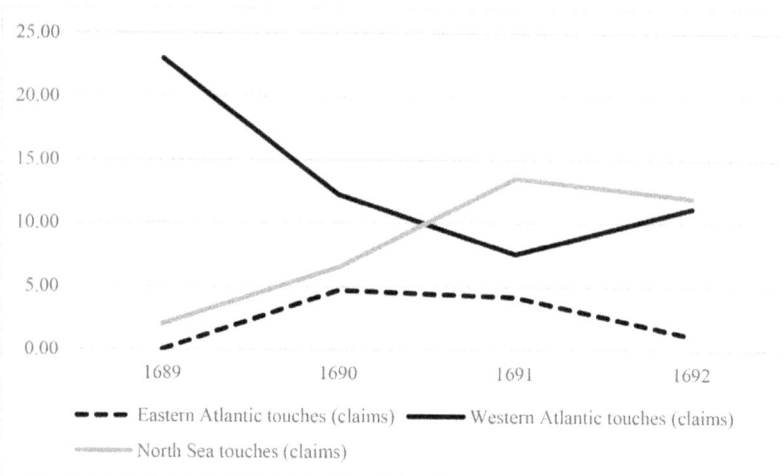

Chart 16 Touches in the eastern Atlantic, western Atlantic and North Sea as a percentage of overall touches in voyages that led to claims from the years 1689–92.

Source: Z/1d/82 and Z/1d/88, AN.

Compounding these losses were those from privateer expeditions. The Company insured and/or gave sea loans to 127 privateer risks in the years 1690 to 1693, having never done so before this point. The details the Company's registers offer on these voyages are frustratingly sparse: what *can* be said, predictably, is that the leading privateer ports – Dunkirk, Saint-Malo, Nantes and Dieppe – figured especially prominently, but in one case, the Company even insured an Irish privateer.[97] In broader narratives of French naval decline in the 1690s, 1695 has traditionally been pinpointed as the decisive moment when the Colbertian *guerre d'escadre* (i.e. war conducted by ships-of-the-line) gave way to the decentralised *guerre de course* (i.e. war conducted by privateers, drawing on private resources to attack enemy commerce). Building on Geoffrey Symcox's work, Benjamin Darnell has recently helped to nuance this analysis: not only was the *guerre d'escadre* central to French naval strategy even as late as the early 1700s, but the *guerre de course* had already been essential since the Dutch War, and grew in importance in the 1690s only because of the unsustainable financial commitment required to keep Colbert's navy in operation.[98] These

---

[97] ATR. As will be discussed in Chapter 6, the Company's claims often offer only the briefest account of what happened to the vessels in question. On Irish participation and investment in privateering during the Nine Years' War, see Talbott, '"Such unjustifiable practices?"', pp. 571–2.

[98] B. Darnell, 'Naval Policy in an Age of Fiscal Overextension', in J. Prest and G. Rowlands (eds), *The Third Reign of Louis XIV, c. 1682–1715*, Abingdon: Routledge, 2017, pp. 68–81; Darnell, 'Reconsidering the *Guerre de Course*', pp. 37–48; Symcox, *The Crisis of French Sea Power*.

were complementary strategies, and just as the English and the Dutch used privateers to great effect alongside their naval fleets to inflict the maximum possible damage on France and its economy, the Company supported French privateers in attacking English and Dutch ships where the French navy could not. Even Seignelay himself had armed four privateer frigates after the outbreak of war in 1688.[99] Malouin privateers alone took more prizes throughout the war than all the English ports put together, pointing to the efficacy of the strategy in supporting French interests.[100]

Nevertheless, privateer expeditions were risky: the hunter often became the hunted. In 1691 and 1692 alone, there were eighteen claims for privateer voyages, with fifteen of these concerning vessels that had been captured by enemies.[101] Two rather ironic claims pertained to the *Vainqueur*, a Malouin privateering vessel seized by two English vessels on 3 September 1691 between twenty-eight and thirty leagues from the Isles of Scilly and then taken to Plymouth to be condemned.[102]

1692–95: overexposure, scaling down and state support

By 1692, losses from Atlantic France, the western Atlantic and the North Sea had taken their toll. With claims peaking in 1691 and 1692,[103] the Company's directors recognised that the institution was in an untenable position.

Table 28 The number of policies signed, and the amounts underwritten (in *livres*), by the Company in the years 1686–93, alongside the number of claims in the years 1686–92.

Year	Total underwritten	Number of policies	Claims*
1686	478,166	117	6
1687	1,491,356	286	27
1688	1,901,135	426	28
1689	1,392,734	427	113
1690	2,801,588	610	108
1691	3,420,920	673	155
1692	2,369,080	549	153
1693	852,302	226	–

* For a full discussion of this column, see Chapters 6 and 8.

Source: Z/1d/82, Z/1d/85 and Z/1d/88, AN.

---

[99] Symcox, *The Crisis of French Sea Power*, p. 76.
[100] W. Meyer, 'English Privateering in the War of 1688 to 1697', *The Mariner's Mirror* 67 (1981), p. 270; see also Hillmann, *The Corsairs of Saint-Malo*. For the number of prizes and ransoms made in Le Havre each year, see Delobette, 'Les mutations du commerce maritime', p. 29.
[101] Z/1d/82 and Z/1d/88, AN.
[102] Z/1d/88, 21v and 22v–23r, AN.
[103] The declaration registers for subsequent years do not seem to have survived.

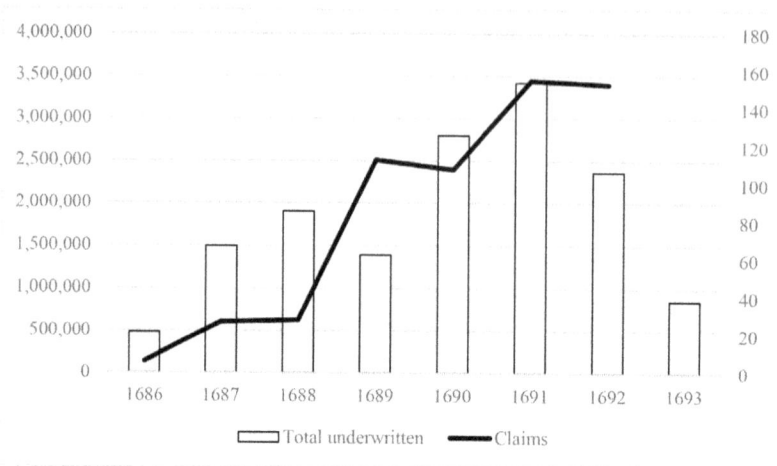

Chart 17 The Company's underwriting in the years 1686–93, in *livres*, alongside its claims from the years 1686–92.

Source: Z/1d/82, Z/1d/85 and Z/1d/88, AN.

What is more, the international climate was only becoming more and more inauspicious. The loss of fifteen vessels at Barfleur and La Hougue in May and June 1692 was a severe blow to the French navy's morale, although naval shipbuilding continued apace in the aftermath.[104] Dunkirk was bombarded following La Hougue; Saint-Malo was subjected to the same treatment in 1693; a failed Anglo-Dutch attack on the French arsenal of Brest in 1694 descended into the bombardment of Dieppe, Le Havre, Calais and Dunkirk; and 1695 also saw the bombardment of Saint-Malo, Granville, Calais and Dunkirk.[105] These attacks targeted ports that had been at the centre of the Company's portfolio. It was in this climate that underwriting was slashed in 1693, 1694 and 1695.

The war had proven grim for French shipping: the records of the Dutch admiralties document 1,059 captures and ransoms of French ships during the war, while the English Court of Admiralty condemned 1,289 enemy

---

[104] Clark, 'The Nine Years' War', pp. 243–4; Darnell, 'Reconsidering the *Guerre de Course*', pp. 40–1.

[105] Clark, 'The Nine Years' War', pp. 248–9; J. Stapleton, 'The Blue-Water Dimension of King William's War: Amphibious Operations and Allied Strategy during the Nine Years' War, 1688–1697', in D. Trim and M. Fissel (eds), *Amphibious Warfare 1000–1700: Commerce, State Formation and European Expansion*, Leiden: Brill, 2005, pp. 337–46.

prizes. France's merchant marine shrunk in the course of the war, whereas that of England, remarkably, grew.[106]

Nevertheless, the Company was not alone in encountering trouble at this point. London and Amsterdam also suffered greatly when the French attacked the 400-strong Anglo-Dutch Smyrna convoy in 1693, with ninety-two merchant vessels, worth over £1 million, being captured or destroyed. The impact on Lloyd's was stark, with thirty-three private underwriters going into bankruptcy. In the words of Wright and Fayle, 'the stability of the marine insurance market had been tested [in 1693] and found wanting'.[107] In response, a parliamentary relief bill was proposed in December 1693 to support the underwriters.[108] Although this bill never passed the House of Lords, mercantile forces in the Commons made clear that 'a notorious and treacherous mismanagement' of the convoy, with a woeful lack of escort ships, had precipitated the disaster.[109] Amsterdam's insurance market was larger, meaning losses were spread across a far larger group of underwriters, but these still totalled somewhere between f 12 and f 14 million.[110]

One could say this was the moment where Seignelay's chickens came home to roost. With a membership restricted to thirty, the Company was worse placed to withstand the effects of the war than London and Amsterdam.

Nevertheless, an open-access institution like the Chamber may not have fared any better: let us not forget the Chamber had only fifty-three regular underwriting entities at its peak, and the institution fell at the first hurdle where the Company did not.[111] Moreover, there is a clear political element to the Company's struggles that needs to be acknowledged. While parliament debated a relief bill for Lloyd's, the Company received no support from Seignelay's successor, Pontchartrain, and the institution faced the consequences of its overexposure alone.[112]

The Company's withdrawal from the market in 1695 had significant consequences for French commerce. At this point, it seems, the Company's

---

[106] Barazzutti, 'La guerre de course hollandaise', pp. 269–80; Clark, 'The Nine Years' War', pp. 243–4; Meyer, 'English Privateering', p. 263. This is not to say, though, that English maritime commerce was not hit hard by the war; it assuredly was; here, see B. Waddell, 'The Economic Crisis of the 1690s in England', *The Historical Journal* (2022), pp. 1–22. doi:10.1017/S0018246X22000309

[107] Wright and Fayle, *A History of Lloyd's*, p. 52.

[108] A. Leonard, 'Underwriting Marine Warfare: Insurance and Conflict in the Eighteenth Century', *International Journal of Maritime History* 25 (2013), pp. 176–7.

[109] Quoted in ibid.

[110] Go, 'Amsterdam 1585–1790', p. 121.

[111] For an imperfect point of comparison, Lloyd's and the Royal Exchange (as distinct from the Royal Exchange Assurance) in London were each said to have had a hundred frequent underwriters in 1720; Wright and Fayle, *A History of Lloyd's*, pp. 50–1.

[112] See Chapter 8.

de facto monopoly in the Atlantic ports was relinquished, allowing merchants to seek coverage abroad. Even so, a group of merchants from La Rochelle – including Theodore Pages, a regular correspondent of Lagny's who had secured coverage with the Company in prior years – lamented their inability to find coverage anywhere in 1695, be it Paris, London or Amsterdam. They successfully petitioned for the right to establish their own company.[113] If we follow Clark in surmising that this company succumbed to the war, this only puts into context the difficulties of underwriting in this period, as well as the vital role the Company had been playing in Rochelais commerce.[114]

With the end of war in 1697, the Company resumed underwriting briefly in 1698, signing thirty-nine insurance policies. It did not underwrite again on any notable scale thereafter.

CONCLUSION

This chapter has offered the first quantitative study of the Company's activities. Like the Chamber before it, the Company underwrote economic activity within, and far beyond, the confines of Europe. In a strict sense, it was a global institution, touching every major ocean space except the Pacific. Nevertheless, the Company's activity dropped off almost entirely east of the Cape of Good Hope – a product of the CIO's monopoly privileges and the lack of diversity in the royal companies more broadly. Although it primarily specialised in insurance, the Company also offered sea loans, especially for capital-intensive voyages touching Newfoundland and the French Caribbean. In sum, the global (dis)connectedness of the Company's activities was the product of France's imperial and commercial frameworks in both the Atlantic and the Indian Ocean. As an institution of state, the Company perpetuated, and was the product of, imperial ambitions.

How are we to understand the Company's fate? On the surface, this is straightforward to answer: like the Chamber, it was a victim of war, losing out in insuring Atlantic and North Sea voyages. But why did it underwrite these voyages? Ignorance or incompetence are inadequate answers. Lagny knew full well what was happening in these spaces: his role as director general of commerce demanded this, and he played an integral role in commercial decision making in both spaces. Furthermore, the Company's directors made prudent decisions at a decisive moment: when claims spiked in 1689, following the outbreak of war in 1688, the directors restructured

---

[113] I, like Clark before me, have found little on this company, besides a series of Parisian admiralty court cases to which it was party in the years 1697–1701; Clark, 'Marine Insurance in Eighteenth-Century La Rochelle', pp. 575–6; Z/1d/88, fol. 94; MAR/B/7/62; Z/1d/111 n.p.; Z/1d/112, n.p., AN.

[114] Indeed, La Rochelle was the most touched port in the Company's portfolio; ATR.

their portfolio, signing smaller policies to ensure they did not unwittingly become overexposed. Moreover, in percentage terms, they increased their portfolio in Atlantic France – familiar territory – to try to pull the portfolio back on track.

Yet losses only grew, and the Company never recovered. To understand why, we must remind ourselves that the Company was never conceived as a profit-making, long-term endeavour. Originally formed for six years, the stated aim of its letters patent was the augmentation and the protection of commerce, in accordance with the public good. With this aim in mind, the Company's letters patent required it to establish a fixed fund dedicated to insurance and sea loans alone. With the same aim in mind, Seignelay treated the Company as a tool of commercial policy, coercing it into giving sea loans for whaling voyages in 1687 and 1688. With the same aim in mind, he promised merchants across France that the Company would entertain all reasonable proposals for coverage.[115]

To be sure, a company that aims at the public good alone is utterly perverse to modern sensibilities. Between 1997 and 2019, the influential Business Roundtable explicitly endorsed 'shareholder primacy', which is the notion that a corporation's duty first and foremost is to maximise returns for shareholders.[116] The argument for the importance of 'credible commitment' in the success of chartered companies, outlined by Harris, bears the imprint of this concept.[117]

Yet, as Richard John has put it, 'corporations maximise shareholder returns – or so goes the conventional wisdom. It was not always so.'[118] Not even the EIC or the VOC were intended, or functioned, strictly as profit-making endeavours in service to their shareholders.[119]

---

[115] See Chapter 2.
[116] Business Roundtable, 'Business Roundtable Redefines the Purpose of a Corporation to Promote "An Economy That Serves All Americans"' [https://www.businessroundtable.org/business-roundtable-redefines-the-purpose-of-a-corporation-to-promote-an-economy-that-serves-all-americans, accessed 21 May 2021].
[117] On Harris' argument, see the Introduction. Harris does not refer to shareholder primacy, but makes clear that 'profit-maximisation' was 'a feature of business firms in all types of organisational forms', including corporations: Harris, *Going the Distance*, p. 252. It is not my intention to say that shareholder primacy and profit maximisation are synonymous: they certainly are not; here, see Ciepley, 'The Anglo-American Misconception', p. 624. Nevertheless, the former presumes the latter, and I argue that the prevailing corporate environment – underpinned by the former – explains the tendency for historians to focus anachronistically on the latter.
[118] R. John, 'After Managerial Capitalism', *Business History Review* 95 (2021), pp. 151–7.
[119] On the EIC as an ambiguous 'company-state', see P. Stern, *The Company-State: Corporate Sovereignty and the Early Modern Foundations of the British Empire in India*, Oxford: Oxford University Press, 2012. Also see the numerous thematic essays

The French case is more striking still. In understanding the Company's portfolio, we must remember that exhaustion was the fate of all of Seignelay's companies. They were designed to leverage private capital for the pursuit of specific state objectives overseas: many had multiple lifespans, and any profits over time were entirely incidental. The Company was no different, and the onset of war did not change the state's intentions for it. Indeed, Lagny framed the Company's losses in the 1690s in the same terms as its letters patent. In a letter to Pontchartrain in 1698,[120] he remarked that 'they [i.e. the Company's members] have supported the little maritime commerce that was done during the war, and they have lost considerable sums'.[121] Yet Lagny treated these losses not as a sign of 'failure', as Boiteux surmised, but as a sign of success: that the Company had been exhausted by the war was not a fault, but the fulfilment of one of its *raisons d'être*.[122] The public good was best served in the 1690s through wealthy *financiers* bearing the burden of war rather than provincial merchants and ship-owners. The Company was thus being exploited as a vessel for the subvention of wartime commerce, effecting the transfer of capital from *financiers* to mercantile and maritime communities. As a weapon of commercial policy, Lagny argued, the Company had served its purpose.

In this way, the Company served 'in the absence rather than the dominance of the state'.[123] Here, I quote Philip Stern: the monopolies of chartered companies, he finds, were often justified through the logic that they operated where the state itself could not maintain a presence. This absence spanned both land and sea, and in our case, neither distant colonies nor near sea spaces could rely on the French state's protection.[124]

Thus, the Company, like other chartered companies under Seignelay, acted where the state could not: it underwrote the French colonies when the state needed to keep the navy closer to home; it underwrote Irish commerce when the state tried, but failed, to keep Ireland in James II's hands; it underwrote neutral shipping when the state hoped to shift the responsibility for protecting North Sea shipping onto the Scandinavian monarchies; and it underwrote French privateers when the cracks were already showing in

---

in Pettigrew and Veevers (eds), *Corporation as a Protagonist*. On the VOC's crucial political function within the context of the Eighty Years' War, see Antunes, 'Birthing Empire'.

[120] This letter is discussed further in Chapter 8.
[121] MAR/C/7/159, n.p., AN.
[122] Boiteux, *L'assurance maritime à Paris*, p. 64.
[123] Stern, 'Companies', p. 188.
[124] On the maritime framing of the VOC and WIC charters – and the infringement of the WIC charter by the VOC – see Antunes and Ekama, 'Mediterranean and Atlantic Maritime Conflict Resolution', pp. 267–83.

the *guerre d'escadre*, with France proving unable to capitalise on its victory at Beachy Head in 1690.[125] The Company was underwriting the kingdom itself, its empire and the neutral shipping that was sustaining it during the war, filling gaps in the state's protection of commerce and the colonies.

Meanwhile, formidable foundations were being built in England to leverage insurance in defence of its commerce in the eighteenth century. The Royal Navy was helping to support the activities of London's underwriters throughout the Nine Years' War by providing naval convoys on particularly lucrative trade routes, thereby helping to reduce premium rates and limit the risks borne by underwriters; in turn, underwriters were supporting these efforts through their policies by requiring vessels to sail in these convoys. The 1693 Smyrna convoy disaster hit Lloyd's hard, to be sure, reflecting broader difficulties in managing convoys throughout the war.[126] Nevertheless, despite the challenges they posed, naval convoys proved a remarkably effective strategy for protecting British commerce throughout the eighteenth century.[127] Thus, while the French state was relying on insurance and neutral shipping as substitutes for naval support for maritime commerce, the English were already recognising that insurance and naval support worked best when deployed in tandem. The extraordinary fiscal system developed in Britain in the eighteenth century ensured this strategy could be implemented and sustained, to the mutual benefit of London's underwriters and the British state.

Although neither the Chamber nor the Company survived the reign of Louis XIV, they left an indelible imprint on the legal landscape of maritime France. This will be the focus of the next chapter.

---

[125] On this, see Symcox, *The Crisis of French Sea Power*, pp. 91–102.
[126] Clark, *The Dutch Alliance*, pp. 62 and 125–6.
[127] Here, see Baugh, 'Naval Power'; Lobo-Guerrero, *Insuring War*; Farber, *Underwriters of the United States*. France also made use of its navy in the eighteenth century to protect Atlantic commerce; Marzagalli, 'Was Warfare Necessary?', pp. 259–60.

Part 3

LAW, CONFLICT RESOLUTION
AND THE ABSOLUTE MONARCHY

6

'IN THE TIME OF THE *ORDONNANCE*': INSURANCE, LAW AND MARITIME JURISDICTION

In January 1750, a marine insurance company was established in Paris. By 1780, it had ceased all meaningful underwriting.[1] *Plus ça change*. One of its members, Balthazard-François de Villeneuve, wrote a *mémoire* around this time asking for 'the protection' of the state in trying to revive its fortunes.[2] In making this case, he harked back to the reign of Louis XIV to argue that insurance had long been of interest to the state: 'the proof is found in the *Ordonnance de la marine* of 1681, which has a specific section for this aspect of commerce [that is] so widely recognised as useful'.[3] The *mémoire* made no reference to the Chamber or the Company. Doubtless, Villeneuve did not wish to draw attention to the ambiguous legacies of these institutions of state while proposing to transform his company into one just like them.

This selective amnesia is symptomatic of a more general abstraction of the *Ordonnance* from its wider historical context. This chapter argues that the *Ordonnance* was the product of the French state's broader strategy to intervene in maritime affairs – a strategy in which the Chamber and the Company played an integral role. The Chamber was consulted during the *Ordonnance*'s compilation, inviting us to move beyond studies of the latter which focus on textual influences alone. Later, the Company presented itself as a model insurance institution as a means of legitimating its activities, setting an example for other French underwriters by referring to the *Ordonnance* at every opportunity. The *Ordonnance* therefore emerged as an essential element of a maritime

---

[1] For a full treatment of the Parisian insurance companies of the 1750s, see Bosher, 'The Paris Business World'. See also J. Savary des Bruslons, *Dictionnaire universel de commerce: contenant tout ce qui concerne le commerce qui se fait dans les quatre parties du monde*, vol. V, Copenhagen: Claude Philibert, 1765, pp. 1697–709.
[2] MAR/B/7/493, n.p., AN.
[3] Ibid.

strategy whose success was far from clear, bringing into focus the contested nature of royal authority in the maritime sphere.

It would be easy to assume that, as insurance institutions, the Chamber and the Company's relationship with the *Ordonnance* centred exclusively on insurance. Yet insurance practice was embedded in various other aspects of maritime activity. Here, I analyse maritime averages to explore the institutions' role in the *Ordonnance*'s compilation and reception.

CUSTOM, LAW AND THE FRENCH STATE

This chapter discusses two types of average: general and particular. Since its inception in antiquity, general average has served as a legal instrument for the proportionate and equitable redistribution of costs in instances of unforeseeable and unavoidable loss during a voyage. These costs are shared because they are directly incurred to ensure the voyage's successful completion. For example, goods may be jettisoned in inclement weather to make the ship more manoeuvrable, thereby avoiding a shipwreck that would have destroyed the rest of the cargo. Having made this sacrifice for the greater good, it is just that the affected merchant does not bear the cost alone: since others have benefited from the sacrifice, they should contribute proportionately.[4] The loss or damage of goods during a voyage does not *per se* give rise to general average compensation; without the element of common sacrifice, the loss is normally considered particular average and borne by the affected merchant alone. Such losses are part and parcel of seafaring, however unfortunate.

In seventeenth-century France, insurers were widely recognised as being liable for general average contributions. In the *Guidon de la mer*, the prevailing text for insurance practice in France from the late sixteenth century to 1681,[5] article 1 of the chapter *Des Avaries* enshrines that 'the insurer is obliged to indemnify the merchant [i.e. policyholder] for [… all] averages', including particular and general average, echoed later in the *Ordonnance* in article 46 of the section *Des Assurances*.[6]

---

[4] W. Ashburner, *The Rhodian Sea Law*, Oxford: Clarendon Press, 1909, p. CCLXXI. The literature on general average is not especially extensive at the time of writing, although Maria Fusaro's ERC-funded project (in which this book has been developed) is addressing this balance; M. Fusaro, A. Addobbati, and L. Piccinno (eds), *General Average and Risk Management in Medieval and Early Modern Maritime Business*, Basingstoke: Palgrave Macmillan, 2023.

[5] This will be discussed later in the chapter. On how the *Guidon* was used and received, especially through Cleirac's *Us et coutumes*, see F. Trivellato, '"Usages and Customs of the Sea": Étienne Cleirac and the Making of Maritime Law in Seventeenth-Century France', *The Legal History Review* 84 (2016), pp. 193–224.

[6] Cleirac, *Us et coutumes*, p. 199; Valin, *Nouveau commentaire*, vol. II, p. 99.

To understand how the Chamber and the Company responded to policyholders' claims for averages, and the significance of these responses for understanding the *Ordonnance*, we need to keep in mind the state's broader maritime strategy, which centred on securing greater jurisdiction in the maritime sphere. This entailed a broad, protracted and contested shift in the legitimacy of privilege: diffuse customary and seigneurial law was adapted and assimilated within the French *ius commune*, shaped by the state itself and premised on its authority.[7]

The origins of this process can be found at the conclusion of the Hundred Years' War (1337–1453). This had transformed the social and political landscape of France, with new provinces being absorbed into the kingdom – each with their own customs – and the reassertion of royal power requiring juridical solutions to adapt to this chaotic legal reality. Martine Grinberg has written a compelling account on the incorporation of seigneurial rights and customs into the French *ius commune*. As Grinberg notes, the distinction between seigneurial rights and customs was often blurred; by the end of the early modern period, jurists such as Nicolas Catherinot characterised local customs[8] and seigneurial rights as legally synonymous insofar as both were, they argued, forms of private law – i.e. consequences of contract.[9] Thus, early modern France witnessed the transfer of what was characterised as private-order contractual relations to law which derived its legitimacy from the state rather than from the distinctive relations engendered by the seigneurial system, where tenants' responsibilities widely diverged from place to place.

This transformation emerged from the *assemblées de redaction*, which, following the 1454 *ordonnance* of Montils-les-Tours, were tasked with collating, editing and recording seigneurial rights and customs across France. The process of writing these down allowed them to be articulated and revised in the legal language and logics typical of *ius civile*: this meant, as Grinberg remarks, that the 'redaction and reformation of customs were at the same time a reality of writing, a juridical event and a political process.'[10]

---

[7] On *ius commune*, see, for example, T. Herzog, *A Short History of European Law: The Last Two and a Half Centuries*, London: Harvard University Press, 2018, pp. 76–93 and 119–31; see also the discussion of universal monarchy, which is relevant here too, in Bosbach, 'The European Debate on Universal Monarchy'.

[8] This was distinct from general customs, which could be regarded, Catherinot argued, as part of *ius commune*; here, see M. Grinberg, *Écrire les coutumes. Les droits seigneuriaux en France*, Paris: Presses universitaires de France, 2006, pp. 110–11.

[9] This blurs the distinction between written and more informal kinds of contract: while written medieval *aveux* outlined the responsibilities (financial or otherwise) of tenants to their *seigneur*, local customs were, by their nature, unrecorded; ibid., pp. 10–11.

[10] Ibid., pp. 3–4.

The mere act of compiling, deliberating on and recording customs transformed them entirely, as their written nature (in French, rather than Latin) and ratification by an *assemblée* gave them a status they had not enjoyed up to that point: timeless custom became time-bound law.[11] The sixteenth-century rise of venal office holding[12] ensured that the office-holding jurists on these *assemblées* upheld the crown's interests, challenging those rights and customs that undermined crown legislation (or, indeed, *ius civile* and/or canon law) while promulgating the king's key role as 'legislator' rather than mere arbiter of justice.[13]

Although this shift fitted into a broader Eurasian dynamic of state formation through greater jurisdictional centralisation, the *assemblées* were unique in late medieval and early modern Europe: no other comparable process of collaborative compilation was witnessed across the continent.[14] However, they did not proceed smoothly and without conflict. Moreover, the shift of ultimate legislative power towards the crown was protracted, pushed back in particular by the French Wars of Religion (1562-98). The return to peace with the reigns of Henri IV and Louis XIII kicked this process off again, but it was neither speedy nor linear.[15]

As Trivellato has found, this was often a reactive rather than proactive endeavour. The shipwrecks of the *São Bartolomeu* and *Santa Helena* off the coast of Guyenne in January 1627 revealed surprising gaps in the state's jurisdiction that it quickly tried to fill. The Portuguese vessels had been carrying an array of exotic goods from the East Indies and Africa valued at

---

[11] French jurists argued that a custom had to fulfil three criteria: it had to be timeless; it had to be consented to by the public, albeit not in an explicit manner; and it had to be widely known; ibid., p. 67. This echoes the definition of custom widely accepted by medieval Roman law jurists such as Bartolus of Sassoferato; E. Kadens, 'The Myth of the Customary Law Merchant', *Texas Law Review* 90 (2012), pp. 1163-4.

[12] This is discussed at length in Chapter 1.

[13] Grinberg, *Écrire les coutumes*, p. 64.

[14] Ibid., p. 71. The literature on Eurasian law and state formation is so rich as to be overwhelming; for only a few notable examples, see P. O'Brien, 'The Formation of States and Transitions to Modern Economies: England, Europe, and Asia Compared', in L. Neal and J. Williamson (eds), *The Cambridge History of Capitalism*, vol. I, Cambridge: Cambridge University Press, 2014, pp. 357-402; C. Antunes and L. Sicking, 'Ports on the Border of the State, 1200-1800: An Introduction', *International Journal of Maritime History* 19 (2007), pp. 273-86; Ormrod, *The Rise of Commercial Empires*.

[15] On the disruption wrought by the French Wars of Religion, see, among many others, Briggs, *Early Modern France*; on Richelieu, see, among many others, Parrott, *1652*, pp. 1-43.

between six and eight million ducats.[16] As the lucrative flotsam emerged on the beaches between Bordeaux and the Spanish border, the question was immediately posed: who had the rights to it? Étienne Cleirac's 1648 work *Us et coutumes de la mer* discusses this utterly unique conundrum. Cleirac was 'a provincial lawyer with a broad humanistic education, a law degree, and extensive professional experience in the city's Admiralty court and the regional appeals court, the *parlement* of Bordeaux'.[17] In this capacity, Cleirac worked alongside Richelieu's emissaries to ascertain the surviving cargo and to appropriately reimburse local lords and peasants for salvaging the flotsam as per the law of wreck. This experience prompted him to later write *Us et coutumes*.[18]

In undertaking this reconnaissance work, Cleirac became aware of the wide array of claims over the rights to the flotsam. Richelieu was ultimately forced to intervene to assert the French crown's tenuous rights to the flotsam and pacify the Spanish crown, which bore heavy losses in the affair. Having made himself *Grand-maître, chef et surintendant général de la navigation et du commerce de France* in October 1626 – giving him control over the admiralties of Guyenne, Bordeaux, and Bayonne – it would seem Richelieu had a strong claim to the flotsam.[19] However, Richelieu was forced to contend with the Governor of Guyenne, Jean-Louis Nogaret de La Valette, duc d'Épernon, who asserted his own authority over the flotsam as the region's seigneurial lord. Épernon thus appealed to the law of wreck outlined in the Rhodian Sea Law, which was at odds with Richelieu's titles and crown decrees that sought to curtail such seigneurial rights.

Drawing on his legal expertise, Cleirac proposed a legal hierarchy whereby the thirteenth-century *Rôles d'Oléron* and other regional customary laws, as part of the *ius gentium*, were subordinate to the law offered by *ius civile* and the crown's ordinances and decrees.[20] But Épernon and other local lords overseeing the recovery process were naturally inclined to dispute this schema, and the legal precedence established in previous centuries offered little clarity.

Cleirac therefore sought to defend the crown's jurisdiction over the flotsam. As part of these efforts, he offered commentaries for influential legal compilations on maritime affairs. Two texts reproduced in *Us et coutumes* were especially significant in the governance of insurance and averages: the *Guidon de la mer* and the *Rôles d'Oléron*.

---

[16] F. Trivellato, '"Amphibious Power": The Law of Wreck, Maritime Customs, and Sovereignty in Richelieu's France', *Law and History Review* 33 (2015), pp. 920–1.

[17] Trivellato, '"Usages and Customs of the Sea"', p. 194.

[18] Ibid., pp. 207–8. Why Cleirac wrote *Us et coutumes* so long after the incident is discussed at length by Trivellato.

[19] Trivellato, '"Amphibious Power"', pp. 922–3.

[20] Ibid., pp. 928–9.

Thirteenth century	*Rôles d'Oléron*
Sixteenth century	*Guidon de la mer*
1648	*Us et coutumes de la mer*
1681	*Ordonnance de la marine*

Figure 2 A timeline of the key legal texts and compilations under discussion.

The *Guidon* was 'a collection of norms concerning primarily marine insurance emanating from Rouen in the late sixteenth century'.[21] Dating originally to between 1204 and 1224, the *Rôles* were supposedly created on the island of Oléron, north of the Gironde estuary. Although the compilation evolved over time, James Shephard emphasises that the *Rôles* were originally a contingent set of rules intended only for the French wine fleet's annual voyages.[22] It was a 'code of conduct' for the merchants, ship-owners, shipmasters and crews involved in this lucrative but very specific maritime venture.[23] However, their terms certainly influenced later practice: in a 1364 *ordonnance*, 'a privilege from King Charles V of France gave Castilian merchants the right to bring their maritime matters before the court of Harfleur and to be judged according to the "coutume de la mer et les droiz de Layron"' (i.e. the *Rôles*), thus acknowledging their legal force in France.[24] They would later be used by Bordeaux's adjudicating courts, to take only one other example.[25]

Cleirac's *Us et coutumes* became a 'bestseller' that would go on to have great influence over French maritime law.[26] It was only published after Richelieu's death, however: in attempting to solve the 1627 incident, Richelieu relied instead on Théodore Godefroy's guidance. Godefroy was an erudite member of the Republic of Letters – a broad network of scholars which shared information through epistolary exchanges – who offered Richelieu his academic expertise to support the development of commercial policy, despite having no prior mercantile experience. Godefroy recognised that early modern economic statecraft revolved around sovereignty, which itself necessarily drew on the

---

[21] Ibid., p. 925.
[22] Shephard finds that early manuscripts documenting the *Rôles* had twenty-four articles, while the later 'Brittany Version' (incorporated into the *Coutumes de Bretagne*) had three additional articles, and the 'Black Book Version' (used by the English Admiralty) had eleven additional articles; J. Shephard, 'The *Rôles d'Oléron*: A *lex mercatoria* of the Sea?', in V. Piergiovanni (ed.), *From* lex mercatoria *to Commercial Law*, Berlin: Duncker & Humblot, 2005, pp. 209–13 and 252.
[23] Ibid., pp. 212–13 and 244–5.
[24] E. Frankot, *'Of Laws of Ships and Shipmen': Medieval Maritime Law and Its Practice in Urban Northern Europe*, Edinburgh: Edinburgh University Press, 2012, p. 12n.
[25] Trivellato, '"Usages and Customs of the Sea"', p. 200.
[26] Ibid.

rich ancient, medieval and early modern literatures on commerce and law.[27] Thus, Godefroy drew on his network to collect, translate, read and assimilate even the rarest and most esoteric texts in service to the crown's needs. But, in keeping with humanist tradition, Godefroy did not merely gather information; he used it to create 'rules and maxims' with 'near-polemical' positions on commerce and maritime practices. These served as 'a theoretical appendage' to the crown's efforts to garner greater authority for itself – or, put another way, they were a legitimation of *raison d'état*.[28] Colbert later constructed his own information network with the support of Godefroy's son – some of Godefroy's own commercial memoranda found their way into Colbert's collection – crystallising the humanist foundations of Colbert's commercial policy.[29]

This humanist muscle was put to the test in the 1627 incident; Godefroy wrote a memorandum asserting the crown's rights over the flotsam. His research was comprehensive: he collected

> ordinances from France, Aragon, Poland, Piedmont, England, and the Holy Roman Empire, the customs of Brittany and Normandy, propositions of the Roman jurist Ulpian, and a treaty between a King of France and a Duke of Brittany. He collected, in addition, the customs of Oleron [sic], the Mediterranean, and Visby, ordinances from kingdoms from Sicily to Scotland, and even a few examples of shipwreck and their legal implication collected from books of voyages to the Orient.[30]

In the end, however, he ultimately proposed that the French crown's recognised *ius naturale* authority to punish pirates as enemies of mankind (*hostes humani generis*) and to extract maritime tolls was an extension of its jurisdiction over the sea; hence, the crown had authority over all flotsam.[31]

Despite Cleirac and Godefroy's efforts to demonstrate the crown's emphatic rights over flotsam, these rights were anything but indisputable. The 1627 incident exposed the intense vulnerability and liminality of French littoral zones, which were subject to ambiguous, overlapping jurisdictional claims. No matter how boldly the crown asserted its authority, it did not

---

[27] E. Thomson, 'Commerce, Law, and Erudite Culture: The Mechanics of Théodore Godefroy's Service to Cardinal Richelieu', *Journal of the History of Ideas* 68 (2007), pp. 409–10.
[28] Ibid., p. 417.
[29] Ibid., pp. 425n–6n. On the influence of humanism in Colbert's commercial policy, see also Soll, *The Information Master*.
[30] Thomson, 'Commerce, Law, and Erudite Culture', pp. 417–18.
[31] Ibid.; G. Calafat, 'Ottoman North Africa and *ius publicum europaeum*: The Case of the Treaties of Peace and Trade (1600–1750)', in A. Alimento (ed.), *War, Trade and Neutrality: Europe and the Mediterranean in the Seventeenth and Eighteenth Centuries*, Milan: FrancoAngeli, 2011, p. 186.

yet have the ability to follow through on its claims; negotiation with local powerholders remained essential.

TRANSFORMING AN AMBIGUOUS LEGAL LANDSCAPE: THE CHAMBER AND THE LEGAL GENEALOGY OF THE *ORDONNANCE*

It was within this ambiguous legal landscape, where the state was yet to successfully assert its will over maritime affairs, that the Chamber conducted its underwriting. Before 1681, the *Guidon* was widely, but not universally, used across France to govern insurance practices, with Dutch practice looming large too – no doubt to Colbert's consternation. One insurance policy signed in Nantes in 1658 specified it would be carried out 'according to, and following, the form of the ordinances made by the states of Holland, and according to the custom of the Bourse of Amsterdam'.[32] In any case, the *Guidon* followed commonplace practice elsewhere in Europe in holding insurers liable for general average contributions: from the sixteenth century, these came to be covered by the insurers of Antwerp, following pertinent legislation from 1551 and 1563 and the publication of commercial manuals that guided practices in the city.[33]

From early on in its existence, the Chamber encountered problems with averages. It held its first ever general assembly[34] on 17 June 1670 to provide a forum for its members to discuss 'the differences of opinion that emerge daily between merchants because of insurance, sea loans, averages and other disputes'.[35] Soon after, the assembly started to give guidance on averages. On 24 January 1669, two separate groups of underwriters in the Chamber signed policies for two different sets of merchandise on the same vessel. The *Esperance de La Tremblade* was set to sail from Bilbao to Le Havre or Rouen. Across the two policies, a total of 7,800 *livres* was insured with a premium rate of 3.5 per cent.[36]

In the course of its voyage, the *Esperance* encountered strong winds between Le Havre and Calais, obliging the crew to cut a cable. The vessel reached Calais,

---

[32] C/760, n.p., *Archives départementales de Loire-Atlantique*. I am indebted to Mallory Hope for providing me with a copy of this policy.
[33] G. Dreijer, 'Maritime Averages and Normative Practice in the Southern Low Countries (15th–16th centuries)', PhD thesis, University of Exeter/Vrije Universiteit Brussel (2021).
[34] For more on this body, see Chapter 7.
[35] Z/1d/73, fols 2r–3r, AN. This laid the foundation for the formalised process of arbitration that will be discussed at length in Chapter 7.
[36] For these policies, see Z/1d/75, fols 58v and 59r, AN. The following discussion draws on Wade, 'Underwriting Empire'.

but not without the loss of some merchandise.[37] General average was assessed in Le Havre on 15 March at 3 per cent for both the ship and the merchandise.[38]

The policyholders sought compensation from the Chamber. The underwriters resisted, however, prompting an arbitration dispute on 15 July 1670 that was escalated to the general assembly on the same day.[39] The underwriters argued, following article 9 of *Du devoir du Greffier des Polices* in the *Guidon*, that the registrar could not accept claims for any averages arising from storms unless they exceeded 5 per cent.[40] Thus, on paper, the insurers made a very straightforward case for not being liable.

Both sets of policyholders came together – referred to hereafter as Jousse *et al.* – to make the argument that this practice was 'contrary not only to [the practices of] Holland, Hamburg and other foreign states, but also to [those of] Rouen and the other principal ports of the kingdom', such as Saint-Malo and Bordeaux, where payment was permitted for averages arising from storms below 5 per cent.[41] To support this claim, Jousse *et al.* submitted a policy signed in Rouen for the same voyage: Rouennais underwriters, it transpires, had made payment on this average without complaint.[42] Moreover, Jousse *et al.* warned that if the underwriters' argument was accepted, policyholders would be incentivised to manage their insured effects poorly after a storm – or even commit fraud – in order to inflate their losses above 5 per cent. The alternative, they claimed, was that interested parties would simply seek coverage elsewhere.

The unusual circumstances of establishing an insurance institution in Paris, thereby bringing new players into the game, unwittingly brought to light instances such as this where the rules of the game on paper differed from how they operated in practice in the ports. The need for the Chamber to align itself with these ports was crucial, but in what way did it need to align? Should a literal reading of legal texts supersede broader legal practice?

In the face of this question, the assembly struggled to make a clear decision. The insurers were ordered to make payment for the average within three days, deferring to the Rouennais' decision to pay out.[43] Furthermore,

---

[37] The precise nature of the loss is not specified.
[38] Z/1d/74, fols 3v–4v; Z/1d/73, fols 4v–5r, AN.
[39] For the arbitration case, see Z/1d/74, fols 3v–4v, AN. For the general assembly, see Z/1d/73, fols 4v–5r, AN.
[40] Z/1d/73, fols 4v–5r, AN. This article holds that a registrar handling insurance policies cannot 'draw up the repartition of any averages if it does not exceed 1 per cent in fees and provisions, and if it does not exceed 5 per cent if the average arises from [a] storm'; Cleirac, *Us et coutumes*, p. 289.
[41] Z/1d/73, fols 4v–5r, AN. For more on Anne Jousse, see Wade, 'Underwriting Empire'.
[42] Z/1d/74, fols 3v–4v, AN.
[43] Ibid.

the assembly ordered policyholders and commission agents who frequently did business in the Chamber to write to their correspondents to inform them that 'all averages that do not exceed 3 per cent will be examined in all rigour' in the future, and, 'in case there is the least [perception of] bad faith, that they will be rejected entirely'.[44] This was to be done 'in order that all [business] can be done with honour according to good faith and to avoid unnecessary disputes over modest sums'.[45]

In handling the dispute, the assembly seemed preoccupied first and foremost with the risk of fraudulent conduct on the part of policyholders. Jousse et al.'s argument for moral hazard – in other words, that the underwriters' position would simply encourage policyholders to act improperly to elevate averages to 5 per cent – was certainly convincing.[46] There seems to have been a lingering fear amongst the assembly members, however, that policyholders in the ports would believe they could submit improper claims for small amounts, based on their perception that insurers would not devote their energy to disputing them. Put another way, the members feared policyholders would seek to pass the buck to the insurers for ordinary fees and costs incurred during voyages. Warning prospective policyholders that even small claims for average would be 'examined in all rigour' was a tepid way of acknowledging this risk.

In essence, this was a dispute that revolved around an asymmetry in theory and practice. While the insurers were correct in arguing that the *Guidon* supported their position, Jousse et al. were able to demonstrate that Rouen itself – the city where the *Guidon* was compiled – did not follow the compilation in this instance. This gives a window into the disparity between texts and practice in maritime law before 1681.

'The honour of giving my opinion': the Chamber and the compilation of the Ordonnance de la marine[47]

The Chamber may have operated within an ambiguous legal landscape in its early years, but this was soon to change. While the 1627 incident brought into focus the state's vulnerability under Richelieu, the efforts surrounding

---

[44] Z/1d/73, fols 4v–5r, AN. Why 3 per cent was set as the limit below which all averages would be scrutinised, rather than the 5 per cent that was the subject of the arbitration proceedings, is unclear.
[45] Ibid.
[46] On moral hazard in insurance, see Kingston, 'Governance and Institutional Change', pp. 1–18.
[47] This subsection is adapted from L. Wade, '"The Honour of Giving My Opinion": General Average, Insurance and the Compilation of the *Ordonnance de la marine* of 1681', in M. Fusaro, A. Addobbati, and L. Piccinno (eds), *General Average and Risk Management in Medieval and Early Modern Maritime Business*, Basingstoke: Palgrave Macmillan, 2023, pp. 415–30.

this provided blueprints for a more propitious push by Colbert for greater state control over legal affairs in 1667 and beyond. This would culminate in the 1681 *Ordonnance de la marine*.

What had changed between 1627 and 1667? Colbert's ability to push for legal codification stemmed from the *détente* that emerged between the crown and the nobility in the aftermath of the *Frondes*.[48] These were a set of uprisings throughout France in the period 1648–53 with roots in municipal and provincial grievances towards Louis XIV's chief minister during his minority, Cardinal Mazarin.[49] After reaching his majority in 1651, Louis pursued a successful policy of amnesty, and his assumption of personal rule in 1661 allowed the crown to re-establish ties with elite groups in the provinces.[50]

Outside of France, the international climate had also shifted substantially. Colbert's newfound capacity to pursue fiscal and maritime reforms was supported by a strong *need* to pursue such reforms in light of the rapid naval development of England and the United Provinces in the 1650s and 1660s. After the 1659 Franco-Spanish Treaty of the Pyrenees, Louis XIV's gaze turned northwards to the new Protestant threats whose presses painted France as a paradigm of popish 'tyranny' for the remainder of the century.[51] Charles-Édouard Levillain has argued that these decades witnessed the emergence of a 'triangular relationship' between France, England and the United Provinces, each with factions trying to play off against others in the pursuit of their own interests. French efforts to intrude on Anglo-Dutch disputes reflected Louis' wish to assume political strength within this new political arena. Moreover, Colbert was truly obsessed with the economic success of the Dutch after 1648 and consciously modelled his commercial projects on Dutch archetypes.[52]

With the crushing of the *Frondes*, Louis XIV's declaration of personal rule and no prospect of significant warfare until the Dutch War (1672–78), Colbert pursued widespread reform with far less resistance than his predecessors had faced. We have seen that Colbert sought to tackle the challenges posed by the

---

[48] This is recognised in B. Allaire, 'Between Oléron and Colbert: The Evolution of French Maritime Law until the Seventeenth Century', in M. Fusaro, B. Allaire, R. Blakemore, and T. Vanneste (eds), *Law, Labour and Empire: Comparative Perspectives on Seafarers, c. 1500–1800*, Basingstoke: Palgrave Macmillan, 2015, p. 99.

[49] Although Mazarin was the central focus of resistance towards Louis XIV's regency government, disaffection had already been growing since the rise of Richelieu as first minister under Louis XIII; on this, see Parrott, *1652*, pp. 1–43.

[50] N. Brière, *La douceur du roi. Le gouvernement de Louis XIV et la fin des Frondes (1648–1661)*, Québec: Presses de l'Université Laval, 2011, pp. 28–9; Parrott, *1652*, pp. 259–80.

[51] Levillain, *Vaincre Louis XIV*, pp. 111 and 363–4.

[52] See Chapter 1.

state debt.[53] He similarly pursued order in naval affairs as finance minister and, after 1669, in his capacity as secretary of state for maritime affairs.[54]

These naval interests dovetailed with Colbert's broader maritime and commercial interests, which were all supported by ambitious legal interventions.[55] Amongst a broader administrative reform – including the 1667 *Ordonnance civile*, the 1669 *Ordonnance sur les eaux et forêts* and the 1670 *Ordonnance criminelle* – came Colbert's famous 1673 *Ordonnance sur le commerce* and 1681 *Ordonnance de la marine*. Together, these codified law across many aspects of French life. The *Ordonnance de la marine*'s 730 articles enshrined the undivided authority of the admiralties in a vast array of maritime disputes, including insurance and averages.[56]

Colbert's approach to jurisdictional reform of maritime affairs was careful: he did not wish to risk unnecessary resistance from maritime communities and regional elites. The *Ordonnance*'s compilers therefore adhered to previous practice where possible, drawing on a wide array of older legal texts. To access these, Colbert and the compilers benefited from an extensive process of information gathering.[57] Nevertheless, the efforts of Richelieu and his humanist circle loomed large in the *Ordonnance*'s compilation. Cleirac and Godefroy may not have succeeded in their efforts under Louis XIII, but their work eventually bore fruit.

For centuries, writers have recognised the influence of these texts on the *Ordonnance*. René-Josué Valin's eighteenth-century commentary strove to understand the *Ordonnance*'s 'principles, sense and spirit' through painstakingly documenting its legal borrowing.[58] Similarly, while the eighteenth-century Marseillais lawyer Balthazard-Marie Émérigon acknowledged in passing that provincial institutions 'were without doubt consulted' on the *Ordonnance*, his emphasis remained on the legal texts preceding it. After introducing an array of medieval compilations,

---

[53] See Chapter 1.
[54] Here, see, among others, É. Taillemitte, 'Colbert et la marine', in R. Mousnier (ed.), *Un nouveau Colbert: actes du Colloque pour le tricentenaire de la mort de Colbert*, Paris: Editions SEDES/CDU, 1985, pp. 217–27; Zysberg, 'Entre soumission et résistance'; Allaire, 'Between Oléron and Colbert'; Darnell, 'Naval Policy'.
[55] These interests are discussed in Chapter 1.
[56] Allaire, 'Between Oléron and Colbert', p. 90.
[57] On the process of information gathering about the admiralties more broadly in the decades before the *Ordonnance*, see Chadelat, 'L'élaboration de l'Ordonnance' I, pp. 74–98. On the process of information gathering about maritime law in the run up to 1681, including the theory that M. Bonaventure de Fourcroy was editor of the *Ordonnance*, see Chadelat, 'L'élaboration de l'Ordonnance' II, pp. 228–53. On the Dutch influences on the *Guidon* and the *Ordonnance*, see Warlomont, 'Les sources néerlandaises', pp. 333–44.
[58] Valin, *Nouveau commentaire*, vol. I, p. VII.

including the *Rôles d'Oléron* and the *Guidon de la mer*, he concluded that 'the 1681 *Ordonnance* is a composite of all these ancient laws'.[59] Later, the nineteenth-century legal scholar Arthur Desjardins wrote that, 'up to Valin, nothing has been written on maritime law that can compare to the *Guidon*, and the editors of the 1681 *grande Ordonnance* had no other model'.[60] In adopting this textual focus, all three men applauded the compilers' deft ability to draw on prior legal compilations to create a coherent and comprehensive document of legal practice.[61]

The significance of these texts is indisputable. How they were used in the compilation of the *Ordonnance* needs to be reinterpreted, however, in light of the Chamber's influence.

Indeed, the Chamber played a key role in the compilation process, as revealed in the preface of Savary's *Le parfait négociant*.[62] Here, Savary justified his decision to not treat extensively on maritime affairs, explaining that, having been informed of the *Ordonnance*'s ongoing process of drafting, he did not wish to make claims that would eventually contradict it. In a piece of self-fashioning common in commercial manuals of the period, Savary added that 'I even had the honour of giving my opinion in the [Royal] Insurance Chamber of this city of Paris' on matters pertaining to the forthcoming *Ordonnance*.[63] This opportunity likely arose from his services as an external arbiter for the Chamber in instances of policy disputes.[64]

The minutes of the Chamber's general assemblies record only one instance of this process. On 7 August 1676 – after *Le parfait négociant* was published, suggesting the Chamber's involvement in the *Ordonnance* was not isolated – a general assembly was held, where Bellinzani asked the members[65] to give their opinion on two questions: first, in instances of the redemption of captured ships where the contribution of the ship and merchandise are obligatory through general average, should the freight also contribute? Secondly, should the merchandise be valued at the rate of purchase, or at their value in the place where they are eventually unloaded?[66]

---

[59] B. Émérigon, *Traité des assurances et des contrats à la grosse*, vol. I, Rennes: Chez Molliex, 1827, p. XIV.

[60] Quoted in Boiteux, *La fortune de mer*, p. 123.

[61] For more on these (and other) jurists and compilers, see É. Roulet, 'Les traités sur l'assurance maritime en France à l'époque moderne', in C. Borde and É. Roulet (eds), *L'assurance maritime XIVe–XXIe siècle*, Aachen: Shaker Verlag, 2017, pp. 125–41.

[62] On *Le parfait négociant*, see Chapters 1 and 7.

[63] Savary, *Le parfait négociant*, vol. I, book I, p. XIII.

[64] Z/1d/73, fol. 21; Z/1d/74, fols 39r–40v, AN.

[65] *Messieurs* Bellettes de Vaux, Pocquelin *frères*, Raguienne, Margas, Froment, Dorigny, Estancelin, Francois, Villain, Maillet, Formont and Mignot were recorded as attendees of the assembly; Z/1d/73, fol. 29v, AN.

[66] Ibid.

The members were eminently qualified to respond to these questions. We have already seen that they frequently grappled with the intricacies of general average. Yet this posed a problem, as the underwriters' technical knowledge of general average was intimately intertwined with their direct stake in the *Ordonnance*'s position: how a contribution to general average was to be determined could radically alter the scale of an insurer's pay-out and the scope for further dispute. The members therefore opted to give clear, decisive answers following a logic that best served their interests.

Answering the first question, the members concluded that the ship – alongside its equipment and 'provisions', the money advanced to the crew and 'generally all which is spent to put the ship to sea' – is liable for contribution, in addition to the merchandise.[67] The freight should not contribute to the average, however, as it is precisely the ship and the associated costs which generate the freight – in other words, the freight constitutes payment for the service provided through these investments. It would therefore be unjust, they argued, if the ship 'was to pay twice [for] the same thing, and it is for this reason that the *ordonnances de la mer* will that it is the ship or the freight which contributes, but not both'.[68]

The phrase '*ordonnances de la mer*' here most likely refers to several maritime compilations from the late medieval period. No doubt the members had the *Rôles d'Oléron* in mind: while the earliest versions of the *Rôles* made no mention of freight, later versions, including the version in *Us et coutumes*, empowered the shipmaster to 'say whether to count the ship or his freightage, at his choice, to compensate the damage'.[69] This was to the benefit of the shipmaster, who could simply choose between the ship and the freight depending on which would require the smallest contribution. The *Ordinancie* of Amsterdam – which heavily influenced the *Waterrecht*, another significant medieval compilation – diverged here in giving this power of choice to the merchants.[70]

In this case, the Chamber members openly defied prior legal compilations by arguing there should be no choice between the ship and the freight in each case: instead, the ship should always contribute while the freight should not. On the surface, this was not a self-interested response, as freight was broadly recognised to be beyond the insurer's remit. In the *Guidon de la mer*, article 1 of the section *Des asseurances sur corps de nef* allows for insurance on the ship and its materials, but 'by no means on the freight', in conformity with the

---

[67] Ibid.
[68] Ibid.
[69] Frankot, '*Of Laws of Ships and Shipmen*', p. 39; Cleirac, *Us et coutumes*.
[70] Frankot, '*Of Laws of Ships and Shipmen*', pp. 42–3.

practices of Antwerp and Amsterdam.[71] If anything, the insurers stood to lose out if their suggestion was implemented, as the contribution demanded by the effects they insured would be greater than if the freight was included. The members sought greater uniformity and clarity in maritime practice here, even if it did not seem to serve their own interests.

This logic fed into the members' answer to the second question, helping us to understand why they took this position in the first place. They suggested that the merchandise subject to contribution should be valued based on how much it cost in the place of purchase rather than its estimated value in the place of unloading, as 'the evaluation of merchandise in the latter place is a variable, uncertain thing and subject to contesting', while the cost in the place of purchase 'is always certain and is justified by invoices and other items'.[72] This was an entirely unconventional recommendation: article 8 of the *Rôles d'Oléron* suggested that merchandise subject to contribution should be valued based on the price received in the place of unloading. This was also the common practice of Antwerp after the sixteenth century, per Quentin Weytsen's famous manual on averages.[73]

Why did the members wish for the *Ordonnance* to go against the grain here? Again, they strove for certainty – but, in this instance, certainty met their own interests. We have seen that merchandise was by far the most insured effect in the Chamber.[74] Thus, the benefits of the Chamber's logic were clear: contributions from merchandise based on the cost in the place of purchase would almost always be lower than those based on the value in the place of unloading. Even though this proposal risked underwriters being liable for greater costs in instances where they insured the ship, the merchandise's contribution would at least be 'certain': valuing the merchandise based on invoices rather than estimates would engender confidence in the validity of the general average calculus. Moreover, set documentary standards would create a clear paper trail alleviating the information asymmetries faced in Paris.[75]

---

[71] Cleirac, *Us et coutumes*, p. 265. The *Ordonnance* proved no different, prohibiting any insurance of the freight in article 15 of the section *Des assurances*; Valin, *Nouveau commentaire*, vol. II, p. 58.

[72] Z/1d/73, fol. 29v, AN.

[73] Cleirac, *Us et coutumes*, pp. 28–9; Valin, *Nouveau commentaire*, vol. II, p. 194. In instances of jettison, Hassan Khalilieh has found that there was often widespread dispute in medieval Islamic discourse as to whether jettisoned goods should be ascribed a value based on the market price in the port of departure, the port of destination, the point of jettison or another point entirely; H. Khalilieh, *Islamic Maritime Law: An Introduction*, Leiden: Brill, 1998, pp. 99–100.

[74] See Chapter 4.

[75] Information asymmetries are discussed at length in Chapter 3.

This sheds light on why the members argued so strongly to exclude freight from contributing to redemption costs. Since they argued that contributing merchandise should be valued based on its cost *before* the redemption, it would have been inconsistent for them to have argued that the freight – paid at the *conclusion* of the voyage – must contribute.[76]

In short, the Chamber stood to benefit from its own proposal. The members argued that the selection and valuation of contributing effects should be derived from documentation produced, and actions made, *before* the redemption of the ship. Consequently, they strove to exclude freight – the payment of which was a by-product of the completed voyage – from general average contributions and to value the merchandise based on its price in the place of purchase. This *ex-ante* logic aimed to limit pay-outs and to create documentary standards that would aid the members' underwriting.

The *Ordonnance* bears the imprint of this input, but the Chamber's logic apparently did not persuade the compilers. Article 20 of the section *Du fret ou nolis* mandates that

> contributions for the redemption [of ships] will be made on [1] the standard price of merchandise in the place of their unloading, deducting fees, and [2] on the total [value] of the ship and freight, deducting consumed provisions and advances made to the sailors, who will also contribute to the benefit of the freight, in proportion to what remains due of their wages.[77]

The *Ordonnance* therefore determined, in defiance of earlier compilations, that both ship and freight should contribute, albeit with specific deductions. The bipartite structuring of the article, reflecting the questions posed to the Chamber, and the precise deductions which were mandated indicate that the Chamber's argument was taken into account, but the *ex-ante* logic it proposed for calculating contributions was rejected. Specifically, the compilers seem to have been receptive to the argument that any voyage involving the freighting of merchandise depends upon a significant upfront investment. The members identified the 'provisions' and the money advanced to the crew as examples of services provided by the shipmaster and/or ship-owners for which the freight is given. While the compilers clearly did not agree with their conclusion that the freight should not contribute, the article specifically deducted 'consumed provisions and advances made to the sailors' from the total value of the ship and the freight. Key aspects from the members' discussion were therefore integrated into the *Ordonnance*, but through an entirely different logic.

---

[76] I am grateful to Sabine Go for her thoughts on this.
[77] Valin, *Nouveau commentaire*, vol. I, p. 663.

What was this logic? While the Chamber's members sought a level of uniformity and transparency that would have supported their underwriting activities, the *Ordonnance* article is more complicated, reflecting the need to address the interests of all the stakeholders in a voyage. Rejecting the Chamber's call to value merchandise based on its price in the place of purchase, the article echoed the *Rôles d'Oléron* and the practices of Antwerp in stipulating that merchandise be valued at the 'standard price' in the place of unloading. This likely aimed to anticipate and respond to the argument that would be posed by shipmasters that, without the ship's redemption, merchandise would never reach the eventual place of unloading; therefore, merchandise should contribute in line with the 'added value' engendered by the ship's redemption. The same logic holds true for the ship and freight: since the shipmaster's control of the ship and the earning of their freight at the end of the voyage depends on the ship's redemption, it is fair that both contribute. This is also why sailors were required to contribute in proportion to their outstanding wages.

Therefore, while the Chamber argued strongly for an *ex-ante* approach to selecting and valuing any contributing effects, the *Ordonnance* enshrined an *ex-post* logic. The *Ordonnance*'s compilers focused on the benefits generated *as a result* of the ship's redemption, thereby concluding that freight ought to contribute and merchandise be valued based on its 'standard price' in the place of unloading. This inversion of logic reflects the different interests that were at stake: the *ex-ante* logic proposed by the Chamber would have served the interests of the insurer, but not of the other parties in the voyage.

The *Ordonnance* echoed the *Guidon de la mer* in holding insurers liable for general average costs in article 46 of the section *Des Assurances*, while article 6 of the section *Des Avaries* defined all costs relating to the redemption of ships and merchandise as being within the remit of general average.[78] The fears of the Chamber's underwriters were realised: the *Ordonnance* held insurers liable for redemption costs incurred by policyholders, and these costs were to be calculated based on the 'variable, uncertain' estimates of contributing merchandise in the place of unloading. Although the crown benefited from the Chamber's expertise while compiling the *Ordonnance*, the Chamber's own interests were not necessarily served in the process.

This is an important corrective to a legal literature that has understandably focused on the *Ordonnance*'s debts to prior texts. I do not wish to suggest this literature is wrong – on the contrary, these legal sources were invaluable to the *Ordonnance*'s construction – but we need to view this process of construction in a new light. As we have seen, these texts were the basis for discussions between the Chamber and the monarchy on how best to serve the needs of

---

[78] Ibid., vol. II, pp. 99 and 165.

different stakeholders in voyages. The Chamber's members recognised they had a large role to play in determining what constituted commonplace practice, but, as the dispute on general average in 1670 made clear, texts were far from perfect vessels of legal wisdom: they required interpretation, upon which hinged the interests of numerous maritime stakeholders. François Olivier-Martin has noted that good counsel was sought for the *Ordonnance du commerce*, and the *Ordonnance* was no different here – but the counsel given in this instance was not accepted in its entirety.[79] The *Ordonnance* was therefore not simply a coherent and disinterested synthesis of prior legal compilations: these compilations were the basis for a broader process of negotiation, whereby the state sought to mediate and reconcile the interests of various stakeholders in the maritime sphere.

THE COMPANY AND THE *ORDONNANCE*: THE LAW OF INSURANCE, AVERAGES AND ABANDONMENT

Before the *Ordonnance* was issued, it was influenced significantly by the Chamber's input, albeit not always with the results the latter had intended. The Chamber's successor would take up the mantle in shaping the *Ordonnance*'s reception across France. The Company's letters patent open with the statement that

> Ever since we began our task of re-establishing maritime commerce – the jurisprudence of which we have set through various regulations and by our *Ordonnance* of the month of August 1681 – many of our subjects have undertaken insurance policies with much advantage, having avoided great losses in return for the modest sums they have paid to insure their vessels and merchandise. It is this that has brought us to encourage several merchants and other knowledgeable people in commerce to come together for the establishment of an insurance chamber, in the form of a Company [with] common funds and signatures, on condition that they contribute a significant fund in order that merchants who would like to use this means of reducing the risks they run in their daily commerce [can] undertake it and continue it with greater ease and security.[80]

The establishment of the Company was a continuation of the broader strategy of maritime legal reform in which the *Ordonnance* was *a* (not *the only*) centrepiece. The letters patent herald the *Ordonnance*'s success in helping merchants to manage risk. Implicit is the assumption, however, that the *Ordonnance* alone could not propel the insurance industry or

---

[79] F. Olivier-Martin, *Histoire du droit français. Des origines à la Révolution*, Paris: CNRS Éditions, 2010, p. 399.
[80] Bornier, *Conférences des ordonnances de Louis XIV*, vol. II, p. 513.

protect merchants: while the admiralty courts could punish underwriters for wrongdoing, the *Ordonnance* itself could not force correct practice. The Company was needed so merchants could seek insurance coverage 'with greater ease and security' than was on offer up to that point. The implication was clear: the Company was to embrace the *Ordonnance* as the model for its underwriting, thereby setting an example for other underwriters in France to follow. This would ensure the protection of mercantile interests, fulfilling the agenda set decades earlier by Colbert.

The Company took this role seriously, engaging systematically with the *Ordonnance* and its provisions. In particular, influences from the *Ordonnance* sections *Des Assurances* and *Des Avaries* are to be found in its insurance policies and registers for declarations of average and abandonment. The remainder of this chapter will analyse the language of these documents alongside the *Ordonnance* and the prior legal compilations that shaped it. These documents attest to the *Ordonnance*'s rigorousness in defining averages and insurance coverage within a single coherent document. They also attest to the Company's value to the state as a model insurance institution with the power to influence insurance practices throughout the kingdom.

The grammar of the policy

The insurance policy was the bedrock of all the Company's activities. It was the document that contractually bound the Company and the policyholder to specific actions that could serve or undermine each party's interests. The Company's articles of association from 1686 recognised the significance of the policy form, stipulating that

> Policy forms will be reduced to only the essential clauses and [will be printed] in a small size, [in order] to be sent more easily by couriers; on the back of the policies will be printed the conditions under which losses and averages will be settled and paid, in order that the public is informed that the Company does not delay in payment, that on the contrary it will make it in advance and provisionally ...[81]

Up to now, the Company's policy form has not been studied. This is perhaps because, so far, there seem to be no policies in the *Archives nationales*. While the alphabetical register helps to fill in some gaps,[82] studying the policy form's grammar requires the full-form policies themselves.

Fortuitously, one has been unearthed. We have seen that Lagny sought Augustin Magy's support for the establishment of commercial links between

---

[81] Ibid., p. 521.
[82] See Chapter 5.

Paris and Marseille in 1686;[83] on 5 November 1687, Magy signed a policy with the institution himself in his capacity as a director of the Mediterranean Company. Recently, after being put on sale by a rare books specialist, this policy was acquired by the Institute and Faculty of Actuaries in London.[84]

The policy was clearly modelled on the *Ordonnance*. First, its structure mirrored article 3 of *Des Assurances*, the *Ordonnance* section on insurance practice. This article stated that

> the policy will contain [1] the name and place of residence of the person seeking insurance, their status as owner or as commission agent, the effects on which the insurance will be made, [2] the name of the ship and master, that of the place where the merchandise will have been or is expected to be loaded, [3] the harbour from which the vessel is expected to leave or will have left, the ports where it is expected to be loaded and unloaded, and all those where it is expected to enter, [4] the time at which the risks will commence and will finish, [5] the sums that they [i.e. the prospective policyholder] mean [i.e. wish] to insure, the premium or the cost of the insurance, [6] the submission of parties to arbiters, in case of contestation, and generally all the other conditions on which they will want to agree.[85]

The *Guidon* offered a clear model here, as these provisions are almost identical to those made by the Rouennais manual.[86]

The policy adhered to these provisions very closely:

1. Magy and Jean Andre Fredian were named, with their elected place of residence stated and their status as directors of the Mediterranean Company indicated. It was then stated that the merchandise being insured was 'for the account' of this company, confirming the directors' direct relationship with this merchandise.
2. The *Armes de France* was named as the ship carrying the goods to be insured, with Jean Jansen as master.
3. Constantinople was listed as the port of departure, with the implication it was also the port where the goods were laden. Marseille was

---

[83] See Chapter 3.
[84] BYQ/517 pam prm3b, Institute and Faculty of Actuaries Library, London. The handwriting matches that of the handwriting in the registers analysed in the rest of the book, indicating that the scribe was the same; moreover, the directors' signatures on the policy match those in the registers. We can therefore be confident about the policy's provenance.
[85] Valin, *Nouveau commentaire*, vol. II, p. 31.
[86] The prescriptions in this article of the *Ordonnance* are, in some parts, word for word copies of the first article of a chapter of the *Guidon* entitled *Ce que doit contenir la Police*; Cleirac, *Us et coutumes*, p. 194.

listed as the port of destination, with no expected stops at other ports indicated.
4. The duration of the risk borne by the Company was explicitly stated, beginning with the departure from Constantinople and ending six days after arrival in Marseille.[87]
5. The premium – calculated as a percentage of the total amount insured, here 8 per cent of 12,000 *livres* – was explicitly acknowledged.
6. The process of arbitration (to which I shall later return) was outlined as one of the policy's conditions.

Not only did the policy contain all the information that article 3 of *Des Assurances* required, but it did so in broadly the same order, indicating it was explicitly designed with a close eye to the *Ordonnance*: the printed portions and the handwritten portions alike adhered systematically to its requirements.

The policy explained that the Company would bear

> all perils, risks and fortunes, all losses and damages for the abovementioned effects, whether [incurred] by storm, grounding, shipwreck, boarding, fire and water, capture by enemies, pirates, or friends, letters of marque, or of reprisals, arrests of Princes or foreign rulers, and all other accidents, impediments and cases of fortune.

It acknowledged that 'the insurers are responsible [for these risks] by the terms of the *Ordonnance* of the month of August 1681'. Indeed, article 26 of *Des Assurances* outlined that insurers were liable for 'all losses and damages which will arrive on [the] sea by storm, shipwreck, groundings, boardings, changes of route, voyage or vessel, jettison, fire, captures, pillaging, arrest of the Prince, declarations of war, reprisals, and generally all other *fortunes de mer*'.[88] The language used by this article and that used by the policy form are almost identical, indicating the former was specifically and consciously used in constructing the latter.

At first glance, insurance historians would not find the extensive list of risks borne by the Company especially surprising. Sixteenth-century Marseillais insurance policies were known to cover all risks 'whether divine or human, [caused by] friends or enemies, familiar or unfamiliar, detention of princes whether ecclesiastical or temporal, reprisals, just or unjust [letters of] marque and countermarque, by [...] fire, wind, [or] jettison into the sea', extending

---

[87] The time lag after the vessel's arrival in Marseille was necessary because even the unloading of ships entailed a risk to the merchandise. This 'risk-trap of entering and leaving port' is discussed in Spooner, *Risks at Sea*, p. 9.
[88] Valin, *Nouveau commentaire*, vol. II, p. 74.

'to all other perils or cases of fortune which could obtain.'[89] This seems to be broadly representative of the risks borne by many French insurers in the decades leading up to the *Ordonnance*: a policy signed in Rouen dated 15 October 1669 (used in the 1671 edition of *Us et coutumes* as a 'formula of the insurance policy following the *Guidon*') stated that the insurers had

> entirely taken on the risk and adventure as our [own] perils and fortunes, whether by peril of sea, fire, wind, friends or enemies, or some other prize, arrest of [the] king or [the] Prince, or some other Seigneur, letters of marque, countermarque, barratry of shipmasters or mariners and generally of all other thought or unthought inconveniences, which could come to the merchandise or portion of it.[90]

Therefore, the risks the Company covered were very similar to those that had been covered by insurers throughout France before 1681 – and, indeed, throughout most of Europe. In this instance, the *Ordonnance* was not especially innovative.

However, the 'losses and damages' for which the Company was responsible were conceived in a manner that reflected the state's novel jurisdictional ambitions. The Company's decision to keep a register at any one time in which policyholders could make declarations of abandonment and/or average acknowledged a legal division between the two that directly reflected the *Ordonnance*'s distinction between losses and damages. If the policyholder declared abandonment, they transferred ownership of the insured effects to the underwriter in exchange for payment on the policy. This gave the underwriter the opportunity to salvage the goods if they wished.[91] By contrast, no transfer of property was entailed in a declaration of average; the underwriter simply made payment to the insured.

What distinguished average and abandonment? In the *Ordonnance*, article 46 of *Des Assurances* established that

> abandonment will only be possible in cases of capture, shipwreck, grounding, arrest of the Prince, or entire loss of the insured effects; and all other damages will be regarded as average, which will be shared

---

[89] Quoted in Boiteux, *La fortune de mer*, p. 152. This was not uncommon for the sixteenth century or earlier centuries: the London Code, written in the late 1570s and early 1580s, covered very similar risks; Rossi, *Insurance in Elizabethan England*, p. 258.

[90] Cleirac, *Us et coutumes*, pp. 290–3. The same risks are borne in an insurance policy from Nantes in 1658; C/760, n.p., *Archives départementales de Loire-Atlantique*. I am again indebted to Mallory Hope for providing me with a copy of this policy.

[91] For an example of this, see Chapter 3.

between the insurers and the insured, in proportion to their interests [i.e. in proportion to the amount of risk borne by each].[92]

This was further clarified in article 1 of *Des Avaries*, where it was determined that 'all damages which will befall it [i.e. the ship and/or merchandise] from its loading and departure up to its return and unloading, will be regarded as averages'.[93] Article 2 offered a clear definition of both general and particular average:

> extraordinary expenses for the ship alone, or for the merchandise alone, and the damage which happens to them in particular, are simple and particular average [*avaries simples et particulieres*]; and the extraordinary expenses made, and the damage suffered for the good and common salvation of the merchandise and the vessel, are general and common average [*avaries grosses et communes*].[94]

Therefore, the *Ordonnance* drew a juridical distinction between 'loss' and 'damage', with abandonment and average being the respective outcomes of the legal processes that followed these events. French insurers, including the Company's underwriters, were liable for both. In the case of both general and particular averages, the insurers were obliged to reimburse policyholders *pro rata*.

Similarly, *pro rata* payment by insurers for averages was established in the *Guidon*, which, as we have seen, was one of the principal normative sources of the *Ordonnance*.[95] However, the *Guidon* offered an analytically blunt definition of averages, without clear reference to abandonments. The first article of the chapter *Des Avaries* in the *Guidon* found that all 'fees [...] averages and devaluation which occurs to the merchandise since it has been loaded [...] is included [i.e. comprised] in this word average'.[96] Thus, while we see that the *Guidon* implicitly moved towards categorising all fees and costs associated with voyages in contradistinction to losses, it still viewed

---

[92] Valin, *Nouveau commentaire*, vol. II, p. 99. The law of wreck was referred to as the *droit de bris et naufrage*; Trivellato, '"Usages and Customs of the Sea"', pp. 200–1.
[93] Valin, *Nouveau commentaire*, vol. II, p. 158.
[94] Ibid., p. 159.
[95] Cleirac, *Us et coutumes*, p. 199. The insurer's responsibility for general average expenses under the *Ordonnance* was in line with European norms up to this point. In the main, insurers had not been liable for general average – even with general peril clauses (whose scope generally depended on the place of insurance in question) – before the sixteenth century. However, as noted above, general average came to be covered by the insurers of Antwerp in the middle of the century. Rossi, *Insurance in Elizabethan England*, p. 259; Cleirac, *Us et coutumes*, pp. 211–12; Boiteux, *La fortune de mer*, pp. 152–3.
[96] Cleirac, *Us et coutumes*, p. 211.

damages as synonymous with averages. The *Ordonnance* regarded them as distinct: an average was the specific result of the legal process undertaken following damages being sustained. In applying the *Ordonnance*, this legal process was twofold, as seen in Figure 3 below. First, the admiralty judge had to establish whether these damages would give rise to particular or to general average, a choice that rested on how he wished to ascribe liability for the damages (if at all); second, in the case of general average, the distribution of the damages had to be calculated.[97] Article 3 of the section *De la Compétence des Juges de l'Amirauté* explicitly outlined that all averages, and the calculations attached to them, came under the remit of the admiralty courts, while article 15 prohibited all other authorities from handling them.[98] Thus, while the *Guidon*'s interest in averages related to insurance practice alone, the *Ordonnance*'s interest served different ends. In defining averages as it did, the *Ordonnance* transformed them into a maritime legal affair henceforth to be dealt with by the admiralty courts alone.

Guidon

Damage = average

Ordonnance

Damage → average =   1. General or particular?
                                          2. Calculation of costs

Loss → Abandonment

Figure 3   A comparison of the conceptualisation of average in the *Guidon* and the *Ordonnance*.

The policy itself acknowledged that the *Ordonnance* required all averages and abandonments to be covered. In the case of damages, an admiralty court would handle the average proceedings and issue the requisite calculations, while the Company would pay out *pro rata*. But the *Ordonnance* did not require the risks borne by the insurer to be outlined in the policy. The Company did so anyway, suggesting it perceived there were benefits

---

[97] By definition, a declaration of general average presumes that nobody is solely liable for the damages, whether through negligence or as otherwise defined in the *Ordonnance*. A declaration of general average therefore presupposes that the shipmaster has not been negligent in the given circumstances; any negligence on the shipmaster's part, as defined in the *Ordonnance*, would have rendered him liable for the damages, which would be declared as a particular average to be borne by him alone. See G. Rossi, 'The Liability of the Shipmaster in Early Modern Law: Comparative (and Practice-Oriented) Remarks', *Historia et ius* 12 (2017), p. 37.

[98] Valin, *Nouveau commentaire*, vol. I, pp. 127 and 155.

to doing so. First, it perhaps ensured that the risks of policy disputes were minimised: while the Company was clearly well acquainted with the provisions of the *Ordonnance*, policyholders may not have had the same understanding. Full transparency was valuable to both parties. Secondly, such close reference to, and explicit acknowledgement of, the *Ordonnance* was just one of several ways in which the Company signalled its status as a state-sponsored institution: adopting the language of the *Ordonnance* acknowledged the ultimate legal authority of the state.

For similar reasons, the policy form dealt carefully with pay-outs and conflict resolution. The form bound the Company to making payment on abandonments and averages three months after the initial declaration, or in advance with a discount.[99] It also outlined a set procedure for arbitration in case of conflict.[100] As noted above, article 3 of the section *Des Assurances* required policies to confirm that disputes will be resolved by external arbiters.[101] This was a delegation of the authority of the admiralty courts, as outlined in articles 2–3 of *De la Compétence*. Article 72 of *Des Assurances* prescribed that all judgments from arbitration proceedings were to be ratified by the regional admiralty court, reflecting the admiralty courts' ultimate authority over maritime affairs; appeals of ratified judgments were ostensibly to be brought before the regional *parlement*, as per article 73.[102]

So how exactly did arbitration work? Articles 70–74 of *Des Assurances* outlined the process. Article 70 required that, if a party to the policy wished to argue before arbiters, the other party was compelled to agree to this and to participate in the process. This process, article 71 indicated, involved

---

[99] This discount was most likely proportionate to the amount of time in advance of the deadline that payment was being made. For abandonments, payment within three months was generally obligatory, as established through article 44 of *Des Assurances*: 'if the time of payment is not set by the policy, the insurer will be responsible to pay the insurance three months after the declaration of abandonment'; Valin, *Nouveau commentaire*, vol. II, p. 98. Although the *Ordonnance* did not specify the repayment period for averages, the Company's letters patent and printed policy form made clear that it was equally bound to pay averages in three months; Bornier, *Conférences des ordonnances de Louis XIV*, vol. II, pp. 513–25. This differed slightly from the *Guidon*, which required that payment be made in two months rather than three; Cleirac, *Us et coutumes*, p. 203.

[100] This will be discussed far more fully in Chapter 8, including the appeal process and the procedure for ratifying the judgments of arbiters.

[101] Valin notes that, in reality, policies which did not confirm this were not necessarily void: it was often still presumed that arbitration would take place in instances of dispute; Valin, *Nouveau commentaire*, vol. II, p. 154.

[102] Ibid., pp. 156–7. As we will see in Chapter 8, the Company was subject to a privileged appeals system.

the nomination of arbiters by the parties.[103] Although avoiding the need to outline the compulsion to participate in these proceedings – the policy form wished to presume good faith from both the Company and the policyholder – the policy form certainly acknowledged the recognised duty for 'each side' to 'name an arbiter' in case 'difficulty' arises. Moreover, as the arbitration process began, the Company was clear that it 'offer[s] to pay provisionally but under caution'. This 'offer' implied a generous concession on the part of the Company, but, in fact, this was another example of it having merely acted in accordance with its obligations per the *Ordonnance*: article 61 stipulated that, even if they disputed the claim, the insurer was 'provisionally condemned to payment of the insured sums' to the policyholder.[104] This adapted a similar requirement for provisional payment in the *Guidon*.[105] Thus, the policy form was adroitly constructed to invoke the *Ordonnance* where it served the Company's interests while, elsewhere, deftly implying its own agency in order to present itself as a moral commercial entity.[106] This careful ambiguity blurred the lines between legal obligation and commercial ethics.

The policy also offers a valuable insight into the information required in establishing a voyage's riskiness. It noted that the *Armes de France* was 'equipped with a French passport in good order'. This established that the ship was legally sailing as a French vessel: the *Ordonnance* granted sole power to issue *congés*, passports, safe-conducts and other similar documents for seafaring to the French admiralties.[107] At least ostensibly, a French passport – offering a ship the right to fly the French flag – granted protection from the corsairs of the Ottoman Regencies with whom France had made protective treaties, such as Algiers and Tunis.[108] In any case, as corsairs were known to ignore passports, this was not an ironclad guarantee of protection. However, it at least offered scope for the ship and its cargo to be declared an illegitimate prize, thereby reducing the risk to the Company of entire loss.[109]

This information was doubtless factored into the calculation of the premium. In this policy, it was 8 per cent: Magy and Fredian paid 960

---

[103] Ibid., pp. 154–5.
[104] Ibid., p. 144.
[105] Cleirac, *Us et coutumes*, p. 207. A key difference, which I will explore further in Chapter 7, is that the *Guidon* required provisional payment only after prescribed documentation was submitted to the insurers; the *Ordonnance*'s requirements here were vague.
[106] The Company's corporate identity will be discussed further in Chapter 8.
[107] Valin, *Nouveau commentaire*, vol. I, p. 66. The exception was passports for the colonies: Lagny alone had the power to issue these; on this, see Chapter 3.
[108] C. Zwierlein, *Imperial Unknowns: The French and British in the Mediterranean, 1650–1750*, Cambridge: Cambridge University Press, 2016, pp. 35–6.
[109] Calafat and Kaiser, 'Le laboratoire méditerranéen', pp. 244–5.

livres for the coverage of 12,000 *livres* of merchandise. However, they also committed to 'pay[ing] a 3 per cent rise in the premium' if 'war breaks out between France and any possible nation (excepting the Saletins [sic] and the Algerians)'. The implication was that, if this augmented premium was not paid, the policy would no longer be binding. The *Ordonnance* did not offer guidance for or against practices like this; the Company clearly introduced this clause to mitigate the risk of the *Armes de France* being caught out if war broke out.[110]

At its heart, the form was leveraging the state's political capital, drawing attention to the *Ordonnance* at every turn to signal the Company's own status as a state-sponsored institution.[111] Yet the form also served state interests. It became a model in Mathieu de la Porte's famous accounting manual, *La Science des Négocians et Teneurs de Livres*. Originally published in 1704, later editions included an edited version of a policy said to have been signed by the Company on 24 March 1709, which was referred to as a 'model insurance policy'.[112] It was not a complete replica of the form, with adaptations and omissions made to provide a model the reader could apply in most scenarios. Nevertheless, the list of risks covered in this model policy was identical to that in the policy of 1687.[113] In this way, the Company led the way for the rest of the kingdom by providing a policy form in full compliance with the *Ordonnance* that others could replicate for their own use.[114]

The influence of the policy form went further than this, however, as can be seen in the Company's extensive underwriting of Breton interests. Brittany was perhaps the most significant battleground in establishing the admiralties' jurisdiction throughout France, as the region fought fiercely to preserve its juridical hierarchy. While Colbert brought the admiralties' powers under the umbrella of the re-established *amirauté de France* in 1669, Brittany's admiralty powers remained in the separate hands of the governor of Brittany until

---

[110] On how the *Ordonnance*'s silence on augmentation clauses was problematic, see Wade, 'Royal Companies'.

[111] The Company's use of its royal patronage to fashion its commercial identity will be discussed further in Chapter 8.

[112] M. de la Porte, *La Science des Négocians et Teneurs de Livres, ou Instruction Générale Pour tout ce qui se pratique dans les Comptoirs des Négocians*, Amsterdam: Aux Dépens de la Compagnie, 1770, p. 477.

[113] The only noteworthy difference throughout was that the process of arbitration was now explicitly acknowledged to be in line with the *Ordonnance*'s provisions.

[114] Certainly, the dissemination of standardised insurance formulae throughout Europe had already been commonplace in prior centuries, but the editors of Porte's posthumous editions of *La Science des Négocians* were making a specific and conscious choice in deciding to print the Company's policy rather than any other.

Louis-Alexandre Bourbon, comte de Toulouse, held the positions of governor of Brittany and *amiral de France* simultaneously from 1695.[115] So strong was this defence of local jurisdictions that the *Ordonnance* only took force in the region after a Breton version was issued in November 1684 which recognised the governor's powers as admiral.[116] In response, the merchants of Nantes promptly issued a *mémoire* on 15 November resisting the *Ordonnance*'s requirements for shipmasters to submit reports to the admiralties about their voyages, arguing that such 'formalities [...] will cause many delays and trials that will ruin several families'.[117]

Within this climate of resistance, the Company had a valuable role to play. While Seignelay pursued a different strategy from Colbert in developing the French insurance industry, both men agreed on the importance of bringing maritime affairs under the state's jurisdiction and pushed for the universal recognition of the *Ordonnance*. We have seen that Seignelay was able to coerce Breton merchants (especially those of Nantes and Saint-Malo) into procuring coverage from the Company when local coverage proved insufficient.[118] Resistance towards the *Ordonnance* in Brittany was therefore undermined through the Company's underwriting in the region: merchants seeking coverage were forced to play by the rules of the game that were established, endorsed and upheld by the state and its legal hierarchy in the maritime sphere.

On a qualitative level, therefore, there is much to be learnt from a single insurance policy. In this case, it has revealed the Company's consistent dialogue with the *Ordonnance* and the impact of this on how the *Ordonnance* was received across France. But did the Company's policy form reflect how insurance was conducted in practice? Its declarations of average and abandonment shed some light on this.

The grammar and practicalities of the declaration

Article 16 of the Company's articles of association specified that

> In the registry, there will be at least seven registers kept by the registry clerk [...] One [...] in which the insured will be made by the clerk to sign all acts of abandonment and average.[119]

---

[115] M. Vary, 'L'État et l'appropriation du littoral sous Louis XIV', in G. Le Bouëdec (ed.), *L'Amirauté en Bretagne. Des origines à la fin du XVIIIe siècle*, Rennes: Presses universitaires de Rennes, 2012, p. 380.

[116] J. Darsel, 'L'Amirauté de Bretagne. Des origines à la Révolution', in G. Le Bouëdec (ed.), *L'Amirauté en Bretagne. Des origines à la fin du XVIIIe siècle*, Rennes: Presses universitaires de Rennes, 2012, p. 262.

[117] MAR/B/7/491, fols 396–413, AN.

[118] See Chapters 2 and 5.

[119] Bornier, *Conférences des ordonnances de Louis XIV*, vol. II, p. 520.

The extant declarations of abandonment and average are kept in two registers, documenting 590 declarations from the years 1686–92.[120] The vast majority of these followed a set formula, with the relevant details inserted in each case. They were written in the first person from the perspective of Jagault, the Company's registrar throughout its existence.[121] The beginning of the declaration typically adhered to the following formula, with occasional unsubstantial variations:

> At the request of Monsieur *[name, profession]*, living on *[road, city]* which he has taken up as his place of residence, having charge and acting for *[name, place]*,[122] I, the undersigned [i.e. Jagault] commit to the exercise of the registry of the [Royal] Insurance Company of France, established in Paris, certifying to have notified and duly brought to the attention of the gentlemen of the Company in speaking to *messieurs [directors]*, directors [of the Company] in their office [on] *rue Quincampoix*, that the ship named *[ship]*, commanded by *[master]* …[123]

The declaration then specified the relationship between the ship and the Company, namely through specifying the date(s) of any insurance policies or sea loans. From here, the declaration outlined the voyage undertaken, the peril encountered, and the damage and/or loss occasioned, before finally announcing the result: an average, an abandonment or both. In the case of an abandonment, the following formula was used, emphasising Jagault's power as registrar in the declaration:

> Through this declaration, I [i.e. Jagault] have made abandonment to the gentlemen of the Company of the interest that Monsieur *[name – the policyholder]* had in the ship, for the value up to the sum insured by them …[124]

In the case of an average, a formula was not used: it was simply stated that the aforementioned events and the accompanying damages had 'cause[d]' an average for which the Company was liable. Some policyholders, who were evidently aware of the *Ordonnance*'s provisions, requested payment on their

---

[120] A further thirty-nine declarations are also made, but these are primarily declarations clarifying policies or other declarations; they are therefore not included in the analysis here. Z/1d/82 and Z/1d/88, AN.
[121] For more on Jagault, see Chapter 2.
[122] Policyholders could make declarations on their own behalf; in such cases, the phrase 'having charge and acting for *[name, place]*' was removed: for example, see Z/1d/82, fol. 5r, AN.
[123] Z/1d/82 and Z/1d/88, AN.
[124] Ibid.

policies 'following the *Ordonnance*' or 'in the time of the *Ordonnance*', making clear this, and not the policy form, was the frame of reference in such matters.[125]

Once the abandonment or average was established, the declaration may have included a statement from the insured party declaring whether they had secured insurance or sea loans elsewhere. If they did, they stated the place(s) where they took out any further contracts and the value(s) of these. As it is, the majority of declarations with such a statement used a variation on the following formula:

> ... declaring moreover that Monsieur *[name]* has not made any other insurance on this merchandise than that dated above [i.e. the policy with the Company] nor taken any sea loans ...[126]

Over-insurance was a perennial risk, so this statement forced policyholders to acknowledge any other policies they had contracted. This served as evidence if they were later found to have fraudulently claimed beyond what was permitted. Unless explicitly expressed in the policy, policyholders were obliged to bear at least 10 per cent of the risk in any given voyage, as per article 16 of *Des Assurances*.[127] An identical requirement was found in the *Guidon*, itself mirroring the norms of Antwerp and Amsterdam.[128] Article 53 of *Des Assurances* therefore obliged policyholders, 'in declaring abandonment, to declare all insurance policies they have made, and sea loans they have taken on the insured effects'.[129] This statement was not obliged in cases of average, perhaps owing to the smaller amounts of capital involved. Nevertheless, occasional instances of average declarations making such affirmative or negative statements can sometimes be found.

Table 29   Types of statement made about external insurance and/or loans in declarations of abandonment to the Company.

Statement within declarations of abandonment	Frequency	%
External insurance or sea loans	80	17.90
No external insurance or sea loans	279	62.42
Statement to be made at a later date	33	7.38
No statement made	55	12.30
Total	447	100

Source: Z/1d/82 and Z/1d/88, AN.

---

[125] For example, see Z/1d/82, fol. 9v, AN.
[126] Z/1d/82 and Z/1d/88, AN.
[127] Valin, *Nouveau commentaire*, vol. II, p. 62.
[128] Cleirac, *Us et coutumes*, p. 200.
[129] Valin, *Nouveau commentaire*, vol. II, p. 135.

Table 29 offers a tantalising insight into mercantile approaches to risk management in this period. Almost 18 per cent of declarations acknowledged securing insurance or sea loans outside of the Company. This suggests risk management tools themselves may have been the subject of risk management strategies. By securing insurance policies with different sets of underwriters, merchants potentially mitigated the risk of underwriters refusing to pay: a single underwriter refusing to pay a fraction of the sum insured overall would be less problematic than a single underwriter refusing to pay the entire insured sum, even if multiple sets of legal proceedings would perhaps be necessary to be fully indemnified. Moreover, as was seen in the Chamber in 1670, a policyholder could leverage the choice of one set of underwriters to indemnify them to pressure another set to make payment without further dispute.

The true percentage of declarations with additional insurance or sea loans was likely higher, but policyholders and commission agents were not always steadfast in acknowledging these. Indeed, from the 447 declarations of abandonment, fifty-five made no statement whatsoever, with another thirty-three promising to make a statement at a later date, together accounting for almost 20 per cent. The thirty-three declarations promising a later statement all came from commission agents making declarations on behalf of principals; they presumably wished to clarify whether their principal(s) had sought insurance or sea loans elsewhere before committing to their legal declaration. The fifty-five declarations offering no statement comprise a mixture of those made by the policyholder and those by commission agents. Of these, only two reached arbitration proceedings, suggesting that the Company was willing to make payment in any case. Why these statements were omitted cannot be easily explained without further evidence; malice or human error could be equally plausible explanations in some or all instances. In any case, they indicate that the Company – while resolute in prescribing procedures for all outcomes from a policy, with the *Ordonnance* as its lodestar – was willing to be flexible in implementing such procedures, recognising, *inter alia*, the difficulties commission agents faced in speaking with full knowledge on behalf of their principals. We see a subtle slide here from the legal and moral grammar used in the policy to the more pragmatic gestures enshrined in the declarations.

The declaration concluded in a self-referential manner, confirming that the Company's directors had been informed of its existence because Jagault had 'left' a copy of it with them.[130] This was necessary because the declaration

---

[130] Z/1d/82 and Z/1d/88, AN.

was, to draw on J.L. Austin, 'performative'.[131] Article 60 of *Des Assurances* confirmed that, 'after serving notice of the abandonment, the insured effects will belong [*pro rata*] to the insurer', thereby enshrining the partial or total transfer of ownership from the policyholder to the Company.[132] As noted above, it also signalled the creation of a legal responsibility for the Company to make payment within three months of the date of abandonment.

Following these statements, the declarations were consistently signed by the figure(s) bringing the request and by Jagault. This confirmed the value of these declarations as legal statements amenable to be used in any future arbitration proceedings.

Table 30   The number of declarations of average and abandonment in the years 1686–92.

Year	Declarations of average	Declarations of abandonment
1686	2	4
1687	17	10
1688	15	13
1689	32	81
1690	17	91
1691	34	122
1692	29	126
Total	146	447

Source: Z/1d/82, and Z/1d/88, AN.

Table 30 allows us to compare the frequency of declarations of average and abandonment. While declarations of average fluctuated over time, abandonments increased consistently from year to year and peaked at 126 in 1692 – over 3.5 times the highest number of averages in any year. A total of 146 declarations of average were made in the years 1686–92, compared to 447 abandonments.[133] As we have seen, it was abandonments resulting from the Nine Years' War that ultimately pulled the Company under; averages were less frequent and, by their nature, almost always less expensive.[134] Nevertheless, averages were not treated trivially: while they comprised

---

[131] J. Austin, *How to Do Things with Words: The William James Lectures Delivered at Harvard University in 1955*, Oxford: Oxford University Press, 1975, p. 6.
[132] Valin, *Nouveau commentaire*, vol. II, p. 143.
[133] Three declarations declared both average and abandonment; they are counted twice in these figures, explaining why the figures total 593 rather than 590.
[134] Colleagues on the AveTransRisk project have found examples of averages totalling more than 100 per cent; I have not. On the losses from the Nine Years' War, see Chapter 5.

29.6 per cent of all declarations, they were the subject of 29.4 per cent of those that proceeded to arbitration. In effect, averages were just as likely to engender disputes as abandonments.[135]

The Parisian merchant Charles Mercier made a model average declaration on 9 May 1687. Mercier made this declaration for goods he had insured for 3,000 *livres* and 6,500 *livres* respectively, through two policies signed on 23 January and 4 April 1687, to be carried on the *St Jean* from Port-Louis to Marseille, set to return later to Rouen.[136] The ship,

> in making its voyage to Marseille, was surprised [by] a large storm that obliged the captain to jettison into the sea around half a ton of wheat with which the ship was loaded, with a cable and other rigging, to lighten the ship and to save it alongside the rest of its load, which caused an average for which the gentlemen [i.e. the directors, mentioned beforehand] are responsible [and] for which M. Mercier understands that he will be paid very promptly.[137]

This was a textbook example of general average emerging through jettison and the sacrifice of ship furniture. As an expense incurred as a direct consequence of perils at sea, the Company was explicitly acknowledged to be responsible for it.

Other declarations were more complex, reflecting the breadth of the insurer's responsibilities. Simon Soaves' declaration on 9 January 1688, on behalf of the Swedish ambassador to France, Count Nils Lillieroot, describes how the *Aigle couronné de Stockholm*, captained by Peter Haveman, had 'wrecked [...] in the strait of the Sound' on its way from Rouen to Stockholm.[138] The 'bundle of merchandise' that the ambassador had sent was recovered, but it 'was opened by the peasants of the coast' in the process, and it was not known if anything had been taken.[139] Soaves asserted Lillieroot's rights to later reimbursement once the integrity of the merchandise was established, as well as for the costs of reloading the merchandise onto another ship to finish the journey to Stockholm. In the meantime, he requested 'the sum of 224 *livres* and six *sols* that was spent in the Sound for extraordinary fees', presumably at least in part for the reimbursement of those same peasants, as per the law of wreck, for recovering the bundle.[140] Article 26 of *Des Assurances* held insurers liable for extraordinary costs following shipwreck, but this was further clarified

---

[135] Z/1d/84, AN.
[136] Z/1d/85, fol. 35r, AN.
[137] Z/1d/82, fol. 5r, AN.
[138] Ibid., fol. 10r. Lillieroot would go on to serve as mediator at Ryswick in 1697, bringing the Nine Years' War to an end; Rule and Trotter, *A World of Paper*, p. 101.
[139] Z/1d/82, fol. 10r, AN.
[140] Ibid.

in article 45, which recognised that, 'in case of shipwreck or grounding, the insured will be able to work towards the recovering of the shipwrecked effects, without prejudice to [...] the reimbursement of their costs [...] up to the value of the recovered effects'.[141] In this way, policyholders were not required to declare abandonment after shipwreck or grounding, although they could later do so if they were unable to recover their goods.[142] Soaves therefore understood the insurers' responsibilities well, and the Company reimbursed Lillieroot without dispute: the *Ordonnance* fully protected the ambassador in this unfortunate series of maritime dramas.

Unfortunately, the registers are not a suitable source for studying how the admiralty courts dealt with averages. From the 146 declarations of average, just twenty-six specified it was general average being declared; none specified particular average.[143] This is perhaps explained by the fact that the Company was liable for all types of average: policyholders may have felt that, so long as they provided the necessary documentation to justify their claim, the type of average was inconsequential. In the absence of this documentation, it is impossible to draw conclusions on the nature of these averages and whether the boundaries between general and particular average that the *Ordonnance* outlined were respected in practice. Study of the extant admiralty court registers across France might yield fruitful insights on this.

CONCLUSION

The years following Louis XIV's proclamation of personal rule in 1661 were unusually idyllic. The *Frondes* were now a memory; war would only return in full force in 1672.[144] Colbert certainly capitalised on this period of calm, pursuing an aggressive agenda of legal reform that would shape French law until the 1804 *Code Napoléon*. Although the Dutch War threatened to reverse Colbert's almost Herculean efforts to restore the French treasury to a healthy state, this did not distract him from his commercial and maritime interests: the 1673 *Ordonnance sur le commerce* and 1681 *Ordonnance de la marine* were the culmination of Colbert's tenure.

The *Ordonnance de la marine*'s place in Colbert's broader maritime strategy has been curiously neglected up to now. We have seen that Colbert promoted the Chamber as an institution with the power to transform the French

---

[141] Valin, *Nouveau commentaire*, vol. II, p. 98.
[142] In this case, following the declaration of abandonment, the policyholder would not be able to recover the costs sustained in trying to salvage the goods.
[143] Z/1d/82 and Z/1d/88, AN.
[144] This is not forgetting the brief War of Devolution in 1667–68, which was a warning of what was to come with the Dutch War of 1672–78.

insurance industry by bringing new players into the game.[145] The Chamber's earliest dispute on averages revolved around these new players and the inconsistencies that they identified between the rules of the game in writing and in practice: not even the Rouennais universally followed their own city's famed insurance compilation. Colbert consulted the Chamber on averages during the compilation of the *Ordonnance*, but its arguments were adapted at its own expense to meet the needs of other maritime stakeholders.

Ascertaining how average costs should be calculated and shared was just one of many contentious judgements the compilers had to make. With wide recourse to prior legal practice, they treaded carefully, avoiding changes that would have upset maritime stakeholders while clearly establishing the admiralty courts' exclusive authority in the maritime sphere. Bringing insurance and averages within this new jurisdictional field of play, the *Ordonnance* proposed a new understanding of abandonments and averages as the outcomes of the legal processes that could be pursued by policyholders for losses and damages respectively. These were outcomes that supported the admiralties' power, which emanated entirely from the state at the expense of seigneurial laws and customs.

Of course, claiming jurisdiction was quite different from enforcing it. Here, the Company embraced its own royal patronage to support the state in selling the *Ordonnance* to the kingdom. Its extensive underwriting of policies in the ports of Brittany, traditionally opposed to royal authority, and the adoption of its policy form as a model in Porte's manual demonstrate that it was an institution with the power to influence commercial practices far beyond Paris. Through closely following the *Ordonnance*'s dictates in its policy form and in its broader practices, the Company effected a triadic relationship between itself, the *Ordonnance* and the monarchy, thereby deriving legitimacy from the latter's political and legal capital as the kingdom's ultimate legal authority.

The *Ordonnance* therefore needs to be reconsidered within the context of state formation under Louis XIV. The documents studied in this chapter evidence the state's substantial push to assert authority over maritime affairs through the *Ordonnance*, and also capture the Chamber and the Company's integral roles within this process. Yet the institutions' ambiguous legacies bring into focus the need to study the reception of the *Ordonnance* across France: to what extent was it truly a success? The Company helped to facilitate at least some degree of successful implementation, namely through its underwriting of Breton interests and its model insurance policy. Nevertheless, only targeted studies of how the *Ordonnance* was

---

[145] See Chapters 1 and 4.

received and implemented in the provinces could provide clearer answers. Here, the records of the provincial admiralty courts in particular would be indispensable.

Indeed, we will see in the next chapter that the French legal system under the Old Regime has received remarkable attention in recent decades, but the admiralty courts have been almost entirely ignored.[146] Conflicts were inevitable in the practice of insurance, so how did the Chamber and the Company manage these? We can only answer this question through studying institutions for conflict resolution, including the Parisian admiralty court.

---

[146] For valuable exceptions to the rule, see the essays in Le Bouëdec (ed.), *L'Amirauté en Bretagne*; R. Grancher, 'Le tribunal de l'amirauté et les usages du métier. Une histoire "par en bas" du monde de la pêche (Dieppe, XVIIIe siècle)', *Revue d'histoire moderne & contemporaine* 65 (2018), pp. 33–58.

7

'IMPAVIDUM FERIENT': REPUTATION, CONFLICT RESOLUTION AND STATE PROPAGANDA IN THE ROYAL INSURANCE CHAMBER, 1668–86

We have seen that Colbert and Seignelay shared some key motivations for intervening in the insurance industry: namely, they strove to challenge Dutch commercial hegemony and redirect specie flows.[1] Another motivation lay just beneath the surface, but came to the fore at crucial moments. Colbert wrote to M. de Sève, intendant in Bordeaux, on 3 March 1673 to discuss the damage inflicted on the insurance industry following the onset of the Dutch War a year earlier. He praised Sève's proposal to establish an insurance chamber in Bordeaux, and promised to offer it the same institutional privileges as those of the Chamber in Paris, so long as Sève could jump over the necessary administrative hurdles. Colbert finished with a note of caution, however, emphasising that 'the principal point' of insurance institutions like the Chamber was 'to prevent, by all sorts of means, any lawsuits in the execution of insurance policies'. Consequently, Colbert advised Sève that he would need to keep an eye on the Bordeaux underwriters' conduct if the proposal came to fruition: 'when chicanery interferes in these types of establishment, they will waste a fortune [in the courts] while never recovering' from their conduct.[2]

Here, we see an inversion of the complex risks of moral hazard first encountered in Chapter 3. There, I focused on the capacity for policy-holders to exploit information asymmetries to deceive underwriters. Yet the underwriter also had the power to deceive by willingly taking insurance premiums, only to refuse to pay out on policies later. In warning against the risks of 'chicanery', Colbert was referring to the underwriters' capacity

---

[1] See Chapters 1 and 2.
[2] Colbert and Clément, *Lettres, instructions, et mémoires de Colbert*, vol. II, book II, p. 675. It is unclear if the Bordeaux chamber was ever established.

to drag their heels in making payment, seeking recourse to every possible legal arena to 'exhaust' the policyholder into abandoning their claim.[3] In invoking this morally charged concept, Colbert presented his fear that underwriters who refused to make timely payments would irredeemably damage the reputation of the institutions in which they were operating, sacrificing the long-term success of these institutions and the good faith of commerce itself for their own short-term gains.

Colbert's morally inflected concerns were not new: the rise of insurance in the fourteenth century had prompted widespread discussion and disagreement amongst scholastic thinkers, who interpreted this commercial innovation through the lens of Christian and Aristotelian frameworks of commerce and *arete* (virtue). Sixteenth-century scholastics such as Domingo de Soto, of the School of Salamanca, ultimately concluded insurance was not usurious (i.e. did not entail the sterility of money)[4] and engendered a common good (i.e. the sharing of risk that facilitated commercial endeavours) that made the instrument morally licit. But earlier scholastic thought, focusing on the aleatory nature of insurance, placed insurance in the same semantic field as gambling, enshrining a broader moral suspicion of insurance (and other similar business instruments such as bills of exchange) across late medieval and early modern Europe.[5] Trivellato has documented the rise in early modern France of the anti-Semitic legend on the origins of insurance and the bill of exchange. In the case of insurance, this was a prejudiced manifestation of society's anxieties about the scope for underwriters to renege on their commitments, to the detriment (or, potentially, the financial ruin) of policyholders.[6]

The state's intervention was therefore driven by a deep-seated and widespread fear of the instrument's capacity to engender chaos in commercial life. In establishing the Chamber, Colbert hoped in part that its members would set standards that could be replicated across France and serve the interests of French commerce.[7]

---

[3] For discussion of chicanery, see G. Calafat, 'Jurisdictional Pluralism in a Litigious Sea (1590–1630): Hard Cases, Multi-Sited Trials and Legal Enforcement between North Africa and Italy', *Past and Present* Supplement 14 (2019), p. 167.

[4] Money is deemed sterile in Aristotelian thought because it is 'only a medium of exchange'; it cannot appreciate in value itself, or else it ceases to be a stable measurement of value; G. Ceccarelli, 'Risky Business: Theological and Canonical Thought on Insurance from the Thirteenth to the Seventeenth Century', *Journal of Medieval and Early Modern Studies* 31 (2001), pp. 601–58.

[5] Ibid. This suspicion was especially commonplace amongst late medieval and early modern governments; Dreijer, 'Maritime Averages'.

[6] Trivellato, *The Promise and Peril of Credit*. For a specific example of anti-Semitism in the discussion of insurance, see Savary des Bruslons, *Dictionnaire universel de commerce*, vol. I, p. 754.

[7] On this, see Chapter 1.

How far was the Chamber able to live up to these expectations? Certainly, the institution went to great lengths in developing its commercial reputation within the moral framework and vocabulary typical of the period. Specifically, it leveraged its royal patronage in order to present itself as a virtuous commercial entity, with underwriters whom merchants across the world could trust to make timely payment. Nevertheless, for the Chamber's underwriters, the *interest* in making timely payment did not always align with their *capacity* to do so.

When conflicts arose in interpreting contracts and prevailing practice, the institution had a strong interest in addressing these in a timely and 'amicable' manner. Recent works have reconceptualised our understanding of conflict resolution, with some incorporating it into broader discussions of conflict management.[8] Despite the recent renaissance in insurance history, disputes have received little attention. Where they have been discussed, it is no surprise, given the influence of neo-institutionalism in recent works, that individual institutions have been the focus.[9] While Amalia Kessler has written on the activities of Paris' merchant court, and its role in transforming the broader discourse on commerce in eighteenth-century France, almost nothing has been written on insurance conflicts in the city.[10]

The key exception has been Boiteux's work. His argument centres on the Chamber's 'simple and rapid' arbitration system, which he regards as a 'merit' of the institution: arbitration obviated the need for parties to engage in onerous litigation.[11]

---

[8] For a recent example, see A. Cordes and P. Höhn, 'Extra-Legal and Legal Conflict Management among Long-Distance Traders (1250–1650)', in H. Pihlajamäki, M. Dubber, and M. Godfrey (eds), *The Oxford Handbook of European Legal History*, Oxford: Oxford University Press, 2018, pp. 509–27. For recent examples, besides Cordes and Höhn, see J. Wubs-Mrozewicz, 'Conflict Management and Interdisciplinary History: Presentation of a New Project and an Analytical Model', *The Low Countries Journal of Social and Economic History* 15 (2018), pp. 89–107; A. Wijffels, 'Introduction: Commercial Quarrels – and How (Not) to Handle Them', *Continuity and Change* 32 (2017), pp. 1–9; L. Sicking and A. Wijffels (eds), *Conflict Management in the Mediterranean and the Atlantic, 1000–1800: Actors, Institutions and Strategies of Dispute Settlement*, Leiden: Brill, 2020.

[9] For example, see S. Go, 'The Amsterdam Chamber of Insurance and Average: A New Phase in Formal Contract Enforcement (Late Sixteenth and Seventeenth Centuries)', *Enterprise and Society* 14 (2013), pp. 511–43. For a valuable exception to the rule described, see G. Dreijer, 'Identity, Conflict and Commercial Law: Legal Strategies of Castilian Merchants in the Low Countries (15th–16th Centuries)', in D. De ruysscher, A. Cordes, S. Dauchy, S. Gialdroni, and H. Pihlajamäki (eds), *Commerce, Citizenship, and Identity in Legal History*, Leiden: Brill, 2021, pp. 118–38.

[10] Kessler, *A Revolution in Commerce*.

[11] Boiteux, *L'assurance maritime à Paris*, pp. 31–2.

This line of argument embraces the 'Manichean distinction' between litigation and arbitration first propagated towards the end of the eighteenth century and still prevalent in legal scholarship.[12] Indeed, arbitration remains a favoured object of analysis in the study of pre-modern mercantile behaviour. Neo-institutionalism has often focused on the 'efficiency' of private order solutions in resolving disputes and policing behaviour. These solutions ostensibly reduced transaction costs by being both quicker and cheaper than litigation. Paul Milgrom, Douglass North and Barry Weingast's famous study of the medieval Champagne fairs suggests that so-called private judges served as 'adjudicator[s] of disputes', allowing merchants to avoid 'the unnecessary costs of dispute resolution' through cheap and speedy justice, enforced through a game theoretical reputation system.[13]

Only in recent decades have historians of pre-modern Europe challenged this conceptualisation of litigation (ostensibly 'formal' and 'public') and arbitration (ostensibly 'informal' and 'private') as diametrically opposed forms of conflict resolution. Indeed, recent works have found that they were often complementary procedures; moreover, arbitration could be decidedly formal and public, with costs similar to litigation.[14] Different forums for conflict resolution thus cannot be abstracted from the broader jurisdictional landscape in which they were situated.

Moreover, these forums must be read within the broader context of the early modern period as a 'golden age of litigation' in Europe: courts across France dealt with an increasing number of cases until the turn of the eighteenth century, when litigation plummeted across the kingdom.[15] Reframing this phenomenon, recent works have rehabilitated the courts at the local and intermediate levels (for example, the *prévôté*, the *balliage*, the *sénéchaussée* and the *présidial* courts), emphasising the competency of their judges and their flexibility in re-establishing 'ruptured equilibria' through

---

[12] C. Burset, 'Merchant Courts, Arbitration, and the Politics of Commercial Litigation in the Eighteenth-Century British Empire', *Law and History Review* 34 (2016), p. 643.

[13] P. Milgrom, D. North, and B. Weingast, 'The Role of Institutions in the Revival of Trade: The Law Merchant, Private Judges, and the Champagne Fairs', *Economics and Politics* 2 (1990), pp. 1–23. See also Greif, *Institutions and the Path to the Modern Economy*. For a rebuttal of Milgrom, North and Weingast's argument – making clear that there were no 'private judges' at the Champagne fairs – see J. Edwards and S. Ogilvie, 'What Lessons for Economic Development Can We Draw from the Champagne Fairs?', *Explorations in Economic History* 49 (2012), pp. 131–48.

[14] For example, see Cordes and Höhn, 'Extra-Legal and Legal Conflict Management', pp. 520 and 523.

[15] Breen, 'Law, Society, and the State', p. 361. On the explosion of litigation in action in seventeenth-century France, see Hardwick, *Family Business*, pp. 57–87.

cheap, speedy and often non-punitive justice.[16] In this light, growing recourse to litigation did not result from increasing social hostility and atomisation, but from the courts' growing capacity to meet litigants' needs as consumers of justice and legitimating agents of state formation.

The implementation of Colbert's legal reforms must be understood within this shifting landscape. While Chapter 6 focused on the *Ordonnance de la marine* as a conscious piece of state formation in which the Chamber and the Company both played a role, we will see that insurance conflicts involving the Chamber were a key driving force behind the conflict resolution procedure the *Ordonnance* would later outline. This stresses, as Breen has observed, the need to recognise the agency of all legal actors in the formation of the Old Regime state.[17]

Therefore, drawing on the findings of these works, this chapter adopts an actor-oriented approach to insurance conflicts in Paris. In studying the choices and strategies of the Chamber's underwriters and policyholders, we can uncover the connections between different forums and the nuanced logics underpinning decision making in insurance conflicts.

Using this model, this chapter suggests that Boiteux's argument ignores the broader jurisdictional climate in Paris up to 1681. The Chamber was forced to introduce compulsory arbitration in the first instance in 1673 because of arbitration's weakness, not its strength. Up to then, arbitration had simply been one of numerous tools that actors used to resolve an array of interconnected insurance conflicts after the onset of war in 1672. We will see that a jurisdictional crisis erupted in 1673, where the city's admiralty court clashed with the merchant court over who had jurisdiction over insurance cases. This proved perilous for some litigants who tried to take their grievances before the latter. In turn, the admiralty court was forced to introduce summary procedure to meet the needs of litigants.

The proliferation of litigation proved to be the Chamber's undoing. It chose to craft its commercial identity as a corporate body rather than as a meeting place for individual and independent underwriters. This was a mistake, as the institution's reputation was irreparably damaged by a handful of underwriters who tried to resist the flood of claims after the onset of war.

---

[16] Here, I paraphrase Fabrice Mauclair, as quoted in Breen, 'Law, Society, and the State', p. 380. For such works, see, for example, J. Hayhoe, *Enlightened Feudalism: Seigneurial Justice and Village Society in Eighteenth-Century Northern Burgundy*, Rochester, NY: University of Rochester Press, 2008; Schneider, *The King's Bench*; H. Piant, *Une Justice ordinaire. Justice civile et criminelle dans la prévôté royale de Vaucouleurs sous l'Ancien Régime*, Rennes: Presses universitaires de Rennes, 2006; Blaufarb, *The Politics of Fiscal Privilege*.

[17] Breen, 'Law, Society, and the State', p. 360.

The introduction of compulsory arbitration in 1673 was a reaction to this state of affairs. In keeping disputes out of the public domain, the Chamber hoped to salvage its tarnished reputation. This strategy was supported by a robust Colbertian propaganda campaign, which has greatly shaped historians' perceptions of the institution to this day. Nevertheless, the strategy did not succeed, and the institution never recovered. In this way, the Chamber's difficulties can be attributed to both institutional and state shortcomings.

MATERIALITY, GESTURE AND REPUTATION IN THE CHAMBER

The Chamber's by-laws from 1671 ordered that the thirty most senior members attending any of its meetings be rewarded with four silver jettons (*jetons*) each.[18] These typically served as aids for calculating commercial transactions. Nevertheless, their functions extended further, as we can see in Image 1.

The jetton's obverse depicts Louis XIV, around which reads 'Louis XIV, by the grace of God king of France and Navarre'.[19] The same inscription appeared on the obverse of the *louis d'or*, the gold coin first minted under Louis XIII.[20] The jetton's reverse depicts a ship sailing through smooth waters, while the sun smiles upon it. The bottom of the coin reads 'CHAMBRE D'ASSURANCE / 1671', with the phrase 'IMPAVIDAM FERIENT' curving around the vessel at the top. This refers to a passage from the *Odes* of the classical poet Horace:

> Not the rage of the people pressing to hurtful measures, not the aspect of a threatening tyrant can shake from his settled purpose the man who is just and determined in his resolution; nor can the south wind, that tumultuous ruler of the restless Adriatic, nor the mighty hand of thundering Jove; if a crushed world should fall in upon him, *the ruins would strike him undismayed* [*impavidum ferient ruinæ*; emphasis mine].[21]

This striking piece of material culture draws on a wide array of motifs. The decision to put Louis on the jetton's obverse made explicit the institution's royal patronage from the moment of its establishment. This allowed the Chamber to leverage the king as a symbol of justice, helping to craft its

---

[18] Z/1d/73, fols 10r–13v, AN.
[19] 'LVDOVICVS XIIII DEI GRATIA FRANCIAE ET NAVARRAE REX'.
[20] M. Snodgrass, *Coins and Currency: An Historical Encyclopedia*, Jefferson: McFarland & Company, 2019, p. 331.
[21] Horace and C. Smart (trans.), *Horace Translated Literally into English Prose*, vol. I, Dublin: P. Wogan, 1793, p. 139.

Image 1   The Chamber's silver jetton from 1671.

Source: CGB Numismatique Paris, 'ASSURANCES La Chambre des assurances, Louis XIV 1671' [https://www.cgb.fr/assurances-la-chambre-des-assurances-louis-xiv-sup,v11_1114,a.html, accessed 1 March 2020]. With thanks to CGB Numismatique Paris for giving permission to reproduce the image. © CGB Numismatique Paris.

own image as a just institution.[22] The reverse reinforces this: the passage from Horace's *Odes* juxtaposes the 'man who is just' and the obstacles that seek to hinder him. In drawing on this passage, the Chamber alluded to the anthropogenic and natural risks it bore, be it the 'threatening tyrant' who unjustly seized ships or 'the south wind, that tumultuous ruler of the restless Adriatic' who led vessels to their demise.[23] Far from faltering in the face of these events coming to pass, the Chamber would withstand them entirely: even 'if a crushed world should fall in upon him, the ruins would strike him undismayed'.

This ability to face adversity is suggested to derive from the institution's virtue – but from where does this virtue come? The image of the vessel, with the anthropomorphised sun, suggests the king himself is the source. The smiling sun no doubt is a reference to Louis XIV himself as the Sun King (*le roi soleil*), but the ship it shines upon is delightfully ambiguous, allowing multiple interpretations at once. In the most classical interpretation, it is the Platonic 'ship of state', led safely in its voyage

---

[22] This was part of a broader phenomenon, whereby the king's symbolic multimedia manifestations across France (in the form of statues, print, medals, among other things) served as 'strategies of glory' for Louis; H. Drévillon, *Le Roi absolu. Louis XIV et les Français (1661–1715)*, Paris: Éditions Belin, 2015, pp. 11–12. See also P. Burke, *The Fabrication of Louis XIV*, New Haven: Yale University Press, 1992.

[23] For more on these risks, see Chapter 6.

through the wisdom bestowed by the sun;[24] it is also the Chamber itself as a vessel of royal patronage; and it is, quite literally, a commercial ship, basking in the light of the king's benevolence in protecting commerce through the Chamber. In appealing to this rich classical imagery, the Chamber reinforced broader understandings of the king's divine power: in protecting merchants from losses, the king exercised his capacity to tame nature itself. The jetton thus propagated the 'myth' of Louis as a truly 'godlike' figure, while establishing the Chamber's glorious role as his 'representative', taking his place in the defence of commercial shipping.[25]

The jetton reflected the Chamber's optimism in 1671. Its business had proven most successful up to this point, and in 1671 it passed its by-laws, with Colbert confirming his desire to 'give new signs of his protection' to the institution.[26] In minting this jetton, the Chamber impressed upon the country its identity as a just institution of protection.

This jetton was not an aberration: the Chamber consistently leveraged materiality in developing its identity, and its by-laws are a testament to this. Around the time they were composed, the Chamber was looking to move to new offices: in its general assembly of 8 January 1672, Pierre Denison was asked to investigate if a building close to the city's merchant court would be suitable for the Chamber's business.[27] The by-laws outlined meticulously how the Chamber's two central rooms were to be laid out and decorated once new premises were secured. From the moment one walked through the door of these new offices, above which was to be inscribed '*Chambre des assurances et grosses aventures* established by the king', there was to be no doubt that this was a chamber where individuals of means did business.[28]

The *grand bureau* would host assemblies of fifty to sixty people. Sixty black leather armchairs would be placed around a table covered in green

---

[24] On the Platonic 'ship of state', and the sun as an allegory for wisdom in Platonic thought, see Plato and T. Griffith (trans.), *The Republic*, Cambridge: Cambridge University Press, 2000; on Richelieu's prior use of the imagery of the 'ship of state', see James, *The Navy and Government*, p. 1.

[25] Burke, *The Fabrication of Louis XIV*, pp. 6–7 and 9. For more on Louis XIV and maritime imagery (especially in relation to the use of Muslim slaves on Mediterranean galleys), see M. Martin and G. Weiss, *The Sun King at Sea: Maritime Art and Galley Slavery in Louis XIV's France*, Los Angeles: Getty Publications, 2022.

[26] Z/1d/73, fols 16r–17r, AN. On the Chamber's activities, see Chapter 4.

[27] Z/1d/73, fols 16r–17r, AN. The offices of the West India Company were already located on the ground floor of the building.

[28] Ibid., fols 10r–13v. Boiteux suggests that, around 1680, the Chamber ultimately moved from its original offices on *rue Quincampoix* to *rue Plastrière*; however, he offers no supporting evidence for this, and I have not been able to corroborate the claim; Boiteux, *L'assurance maritime à Paris*, p. 27.

leather, thirty of which would be reserved for the first rung of members (i.e. the most senior) while the other thirty would be free for the second rung of members to use.[29] Meanwhile, the room would be 'very clean', decorated with 'a crucifix and a portrait of the king', alongside 'maritime maps' and six silver candlesticks.[30] As president, Francesco Bellinzani would always sit opposite the crucifix.[31]

Adjoining the *grand bureau* would be the *chambre du conseil*, where arbitration proceedings would be handled. This would also be decorated with a crucifix, alongside a table, tapestry, writing case, paper, pens and ink, a purse of jettons and eleven armchairs. This too would 'always be kept clean'.[32]

These decorative details were far from trivial. Following the issuing of its by-laws, the Chamber agreed that, since 'nothing can contribute more to the augmentation of the Chamber than establishing its reputation', the by-laws 'will be printed in French and several foreign languages like German, English, Spanish and Italian', to be 'distributed in all the places of commerce and seaports of Europe', thereby 'making known to foreigners the good order being observed here'.[33] Not just an internal document, the by-laws were a carefully crafted piece of propaganda too, intending to present the Chamber's solvency and credit to merchants across Europe. The future *grand bureau* was thus a tailored statement of tasteful luxury: hanging a portrait of the king signalled again the Chamber's royal patronage, while the use of green and black leather to decorate the table and armchairs was a conspicuous statement of luxury. Silver candlesticks were a somewhat crude, but effective, way of demonstrating the Chamber's liquidity.[34]

This emphasis on materiality also intended to shape the conduct of the Chamber's members. By describing the hierarchical layout of the *grand bureau* so carefully, the institution was crafting a corporate identity in some ways reminiscent of a craft guild: its goal was to create and wield the

---

[29] On these rungs, see Chapter 1.
[30] Z/1d/73, fols 10r–13v. On Paris' significance as a centre for the patronage and production of maps, see Regourd, 'Capitale savante, capitale coloniale', pp. 121–51.
[31] The attention given to the hierarchies created and sustained through these spatial and material configurations reflects the broader place of ceremony and ritual in shaping status interaction in Old Regime France (and beyond); on the ambiguities and the contested nature of status interaction, see G. Sternberg, *Status Interaction during the Reign of Louis XIV*, Oxford: Oxford University Press, 2014.
[32] Z/1d/73, fols 10r–13v, AN.
[33] Ibid., fols 14r–15v, AN.
[34] Here, see, for example, Muldrew, '"Hard Food for Midas"', p. 109. On credit in seventeenth- and eighteenth-century French discourse, see Trivellato, *The Promise and Peril of Credit*; on credit in seventeenth-century French practice, see Hardwick, *Family Business*, pp. 128–82.

'social capital' needed to establish and enforce the sorts of norms that would promote the institution's long-term wellbeing.[35]

Crucifixes were placed in both rooms for similar reasons. These signals of the institution's religiosity were supported by the by-laws, which decreed that, 'in order that it pleases God to bless the establishment and the safety of the [Royal] Insurance Chamber', two services would be held each year at Notre-Dame-des-Victoires in Paris for those associated with the institution.[36] On 2 January, a service would be held at 10:00am for the living, while a service would be held on 31 December at 10:00am for the dead. The church would be paid thirty *livres* per year for the two services. While such displays of Catholic piety were doubtless sincere, they also served the Chamber in fashioning its commercial identity, consistent with broader understandings of insurance as an instrument of virtue capable of supporting the cohesiveness of the mercantile community.[37] As such, these displays intended to create what Sheilagh Ogilvie calls 'multiplex ties' between the Chamber's members: it was surely hoped that these religious bonds, when married with shared economic interests, would facilitate correct practice amongst and between the members.[38]

AD HOC BEGINNINGS: EARLY CONFLICT RESOLUTION AND REPUTATION MANAGEMENT IN THE CHAMBER

The Chamber's careful attention to gesture and materiality makes sense only within the matrix of early modern commerce itself. Put another way, gesture and materiality were socially codified and could not be abstracted from broader commercial practice. They could support and display virtuous commercial conduct, but they were efficacious only if the Chamber's underwriters kept their commitments. This required the institution to approach conflict resolution with the utmost care: if underwriters believed they were not liable for a given claim, the ensuing dialogue with the policyholder had

---

[35] S. Ogilvie, *The European Guilds: An Economic Analysis*, Princeton: Princeton University Press, 2019, pp. 6 and 18–19. On the Parisian craft guilds, see Kessler, *A Revolution in Commerce*.
[36] Z/1d/73, fols 10r–13v, AN. Notre-Dame-des-Victoires was (and is) located only two streets away from the *Hôtel Colbert*. The *Compañía Española de Seguros*, established in Cádiz in 1791, made similar provisions; Baskes, *Staying Afloat*, p. 197.
[37] For more on the intersection of religion and insurance, see Ceccarelli, 'Risky Business', especially pp. 629–30, which articulates the argument of the sixteenth-century Scottish theologian John Major that insurance was connected to 'the Christian duty of mutual aid and solidarity', thus 'tying businessmen to a complex social network involving the community as a whole'.
[38] Ogilvie, *The European Guilds*, pp. 18–19. On the efficacy of such ties in governing behaviour in guilds, see the remainder of Ogilvie.

to be handled in a manner that protected the institution's long-term interests. In an ideal world, conflicts would have been resolved amicably with the assent of both parties, but the reality was often messier.

This is where the Chamber's arbitration system came into play, built on a carefully selected moral vocabulary. On 17 June 1670, the Chamber's general assembly met, agreeing that there would be 'nothing more important for the reputation of the Chamber nor more advantageous for commerce' than to use the body to 'amicably' consider and resolve disputes on insurance, sea loans, averages and other affairs.[39] The body had already handled some disputes up to this point, but without a set procedure for (or record of) them. It was agreed that 'it would be glorious for the Chamber, and advantageous to merchants, to set the days of these assemblies, and to establish a fixed and certain procedure' for conflict resolution.[40]

To this end, it was ordered that the general assembly would henceforth meet the first and third Tuesday of each month at 3:00pm. Forms were to be printed allowing disputing parties to request to have their cases heard before the assembly or, alternatively, before arbiters who would report their decisions to the assembly. The registrar was asked to maintain a register to record the outcomes of all these disputes.[41]

One would be forgiven for thinking this was decidedly vague. Recognising that it was 'necessary to explain the procedure [for addressing conflicts] clearly', the Chamber issued a clarification on 1 July.[42] It was resolved that, once parties reported their dispute to the Chamber, the institution would appoint arbiters to handle it, who would then deliver their decision to the assembly.[43]

The process was further refined through the 1671 by-laws. These ordered that, for affairs which were likely to be resolved in a 'summary' manner,[44] the Chamber would appoint five arbiters to resolve the dispute; for those requiring further investigation, seven; and for 'the most important' and most difficult of disputes, nine.[45] While 'good faith' was emphasised as the 'principal foundation of justice', arbiters were enjoined to follow the 'written conditions' of policies 'exactly', 'following also the ordinances and regulations of *Us et coutumes de la mer*'.[46]

---

[39] Z/1d/73, fols 2–3r, AN.
[40] Ibid.
[41] Ibid.
[42] Ibid., fol. 4r.
[43] Ibid., fol. 4r. In reality, the general assembly continued to be consulted in some instances instead of arbiters.
[44] This should not be confused with summary procedure in courts, which is a separate matter entirely.
[45] Z/1d/73, fols 10–13v, AN.
[46] Ibid.

The by-laws also charged the registrar, Christophe Lalive, with upholding the institution's reputation in the course of arbitration. Upon request, Lalive was required to provide copies or extracts of all paperwork relevant to a given dispute. Through these means, the Chamber would witness 'honourable behaviour' and 'all chicaneries and ill legal proceedings' would be avoided.[47] Moreover, Lalive was instructed to take 'an exact care' to inform underwriters when judgments were issued that ordered them to make payment. This practice would uphold 'the honour and reputation of the Chamber, which through these means will grow from year to year and will draw not only the insured of Paris, and of several maritime cities in the kingdom, but even foreigners', attracted 'by the security of payments from Parisian merchants'.[48] In keeping with this, insurers were bound to pay out on all claims within three months, as would later be enshrined in the *Ordonnance de la marine*.[49]

The arbitration system soon became one of the pillars of the Chamber. Boiteux notes that the by-laws instructed arbiters to follow the conditions of contracts and customary practice precisely; nevertheless, he argues that, 'in reality, their decisions were not motivated by law'. Instead, they 'were inspired especially by the jurisprudence of Solomon – but it did not matter, since the parties were pleased' with the decisions that were made.[50]

It is an unfounded assumption that all parties were pleased with the arbitration system and the judgments that resulted from it. The nature of the arbiters' judgments, however, deserves to be tested. By the end of 1672, forty-six arbitration cases had taken place, as seen in Table 31. The Chamber's arbitration register recorded the arguments in each case and the judgments rendered.

Table 31   The frequency of arbitration cases in the years 1670–72.*

Year	Number of arbitration cases
1670	11
1671	19
1672	16
Total	46

* NB two cases recorded in the register from 1670, but not pertaining to the Chamber's underwriting, are not included here. Cases in which the general assembly pronounced judgment rather than specific arbiters are included.

Source: Z/1d/74, AN.

---

[47] Ibid.
[48] Ibid.
[49] An appeals process was introduced on 22 January 1672, but I have found no evidence it was ever used; Z/1d/73, 17v–18r and 21, AN.
[50] Boiteux, *L'assurance maritime à Paris*, p. 48.

Escalating to arbitration to de-escalate conflicts

Some cases were delightfully straightforward to resolve. On 11 January 1670, a group of insurers underwrote 5,000 *livres* for the *Saint Anthoine de Padouë*'s voyage from Bayonne to Lisbon. During the voyage, the vessel was forced to stop at Aldán in Spain. On leaving port, it struck a rock or sandbank, and the vessel and its cargo were lost.[51]

On 19 August, the underwriters were pursued for payment in arbitration by Romul Valenty, the commission agent for the policyholders in Bayonne. Valenty provided numerous documents to justify the policyholders' interest in the voyage and the loss that had occurred.

This was unnecessary, because the underwriters did not dispute the loss: there had simply been a miscommunication over payment. As noted above, the underwriters were required to make payment on losses within three months of being informed of it. In response to Valenty, the underwriters said that they had 'each [already] offered to pay in cash the sums insured by them', but with a discount for making payment before the three months had elapsed.[52] Valenty replied, simply, that his principals had not given him any orders to accept a discount. Consequently, he had waited for the three months to elapse in order to receive full payment. With no defence from the underwriters, the judgment was predictable.

The result was similar following an arbitration case on 18 November 1670. On 2 June, twenty separate underwriting entities had underwritten the *Esperance*'s voyage from Le Havre to Cádiz. Before the arbiters, Anne Jousse and Jean-Anthoine Vanopstal (commission agents for a company in Orléans) presented abundant evidence to substantiate the vessel's capture by Salé corsairs. This included a certificate issued by Julien Parasol, consul to the French nation in Salé, acknowledging the capture. They also submitted bills of lading and other documents to justify the company's interest in the adventure. In the face of this evidence, the underwriters made no argument, and the judgment requiring them to make payment duly followed.[53]

As trivial as they seem, arbitration helped to de-escalate these conflicts in the long run. With twenty separate entities underwriting the *Esperance*, it is easy to imagine that Jousse and Vanopstal could not easily communicate their supporting documents to each and every underwriter. Arbitration thus brought the parties into one space to ensure losses were justified to the underwriters' satisfaction, preventing such disputes from going before the courts at a later date.

---

[51] Z/1d/74, fol. 9v, AN.
[52] Ibid.
[53] Ibid., fol. 13r. This paragraph draws from Wade, 'Underwriting Empire'.

The droit de restorne

Other disputes emerged when the conditions of contracts were not met. On 23 February and 7 August 1671, a group of insurers underwrote the merchandise on the *Ville de Paris* for a voyage from the French Caribbean to Dieppe or Dunkirk. It later transpired that no merchandise had been loaded on board. Since the underwriters had not borne the risk for which they had signed, the policyholders sought the return of their premium in an arbitration case of 8 January 1672. For the August policy, the arbiters duly ordered the return of the premium, subtracting half a per cent for the *droit de restorne*.[54] This was the percentage the underwriter was allowed to keep in such situations to compensate them for the inconvenience incurred, as recognised in the *Guidon de la mer* (and, later, the *Ordonnance de la marine*). Other cases like this had similar results.[55]

Mediterranean captivity and the verification of captures

Conflicts frequently emerged when insured vessels were captured by North African corsairs. On 17 June and 2 July 1669, 6,000 *livres* was underwritten on merchandise loaded on the *Concorde* for its voyage from Bordeaux to Marseille. On 1 July, between Gibraltar and Málaga, the *Concorde* was boarded and captured by 'a Turkish ship'.[56] The crew had managed to escape using 'the skiff', leaving the shipmaster, Nicolas Dolonne, to face the aggressors alone.[57] The North African shipmaster enslaved Dolonne as a crewmate while sailing the Mediterranean for another six weeks in search of further prizes, before returning to Algiers. Dolonne remained captive in Algiers for seven months, before being released through 'the compromise made by His Majesty with these barbarians', most likely referring to the treaty signed that year between France and Algiers.[58] However, in defiance of this treaty, the lead shot with which the *Concorde* had been loaded was seized; part of the glass on board was smashed, while the other part was lost. Dolonne found his way back to Marseille, where he testified on 26 April 1670. Pierre Formont, the policyholder, sought full reimbursement for the damages before arbiters on 7 October.

The underwriters objected to fully reimbursing Formont, arguing that Dolonne had been given 1,400 piastres for the lead shot that was seized.

---

[54] Z/1d/74, fol. 28v, AN.
[55] The arbiters demanded further documentation for the February policy before they could make a decision, although how this policy differed from the August policy is unclear; ibid. For other examples of the *droit de restorne*, see ibid., fols 5, 9r, 10v–11.
[56] Ibid., fols 11v–12r.
[57] Ibid., fols 11v–12r.
[58] Ibid., fols 11v–12r; Weiss, *Captives and Corsairs*, appendix 1.

Furthermore, they objected to Formont's demand that he be reimbursed for the loss of profits entailed by the breaking of the glass: 'this is practiced only in case of jettison into the sea to save men, the ship and the merchandise [when faced with] the evident peril of shipwreck'.[59] Since this was not the case, the loss of the merchandise should be distributed *pro rata* between Formont and the insurers based on its original cost. Nevertheless, the insurers offered to pay 50 per cent (3,000 *livres*) of the full sum insured. Formont objected to this, arguing that, by his calculations, the damages amounted to 78 per cent of the amount insured. The arbiters ultimately ordered the underwriters to pay 4,000 *livres*, two-thirds of the sum insured.[60]

The events precipitating an arbitration case from 1671 were similar, but the grounds for the dispute were quite different. On 22 May 1670, 12,000 *livres* was underwritten in a voyage from Bordeaux to Lisbon and Madeira. On 18 September, *sieur* Dupré, a passenger on board, wrote three letters to confirm that, after leaving Lisbon for Madeira in August, the vessel had been captured by the corsairs of Salé and he was now being held captive in the port. In requesting payment before the arbiters on 20 March 1671, Pierre Cadelan, commission agent for a Bordeaux merchant named Saluy Rabier, submitted these letters alongside various pieces of paperwork to justify Rabier's interest in the voyage. This does not seem to have entirely satisfied the arbiters, however, who agreed to order the insurers to make payment within a week, but also required Cadelan within six months to produce a 'certificate in good form from the French consul of Salé or other trustworthy figure of the French nation, [certifying that] the ship in question was taken there by corsairs, confiscated and sold, and [providing] the day of the capture of the ship'.[61] The capture of ships by North African corsairs often precipitated disputes like this: insurers demanded concrete information on precisely how a ship was captured, but by virtue of the circumstances surrounding such captures, verification of these losses was an eminent challenge.

Insurers as particular average adjusters

Some of the more complex cases revolved around averages.[62] While a total loss with an ample paper trail was easy all around – the insurers simply paid the full amount they insured – averages were more intricate, requiring an array of paperwork and a series of calculations to work out how much each insurer should pay.

---

[59] Z/1d/74, fols 11v–12r, AN.
[60] Ibid.
[61] Ibid., fols 19–20r.
[62] On averages, see Chapter 6.

On 9 July 1669, 10,000 *livres* was underwritten on the *Satisfaction de Darmouth* for a voyage from Newfoundland to Barcelona. On 28 October, witnesses from the ship testified in Cartagena in Spain that, near Cape St Vincent in southern Portugal, the ship had encountered a storm and a part of it was damaged, allowing seawater to flood in and spoil the 235 *quintaux* of Newfoundland cod on board, which was valued at 1,344 *livres* 1 *sol* 6 *deniers*. Before the general assembly on 16 January 1671, the policyholders, M. Soulet and Nicolas Chanlatte, requested that the underwriters pay a particular average of 13 per cent.[63]

The underwriters acknowledged the average, but felt that the calculation had been made incorrectly. By requesting an average of 13 per cent (1,300 *livres*), the policyholders were asking the insurers to bear almost total liability for the damage to the cod. Since total insurance coverage was rare throughout the early modern period, the underwriters argued that it was not 'just' for them to bear the average 'alone': Soulet and Chanlatte needed to also bear the average proportionately.[64] From this, the insurers calculated that their own share of the average would be 10 per cent of the insured sum. Nevertheless, they argued they should only pay 4 per cent, as the spoiling of fish during a voyage was an inherent vice (i.e. the natural by-product of fish being a perishable foodstuff) and therefore was not the responsibility of insurers.[65] Working together, the general assembly examined the documents provided to them and, by majority vote, concluded that the underwriters should pay 6 per cent of the insured sum, making a total of 600 *livres*.[66]

In some cases, the responsibility for calculating averages was entrusted to a respected and experienced underwriter with no interest in the policy. In the case of the *Fortune dorée* from 2 May 1671, the arbiters settled the average based on Jacques Rey's calculations; Henri Desanteul joined Rey the same day to calculate the particular average contributions for the *Saint Victor*.[67]

Arbitration therefore provided a space for the resolution of a variety of conflicts: some were straightforward, others more complicated, centring on the verification of events that took place far beyond the ports of France. While policyholders were often diligent in submitting paperwork, in some cases it was difficult to fully substantiate the fate of an adventure, prompting

---

[63] Z/1d/74, fols 14v–15r, AN.
[64] Ibid. For an explanation of why total coverage was rare, see Chapter 6.
[65] On inherent vice, and how it was applied in the Atlantic slave trade, see A. Rupprecht, '"Inherent Vice": Marine Insurance, Slave Ship Rebellion and the Law', *Race and Class* 57 (2016), pp. 31–44.
[66] Z/1d/74, fols 14v–15r, AN. This calculation was applied to another case before the general assembly on the same day, where Chanlatte pursued the insurers for an additional policy signed on 29 July 1669 for the same voyage; Z/1d/74, fols 17v–18r, AN.
[67] Ibid., fol. 18. For other cases involving averages, see ibid., fols 9r, 12v and 20v.

arbiters to ask for further evidence. In instances of average, disputes often centred on precisely how far underwriters should bear these. In these circumstances, insurers were ordered to pay some conveniently round numbers, suggesting the arbiters engaged less with the wise 'jurisprudence' of Solomon, as Boiteux calls it, than in guesswork.[68]

Strategies for resolving conflicts in the dispute crisis of 1673

If prayers were made on 2 January 1672 for the year to bring good fortune to the Chamber, these were not answered. As we have seen, the onset of the Dutch War in 1672 led to great losses for some underwriters, with the fallout from this following in 1673.[69] Arbitration cases almost doubled between 1672 and 1673, making it the year with the highest number of cases on record by far.[70]

Table 32 The frequency of arbitration cases in the years 1670–74.*

Year	Number of arbitration cases
1670	11
1671	19
1672	16
1673	29
1674	11
Total	86

* NB two cases recorded in the register from 1670, but not pertaining to the Chamber's underwriting, are not included here. Cases in which the general assembly pronounced judgment rather than specific arbiters are included. The record for 1674 is incomplete.

Source: Z/1d/74, 1 AN.

Conflict resolution strategies

Nevertheless, arbitration was only one of a series of forums and tools for resolving insurance conflicts. In some instances, parties were able to come together of their own volition to find a mutually agreeable solution to their disagreements. The Chamber's arbitration register documents four such compromises: the first of these, on 3 March, came after an arbitration judgment had

---

68   Whether this was motivated by a lack of information, ability and/or will to make more precise calculations and judgments is unclear.
69   See Chapter 4.
70   The Chamber's arbitration register inexplicably stops midway through a case that followed one of 25 May 1674, making it impossible to gauge precisely the frequency of arbitration after 1673; Z/1d/74, fols 102–4r, AN.

been made on the dispute the same day.[71] The parties agreed not to execute the judgment and to follow their own agreement (half payment on the policy) in order to avoid an appeal.[72] Clearly, neither party was satisfied with the judgment: their agreement ensured the conflict did not escalate further.

When private agreements and arbitration proved insufficient, the courts became involved. Here, the Chamber found itself sucked into a jurisdictional minefield. Colbert's *Ordonnance sur le commerce* was issued in March 1673: article 7 of the section *De la jurisdiction de Consuls* granted merchant courts exclusive jurisdiction in the first instance over disputes on 'insurance, sea loans, promises, obligations and contracts concerning maritime commerce and the freighting of vessels'.[73] A *volte-face* soon followed: an order of the Council of State on 28 June suspended this article, with the admiralty courts instructed to preside over these cases 'as they had done beforehand'.[74] The merchant courts were henceforth prohibited from taking such cases themselves.[75]

The extant records of the Parisian admiralty court attest to this jurisdictional confusion and the acutely challenging year the Chamber faced. These records are, put simply, a nightmare for the historian: they comprise bundles of scraps of paper in various shapes and sizes, kept in a random order, giving every indication that sheets have gone missing over the centuries. Moreover, as is so often the case with early modern court records, it was rare for the details of the dispute, or the logic underpinning judgments, to be explained. Any account of litigation in the admiralty court will, by necessity, be incomplete.

This said, I have found nineteen cases from 1673 where policyholders sought payment on policies they contracted in the Chamber. These cases are summarised in Table 33. Although the ultimate judgment was not recorded in every case, the records nevertheless give a window into this challenging year.

There are some clear patterns to the cases. François Moreau de Launay was plaintiff in four of the cases; Paul Aceré des Forges was plaintiff in six; Louis Bigot of Bordeaux and Pierre Dhariet of Bayonne were each plaintiffs for two; and the remaining seven were plaintiffs in a single case. Where judgments were awarded in the policyholders' favour, the underwriters were ordered to pay interest on the amount they had insured alongside legal

---

[71] Z/1d/74, fols 49v–50r, 52, 58v–59, 64v–65r, AN.
[72] Ibid., fols 49v–50r. As a result of the agreement, the arbitration judgment does not seem to have been recorded.
[73] J. Sallé (ed.), *L'esprit des ordonnances de Louis XIV*, vol. II, Paris: Chez Samson, 1758, p. 437.
[74] Z/1d/106, n.p., AN.
[75] This was clarified in a later order of the Council of State of 23 July; Valin, *Nouveau commentaire*, p. 122.

Table 33 Insurance cases brought by policyholders against the Chamber's underwriters before the *table de marbre* of the seat of the admiralty of France in Paris in 1673.

Date of court record, 1673	Vessel/s	Type and date of policy/ies	Plaintiff seeking reimbursement*	Insurers/reinsurers (and the amount the plaintiff sought)**	Result (where known)
28-Mar	*Madonna del Carmine*	Insurance 4 April 1672	Philippes Pocquelin, on behalf of Pierre de la Roche (Venice)	Jacques Rey (interest) Jacques Richard (interest) André Petit (interest) Henri Desanteul (interest) Anne Jousse and Jean-Anthoine Vanopstal (interest) Charles Lhuillier de Creabé (interest)	Parties ordered to proceed before arbiters
14-Apr	*Saint Leon*	Insurance 17 August 1672	François Moreau de Launay (Paris)	Guillaume Hallé and Bonnaventure Rebillé (400*lt*)	Judgment in plaintiff's favour for the full amount requested
18-Apr	*Saint Pierre*	Insurance 14 June 1672	François Moreau de Launay, on behalf of Julien Eon de la Villebague and Helaine de Launay (Saint-Malo)	Henri Desanteul and Elisabeth Hélissant (6,000*lt*)	Default judgment in plaintiff's favour for the full amount requested
18-Apr	*Orrore*	Insurance 18 June 1672	François Moreau de Launay, on behalf of *Sieur* Lebreton and Julien Eon de la Villebague (Saint-Malo)	Henri Desanteul, Elisabeth Hélissant and Pierre Desanteul (4,000*lt*)	Default judgment in plaintiff's favour for the full amount requested

Date of court record, 1673	Vessel/s	Type and date of policy/ies	Plaintiff seeking reimbursement	Insurers/reinsurers (and the amount the plaintiff sought)	Result (where known)
3-May	*Saint Pierre*	Insurance 29 September 1672	François Moreau de Launay, on behalf of Nicolas Clotel-lien Lesnaudieres (Saint-Malo)	Henri Desanteul and friend (500*lt*) François Gueston for his brother (500*lt*) Oudard Thomas de Lisle (500*lt*)	
30-May	*Catherine*	Insurance 13 August 1672	Paul Aceré des Forges (Paris?)	Nicolas Maillet (200*lt*) Henri de Vaux (200*lt*) François Lefèbvre (200*lt*) André Petit (200*lt*) Antoine Lachasse (200*lt*) Charles Lhuillier de Creabé (200*lt*) Henri Desanteul (200*lt*) Gilles Mignot (200*lt*)	
30-May	*Saint Joseph Nostre Dame de bonne esperance Sainte Anne Niuerve? Saint Pierre Saint Esprit Saint Leon*	Insurance 13 August 1672	Paul Aceré des Forges (Paris?)	Nicolas Maillet (350*lt*) Henri de Vaux (350*lt*) François Lefèbvre (420*lt*) Jacques Rey (420*lt*) André Petit (420*lt*) Antoine Lachasse (420*lt*) Charles Lhuillier de Creabé (420*lt*) Alexandre Vinx (420*lt*) Henri Desanteul (420*lt*) Gilles Mignot (1050*lt*) Jacques Petit (1400*lt*) Étienne Rouxelin (350*lt*)	Plaintiff ordered to substantiate the loss of *Saint Esprit* within three months (see the text)

31-May	*Nostre Dame de bonne esperance* *Sainte Anne Marie* *Saint Pierre* *Saint Esprit* *Saint Leon* *Saint Joseph*	Insurance 13 August 1672	Paul Aceré des Forges (Paris?)	Denis Rousseau (350*lt*) Elisabeth Hélissant (210*lt*) Étienne Rouxelin (350*lt*)	Default judgment in plaintiff's favour for the full amount requested
31-May	*Catherine Esperance notre dame*	Insurance 13 August 1672	Paul Aceré des Forges (Paris?)	Denis Rousseau (200*lt*) Elisabeth Hélissant (66*lt* 3s 4d) Jean Roussel (130*lt* 6s 8d)	Default judgment in plaintiff's favour for the full amount requested
4-Jul	*Saint Jean*	Reinsurance 11 and 12 October 1672	Paul Aceré des Forges (Paris?) and Pierre Dhariet (Bayonne)	Jean-Baptiste Forne and Isaac Pierre Jouan (300*lt*) Robert Sanson (300*lt*) Étienne Rouxelin (300*lt*) Oudard Thomas de Lisle (300*lt*) Elisabeth Lefebvre (300*lt*)	Reinsurance policies declared null; reinsurers ordered to return premiums
4-Jul	*Saint Joseph* *Nostre Dame de bonne esperance* *Sainte Anne Marie* *Saint Esprit* *Saint Leon*	Insurance 13 August 1672	Paul Aceré des Forges (Paris?)	Nicolas Maillet (300*lt*) Henri de Vaux (300*lt*) François Lefebvre (360*lt*) Jacques Rey (360*lt*) André Petit (360*lt*) Antoine Lachasse (360*lt*) Charles Lhuillier de Creabé (360*lt*) Alexandre Vinx (360*lt*) Henri Desanteul (360*lt*) Gilles Mignot (900*lt*) Jacques Petit (1,200*lt*)	

Date of court record, 1673	Vessel/s	Type and date of policy/ies	Plaintiff seeking reimbursement	Insurers/reinsurers (and the amount the plaintiff sought)	Result (where known)
31-Jul	*Sainte Anne*	Insurance 9 March 1672	Catherine de Lasson (Saint-Jean-de-Luz)	André Petit (1,000*lt*) Simon Boirat (500*lt*) Mathieu Marchand (500*lt*) Antoine Lachasse (500*lt*) Louis Marchand (500*lt*)	Default judgment in plaintiff's favour for the full amount requested
9-Aug	*Sainte Anne*	Reinsurance 10 October 1672	Pierre Dhariet (Bayonne)	Étienne Rouxelin (200*lt*) Robert Sanson (200*lt*)	Judgment in plaintiff's favour for the full amount requested
1-Sep	*Marie* *Nostre Dame de bonne esperance* *Saint Francois* *Saint Joseph* *Saint Esprit* *Saint Leon*	Insurance 1 October 1672	Louis Bigot (Bordeaux)	Charles Lhuillier de Creabé (3,500*lt*)	
6-Sep	*Marie* *Sainte Anne* *Saint Joseph* *Saint Esprit*	Insurance 3 October 1672	Louis Bigot (Bordeaux)	Guillaume Hallé and Bonnaventure Rebillé (1,050*lt*)	
6-Sep	*Marie*	Insurance 19 March 1672	Jacques La Roude (La Rochelle)	André Petit (1,000*lt*) Antoine Lachasse (600*lt*) Charles Lhuillier de Creabé (1,000*lt*) Denis Rosseau (750*lt*) Jacques Petit (550*lt*) Henri Desanteul (1,000*lt*) François Lefèbvre (500*lt*)	Default judgment in plaintiff's favour for the full amount requested

9-Sep	Saint Pierre	Insurance 22 September 1672 18 October 1672	Jean Minuille (Bayonne)	Henri de Vaux (500lt) Henri Desanteul and Elisabeth Hélissant (400lt) M. Marchand (200lt) Alexandre Vinx (600lt) Charles Lhuillier de Creabé (300lt) Pierre Desanteul (200lt) André Petit (1,000lt) Antoine Lachasse (1,000lt) François Lefebvre (400lt) Elisabeth Lefebvre (400lt)	
20-Sep	Nostre Dame du rosaire	Reinsurance 17 October 1672	Jean-Baptiste Forne, Isaac Pierre Jouan and company, on behalf of an anonymous principal (on an insurance policy signed in Livorno)	André Petit (800lt) Denis Rousseau (600lt)	Plaintiff ordered to substantiate the underwriter's interest in the original insurance policy from Livorno within three months
5-Oct	Dauphin	Insurance 18 July 1672	Pierre Cadelan (Paris)	Henri Desanteul (unstated share of average)	Plaintiff ordered to substantiate the time of the vessel's capture

*I include the location of the principal where it is noted.
**This excludes interest and expenses (which was requested in every case) except in the first case, where interest alone was sought.

Source: Z/1d/106, n.p., AN.

expenses.[76] These expenses were not trivial: when the court made judgment on 31 July 1673 in favour of Catherine de Lasson of Saint-Jean-de-Luz, her underwriters were ordered to pay 2,800 *livres*, alongside interest and expenses. On 16 December, she submitted a list of her expenses with over twenty items, totalling 50 *livres* 14 *sols*.[77]

Leaving Moreau and Acéré (the court's most prolific users) aside for now, the other plaintiffs seem to have been merchants who simply wished to see the underwriters fulfil their contractual duties. The first item listed in Lasson's expense report was 30 *livres* for the cost of sending a horseman from Saint-Jean-de-Luz to Paris to submit her petition.[78] Besides Paris and Saint-Jean-de-Luz, French plaintiffs in the admiralty court were based in Saint-Malo, Bordeaux, La Rochelle and Bayonne. A case of 20 September centred on an unnamed party who had secured 800 *livres* of reinsurance with the Chamber through Jean-Baptiste Forne, Isaac Pierre Jouan and company. The anonymous party had signed an insurance policy in Livorno, covering a sea loan for a return voyage from the *porto franco* to Cagliari.[79]

Despite plaintiffs going to such lengths to bring proceedings before the admiralty court, the Chamber's underwriters did not respond to their summons in six of the nineteen cases, leading to default judgments against them. We can only speculate on the reasons for this: underwriters perhaps wanted to avoid the expense of hiring a lawyer to represent them in some cases, especially if they knew they had no defence.

But this was not always the case. On 18 April, two default judgments were issued in Moreau's favour against Henri Desanteul and Elisabeth Hélissant for 10,000 *livres*.[80] In the second order, for the *Orrore*, the court noted it was simply enforcing the judgment made by the Chamber's arbiters on 20 January.[81] It was surely embarrassing to the Chamber that, even after

---

[76] The exact amount to be paid in interest depended on the length of time between the starting date set by the judgment and the date on which the underwriters ultimately made payment.

[77] Z/1d/106, n.p., AN.

[78] Ibid.

[79] Ibid. Risk management tools could clearly be complementary, and further research is needed on this. On this, see Dreijer, 'Identity, Conflict and Commercial Law'. Forne, Jouan and company also went before arbiters on 1 September 1673 on a different policy; Z/1d/74, fols 75v–76, AN.

[80] Pierre Desanteul was also ordered to contribute to 4,000 *livres* of this. For more on Hélissant, see Chapter 4; and Wade, 'Underwriting Empire'. Hélissant and Desanteul were siblings-in-law.

[81] For reasons unknown, this case was not recorded in the arbitration register; if this was any regular occurrence, then the arbitration figures for the Chamber were perhaps quite considerably higher than Table 32 suggests; Z/1d/74, AN.

arbitration had taken place, Moreau was forced to pursue two of the institution's leading underwriters in court for payment.

We should not assume Desanteul and Hélissant were behaving viciously. We have seen that, as prolific underwriters in the Chamber, both were able to avoid the severe losses that some of the occasional underwriters sustained.[82] Nevertheless, the sudden influx of claims may have caught them off guard, especially if they had invested their premium income on receipt: delay tactics may have been necessary for them – and other underwriters in the Chamber – to draw on their credit resources to make payment. Such delays came at a price though: the judgment for the *Orrore* was unique in specifying that interest payments were to be calculated 'from the day of the sentence in the Chamber' until the day the ordered sums were ultimately paid.[83] If Desanteul and Hélissant had paid immediately, they would have been liable for almost three months of interest.

But they did not pay immediately. Instead, they submitted petitions to the admiralty court to appeal. The nature of the two petitions was the same: they accused Moreau of failing in both cases to provide 'supporting documents', such as the 'sentence of confiscation', to justify the 'claimed loss'.[84] Although there is no record of what followed this, it is clear that Desanteul and Hélissant were willing to pursue every legal avenue in the hopes of being discharged from the policies they had signed.[85]

For Moreau, recourse to the admiralty court had been necessary to enforce the arbitration judgment against Desanteul and Helissant on 20 January. This was part of his broader strategy to resolve conflicts over a series of claims.

Moreau was a Parisian merchant-banker with deep ties to Saint-Malo.[86] As both a policyholder and commission agent, he adopted a nuanced strategy for securing payment on different policies: he proved willing to take underwriters to the admiralty and merchant courts to secure payment, both for his own account and for principals.[87] Nevertheless, in taking these cases to court, Moreau was not necessarily voting with his feet. For

---

[82] See Chapter 4.
[83] Z/1d/106, n.p., AN.
[84] Ibid.
[85] The prior three paragraphs draw on Wade, 'Underwriting Empire'.
[86] For clear examples of these ties, see the Chamber's policy registers; Z/1d/75–8, AN. See also his declarations of average and abandonment with the Company in later decades; Z/1d/82 and Z/1d/88, AN.
[87] He tried to make use of the merchant court through filing a petition there on 28 February but, as we will see below, this attempt to leverage every possible forum in the city backfired on him.

him, arbitration remained a legitimate tool of conflict resolution. Moreau appeared before arbiters in the Chamber on 20 January and 13 March to resolve policies in which he was the commission agent.[88] Shortly after, on 17 March, Moreau served as an arbiter for a dispute in the Chamber.[89] In this way, the man who was embroiled in several insurance conflicts became a 'manager' in others.[90]

This use of multiple forums can be interpreted in several ways. Litigation was perhaps necessary in some disputes because the underwriters were unwilling to engage in private discussions or take their conflict before arbiters. For those policies where Moreau was a commission agent, he perhaps followed the instructions of principals in deciding whether to pursue a claim for payment and, if so, in choosing which forum to use.

As the node in this web of conflicts, however, Moreau was surely a more active participant than these possibilities suggest. The 'multitude of forums' on offer gave great scope for 'choice' and 'design' in resolving these conflicts, so it seems most likely that Moreau engaged in an extensive dialogue with principals and underwriters in developing a broader strategy for resolving them.[91]

Within pre-modern mercantile conflict management, Albrecht Cordes and Philipp Höhn have recently observed that 'pending [court] claims could in fact have advantages because they opened up room for negotiation'.[92] When Desanteul and Hélissant refused to accept the arbitration judgment on the *Orrore*, Moreau escalated this conflict to court, most likely in the hopes that underwriters on other policies would be more inclined to engage with him out of court. Therefore, these conflicts did not exist in a vacuum: they frequently overlapped and interacted, often messily, with others. Escalating one or a handful of conflicts as a display of one's strength may have helped to de-escalate others in the long run.[93]

Acéré, the other major user of the admiralty court, was able to escalate and de-escalate his conflicts to meet his short- and long-term interests. Unlike Moreau, Acéré only sought reimbursement for policies he signed on his own account (in one case jointly with Pierre Dhariet). Excepting the policy with Dhariet, these policies covered the sea loans Acéré had given for cod fishing in Newfoundland and whaling in Greenland.[94] Since his interests alone were at stake, he tailored his strategy for securing payment accordingly: he immediately escalated his claims for payment to court,

---

[88] Z/1d/74, fols 50v–52r; Z/1d/106, n.p., AN.
[89] Z/1d/74, fols 53–54r, AN.
[90] Wubs-Mrozewicz, 'Conflict Management', pp. 91–2.
[91] Cordes and Höhn, 'Extra-Legal and Legal Conflict Management', p. 513.
[92] Ibid., p. 524.
[93] Wubs-Mrozewicz, 'Conflict Management', p. 102.
[94] Z/1d/77, fol. 226, AN. The policies covered return voyages to France.

trying first to petition the merchant court (as we will see below) and then the admiralty court to this effect.

Aceré pursued multiple claims in the admiralty court on the *Saint Esprit*. On one of these claims, he received a default judgment in his favour on 31 May. On another judged the day before, he was ordered to return to the court before the end of August with further evidence of the ship's loss.[95]

In the end, this case was not concluded in court: the parties appeared before arbiters in the Chamber on 23 August to settle the dispute.[96] It transpires that the underwriters were unhappy with making payment on the *Saint Esprit*, whose shipmaster was Esteben Bernard, when it was the *Saint Pierre*, whose shipmaster was Esteben de Renard, which had been captured instead. Aceré submitted that this was simply an error in the policy and provided evidence that, while he had given a sea loan to the *Saint Pierre*, he had made no such loan for the *Saint Esprit*. Ignoring this evidence, Henri Desanteul and Henri de Vaux alleged on behalf of the other underwriters that Aceré had intended all along to insure the *Saint Esprit* and could not now make a claim on the *Saint Pierre*.

Strangely, the arbiters chose to side with neither party, instead ruling without a clear logic that the underwriters should make half payment on the policy. The underwriters were also discharged from the fees ordered in the earlier court judgments, and the pending case in the admiralty court was duly withdrawn.[97]

With a dissatisfying verdict like this, Aceré may have regretted agreeing to go before arbiters. Nevertheless, de-escalating the conflict to arbitration allowed Aceré and the underwriters to address outstanding points of contention outside of court. For Aceré, this was valuable in protecting his long-term interests: using the admiralty court alone would have risked underwriters refusing to do business with him in the future. Although Desanteul and Vaux accused him of deception, his willingness to go before arbiters, despite the pending case in the admiralty court, displayed his desire to settle the dispute amicably. 'Good faith' was very much a matter of prudential self-interest in this instance, leaving the door open for Aceré to insure with the Chamber in the future if he so desired.

Moreau and Aceré's strategies illustrate that neither arbitration nor litigation were silver bullets in resolving the 1673 dispute crisis. These were complementary tools, allowing actors to escalate and de-escalate specific conflicts in order to resolve broader sets of disputes. For Moreau, carefully

---

[95] See Table 33.
[96] The arbitration record made clear that the case was settling the case 'pending before the judges of the admiralty of France [...] in Paris': Z/1d/74, fols 72–3, AN.
[97] Ibid.

picking his battles allowed him to secure court judgments in his favour while also participating in arbitration as disputant and arbiter. For Acéré, conflict resolution entailed more than simply receiving payment, prompting him to de-escalate the dispute over the *Saint Esprit* to arbitration in accordance with his long-term commercial interests. These strategies thus accord with Wijffels' observation that 'arbitration [...] is often presented as a faster, more cost-effective and less damaging option than litigation. In practice, it was often combined with litigation.'[98]

While Moreau and Acéré used the admiralty court to great effect, Desanteul and Hélissant were far from being the only underwriters to use the court to push back against policyholders and debtors. Records from 9 and 13 September note that Desanteul, Mathieu Marchand, Denis Rousseau and Henri Herlan had petitioned the court to discharge them from a series of policies signed with Louis Bigot in Bordeaux worth upwards of 4,000 *livres*.[99] A few days later, on 15 September, Gilles Mignot and François Lefebvre secured a default judgment against Elisabeth Marie Phillipes, requiring her to pay them 232 *livres* 10 *sols* for additional coverage on a time policy.[100] Meanwhile, on 26 January, Pierre Boullard, Charles Lhuillier de Creabé, Lefebvre and Mignot had successfully enforced an arbitration judgment against Anthoine de Gaumont and Martin Bernier through the court.[101]

Even Lalive went to court in his capacity as the Chamber's registrar. This became necessary after a general assembly on 7 January. Up to that point, it was Lalive who had collected premiums from policyholders/commission agents and then released them to the underwriters. Premiums were not always paid the moment that policies were signed, however, raising concerns about who was ultimately responsible for them. The assembly agreed that, in handling premiums, Lalive was the underwriters' 'agent'. Consequently, they 'will have no other debtor for their premiums than the registrar from the moment they have signed' any policies.[102] If policyholders refused to pay their premiums, Lalive agreed that this would be 'his own matter' to resolve.[103]

Shortly after this resolution, Lalive petitioned the city's merchant court, seeking 16,150 *livres* 10 *sols* 6 *deniers* 'owed for the premiums and duties of

---

[98] Wijffels, 'Commercial Quarrels', p. 6.
[99] Z/1d/106, n.p., AN. For the record of 9 September, it is unclear if the policy was worth 'deux mil livres' (2,000 *livres*) or 'dix mil livres' (10,000 *livres*); the remainder of the record does not give a date for the policy, or the name of the vessel insured, which makes it impossible to check.
[100] Ibid.
[101] Ibid.
[102] Z/1d/73, fols 25v–26, AN.
[103] Ibid. For the similar role of brokers in late medieval and early modern Italy, see Addobbati, 'Italy 1500–1800', pp. 57–9.

the insurance registry that the plaintiff had paid' on behalf of Pierre Cadelan.[104] However, Cadelan submitted to the admiralty court on 9 February that this was a breach of its jurisdiction over insurance disputes. Consequently, he petitioned for the case to be transferred to the admiralty court to be judged by it and it alone. Lalive agreed to this, and the admiralty court ultimately ordered Cadelan to pay 6,230 *livres*, with the balance of Lalive's claim to be decided by arbiters.[105]

'Distraction of jurisdiction' and summary procedure: the Chamber's role in the dispute crisis

This was only one of several instances in 1673 where the Chamber found itself caught up in the power struggle between the admiralty court and the merchant court for jurisdiction over insurance disputes. On 25 February, Moreau petitioned the merchant court to oversee his claim against François Lefebvre, Simon Boirat, Gilles Mignot and Étienne Suplegeau. The attorney general (*procureur du roi*) of the Parisian admiralty court intervened personally to protest this.[106] On 28 February, he explained that the merchant court was 'entirely incompetent' in matters of insurance, and therefore moved 'to have Moreau assigned before us', i.e. the admiralty court.[107] Moreau was given a hefty fine of 500 *livres* for 'distraction of jurisdiction', i.e. for undermining the admiralty court's authority by bringing the case before the wrong court.[108] The parties were ordered to proceed with their case at the admiralty court rather than 'before the consular judges' or any other authority.[109] Moreau's strategy of escalation had backfired here amidst this jurisdictional tension.

This intervention came just before the *Ordonnance sur le commerce* was issued in March, granting jurisdiction over insurance disputes to the merchant courts. The *volte-face* followed in June. Amidst the confusion, chaos ensued. Acéré petitioned the merchant court on 8 April to hear his grievances with two sets of underwriters, believing it was competent in insurance disputes. The attorney general intervened again on 10 April to assert the admiralty court's jurisdiction over these cases, but he only moved one of them over. Acéré submitted to the admiralty court on 13 April that 'it

---

[104] Z/1d/106, n.p., AN.
[105] Ibid.
[106] I have been unable to find the name of the attorney general.
[107] Z/1d/106, n.p., AN.
[108] Ibid.
[109] Ibid.

would not be just to proceed on the same offence in two different jurisdictions' and asked that the other case be heard before it as well.¹¹⁰

The transfer of cases continued. On 7 July, the widow of Jean Gler petitioned the merchant court to hear her claim against Maillet, Pocquelin and company and Étienne Rouxelin; the attorney general intervened on 8 July, resulting in the widow being fined 500 *livres* for 'distraction of jurisdiction'. This time, the attorney general made expressly clear that the order of the Council of State of 28 June had restored full and exclusive jurisdiction over insurance disputes to the admiralty courts.¹¹¹ On 21 August, he issued an almost word-for-word replica of this declaration while fining Guillaume de Voulges for submitting a claim against François Lefebvre and Pierre Robelot in the merchant court. Both of these cases were transferred to the admiralty court. The attorney general, it seems, was determined to uphold the admiralty court's jurisdiction at any cost.¹¹²

With so many cases coming before the admiralty court, however, the attorney general recognised that speedy justice was needed to pacify underwriters and policyholders alike. Although the extant records are unclear on the matter, it seems that the court had been using the full civil procedure in addressing insurance disputes up to August, when Voulges was fined.¹¹³ On the attorney general's prompting, the admiralty court issued a statement on 29 August acknowledging that 'disputes concerning maritime commerce must be treated summarily and cannot suffer the delays observed ordinarily in other principal affairs when they are treated in the first instance'.¹¹⁴ Thus, at 'the good pleasure of the king', the court announced that summary procedure would be introduced to expedite cost-efficient maritime commercial dispute resolution: hearings for maritime commercial disputes were thereafter to take place every Monday, Wednesday and Friday morning from 10:00am to 12:00pm, and new fixed procedures were introduced, designed to ensure prompt justice and prevent litigants from intentionally stalling proceedings.¹¹⁵

---

[110] Ibid. Whether this petition was successful or not is unclear, nor is it clear whether Aceré received a fine; since article 7 of the section *De la jurisdiction de Consuls* of the *Ordonnance sur le commerce* had not yet been suspended when the attorney general intervened, his right to assert jurisdiction seems to have been very tenuous.

[111] Ibid.

[112] Ibid.

[113] It was common practice across continental Europe for commercial affairs to be treated in a summary fashion; why this was not the case in the admiralty court until the attorney general's intervention is unclear; M. Fusaro, 'Politics of Justice/Politics of Trade: Foreign Merchants and the Administration of Justice from the Records of Venice's *Giudici del Forestier*', *Mélanges de l'École française de Rome* 126 (2014), pp. 139–60.

[114] Z/1d/106, n.p., AN.

[115] Ibid.

Parties could be heard without representation if they wished, thereby limiting their expenses.

Tellingly, the court ordered for the new procedures to be advertised in two places: 'in the registry of the community of lawyers and prosecutors of the *parlement* [of Paris] and the registry of the [Royal] Insurance Chamber of Paris'.[116]

This brings into stark relief the proliferation of insurance disputes in 1673, the Chamber's central role in the battle of jurisdictions and the precariousness of the admiralty court's position. While Colbert's reforms up to his death centred on clarifying jurisdictional ambiguities in all aspects of French life, legitimacy did not simply come from above: a court could boast royal credentials, but its power was entirely illusory if people chose not to take their conflicts there. The 1670 *Ordonnance civile* recognised this at the local level by mandating the 'use of summary, oral procedure for a wide variety of cases': in seigneurial courts, for example, all private matters involving less than 200 *livres* were resolved in this manner thereafter. This ensured the local courts' popularity, thereby facilitating 'state formation from below': magistrates were able to respond to litigants' needs by making quick and inexpensive judgments.[117] Following this logic to its conclusion, the attorney general recognised that the admiralty court could only defend its jurisdiction over insurance cases if it could respond in a prompt and supple manner to the Chamber's disputes. Without the introduction of summary procedure, he realised, litigants would simply continue trying to bring their cases before the merchant court, which, as Kessler puts it, offered 'the speedy, simple procedure that merchants craved'.[118] The year 1673 thus proved to be an unwelcome stress test not only of the Chamber, but of Colbert's new commercial jurisdictional framework as well.

'FOR THE ENTIRE AND JUST PRESERVATION OF ITS SPLENDOUR': THE STATE PROPAGANDA CAMPAIGN AFTER THE DISPUTE CRISIS

The avalanche of court cases hit the Chamber hard. Slow proceedings may have suited the short-term interests of overexposed underwriters, but they carried the cost of legal fees and interest penalties when the court finally ruled.

---

[116] Ibid.
[117] Hayhoe, *Enlightened Feudalism*, pp. 155–6; Breen, 'Law, Society, and the State', p. 380. For this bottom-up understanding of courts and the source of their authority, see Schneider, *The King's Bench*; Breen, 'Law, Society, and the State', pp. 365–85; Piant, *Une Justice ordinaire*; Hardwick, *Family Business*.
[118] Kessler, *A Revolution in Commerce*, p. 30.

They also came at a cost to the Chamber's reputation. The institution had already been forced on 30 September 1672 to acknowledge grievances that had arisen due to underwriters loitering in the registry: the presence of these underwriters pressured policyholders/commission agents into accepting coverage from them even if the latter did not wish to do business with them. The Chamber thus henceforth forebade policies from being signed in the registry itself, requiring clerks to bring policies to the homes of underwriters instead to be signed. This would allow the registry to discreetly take into account the wishes of policyholders/commission agents on who would (not) provide coverage.[119] That this judgment was necessary speaks to the reality that policyholders and commission agents were losing faith in some of the underwriters and hoped to avoid dealing with them in the future. Moreover, that these disagreements came even before the onslaught of court cases in 1673 did not bode well for the institution's long-term wellbeing.

By August 1673, when the jurisdictional tug-of-war in the city came to a head on the back of the Chamber's conflicts, its members knew that damage control was needed to salvage its reputation. On 26 August – just three days before summary procedure was introduced in the admiralty court – the Chamber made a significant change to its dispute resolution mechanisms.

This change addressed the risk of a future glut of court cases. All policies signed after 1 October 1673 were to contain a clause obliging parties to bring their disputes before arbiters, preventing them from seeking redress in the courts in the first instance. The members justified this measure by suggesting that, since the Chamber 'is filled with the most enlightened people in commerce', disputes within the Chamber 'can easily be settled amongst [the members] themselves, without fees and more promptly' than in the courts.[120]

The deliberation was trying to square several circles at once. Certainly, the new clause was not just a future-proofing exercise: the Chamber's short-term interests were very much at stake, as the washing of its dirty laundry in the courts had clearly damaged its reputation. There was the risk that prospective policyholders would no longer bring business to Paris, deterred by the time and money commitment necessary to secure payment on their policies.

Even so, policyholders did not bring their disputes before the courts in 1673 for lack of an alternative. The deliberation itself boasted that the Chamber had pioneered 'the way of compromises and arbitration', and the proliferation of arbitration cases that year indicates that it was an option pursued by some. Nevertheless, *pace* Boiteux, it was not preferred by all:

[119] Z/1d/73, fols 24v–25r, AN.
[120] Ibid., fol. 27.

numerous policyholders chose to take their cases before the courts instead. Lasson sent a horse from Saint-Jean-de-Luz to submit a petition to the Parisian admiralty court for a reason. While the Chamber's deliberation stressed the efficiency of arbitration, policyholders like Lasson had greater confidence in the admiralty court than arbitration. Moreover, for those like Moreau and Acéré who sought payment on multiple insurance policies, the courts were essential in their strategies for resolving multiple conflicts at once. In brief, policyholders leveraged their freedom to choose their forum in the pursuit of their interests.

Nevertheless, the deliberation suggested that policyholders were the winners from the new clause: the widespread recourse to the courts in 1673 was said to be 'of a very dangerous consequence for merchants in particular'. In reality, the court activity in 1673 was of a greater consequence to the underwriters.

In this light, the deliberation reveals itself to be a survival tactic in disguise: it was designed to forestall the ongoing mass exodus of underwriters by keeping them from being embroiled in expensive court cases in the future, while also limiting any further damage to the Chamber's reputation by keeping future disputes out of the public eye. The result of this was that, on the one hand, the deliberation restricted the legal rights of policyholders while, on the other, trying to encourage them to bring their business to the Chamber for precisely this reason.

The deliberation overlooked that two admiralty court judgments had concerned arbitration sentences the losing party had not respected. Indeed, Desanteul and Hélissant not only refused to respect the arbitration sentence against them from 20 January, but also the admiralty court's judgment against them from 18 April. This suggests that the Chamber faced a broader problem with enforcement: good faith alone was insufficient, and the institution lacked the teeth to enforce arbitration sentences. When these were ignored, parties were forced to go before the admiralty court.

Despite these peculiarities, Moreau himself signed the deliberation. We should not presume from this gesture that he fully endorsed what was written. Nevertheless, with his hefty fine for 'distraction of jurisdiction' in mind, he may have believed that mandatory arbitration in the first instance was preferable to trying to navigate the minefield of jurisdiction within the city.[121]

The decision to print and distribute the deliberation across Europe transformed an already charged record into a public statement. The deliberation was tailored to its audience and intended purpose, drawing attention to the Chamber being 'filled with the most enlightened people in commerce' while playing down the proliferation of litigation by suggesting only 'some people'

---

[121] Ibid., fol. 27.

had brought cases to court. Moreover, it suggested that the widespread use of arbitration had 'augmented considerably the Chamber's reputation and drawn here business from all parts of Europe'.[122] This not only implied that the proliferation of court cases was an aberration entirely out of the Chamber's control, but also that the compulsory arbitration clause would ensure a return to the orderly, harmonious norm.

With the introduction of summary procedure in the admiralty court looming, the Chamber took the opportunity to mitigate the damage that the year had inflicted. Nevertheless, Colbert himself was forced to step in to further mitigate the fallout, kicking off a propaganda campaign that was to last until the end of the decade.

Part I: the royal orders

On 16 December 1673, an order of the Council of State was issued ratifying the Chamber's new obligatory arbitration clause.[123] In essence, this was cheap royal propaganda in every sense: the order was distributed and registered throughout France at no expense to the Chamber, legitimating the institution at its lowest ebb by signalling the state's continued support for it. In many ways, the Chamber was presented as a manifestation of the king's glory that had lost none of its lustre: indeed, the order suggested that the clause was being introduced to preserve the institution's 'splendour' by 'conserv[ing] the order and unity that must be observed' amongst its members in handling disputes.[124] Far from panicking in response to a crisis of its own making, the Chamber was portrayed to be future-proofing its activities, wisely and ably righting the ship in response to exogenous forces. Moreover, in observing that 'great sums can be consumed by the length of legal proceedings', the order reinforced the Chamber's message that cheap and speedy justice in the first instance was an equal benefit to all parties, deftly glossing over the fact that this limited the rights of policyholders to select the forum in which to pursue their claims.[125] The order also ignored the reality that these lengthy court proceedings were, at heart, a failure of the state.

The Chamber's compulsory arbitration clause seems to have been an innovation in French insurance practice, later enshrined in the 1681 *Ordonnance de la marine*.[126] Through articles 3 and 70–4 of the section *Des*

---

[122] Ibid., fol. 27.
[123] Pouilloux, *Mémoires d'assurances*, pp. 428–9.
[124] Ibid.
[125] Ibid.
[126] I have found no evidence of compulsory arbitration clauses in any French policy forms before 1673. Mallory Hope has found numerous insurance policies for Nantes before and after 1681; only those after 1681 included compulsory arbitration clauses,

Assurances, recourse to arbitration became obligatory in the first instance; arbitration judgments were merely to be ratified (and, where necessary, enforced) by the admiralty courts.[127] By shifting the burden for handling insurance disputes onto arbiters, the *Ordonnance*'s compilers ensured that France's admiralty courts would not be inundated with disputes on maritime commerce every time war broke out.[128] We will see in the next chapter that this 'institutionalisation of arbitration' was a deft manner of delegating, rather than giving up, state power, but it seems very likely that the *Ordonnance*'s compilers were drawing from the Chamber's experiences in creating this system.[129] Put another way, this new system emerged from the state's weakness in handling the 1673 crisis.

Pointing further to the precariousness of the Chamber's position, another order was issued on the same day by the Council of State, responding to concerns raised by Lalive about the registration of policies. Lalive warned that Parisians had begun to negotiate contracts outside the Chamber, registering them with notaries rather than in the Chamber's registry. The order warned that, 'if this was permitted', the practice would bring about 'the Chamber's entire destruction'.[130] The order prohibited all notaries and other authorities from registering policies in Paris, requiring them to be registered instead with Lalive in the Chamber, with the requisite registry fees paid. That this order was needed at all suggests merchants had begun to lose faith in the Chamber and were now opting to do their underwriting beyond its confines.

Part II: Savary and the Chamber as a model Colbertian institution

This was unacceptable to Colbert, who was determined to see the Chamber succeed again. Perception is a form of reality, and Colbert knew this well: when he introduced his plans for the CIO in 1664, Colbert had turned to François Charpentier to act as the state's 'glory salesman'. Charpentier led the propaganda campaign for the project, writing two tracts encouraging Frenchmen to invest in the CIO as a patriotic gesture that would unite the country in a shared manifestation of the king's glory.[131] True to form,

---

in conformity with the *Ordonnance de la marine*. In Marseille, a compulsory arbitration clause was never introduced to the city's policy form during the Old Regime; Hope, 'Underwriting Risk'.

[127] Valin, *Nouveau commentaire*, vol. II, pp. 31 and 154–7.
[128] The authorities of La Rochelle noted in 1764 that the compulsory arbitration clause in insurance contracts was 'for the greater good of commerce, nipping lawsuits in the bud': quoted in Hope, 'Underwriting Risk'.
[129] Cordes and Höhn, 'Extra-Legal and Legal Conflict Management', pp. 520–1.
[130] Pouilloux, *Mémoires d'assurances*, pp. 429–30.
[131] Clark, *Compass of Society*, pp. 39–5; Ames, *Colbert*.

Colbert turned to Savary to lead the charge in the next stage of the propaganda campaign for re-establishing the Chamber's reputation. Savary dedicated his 1675 merchant manual, *Le parfait négociant*, to Colbert himself.

In this manual, Savary offered a glowing endorsement of the Chamber – 'the most famous [insurance chamber] that there has ever been in Europe, where even the Dutch come to insure their vessels' – structured around several themes dear to Colbert.[132] In the first two paragraphs of his discussion on underwriting, he warned the reader to be 'careful' when choosing an underwriter, highlighting the capacity for underwriters to engage in chicanery to avoid making payment on claims; in the following two paragraphs, he introduced the Chamber and its activities; and in the final paragraph, he encouraged the reader to insure with the Chamber above all other underwriters.[133] In shifting so skilfully from the risks posed by the immoral underwriter to the security and ease of indemnity offered by the Chamber's supposedly virtuous underwriters, Savary was able to contrast the two to great effect. In calling the Chamber's underwriters 'intelligent', 'of such good faith', 'so reasonable' and 'more solvent' than underwriters based elsewhere, Savary appealed to a moral vocabulary so typical of the period that established the Chamber's underwriters as virtuous and trustworthy.[134]

Savary also praised the supposed scale of the Chamber's underwriting and its foreign clientele, speaking to Colbert's interest in developing the French insurance industry at the expense of the Dutch. Yet, by 1675, the Chamber was close to ruin after the 1673 dispute crisis. Savary played on this intelligently, using the losses incurred during the war as a demonstration of the insurers' supposed moral rectitude: even in the face of such devastating losses, Savary claimed, the Chamber made prompt payment to all policyholders without recourse to lawsuits. This drew on, and reinforced, the Chamber's own motto from the 1671 jetton: a crushed world fell in upon the institution in 1672, but (so Savary claimed) the ruins struck it undismayed. In suggesting this, Savary turned the Chamber's losses into a strength that appealed once again to Colbertian sensitivities: the Chamber had not resorted to the 'chicanery' that Colbert and Savary had both warned against. In drawing on Colbert's anti-Dutch sentiments, and in dubiously reframing the institution's losses in 1672, Savary sold the Chamber as a model Colbertian insurance institution.

The Chamber could have received neither a more influential endorsement nor a better advertisement: *Le parfait négociant* was an instant bestseller, becoming 'the most reprinted, translated, and plagiarised merchant

---

[132] Savary, *Le parfait négociant*, vol. I, book II, pp. 200–1.
[133] Ibid., pp. 112–13.
[134] Ibid., pp. 112–13.

manual of early modern Europe'. It received translations into German and Dutch in 1676 and 1683 respectively and ran to at least twenty-nine editions in French by 1800.[135]

Indeed, this endorsement has left a lasting imprint on the historiography. Based on Savary's account, Barbour has argued that, alongside Amsterdam's *Kamer van Assurantie*, the 'Chamber established by Colbert at Paris could boast a good name' in resolving disputes amicably.[136] Similarly, Boiteux quotes Savary at length in arguing that the Chamber 'kept all its commitments' after 'the disaster of 1672'.[137] Moreover, he lauds the Chamber's 'simple and rapid' arbitration system as 'a solution' to the 'difficulties' posed by onerous litigation, with the shift towards compulsory arbitration being part of this good institutional practice.[138] He argues that

> From 1670 to 1674 (the only period for which there remains evidence) the Chamber produced less than a hundred arbitration cases, bearing often on elevated [levels of] capital and, it seems, to the entire satisfaction of the parties, since we often see them refusing the offer made to them by the admiralty judges to settle their disputes.[139]

This characterisation of the period, we have seen, does not accord with the reality of conflict resolution in the Chamber in these years.

Part III: Irson and the model Colbertian commercial universe

The propaganda campaign only ended later in the decade. Colbert commissioned Claude Irson to write a manual for maintaining model commercial registers following the maxims of double-entry bookkeeping. Once Irson finished it, Colbert ordered the Chamber to certify it was 'worthy' of his

---

[135] Trivellato, *The Promise and Peril of Credit*, pp. 99 and 103. Jean Toubeau's *Les institutes du droit consulaire*, first published in 1682, replicated Savary's account of the Chamber almost entirely, adding only that the underwriters had reimbursed the policyholders 'with honour'; J. Toubeau, *Les institutes du droit consulaire, ou La jurisprudence des marchands*, vol. I, Paris: Nicolas Gosselin, 1700, pp. 267–8.

[136] Barbour glosses over the radical structural differences between the Chamber and the *Kamer*; she also incorrectly dates the establishment of the Chamber to 1671 rather than 1668; Barbour, 'Marine Risks', pp. 573 and 575. Citing Barbour, this date is also given in Trivellato, *The Promise and Peril of Credit*, p. 23. For another account taking Savary at face value, see Cole, *Colbert*, vol. I, p. 385.

[137] Boiteux, *L'assurance maritime à Paris*, p. 47.

[138] Ibid., pp. 31–2. Boiteux lauded the Chamber for adopting this arbitration system from the insurance chambers of the Netherlands, but the most significant of these – the *Kamer van Assurantie* in Amsterdam – was a subordinate court, not an arbitration tribunal; Go, 'Amsterdam 1585–1790', pp. 113–14.

[139] Boiteux, *L'assurance maritime à Paris*, pp. 47–8.

patronage.[140] On 11 February 1678, Bellinzani, Lalive and a handful of the Chamber's members met and confirmed that the manual 'is very useful and conforms to the usage practiced throughout Europe'.[141] The Chamber's endorsement was the first of three to be printed when the manual was published. Irson repaid this favour by giving the Chamber free advertising in his model entries: in the model entry for premiums due to Irson for a series of policies he had underwritten, he used the Chamber as the example debtor. Similarly, in the model entry for the premium and registry fees he owed after having his merchandise underwritten, he used the Chamber as the example creditor, even specifying that the premium was owed to Robelot, the cashier of the Chamber, and the registry fees owed to Lalive, its registrar.[142] While Savary had presented the Chamber as a model insurance institution, Irson went further by incorporating it into a model commercial universe.

Alas, this model universe was not real and could do little to change the Chamber's plight. While Savary has convinced unwitting historians of the 'good faith' of the Chamber's underwriters, he could not convince the very merchants for whom his manual was written. As we have seen, the Chamber never recovered from the 1673 crisis, even if its influence continued long after then.[143]

CONCLUSION

In early modern France, commerce was perceived with distrust. If left to its own devices, chaos and ruin were believed to be the inevitable results. Insurance occupied an especially precarious position in this discourse: if both underwriter and policyholder behaved correctly, the benefits to commerce were great; if either party engaged in 'bad faith', especially during a time of crisis, the scope for chaos in the courts – and in the commercial sphere more broadly – was very real.

Reputation and conflict resolution were therefore intimately intertwined. Accordingly, the Chamber went to great lengths to shape its commercial identity through its approaches to conflict resolution. It leveraged its royal patronage to style itself as a virtuous and trustworthy institution whose underwriters could be relied on to make prompt payment or, otherwise, meet with policyholders before arbiters to resolve any disputes quickly and amicably.

---

[140] C. Irson, *Méthode pour bien dresser toutes sortes de comptes à parties doubles*, Paris: Claude Irson and Jean Cusson, 1678, n.p.
[141] Ibid.
[142] Ibid., pp. 10 and 67.
[143] On the Chamber's inability to recover, see Chapter 4. On its influence after 1673, see Chapter 6.

The reality was decidedly messier, especially in 1673. We can no longer accept Boiteux's assessment of the Chamber's arbitration system as a triumph of private ordering: eschewing the longstanding dichotomy between formal and informal conflict resolution, this chapter has found that policyholders drew extensively on Paris' diverse market for conflict resolution. Arbitration thus complemented litigation in some instances, and vice versa. As both a policyholder and a commission agent, Moreau adopted a mixed strategy, escalating particular conflicts to court while simultaneously participating in the Chamber's arbitration system as both disputant and arbiter. Aceré escalated his claims for payment early on, before de-escalating a specific dispute to arbitration to protect his long-term commercial interests. In short, policyholders could take their grievances before the forum that best served their needs and interests, or even craft their own conflict resolution strategies that incorporated multiple forums.

Nevertheless, the city's fractious jurisdictional landscape exacerbated conflicts within the Chamber. In the jurisdictional confusion arising from the *Ordonnance sur le commerce*, Moreau was one of several who were caught out, receiving a stringent fine from the admiralty court for trying to take a case before the city's merchant court. Yet the admiralty court was ill-equipped to manage the influx of cases from the Chamber in 1673, and by the end of August was forced to implement summary procedure for insurance disputes. The court's belligerent defence of its jurisdiction thus exposed its position of vulnerability: its jurisdiction rested on its ability to meet the needs of policyholders and underwriters alike. Viewed from the top-down, the court wielded the delegated power of the state; viewed from the bottom-up, the court wielded the delegated power of the litigants themselves.[144]

The plethora of cases against the underwriters in 1673, and the introduction of summary proceedings in the admiralty court to handle these, casts Savary's endorsement of the Chamber in a new light. This endorsement was part of a broader Colbertian propaganda campaign to salvage the Chamber's tarnished reputation. In *Le parfait négociant*, Savary framed his discussion in a way that appealed to Colbertian sensitivities while also touching on the fundamental values of 'good faith' at the heart of early modern commerce itself.

In this way, Savary drew on and supported the Chamber's earlier efforts to establish its reputation. Discourse, gesture and materiality were artefacts of early modern commerce that the Chamber leveraged consciously and consistently, but they had meaning only if the fundamental value system

---

[144] In many ways, this supports Rafe Blaufarb's argument that 'law was politics in early modern France' and reinforces his assessment of the 'importance of the judicial aspect of absolutist sovereignty'; Blaufarb, *The Politics of Fiscal Privilege*, pp. 265–6.

they spoke to was upheld. The Chamber's leading underwriter on paper, Henri Desanteul, chose to prolong numerous insurance disputes in 1673, ignoring an arbitration sentence and admiralty court judgment in the process. He was far from alone. When the underwriters failed to live up to their commitments, discourse, gesture and materiality became worthless tools. Savary may have pleased Colbert with his endorsement of the Chamber, and even led later historians astray, but the many merchants across Europe who had a copy of *Le parfait négociant* on their desk were not persuaded to bring their business to the institution. In this light, Colbert's letter from early 1673 seems most prescient: he warned that, when insurance institutions like the Chamber become embroiled in 'chicanery', 'they will waste a fortune [in the courts] while never recovering' from the damage to their reputation. His later propaganda campaign notwithstanding, this proved true of the Chamber. The 1684 counterfeiting scandal, which implicated Bellinzani and Lalive, simply brought about the disgraceful demise of an institution already beyond repair.[145]

Of course, not every underwriter in the Chamber was as belligerent as Desanteul – but this mattered little. To understand why, we must acknowledge the incompatibility between the institution's structure and its commercial identity. The Chamber's appeal lay in its flexible structure: members could join or withdraw from the market at will, bearing only the risks they signed for themselves.[146] The Chamber was a collection of private underwriters, each with different reputations and credit. Yet it fashioned its commercial identity as a corporate body, with the intention of creating and leveraging social capital to maintain righteous conduct amongst its members. Social capital proved ineffective, however, which left the Chamber vulnerable to its members' actions: in withholding payment on so many policies, Desanteul and others undermined the whole Chamber's reputation. Social pressures created by underwriters loitering in the registry, which were only addressed in mid-1672, prevented policyholders from effectively punishing rogue underwriters by refusing to do business with them in the future. Without such self-policing mechanisms in place, the Chamber could only be as trustworthy as its least creditworthy and/or most unscrupulous underwriter.[147]

This vulnerability was compounded by the introduction of the compulsory arbitration clause. Despite the Chamber's stated intentions, introducing it did not serve the interests of policyholders: it aimed instead to mitigate the damage inflicted on the institution's reputation after a bruising year of

---

[145] On this scandal, see Chapter 2.
[146] See Chapter 1.
[147] On mechanisms like this, see Greif, *Institutions and the Path to the Modern Economy*.

disputes scattered across the city's courts. The Chamber had hoped to restore its reputation and even encourage new business in the aftermath of the dispute crisis, but denying policyholders the agency to choose their underwriters or their forum for addressing conflicts was not a winning strategy.

In essence, the Chamber could not square the circle between its corporate identity and its private structure. When storm clouds obscured the sun and the ship faced choppy waters, it was every man and woman for themselves.

8

'NEC HOSTES NEC MARE TERRENT': REPUTATION, CONFLICT RESOLUTION AND PRIVILEGE IN THE ROYAL INSURANCE COMPANY, 1686–1701

Continuing from the last chapter, and with its theoretical frameworks, this chapter analyses the evolution of conflict resolution in Paris while the Company conducted business. The difficulties of 1673 seem to have influenced the *Ordonnance de la marine*, which followed the Chamber's lead in requiring insurance disputes to be resolved through arbitration in the first instance. Yet the state had not given away legal authority to arbiters, but simply delegated it to them, with the admiralty courts overseeing arbitration proceedings and ratifying their judgments. This was the 'institutionalisation of arbitration' writ large.[1] Nevertheless, it was not simply arbitration that had been transformed, but the admiralty court too: it became a mediator more than a judge of conflicts, bringing parties to the table to negotiate their conflicts privately or appoint arbiters for arbitration. In this way, the Parisian admiralty court was now better able to meet the needs of disputants: its role now aligned more closely with that of the local civil courts – where judges often strove to mediate a conciliatory outcome rather than mete out punitive judgments – and even that of the Parisian merchant court with which it had battled for jurisdiction in 1673.[2]

The Company was able to navigate this new, clearer jurisdictional landscape without difficulty, at least until insurance claims skyrocketed in 1691 and 1692. The admiralty court took on several cases involving the Company in 1694 and 1695, pointing to the discretion it continued to exercise in handling insurance conflicts.

---

[1] Cordes and Höhn, 'Extra-Legal and Legal Conflict Management', pp. 520–1.
[2] Breen, 'Law, Society, and the State', pp. 374–80; Kessler, *A Revolution in Commerce*, p. 31; Schneider, *The King's Bench*; Piant, *Une Justice ordinaire*.

Unlike its predecessor, however, the Company received no support from the state in the wake of these difficulties. The Company's fate was sealed at the turn of the century when it was subjected to a state-sponsored smear campaign. Fuelled by high politics, this campaign drew on common tropes of commercial morality to impugn the Company's reputation. This brings into focus the state's pivotal role in the Company's eventual demise.

THE COMPANY AND THE FASHIONING OF REPUTATION

The Company's articles of association enshrined that the attendees of its general assemblies would each receive two silver jettons. When the directors met to discuss the Company's affairs, they would each be given six jettons.[3]

There was some clear continuity from the Chamber's jetton: the obverse remained unchanged, depicting Louis XIV as a representation of the institution's royal patronage. The reverse, however, was quite different. A catalogue from 1715 described the image in the centre as 'a Fortification upon a Precipice near the Sea'.[4] Gone are the calm waters and the benevolent gaze of the Sun King depicted in the Chamber's jetton; in its place, rough waters batter a precipice with storm clouds above. The image's precariousness is contrasted only by the fortification in the centre and the phrase that encircles it: 'they fear neither enemies nor the sea'.[5] In this way, the Company's jetton drew on similar tropes to the Chamber's: the ability to withstand natural and anthropogenic hazards was once again invoked. The image was decidedly harsher, however, with the fortification in the centre sitting in stark contrast to the chaos surrounding it.

To a degree, this shift away from optimism reflected the transformation in international climate by 1686. In 1671, France's prospects were most sunny; by 1686, it was bracing for the barrage from the League of Augsburg. The Company's forthright motto, leaving no ambiguity that it would face down all threats from France's enemies, presented the institution's strength and defiance in the face of the shifting political landscape. Just as the state's strategy for insurance adapted to the times, so also did the Company's jetton.[6]

---

[3] Bornier, *Conférences des ordonnances de Louis XIV*, vol. II, pp. 513–25. These jettons were worth twenty *sols* each.
[4] R. Thoresby, *Ducatus Leodiensis, Or, The Topography of the Ancient and Populous Town and Parish of Leeds*, London: Maurice Atkins, 1715, p. 405.
[5] 'NEC HOSTES NEC MARE TERRENT'; I am grateful to Robyn Summers for this translation.
[6] On how this strategy changed over time, see Chapter 2.

Image 2   The Company's silver jetton, after 1686.

Source: Jetons-Médailles Frédéric Boyer, 'Jeton Louis XIV chambre des assurances s.d.' [https://www.jetons-medailles.com/fr/louis-xiv/260-jeton-louis-xiv-chambre-des-assurances-sd.html, accessed 1 March 2020]. With thanks to Jetons-Médailles Frédéric Boyer for giving permission to reproduce the image.

UNCLEAN HANDS: THE 'EXCLUSIVE SYSTEM' AND THE ROLE OF THE STATE IN INFORMAL CONFLICT RESOLUTION

Nevertheless, some things did not change. As with the Chamber, the state supported the Company's efforts to craft its identity as a moral commercial entity.[7] Indeed, this was one of the institution's *raisons d'être*. Yet this left it especially vulnerable to charges of immoral conduct. This vulnerability was revealed in dramatic fashion by Lagny's own correspondent in Saint-Malo, Jean Magon de la Lande.[8] Magon had frequently insured in the Chamber through Moreau, so he was already comfortable with seeking coverage in Paris.[9] Discussions between Lagny and Magon started out cordially, but by June 1687, the relationship had begun to sour.[10] Our knowledge on this affair is limited to a summary of a letter Magon wrote

[7] See Chapters 2, 3 and 6.
[8] On Magon and his correspondence with Lagny, see Chapter 3.
[9] For example, see Z/1d/75, fol. 170v, AN. See Chapter 4.
[10] When posed a question by Magon on the Company, Lagny responded on 30 August 1686 that 'I have not been able to respond to the question that you have given to me touching insurance because I have not been able to go to the Chamber since I received your letter, having almost always been in Versailles'; MAR/B/7/58, fols 245–6, AN.

to Seignelay on 8 June 1687.[11] Although the precise details are unclear, the summary conveys Magon's furiousness at Lagny and the Company: Magon claimed that, since the institution's establishment, he 'had written to his correspondents in foreign countries' to establish 'their entire trust' in it. Based on this, Magon's 'Spanish friends – owners of vessels [coming] from Buenos Aires – had given him an order to insure 150,000 *livres*'. Moreau consented to serving as Magon's commission agent for these policies, 'agree[ing] a premium of 9 per cent' with Lagny. Magon claimed that the Company subsequently 'demanded 10 per cent from him' for the premium, 'without having any regard' for the rate agreed with Moreau.[12] With apparently no resolution for this disagreement reached, the ships had no coverage when they arrived in Europe.

As a consequence of this affair, Magon asked Seignelay 'to consider how much this conduct is contrary to the good faith of commerce', since Magon's Spanish correspondents would have been entirely liable for any damages or losses to the vessels.[13] The summary of Magon's final point is emphatic: 'all trust in the insurers of Paris will be lost if they continue to act in this manner'.[14]

In writing this letter, Magon opted against trying to resolve the incident with Lagny personally and escalated his grievances directly to Seignelay. He framed his criticisms of the Company in a very familiar vocabulary. In trying to raise the premium after it had ostensibly been agreed, Magon accused the Company of an act 'contrary to the good faith of commerce' that imperilled the commercial interests of his Spanish correspondents. His conclusion that 'all trust in the insurers of Paris will be lost if they continue to act in this manner' was designed to pressure Seignelay to intervene in the Company's affairs: if its establishment really followed from the king's duty to protect merchants from the immoral conduct of foreign insurers, as the crown had argued and would continue to argue, then it was Seignelay's responsibility to ensure the Company was living up to one of its *raisons d'être*.[15]

This fraught confusion – an occupational hazard in business transactions across long distances – soon developed into a full-blown standoff. On 12 November 1687, Magon wrote to Seignelay, explaining that he had sought 80,000 *livres* of coverage from the Company for cargo worth a total of 204,662 *livres* on the *Galand*, for a return trip from Saint-Malo to the

---

[11] Summarising letters was common practice in the secretariat of state for maritime affairs, and these summaries no doubt served as a valuable tool for those clerks searching for particular topics or events, but they are a poor substitute for the full letters.
[12] MAR/B/7/492, fol. 438, AN.
[13] Ibid.
[14] Ibid.
[15] On this understanding of the king's duty, see Chapter 2.

Caribbean.¹⁶ Echoing his letter in June, Magon accused the Company of demanding a premium of 9 per cent for six months of coverage after having already settled on a rate of 8 per cent. He viewed this as an unreasonable demand, as the *Galand* had already left Saint-Malo and avoided problems in the Channel – in other words, it had navigated what Frank Spooner calls the 'risk-trap' of leaving port, a constant consideration in deciding insurance premiums.¹⁷ More pressingly, however, Magon attested that the Company was being unreasonable in inserting a deliberately ambiguous clause into the policy, absolving it of all responsibility for losses caused by Spanish or piratical forces. Without Seignelay's intervention to resolve the two points of contention, Magon threatened to 'find the surplus [coverage for the *Galand*] in this town or elsewhere', implying his willingness to contravene the ban on foreign insurance Seignelay had imposed in September.¹⁸

The morally charged vocabulary of the June letter can be found again here: as a result of the Company's unwillingness to insure the *Galand* 'purely and fully', Magon suggested that 'it will not be possible to have trust' in the institution.¹⁹ He felt able to question its trustworthiness because of the clause it had proposed for the policy: Magon suggested that the Company would seize on the clause's ambiguity to give a 'thousand [different] excuses' for not paying out on any claims. The implication that the Company would engage in chicanery, tying up any claims in arduous and lengthy legal proceedings based on this ambiguity, lay just beneath the surface of this accusation.

Within this passionate plea for Seignelay to intercede, Magon conveniently omitted a significant detail. Accompanying his letter was a copy of the *mémoire* he had sent to the Company's directors, giving a description of the *Galand* for them to analyse. They sent this note back to Magon, annotated with their conditions and the premium rate they proposed for the policy. This *mémoire* runs as follows (NB the emphasised portions are the directors' additions):

> Insurance proposed of 80,000 *livres* on the ship the *Galand* – heretofore the ship named the *Seignelay* of around 300 tons, armed with 36 pieces of cannon, four pieces of cast iron, a crew of 94 men led by François Vivien, sieur de la Vicomté – on merchandise loaded on the ship by the widow Moreau and son for their own account and risk (and that of their associates) in said cargo of whatever nature it may be, to go from Saint-Malo to the islands and coasts of America, to enter one or several ports of these places to do business with the inhabitants […] **on condition that the insurers will not be liable for arrests or other acts by individuals, governors or commanders of ports and forts under Spanish control (or under the control of another foreign**

---

¹⁶ MAR/B/7/492, fols 439–43, AN.
¹⁷ Spooner, *Risks at Sea*, p. 9.
¹⁸ MAR/B/7/492, fols 439–43, AN. On this ban, see Chapter 2.
¹⁹ MAR/B/7/492, fols 439–43, AN.

power) in which it is not permitted for the French to trade, with power to make all forced stops or such that Vivien will judge necessary **following the conditions stated above**, and make its return to Saint-Malo; commencing the risks on 29 September, when the ship left Saint-Malo, either for a flat rate or insured per month for five or six months.

At 1.5 per cent per month for six months insured, [with freedom] to continue.[20]

The situation was rather different from what Magon had suggested. His letter indicates that Seignelay had given orders to the Company to insure the cargo, in keeping with the sorts of interventions we encountered in Chapter 2. In quibbling over the premium and other details, it seems that the Company did not want to sign the policy – only once in its existence did it cover more than 60,000 *livres* on a single policy[21] – and the conditions it proposed were an ingenious means of delaying the process further while not openly disobeying Seignelay's orders. The Company, in fact, refused to bear the risks of any arrests made by a foreign or piratical power in a port 'in which it is not permitted for the French to trade'. Magon suggested that the condition was so vague as to allow the Company to argue against being liable for any damages or losses in the Caribbean, but in reality, the condition was an obstacle because the *Galand* was almost certainly intending to conduct illegal trade in Spanish Caribbean ports. In implementing the 'exclusive system', the crown had intended to keep trade between the French colonies and metropolitan France in French hands: foreign ships were excluded from trading in French colonial ports, while French ships were banned from trading in foreign colonial ports. Nevertheless, it was an open secret that French ships would often engage in short contraband trips between the Caribbean islands in the course of their journey.[22] In a letter of 1 September 1688, the king himself acknowledged his awareness of smuggling routes between various French Caribbean islands and those under the control of other European powers.[23]

By refusing to be liable for any arrests made in ports where the French could not legally trade, the Company intended to expose the voyage's illicit nature, thereby playing on the state's diverse, and often contradictory, interests. We have seen that Seignelay treated the Company as a tool of commercial policy, and had instructed the Company accordingly to consider all 'reasonable propositions' for insurance.[24] But was Magon's proposition reasonable?

[20] MAR/B/7/492, fol. 441r, AN.
[21] Z/1d/85, AN.
[22] Lespagnol, *Messieurs de Saint-Malo*, vol. II, pp. 512–13. On the reality of the need for flexibility in this system, see Marzagalli, 'Was Warfare Necessary?', pp. 253–77.
[23] Pritchard, *In Search of Empire*, p. 204.
[24] See Chapter 2.

Could the Company be asked to knowingly insure an illegal voyage? This was the tension that Seignelay needed to resolve. In the end, the interests of the exclusive system prevailed over those of Magon, as the Company never insured the voyage.[25] The institution's tactic had succeeded.

Incidents like these – where the crown was asked to facilitate informal conflict resolution – point to the precariousness of the Company's position. As an institution with royal patronage, it endeavoured to present itself as a moral commercial entity, just as the Chamber had done. It could not control the actions of other agents, however, who could bring it into complicated disputes and threaten to undermine its standing in commercial circles if they did not get their way. As much in the court of public opinion as in the 'opaque' Braudelian sphere of capitalism in which the Company and Magon operated, an accusation of 'bad faith' on the Company's part (whether warranted or not) had the potential to be very damaging to its reputation.[26] As we will see, this played out at the turn of the century, when the state disowned the Company.

'WISHING TO AMICABLY PUT AN END TO THEIR DISPUTES AND DIFFERENCES': THE COMPANY'S PRIVILEGED SYSTEM OF CONFLICT RESOLUTION

The disputes with Magon were rare examples of those that emerged before a contract had even been signed. Once a contract had been signed, there was a fixed system in place to handle disagreements. The Company's approach to conflict resolution was shaped by the prescriptions of the 1681 *Ordonnance de la marine*. Article 3 of the section *Des Assurances* required policies to confirm that any disputes would be resolved by external arbiters in the first instance.[27] Article 70 stipulated that, if a party to the policy wished to argue before arbiters, the other party was compelled to agree to this and to participate in the process. This process, article 71 indicated, involved the nomination of arbiters by the parties.[28]

This arbitration process was a delegation of the authority of the admiralty courts, as outlined in articles 2–3 of *De la Compétence des Juges de l'Amirauté*: article 72 of *Des Assurances* prescribed that all judgments from

---

[25] The ship would later be insured on 13 September 1688 for an unspecified voyage, but for only the very modest sum of 2,000 *livres*; Z/1d/85, fol. 81r, AN.

[26] I. Wallerstein, 'Braudel on Capitalism, or Everything Upside Down', *The Journal of Modern History* 63 (1991), pp. 354–61; see also Braudel, *Civilisation and Capitalism*, vols I–III.

[27] Valin notes that, in reality, policies which did not confirm this were not necessarily void: it was often still presumed that arbitration would take place in instances of dispute; Valin, *Nouveau commentaire*, vol. II, p. 154.

[28] Ibid., pp. 154–5. Parts of this discussion, and parts of the discussion to follow, draw from Wade, 'Royal Companies'.

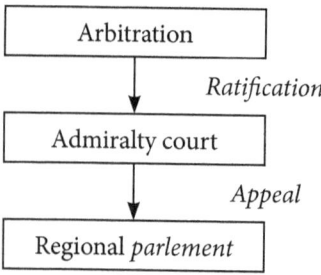

Figure 4   The procedure for resolving insurance conflicts, as outlined in the 1681 Ordonnance.

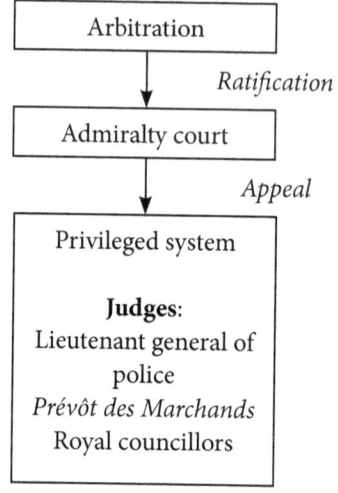

Figure 5   The Company's procedure for resolving insurance conflicts, following its letters patent from 1686.

arbitration proceedings were to be ratified by the admiralty court.[29] Article 73 required all appeals of ratified arbitration judgments to be brought before the regional *parlement*.[30]

The Company's letters patent confirmed, and largely conformed to, this process. They required all its policies to contain a statement confirming all disputes would be taken before arbiters in the first instance. In case of dispute, the Company and policyholder would each name an arbiter – a 'merchant' or 'banker' with no stake in the risk under dispute – or, otherwise, the lieutenant general (*lieutenant général*) of Paris' admiralty court would choose for them. Arbiters were tasked with looking over the documents released to them by the parties and coming to a verdict, which would be given at the Company's office. The verdict would then be ratified (and, if necessary, enforced) by Paris' admiralty court.[31]

---

[29]   Valin, *Nouveau commentaire*, vol. II, p. 156.
[30]   Ibid., p. 157.
[31]   Bornier, *Conférences des ordonnances de Louis XIV*, vol. II, pp. 513–25. Before arbitration took place, the Company was obliged to pay the policyholder provisionally, so long as the latter wished to be paid. The policyholder could only accept this payment with the understanding that they would be expected to return the principal if the arbiters found in the Company's favour, alongside 6 per cent of interest on the principal, calculated from the day the provisional payment was made to the day of the arbitration sentence. This was broadly in keeping with article 61 of the

The Company's procedure only deviated from the *Ordonnance* at the appeals phase. Instead of being judged by the *parlement* of Paris, the institution's letters patent dictated that any appeals would be 'judged in the last resort by the lieutenant general of police, the *Prévôt des Marchands* of our good city of Paris, and some of our councillors from our [royal] councils and Council of State', as chosen by the crown.[32] The appeal would take place only after a report on the dispute was issued by the lieutenant general of Paris' admiralty court.[33]

From the outset, then, the Company had a far more transparent process for handling conflicts than the Chamber. While the Chamber developed its arbitration system over time as needs required, the Company – with the *Ordonnance* providing a clear path – had the same, fixed arbitration and appeal system throughout its existence.

Table 34   The frequency of arbitration cases in the years 1687–1700.*

Year	Number of arbitration cases
1687	5
1688	–
1689	4
1690	2
1691	1
1692	5
1693	7
1694	5
1695	5
1696	4
1697	1
1698	3
1699	–
1700	2
Total	44

* NB a case from 1693, where the Company was not a party, is not included here.

Source: Z/1d/84, AN.

Ordonnance section *Des Assurances*, which required the insurer to make provisional payment even in instances of dispute, but the accumulation of interest on this was a novelty; Bornier, *Conférences des ordonnances de Louis XIV*, vol. II, pp. 513–25; Valin, *Nouveau commentaire*, vol. II, p. 144.

[32] Bornier, *Conférences des ordonnances de Louis XIV*, vol. II, pp. 513–25.
[33] I have not been able to locate any appeals. Owing to their privileged structure, it is unclear how and where appeals would have been recorded. In any case, I have found only one instance where the Company signalled its intention to appeal an arbitration sentence, but they ultimately did not proceed with this; this came in a particularly contentious dispute; see Wade, 'Royal Companies'.

We are blessed with a register containing all of the Company's arbitration cases. In the course of its existence, the Company was party to forty-four cases – just over half of the number of recorded arbitration cases in the Chamber from 1670 to May 1674 alone.

This gulf cannot be put down to the Chamber's sample being unrepresentative. True, the period 1670 to 1674 saw the fallout from the outbreak of the Dutch War, but the Company was plagued for almost the entirety of its existence by the Nine Years' War. Arbitration cases peaked for the Company in 1693; this followed two peak years in capital underwritten and, in turn, two peak years in claims.[34] Even so, 1693 saw fewer cases than any recorded year for the Chamber. This is all the more striking when we take into account that arbitration was, at least theoretically, compulsory in the first instance for all the Company's policy disputes, which was only the case in the Chamber for disputes about policies signed after 1 October 1673.

Reaffirming that the *Ordonnance de la marine* had not revolutionised insurance practice, many of the overarching themes in the Company's arbitration cases are similar to those found in the Chamber's. For the Company, however, a particular rule loomed especially large.

The 'league-and-a-half per hour' rule and the value of expertise

The Company's first arbitration case took place on 22 March 1687. It revolved around a policy signed with Alexandre Lallier, a broker in the city, for the account of Charles de Caux of Dunkirk on 9 September 1686. The policy insured the *Saint André*'s voyage from Madeira to São Miguel (in the Azores), Lisbon and Dunkirk.[35]

By the time Lallier signed this policy, the voyage had already failed. On 15 October 1686, Jean Herbant, the vessel's boatswain (*contre-maître*), testified in a deposition in Dunkirk that, at around 9:00pm on 16 August, the ship had wrecked off the coast of São Miguel, where only 150 *livres* of debris could be salvaged. On 18 November, Lallier submitted a claim to the Company.[36]

The Company objected to payment. In the arbitration case, the directors submitted two certificates, issued by Guillaume Sanson on 21 March. Sanson was the famous author of the 1681 text *Introduction à la Géographie* and served as the king's cartographer (*géographe du roi*), operating

---

[34] On this, see Chapter 5 and Table 35.
[35] Z/1d/84, fol. 1, AN.
[36] Ibid.

from a site granted to him in the great gallery of the Louvre.[37] Sanson's certificates attested that

> from the port of the island of São Miguel, one of the islands of the Azores, to Le Havre, there are 530 leagues; that from Le Havre to Paris by river, there are 65 leagues; and that from the port of the island of São Miguel to Dunkirk, there are 570 leagues of 3,000 geometric paces each.[38]

Like the *Guidon de la mer*, the *Ordonnance* enshrined the 'league-and-a-half per hour' rule. Article 38 of the section *Des Assurances* declared 'null' all insurance 'made after the loss or arrival of the insured effects, if the insured knew or could have known of the loss, or the insurer of the arrival, before the signing of the policy'.[39] Articles 39 and 40 clarified that

> the insured will be presumed to have known of the loss, and the insurer the arrival of the insured effects, if it is found that, from the place of loss or the approach of the vessel, the news had been able to be carried [i.e. transmitted] before the signing of the policy to the place where it was concluded, in counting one and a half leagues per hour, without prejudice to other proofs.[40]

In applying the 'league-and-a-half per hour' rule to Sanson's calculations, news of the *Saint André*'s loss was presumed to have reached Caux in Dunkirk on 1 September at 5:00pm and Lallier in Paris on 2 September at 9:40am, a week before the policy was signed.

This was all the evidence that was needed to discharge the Company from the policy. Caux swore before a notary in Dunkirk on 13 February 1687 that he had only learnt of the loss of the vessel when Herbant testified in the city in October 1686. This was a generous gesture, intended to demonstrate his good faith, but it was legally futile: the *Ordonnance* required that the 'league-and-a-half per hour' rule be applied notwithstanding the parties' good faith. The arbiters ruled in the Company's favour, requiring them to return the premium to Lallier, save for half a per cent for the *droit de restorne*.[41]

We have seen that the Company benefited from extensive flows of information between Paris and the colonies. Here, royal patronage of insurance intersected with royal patronage of the sciences: a royal

---

[37] N. Verdier, 'Entre diffusion de la carte et affirmation des savoirs géographiques en France. Les paradoxes de la mise en place de la carte géographique au XVIIIe siècle', *L'Espace géographique* 44 (2015), p. 42.
[38] Z/1d/84, fol. 1, AN.
[39] Valin, *Nouveau commentaire*, vol. II, p. 93.
[40] Ibid., p. 94.
[41] Ibid., p. 94. On the *droit de restorne*, see Chapter 7.

cartographer provided the scholarly testimony necessary to discharge the Company from the policy. Learned culture had practical applications in the city's commercial sphere.

The 'league-and-a-half per hour' rule continued to be applied religiously, even when faced with the complications of particular contractual clauses. On 18 February 1689, the Company underwrote 500 *livres* for the *Saint Bernard*'s voyage from Alicante to Le Havre, agreeing to retroactively bear any risks from 16 December 1688. However, the *Saint Bernard* had already sunk: on 4 February 1689, Joseph de Vigault, vice-consul to the French nation in Santiago de Compostela in north-west Spain, had written to *sieur* de Miannay, the policyholder in Abbeville, to inform him that the ship had sunk on 24 January off the coast of 'Courribede', a port fifteen leagues from Santiago de Compostela.[42]

The Company disputed payment, arguing that the 'league-and-a-half per hour' rule discharged them from the policy. Sure enough, the arbiters reasoned that 'the shipwreck took place twenty-four days before the insurance in question [was signed]: at thirty-six leagues per day for the league-and-a-half per hour [rule, this] makes 864 leagues, while only ten days were necessary [to cover] the distance of 360 leagues from the port of the shipwreck to the place where the insurance was made', meaning news of the loss was presumed to have arrived in Paris fourteen days before the policy was signed.[43] Speaking on Miannay's behalf before the arbiters, a man named M. Bruslé argued that the rule should not be applied here, as the Company agreed to bear any loss that took place after 16 December 1688: the shipwreck occurred in January 1689, making the insurers liable. The arbiters disagreed: 'the clause [...] is of no consideration and cannot undermine' the rule, because, 'supposing that one could know or knew the news' of a vessel's loss, 'it would be easy' to circumvent the rule by negotiating a policy agreeing to retroactively bear the risks from a date before the loss took place.[44] The rule needed to be applied, notwithstanding other clauses, or else information asymmetries would engender moral hazard. Accordingly, the arbiters found in the Company's favour and discharged it from the policy, requiring the directors to return the premium to the policyholder. The records of other cases did not spell out the arbiters' calculations, but nevertheless saw them discharge the Company from policies on the basis of the same rule.[45]

---

[42] Z/1d/84, fols 10v–11r, AN. Perhaps 'Courribede' is Corcubión?
[43] Ibid.
[44] Ibid.
[45] For example, see ibid., fols 1v–2r, 13.

Particular average and the need for information

For the 'league-and-a-half per hour' rule to be applied, precise information about the time and place of a maritime incident was needed. In the case of abandonments, there were obvious challenges if a ship was lost and no witnesses were able to substantiate what had happened. In the case of particular averages, it could be especially hard to establish precisely when damages were sustained during a voyage.

On 21 November 1687, the Company signed a policy with Antoine and Jacques Martins Demoura, Parisian bankers, for 12,000 *livres* of wool loaded on the *Sainte Anne* for its voyage from Bilbao to Rouen. Once the voyage had concluded, the shipmaster, André Flandrin, submitted a report to the registry of the admiralty of Rouen on 19 March 1688. Within this report, he noted seawater damage to the cargo. This prompted a bailiff of the admiralty court to inspect the cargo while it was unloaded on 22, 23 and 24 March: he concluded that, of the seventy-nine bales of wool loaded on the ship, thirty-one had been soaked and damaged by seawater entirely, while nine others had been soaked on the ends and the sides.[46] All bar one of these bales had been loaded on the ship in Bilbao for the account of the Demoura brothers.

The court discharged Flandrin of any liability for the damages to the wool on 30 March, shifting the burden for them onto the Company. In total, the particular average amounted to 4,359 *livres* 4 *sols*, or 19 *livres* 11 *sols* 7 *deniers* per cent. Accordingly, the Demoura brothers sought payment of 2,359 *livres* 10 *sols* from the Company, based on the 12,000 *livres* it had insured.[47]

The directors disputed the claim, and arbiters were convened on 24 April 1690 to settle the dispute. The directors' argument revolved around a report submitted by Flandrin to the admiralty of Quimper in Brittany on 16 November 1687, a copy of which they were able to obtain for the arbitration case. In this report, Flandrin submitted that the *Sainte Anne* had encountered a storm on the night of 12 November, resulting in the ship being thrown onto the rocks surrounding Île-Tudy, near Quimper, at 11:00pm. This damaged the keel and rudder of the ship and allowed water to enter at its front and end. The directors argued that it was this incident that led to the wool being soaked; while Flandrin's report to the admiralty of Rouen noted that the *Sainte Anne* had encountered a storm on 30 December, Flandrin did not note the entry of any water, which meant the damage to the wool could only have come through the incident at Île-Tudy. Through application of the 'league-and-a-half per hour' rule, this meant that news of

---

[46] Ibid., fols 11–12r.
[47] Ibid., fols 11–12r.

the damage was deemed to have reached Paris 'three days before the insurance [was] made'.[48]

In response, the Demoura brothers argued that Flandrin's declaration before the admiralty of Quimper made no reference to soaked merchandise. This suggested the storm of 30 December was indeed the cause of the damage.

Faced with these arguments, the arbiters were unusually candid:

> [S]ince Flandrin did not declare if the wool was soaked before or after [...] the night of 12 to 13 November at Île-Tudy, we cannot establish a fixed and certain judgment, because if there was certainty that the wool had been soaked by the storm the ship suffered the day of 12 November 1687, we would have no difficulty in pronouncing the discharge of the insurers [from the policy] who are [covered] in that case by the 'league-and-a-half per hour' [rule]. By contrast, if the wool was soaked since 21 November 1687 – the day of the insurance policy – the insurers would owe the average entirely.[49]

With the parties' consent, the arbiters proposed a compromise from ignorance, in which the average was set at 6.5 per cent and the Company was liable to pay a total of 780 *livres*.

This was a failure of information: without knowing when the wool was soaked, the arbiters could not come to a 'fixed and certain' judgment. Without the obligation or capacity to inspect a ship in full after every incident, it could not always be known when cargoes sustained damage. Yet, as this case demonstrates, much could hinge on precisely when a set of damages occurred: the arbiters made clear that, had this information been known, a definitive judgment would have been made on the claim without hesitation.[50] The 'league-and-a-half per hour' rule was a common feature of the Company's cases, but without the requisite information at hand for the arbiters to be able to implement it, the Company had no choice but to accept the compromise that was proposed.

Conflict resolution in the admiralty court

The admiralty court also supported the Company in handlings its conflicts. Nevertheless, the court's records testify to the transformation and diversification of its role in resolving insurance conflicts after the 1673 dispute crisis. We have seen that declarations of average and abandonment (i.e. claims) peaked in 1691 and 1692.[51] The court had a valuable role to play in

---

[48] Ibid., fols 11–12r.
[49] Ibid., fols 11–12r.
[50] Ibid., fols 11–12r.
[51] See Chapters 5 and 6.

facilitating arbitration in the years that followed: from its records for 1693 to 1695, I have found twenty records pertaining to arbitration proceedings involving the Company, be they orders for the disputants to select arbiters, confirmations of the arbiters they chose (or difficulties encountered in this process), or sentences ratifying arbitration judgments. Various arbitration judgments were copied verbatim by Jagault, before being submitted to the court to be ratified and executed.[52] But far from simply ratifying arbitration judgments, as the *Ordonnance* required, the admiralty court was now fulfilling a valuable role in serving as guarantors of the arbitration process, bringing parties together to make timely and constructive decisions on who to select as an arbiter. In this way, arbitration was integrated into the formal framework for handling insurance conflicts, while the admiralty court now served as a mediator of these disputes more often than as a judge.

In this capacity, the court facilitated the informal settlement of disputes. On 30 October 1692, Nicolas Desanteul submitted a claim to the Company on behalf of the Rochelais merchant Nicolas Claessen for the *Infante*; the ship was captured just as it was about to leave Saint-Domingue to return to La Rochelle.[53] When payment on the claim was not forthcoming, Claessen made a submission to the admiralty court on 20 February 1693, naming an arbiter and formally requesting the Company to name one in turn so that arbitration proceedings could be arranged. Yet there is no record these proceedings ever took place, nor did any case follow in the admiralty court. This was not a unique occurrence: it seems that pushing the Company to name an arbiter, under the court's gaze, encouraged the directors on some occasions to meet with policyholders privately to come to terms. As Cordes and Höhn note, legal submissions could be powerful, as they demonstrated an actor's 'will to enforce [their] legal interests'.[54] In this way, the court's gentle oversight helped to bring together parties in some instances to settle disputes without need for further intervention from conflict managers.[55]

Theoretically, the court should not have taken on insurance cases in the first instance, but it seems to have done so occasionally at its discretion. Precisely what motivated this could only be speculated.

This discretion was only exercised on any notable scale in 1694 and 1695: for these two years, I have found sixteen cases that were brought by

---

[52] Z/1d/110, n.p., AN. For example, on 20 May 1693, the Company's directors submitted a copy of an arbitration sentence from 24 December 1692 to the court to be ratified.
[53] Z/1d/88, fol. 85, AN.
[54] Cordes and Höhn, 'Extra-Legal and Legal Conflict Management', p. 524.
[55] For the example of Claessen, and others, see Z/1d/110, n.p., AN.

the Company's policyholders, while its directors also served as plaintiff in six further cases in these years.[56]

What resulted from these cases is documented in only a few instances. On 28 July and 6 September 1694, Jeanne Pertrus, widow of Mathurin Bruneau of Nantes, petitioned the court: she sought payment on the policies the Company had signed on 10 and 22 December 1691 (600 *livres* in total) alongside interest. The attorney general made judgment in Pertrus' favour on 2 October 1694. He similarly made judgment in favour of Nicolas Magon on 21 May 1695 and of Pierre Loquette and Jacques Ratier of Bordeaux on 2 July.[57] These are the only judgments that are recorded.[58]

Clearly, 1694 and 1695 were busy years for the directors. Resolving so many disputes in court and in arbitration (thirty-two in total) no doubt became a burden on their time and resources. Although the inauspicious international climate no doubt factored heavily into the directors' decision to pause underwriting in 1695, the need to address these cases likely played a role too.[59]

The death of a dream: high politics and the decline of the Company

The early 1690s had hit the European insurance industry hard. There was sympathy in parliament for the struggles of Lloyd's: the proposal in December 1693 of a 'Bill to Enable Divers Merchants-Insurers, that Have Sustained Great Losses by the Present War with France, the Better to Satisfy Their Several Creditors' passed the Commons, only to fail in the Lords. This bill had proposed bankruptcy protection measures, helping the most affected underwriters to better address their creditors' claims.[60]

While the Commons proved sympathetic to the interests of Lloyd's in this difficult period, the Company became victim of a cruel piece of irony. Being so bound to the state meant it was vulnerable to the oscillations of high politics in Versailles. Seignelay's sudden death in 1690 had robbed the Company of its patron just as risks at sea were reaching their peak. It could not rely on Seignelay's successor as secretary of state for maritime affairs, Louis Phélypeaux, comte de Pontchartrain, to support its activities. Threatening to undermine the Company's business, Pontchartrain sought to establish insurance institutions in several cities across France with the support of royal funds. Thomas Legendre, one of Rouen's leading

---

[56] Ibid. Jagault, the Company's registrar, also served as plaintiff in two cases, suing Alexandre Lallier for the premiums on a series of policies.
[57] These two cases involved individual underwriters who had signed the policies alongside the Company and were also condemned to payment.
[58] Z/1d/110, n.p., AN.
[59] On the inauspicious geopolitical climate, see Chapter 5.
[60] Leonard, 'Underwriting Marine Warfare', pp. 176–7.

merchants, was asked to weigh in on these plans in January 1691 and gave them his approval.[61] I have found no evidence that these institutions were established, but in any case, Pontchartrain was rejecting Seignelay's strategy of entrusting insurance coverage to a single insurance institution.

With the Company scaling back its activities in 1695, it was only at the end of 1698 – with the Company underwriting again, albeit modestly, after the return of peace in 1697 – that Lagny discussed insurance again with Pontchartrain. On 18 December, at Pontchartrain's request, Lagny wrote him a letter painting a precise, yet peculiarly optimistic picture of the insurance industry.[62] Betraying Pontchartrain's longstanding lack of interest in the Company's affairs, Lagny informed him that it had 'supported the little maritime commerce that was made during the war, and they have lost considerable sums in this'. This very much tallies with the findings of Chapter 5. Yet within the letter's broader scope, Lagny presented the Company's losses as a strength: it had borne the losses of war so that French merchants did not have to do so themselves. The public good, not profit, was the measure of success; with this criterion, Lagny argued, the Company had succeeded.[63]

With the end of war, Lagny was hopeful: mutual underwriting had recommenced in the ports, and any policies requiring further coverage could go to the Company in Paris. Although he was happy to lead a restructuring of the Company to bring in new members and/or capital, Lagny was resolute that the Company's members had done their duty up to now and that 'there are not better people' in Paris than those who were already in the institution. In proposing this restructuring, Lagny was endorsing Seignelay's approach to the privileged companies: following this model, these companies were designed to have several life cycles, being exhausted and recapitalised several times over.

Nevertheless, Pontchartrain did not share Lagny's enthusiasm for this model, nor for what the Company had achieved throughout the war. Lagny came to the striking conclusion that 'insurance is not being made in foreign countries, which is what we must uniquely avoid' (NB the emphasis is not mine). This caught Pontchartrain's attention. In the margin next to this, he (or a clerk to whom he was dictating) wrote tersely that, 'if that was [the case], you would have a point, but we are [still] insuring much of our commerce in Holland'.[64] Thirty-four years on from Clerville's mission to Rouen, the state's language and goals in supporting insurance had scarcely

61 A. Boislisle, *Correspondance des contrôleurs généraux des finances avec les intendants des provinces*, vol. I, Paris: Imprimerie Nationale, 1874, p. 232.
62 MAR/C/7/159, n.p., AN.
63 This echoes the argument made by Jacques Savary in defence of the Chamber after its losses in 1672; on this, see Chapter 7.
64 MAR/C/7/159, n.p., AN.

changed: the goal remained to deprive the Dutch of insurance premiums.[65] Thirty-four years on, and two royal projects later, the Dutch still ruled supreme in European insurance.

Although Pontchartrain asked Lagny to draft a *mémoire* laying out his plans to bring a new lease of life to the Company, the institution's limited activity after this letter suggests that, in reality, Pontchartrain's interest was tepid. This is no surprise, as the Company was Seignelay's project, and it was not in Pontchartrain's dynastic interests to see it succeed. Colbert's death in 1683 precipitated a fierce struggle in government between the Colbert, Le Tellier and Phélypeaux clans, with significant repercussions.[66] The roles of secretary of state for maritime affairs and controller general of finances, which had been held simultaneously by Colbert, were separated out, and Pontchartrain would take the latter role on 20 September 1689. A day later, Seignelay wrote a strongly worded *mémoire*, accusing his political enemy of encroaching on maritime and commercial affairs and demanding that these be left for him to administer alone.[67] The Company was thus a victim of both the Nine Years' War and this high political manoeuvring.

THE COMPANY AND THE SMEAR CAMPAIGN OF 1701

With the Phélypeaux clan now in charge of the secretariat, the state went so far as to disown the Company entirely after Lagny's death in early December 1700.[68] Here, we must return to a document we first encountered in Chapter 3: a letter written by Jérôme Phélypeaux, comte de Pontchartrain (hereafter Pontchartrain *fils*), on 12 January 1701. Pontchartrain *fils* served as secretary of state for maritime affairs from 1699 onward. Chapter 3 problematised his argument that the Company was unable to gather the information it needed to conduct its underwriting successfully. In the same letter, he offered another reason to explain the Company's failure – namely, 'the difficulty the insured had in getting paid'. He suggested that the Company relied on its royal 'protection' to pursue lengthy 'lawsuits' on a frequent basis.[69]

This argument was supported by a *mémoire* submitted later the same year by Noé Piécourt, one of Dunkirk's deputies on the newly established Council of Commerce (*Conseil de commerce*). The council brought together

---

[65] On Clerville's mission, see Chapter 1.
[66] Soll, *The Information Master*, pp. 154–7.
[67] MAR/B/7/495, fols 550–2, AN.
[68] On Lagny's death, see *Mercure Galant*, pp. 143–4.
[69] Quoted in Boiteux, *L'assurance maritime à Paris*, pp. 64–5. This letter is kept in the Archives CCI in Marseille; the COVID-19 pandemic prevented me from consulting it. One wonders if Pontchartrain *fils* was implicating Lagny as the source of this royal 'protection'.

merchants, royal allies and *financiers* from across France to advise the state on its commercial policy throughout the eighteenth century.[70] As part of its early activities, the council's deputies (representatives of cities across France) were asked on 24 November 1700 to write individual *mémoires* discussing the general state of French commerce and the measures they believed were necessary to improve it.[71]

Piécourt dedicated part of his *mémoire* to attacking the Company in the strongest terms. He argued that, instead of imitating the Dutch by displaying 'good faith' in their underwriting, the Company had 'put all [the tools at its disposal] to use to prevent payment of the sums [it] insured'. He even went so far as to accuse the Company of engaging in conspiracy to secure favourable verdicts.[72]

Pontchartrain *fils* and Piécourt thus blamed the Company itself for its failure, arguing that its royal patronage had emboldened it to make excessive use of arbitration and legal proceedings in order to avoid keeping its commitments. Not heeding Colbert's warning from 1673, the Company's chicanery had apparently led to its ruin. Moral and commercial failure were inextricably bound in the early modern commercial cosmos.

Rate of conflict

The evidence does not corroborate these assessments, however. Using the extant claims from 1686 to 1692, alongside the institution's complete arbitration register and the admiralty court records, we are able to calculate an overall 'rate of conflict' for these years, i.e. the percentage of claims recorded to have resulted in arbitration and/or litigation.

Table 35 is the result of this exercise. In total, twenty-three of the 590 claims made in the years 1686 to 1692 resulted in arbitration, an admiralty case or both. This yields a rate of conflict of 3.9 per cent – in other words, fewer than four in every hundred claims in this period resulted in disputes requiring the intervention of external conflict managers. It is impossible to make a like-for-like comparison with other insurance institutions, but this rate of conflict seems very modest. Of course, this does not account for informal conflicts, but the very nature of such conflicts – namely, that they did not require the intervention of external conflict managers – points

---

70 Schaeper, *The French Council of Commerce*. The council was dissolved in 1791. On the Council, see also Smith, 'Structuring Politics'.
71 M. Isenmann, 'From Privilege to Economic Law: Vested Interests and the Origins of Free Trade Theory in France (1687–1701)', in P. Rössner (ed.), *Economic Growth and the Origins of Modern Political Economy: Economic Reasons of State, 1500–2000*, London: Routledge, 2016, pp. 113–14.
72 Quoted in Boiteux, *L'assurance maritime à Paris*, p. 65.

Table 35 The amounts underwritten by the Company in the years 1686–92 (in *livres*), the number of policies/loans it offered, the frequency of claims in these years, the frequency of such claims leading to arbitration proceedings, the frequency of such claims leading to admiralty cases, and the frequency of such claims leading to arbitration proceedings and/or admiralty cases.

Year	Amount underwritten	Number of policies/loans*	Claims**	Claims leading to arbitration proceedings	Claims leading to admiralty cases	Total claims leading to arbitration and/or court***
1686	478,166	133	6	2	–	2
1687	1,491,356	321	27	3	–	3
1688	1,901,135	457	28	1	–	1
1689	1,392,734	437	113	6	1	6
1690	2,801,588	629	108	1	–	1
1691	3,420,920	688	155	1	2	2
1692	2,369,080	555	153	3	5	8
Total	13,854,979	3,220	590	17	8	23

* For a full discussion of this column, and the 'Amount underwritten' column, see Chapter 4.

** For a full discussion of this column, see Chapter 6.

*** NB some claims led to both arbitration and admiralty cases, meaning this column is not simply the sum of the two prior columns.

Source: Z/1d/82, Z/1d/84, Z/1d/85, Z/1d/88, Z/1d/109, Z/1d/110 and Z/1d/111, AN.

to the Company's ability to work with policyholders on a frequent basis to resolve points of contention to their mutual satisfaction. If the Company had frequently been 'deceived' and had become 'mistrustful through its losses', as Pontchartrain *fils* suggested in 1701, then one would expect the institution to have had frequent recourse to arbitration and litigation in order to challenge dubious claims or even to try to exhaust policyholders into abandoning legitimate claims.[73] As it is, the rate of conflict does not corroborate this assessment: it points instead to the efficiency of the Company's information-gathering apparatus in providing the documentation necessary to substantiate – and, where necessary, challenge – submitted claims. Put simply, this was an institution that typically kept its commitments.

The Piécourt dispute

This calls into question Pontchartrain *fils* and Piécourt's accounts. The Company's rate of conflict up to 1692 was modest, and while the institution was the subject of heightened activity in the admiralty court in 1694 and 1695, most cases were submitted by the policyholders themselves rather than the Company. Simply put, the Company does not seem to have been unduly litigious. We have seen that Pontchartrain *fils* had a vested interest in placing the blame for the Company's failure at the institution's own door (with Lagny's death paving the way for him to implement this agenda), but how should we understand and interpret Piécourt's assessment?[74] We must look to his own experience with the institution. He was an interested party in an insurance claim that was not resolved amicably.

On 15 September 1691, Pierre Durand had signed a policy with the Company on behalf of Daniel Denis and Piécourt, both of whom seem to have been based in Bordeaux at the time. This was a hull and cargo policy worth 5,000 *livres*, covering the *Licorne de Houssen*'s voyage from La Tremblade to Kopervik or another Norwegian port.[75] The voyage had already come to an end, however: its shipmaster, Joachin Mayer, had sworn under oath on 13 September that the vessel had been captured by 'two English frigates'.[76] Durand informed the Company of this on 13 December in his declaration of abandonment, before asking permission from the directors to nullify this declaration on 5 January 1692 so that Denis and Piécourt could try to recover the vessel. The directors agreed to this, and agreed

---

[73] Ibid., pp. 64–5.
[74] On this vested interest, see Chapter 3.
[75] Z/1d/85, fol. 45r, AN.
[76] Z/1d/84, fols 34v–35; Z/1d/88, fol. 30, AN.

also to reimburse any fees Denis and Piécourt incurred in this process 'in proportion to the sum insured by them'.[77]

For a long time, the record becomes silent.[78] Only on 28 January 1694 do we find that Durand agreed to arbitration proceedings with the Company. The proceedings were noted to have been delayed twice by mutual agreement, with the last record on 2 August 1695 agreeing to another two months of delay.[79]

Apparently dissatisfied with the prospect of any further delay, Durand petitioned the admiralty court to hear the dispute so the claim could be paid. In response, the directors asked the court on 24 October 1696 to comply with the *Ordonnance* by ordering the parties to select arbiters so the dispute could be settled.[80] The court agreed with the directors, confirming on 22 April 1697 that Pierre Chabert, the former consul of the French nation in Amsterdam, and Charles Le Vasseur, a Parisian merchant, had been selected as arbiters.[81]

Why was the Company disputing the claim? In their sworn statements of 13 September 1691, the shipmaster, Mayer, and two members of the crew had stipulated that 'they had been ordered to go to Dunkirk', not to Kopervik or any other Norwegian port.[82] The directors therefore argued that the Company was not liable for any damages or losses incurred during a voyage it had not insured.

With the arbiters selected, the wait continued – but it was the Company which was waiting now, not the policyholders. On 21 June, the directors petitioned the *Châtelet de Paris* to allow Chabert and Le Vasseur to bring the dispute to a close by scheduling the arbitration proceedings. Denis and Piécourt's lawyer in Paris was informed on 27 June that the proceedings would take place on 2 July, but the policyholders did not attend in person,[83] nor did they send Durand or anybody else to argue on their behalf. On 4 July, the delayed proceedings finally took place, but again, Denis, Piécourt and Durand were absent. The arbiters ruled in the Company's favour by default, discharging the institution of any liability for the loss in exchange for reimbursement of the premium, save for the half per cent that was customary for the *droit de restorne*. On 10 July, the admiralty court ratified the arbiters' decision.[84]

This dispute had been drawn out at different points by both parties. In this light, Piécourt's claims should be treated with care. His accusation that the Company engaged in conspiracy to get favourable judgments seems

---

[77] Z/1d/84, fols 34v–35, AN.
[78] This is unsurprising, as the recovery of ships in times of war could be a lengthy process.
[79] Z/1d/83, fol. 30, AN.
[80] Z/1d/111, n.p., AN.
[81] I have not found this order myself, but it is referred to in Z/1d/84, fols 34v–35, AN.
[82] Ibid.
[83] This is not surprising, as neither was based in Paris.
[84] Z/1d/111, n.p., AN.

particularly dubious: this dispute ended in the Company's favour by default precisely because Denis and Piécourt twice failed to send a representative to argue their case. If Durand's petition to the admiralty court might have suggested that the Company was dragging its feet, the dispute's conclusion indicated entirely the opposite.[85]

Simply put, Piécourt's *mémoire* was propagating a smear campaign. While the Chamber could rely on Colbert to defend the institution from such attacks, the Company had no such protection, especially by 1701. Indeed, Pontchartrain *fils* himself had pre-empted Piécourt's sentiments.

We must also understand Piécourt's attack within the broader context of the Council of Commerce. Piécourt's *mémoire* posited that 'exclusive privileges must be counted among the causes of the ruin of commerce and shipping'. Privileges 'constrain[ed] liberty in according the power to exercise a kind of commerce to a [limited] number of people', ensuring that 'other subjects are deprived of [the ability to] practice it'. Piécourt believed that this was detrimental to France's interests, because other subjects had the 'industry' and resources to practise commerce better 'in all the parts of the world than those to whom privileges are granted'.[86]

Certainly, there was a time when historians saw the Council of Commerce as a revolutionary commercial body, rejecting Colbert's alleged penchant for monopolies in favour of unfettered liberty of commerce. Lionel Rothkrug famously presented it as the apogee of a growing mercantile 'antagonism' towards Colbertianism, where, with the conclusion of the Nine Years' War, merchants 'unleashed a torrent of pent-up criticism' towards the crown through airing 'radical anti-mercantilist arguments'.[87] Claude-Frederic Levy declared that the deputies' early *mémoires* presented 'a manifesto of Physiocratic liberalism'.[88] Thomas Schaeper was among the first to resist this line of argument, demonstrating that the deputies were no Physiocrats and certainly not advocates of anything close to *laissez-faire* economics.[89]

Piécourt's *mémoire* is a case in point. Since the Company had ceased all meaningful underwriting by 1700, and Lagny had died that year, Piécourt saw it as an easy target in a broader attack on monopoly companies, arguing hyperbolically, in Schaeper's words, that 'if the number of monopolies in France continued to grow, one would have to purchase

---

[85] Piécourt received prompt reimbursement from the Company without dispute on a claim made on his behalf on 2 October 1692 for 1,300 *livres*; Z/1d/85, fol. 40r; Z/1d/88, fols 94v–95r, AN.
[86] Quoted in Boiteux, *L'assurance maritime à Paris*, pp. 65–6.
[87] Rothkrug, *Opposition to Louis XIV*, pp. 194, 373 and 411.
[88] Quoted in Schaeper, *The French Council of Commerce*, pp. 53–4.
[89] Ibid., pp. 55–6.

from the government the right to enter into any kind of trade whatever'.[90] Such railing against monopolies and privilege in the economic sphere was entirely self-interested, however. As Schaeper notes:

> [T]he deputies were rather hypermetropic, seeing clearly the abuses and privileges of other cities but overlooking or even defending the favours and monopolies of their own localities. The excuse was always that it was in the interest of the common good: each deputy's city or region was so well-endowed or conveniently located for a particular trade that it merited special consideration.[91]

Piécourt was willing to criticise specific monopolies and privileges, such as those of the Company, but the economic wellbeing of Dunkirk – the city he represented – rested on its free port privileges.[92] He was, understandably, no advocate for removing these privileges from the port. The deputies were, after all, elected by their local communities to present local grievances and defend local interests. Simply put, this was not a venue for a revolution in economic thought, where deputies could unite to present a radical mercantile agenda. Moritz Isenmann argues instead that, at its heart, the Council became a space for a debate over France's tariff regime, where deputies with a vested interest in protecting French agriculture opposed those with a vested interest in protecting French industry.[93]

Piécourt's criticism of the Company must be understood within this context. He targeted the Company as part of a broader criticism of monopolies that was typical of the Council's early *mémoires*, where the deputies jostled to protect their own regional interests and attack those of others. The 'liberty' for which Piécourt advocated in making this argument was, as Horn has argued, part of the lexicon of privilege itself.[94]

CONCLUSION

Unsurprisingly, there was no revolution in the nature of reputation and trust between 1668 and 1701. Accordingly, the Company followed the Chamber's example in several ways in shaping its commercial identity, for example in appealing to its royal patronage. Conflicts needed to be handled, however,

---

[90] Ibid., p. 55.
[91] Ibid., p. 62.
[92] On this, see Chapter 2.
[93] Isenmann, 'From Privilege to Economic Law', pp. 113–14.
[94] Horn, *Economic Development in Early Modern France*. Here, also see the discussions on protection and liberty as compatible in J. Shovlin, *Trading with the Enemy: Britain, France, and the 18th-Century Quest for a Peaceful World Order*, New Haven: Yale University Press, 2021, pp. 22–3; Hirsch and Minard, '"Laissez-nous faire"'.

and there was indeed a shift here between the two institutions. In response to the dispute crisis, the Chamber had introduced its compulsory arbitration clause in August 1673. Compulsory arbitration in the first instance was enshrined in the *Ordonnance* in 1681, which informed the Company's approach to conflict resolution, although it is clear that the admiralty court still exercised discretion in taking on insurance cases. Nevertheless, the admiralty court's primary role had been transformed from judging disputes to mediating them, overseeing the selection of arbiters for arbitration cases and facilitating out-of-court agreements.

We have seen that the Company operated where the state could not.[95] Eventually, this brought it to its knees. Yet this need not have been the end: the genius of Seignelay's creation was that only thirty individuals had been involved in it. When Louis XIV once asked whether the system of venal offices was sustainable, Pontchartrain is said to have responded wryly that, 'whenever it pleases Your Majesty to create an office, God creates a fool to buy it'.[96] The facetiousness of the comment aside, it points to the prevailing power of privilege in French life and, in turn, to the value that the Company still possessed as an institution with quasi-venal offices. In 1698, Lagny offered to bring in new investors to recapitalise the institution, just as Seignelay had done for the CIO in 1685.[97] New capital from new members, who would have been able to exploit the institution's privileges all over again, may have given the Company a new lease of life. Nevertheless, it was left to atrophy.

The Company was subsequently subjected to a state-sponsored smear campaign at the turn of the century, caught in the midst of broader debates on the deployment of privilege in the commercial sphere. Its rate of conflict was low, suggesting it was not overly litigious. Nevertheless, the language that the institution used to construct its commercial identity was used against it by its opponents. Magon's criticisms of the Company in 1687, laced with a potent commercial rhetoric that disguised his ulterior motives, foreshadowed the smear campaign: while Colbert used Savary and Irson to try to bolster the Chamber's reputation after the dispute crisis in 1673, Pontchartrain *fils* disowned the Company entirely. Piécourt centred his single dispute with the Company within a broader criticism of monopolies at the Council of Commerce. In the face of this concerted smear campaign, the Company had no defence. The reality of how the institution had approached conflict resolution during the 1690s became inconsequential, because perception had a reality of its own.

---

[95] See Chapter 5.
[96] Bernard, *The Emerging City*, p. 111; Dessert, *Le royaume de Monsieur Colbert*, p. 19.
[97] MAR/C/7/159, n.p., AN.

This campaign was a mistake: nascent insurance markets needed consistent state and/or municipal support to achieve lift-off, as Amsterdam and London ultimately did. Of course, it is impossible to know how a recapitalised Company would have fared – the onset of the War of the Spanish Succession at the turn of the century suggests it would have run into familiar challenges – but, as France began to offer more frequent naval convoys in times of war, the Company may have come to work *in tandem* with the French navy, as was the case with Lloyd's and the Royal Navy during the eighteenth century, rather than in its absence. While other royal companies in France enjoyed multiple lives in various forms, the Company was unfortunate enough to live only once; while the Sun King had tried to protect the ship in the course of its voyage, the fortification on the precipice was left to feel the full force of the storm.

CONCLUSION: PRIVILEGE AT A PREMIUM

This book has undertaken the first in-depth analysis of Louis XIV's insurance institutions, the Royal Insurance Chamber and the Royal Insurance Company, in over seventy-five years. Drawing on the registers these institutions have left, the book has treated *louisquatorzien* Paris as a laboratory for analysing the rise and fall of its insurance market, thereby allowing us to test key principles from neo-institutionalism that have underpinned recent studies of pre-modern insurance. Moreover, it has assimilated and developed the findings of various other fields of analysis: fiscal policy, commercial policy, state formation and conflict resolution, to name only the key examples. In reflecting on the key findings of the book, I return first to the comparative analytical framework I proposed in the introduction.

PARIS: AN INCOMPLETE TRIANGLE

The insurance markets of Amsterdam and London took off because the insurance triangle (an adequate capital market, adequate institutions, and adequate support at municipal and/or state level) was complete in both cities.[1] The French state under Louis XIV tried in two very different ways to overcome natural market deficiencies to support Paris in challenging these markets. Nevertheless, the insurance triangle was never complete. Understanding why yields new insights into commercial policy under Louis XIV, early modern economic development and the nature of the absolute monarchy.

The Chamber

> Parisian wealth was *mal engagée* […] the proprietor classes [were] too caught up in offices and land, operations socially rewarding, individually lucrative, economically parasitical.[2]

Surprisingly, these are not the words of Colbert, but of Braudel. Nevertheless, they encapsulate the logic underpinning Colbert's multifaceted project of fiscal

---

[1] See p. 16.
[2] Quoted in Kaplan, 'Long Run Lamentations', p. 351.

reform in the 1660s. In his eyes, the French culture of privilege – and specifically, widespread investment in the state debt through venal office holding and *rentes* on the *Hôtel de Ville de Paris* – was an impediment to a sustainable fiscal policy and inhibited economic growth by starving the commercial, industrial and agricultural sectors of capital.

This much has long been known, but this book has taken the crucial step of articulating the role of insurance as a nexus in Colbert's commercial and fiscal reforms. The insurance industry was suffering from a severe lack of capital: Louis Nicolas de Clerville reported in 1664 that even Rouen, the birthplace of the *Guidon de la mer*, was reliant on London and Amsterdam for larger risks. This led to outflows of specie in the form of premiums, further fuelling the country's bullion crisis while supporting the activities of France's commercial enemies.

The Chamber emerged as Colbert's attempt to address these countrywide challenges and undermine Amsterdam and London's hegemony – a valuable reminder that absolutism can only be understood within the broader context of political and economic competition. Although the impetus for the Chamber first came from Parisian notables, Colbert recognised the institution's potential within his broader commercial policy and championed it throughout its existence. In supporting it, he sought to create an insurance market in Paris *ex nihilo*: the city had ample *capital*, but not an adequate capital *market*, as Hoffman, Postel-Vinay and Rosenthal have demonstrated, since the necessary institutions were not in place to link up supply with demand and overcome information asymmetries.

A single institution could perform multiple roles, each with a varying degree of success.[3] In establishing the Chamber, Colbert was trying to overcome, and compensate for, multiple market deficiencies. As an open-access institution, entirely consistent with Colbert's flexible commercial policy, the Chamber served as a fixed space for the circulation of information on maritime affairs and market participants, helping to overcome information asymmetries that had hitherto prevented greater commercial investment. Colbert supported the Chamber here by tasking the admiralties and Mediterranean consulates with sending up-to-date information on ship movements at their own expense.

The Chamber was therefore a significant attempt to institutionalise the Parisian capital market, overlooked in Hoffman, Postel-Vinay and Rosenthal's analysis. Through the intermediation of commission agents, who could vouch for the creditworthiness of prospective policyholders and debtors, it facilitated the negotiation of insurance and sea loans for individuals and organisations across Europe. Furthermore, it established and maintained a system of arbitration to support the cost-effective and amicable resolution of conflicts.

---

[3] Ogilvie, '"Whatever Is, Is Right"?', p. 668.

Through these institutional mechanisms, Colbert hoped to redirect capital flows in Paris away from the state debt towards maritime and colonial commerce.[4] With the right institutions in place, insurance could be a valuable way to diversify one's commercial portfolio. Yet members were perhaps more enticed by the flexible access to royal power that the Chamber offered through Francesco Bellinzani, the institution's president and Colbert's right-hand man in commercial affairs. Bellinzani proved willing to intercede in commercial and financial affairs on behalf of the Chamber's members. Nevertheless, the 'soft' benefits of membership could prove a double-edged sword: when the Chamber's members were consulted in the course of the compilation of the *Ordonnance de la marine*, their advice was incorporated within a legal logic that privileged the heterogeneous interests of different stakeholders in the maritime realm over those of insurers.

The early years of underwriting in the Chamber were broadly successful. Men and women from a variety of backgrounds developed profitable portfolios up to 1672, covering an extraordinary range of intercontinental voyages: the volume of underwriting in the institution grew consistently year on year.

It all went wrong in 1672. In the face of the outbreak of war, underwriters made risky decisions: Newfoundland fishing voyages in particular became the dominant source of losses, alongside Greenland whaling voyages and Mediterranean voyages. While the most prolific underwriters, such as Gilles Mignot, weathered the storm by keeping a suitably large portfolio, underwriters with smaller portfolios accepted the risk of large losses. With such uncertainty for the infrequent underwriters, and such meagre returns for the most frequent, there was little incentive for them to continue business for the rest of the war.

This need not have been the end of the road for the Chamber: London and Amsterdam both suffered periods of crisis, but were able to navigate them. Paris could not, however, due to the institutional deficiencies of the Chamber and the courts. First, the Chamber fashioned its reputation through developing a corporate identity, with the aim of creating and wielding social capital to enforce righteous conduct amongst its members. Yet any social capital the Chamber had created proved ineffective in incentivising correct conduct: with limited scope for self-policing mechanisms until mid-1672, owing to social pressures created by the registry's use as a space for signing policies, policyholders were powerless to punish rogue underwriters. Moreover, the Chamber proved unable to cleave such underwriters from the herd. The institution's reputation thus hung on the conduct of its least creditworthy and/or most unscrupulous underwriters.

---

[4] For a more explicit presentation of the Chamber as an institution for the promotion of colonial commerce under Colbert than was offered in Chapter 4, see Wade, 'Underwriting Empire'.

Unsurprisingly, the Chamber's reputation collapsed during the 1673 dispute crisis. Rather than keep their commitments, a series of underwriters – including Henri Desanteul, nominally the institution's leading underwriter – chose to withhold payment on numerous policies even in the face of legal action. The explosion of litigation in the city was complicated greatly by the confusion arising from the 1673 *Ordonnance sur le commerce*, which left policyholders stranded in a jurisdictional minefield: the city's admiralty and merchant courts each claimed jurisdiction over insurance disputes, and some who took their cases before the latter were subjected to significant fines for undermining the ostensible jurisdiction of the former. In defending its jurisdiction, the admiralty court was forced to introduce summary procedure to meet litigants' needs, acknowledging the power of actors in the Chamber as agents in the formation of the state.

The Chamber had already created and maintained its own arbitration framework up to the outbreak of war, but in 1673, it fully internalised its conflict resolution by introducing a compulsory arbitration clause into its contracts. Far from being a sign of the strength of its arbitration system, as Boiteux suggests, this was a panicked reaction to the damage that had been inflicted on the Chamber's reputation through the explosion of litigation. Yet by internalising conflict resolution, the Chamber limited the legal options of policyholders. This simply incentivised merchants and shipowners to seek coverage in other insurance centres: Amsterdam had built its reputation on the honourability of its underwriters and the quality of service offered by the *Kamer van Assurantie* in resolving disputes.

A rump of underwriters remained even after 1673, but the Chamber lacked business. While Colbert instigated an extensive propaganda campaign to try to restore the Chamber's reputation, the damage had already been done. Savary's praise for the Chamber in his bestselling *Le parfait négociant* convinced unwitting historians in future centuries of the institution's creditworthiness, but it made little difference at the time: merchants across Europe who owned a copy of the indispensable commercial manual were unconvinced, and the Chamber never recovered.

The insurance triangle, therefore, was incomplete, owing to institutional inadequacies stemming from, and exacerbated by, state shortcomings. To be sure, state support helped to overcome some, but not all, of the Parisian market's deficiencies: as a space for market participants to meet, and for the circulation of the information necessary to facilitate impersonal transactions, the Chamber was successful. Yet the Chamber's conflict resolution mechanisms proved inadequate, compounded by the inability of its members to self-police and the jurisdictional confusion sown by the *Ordonnance sur le commerce*. Put simply, the Chamber could not reconcile its open-access institutional framework with its corporate commercial identity.

The Company

In stressing the striking differences between the Chamber and the Company, this book has heeded a recent clarion call to re-evaluate the royal ministers serving in the latter decades of Louis XIV's reign. As such, I have argued that Seignelay and his commercial policy need to be considered anew.

Colbert had created chartered companies for specific purposes: to establish the diplomatic, commercial and/or colonial frameworks to sustain French trade in distant markets. They were conceived and justified as short-term measures. Yet upon his death, the logic changed: the shift in international climate after 1683 forced the state to lean more and more heavily on venal offices as a fiscal expedient. It was in this climate that Seignelay leveraged privilege to support state ambitions in the commercial and maritime spheres: now that frameworks were established overseas, they needed to be maintained as matters of geopolitical urgency, and Seignelay drew on private resources to do so through exploiting the power of privilege.

While the CIO and other chartered companies established and restructured under Seignelay gave members access to markets under monopoly, the Company was unique in being a chartered company operating within the bounds of metropolitan France with no lucrative market for members to exploit. The Company's experience thus offers a unique perspective on how the corporate form was deployed as a tool of commercial policy. Seignelay offered its prospective members an array of privileges entirely divorced from the insurance market, including the opportunity to become a director of the CIO or a judge on Paris' merchant court. This refocuses our attention on chartered companies as the product of the culture of privilege: discussion of monopolies should not be abstracted from this broader culture. Consequently, I suggest that we should reconceptualise membership of the companies as a form of quasi-venal office holding, where 'the return was a different kind, one measured not in money but in the psychic satisfaction found in enhanced social standing'.[5] In structuring the companies in this way, Seignelay sought to make them attractive to investors where his father had failed.

The companies carried out the tasks set for them – tasks that were fundamentally different from those Colbert had set. This was not a continuation of Colbertianism nor a more extreme version of it, as Cole suggests: Seignelay and Pontchartrain may have been drawing on mercantilist ideas too, but they were doing so in a very different international context that reshaped French state interests in the international arena. While Colbert was trying to fix the roof while the sun was shining, those who succeeded him were trying to keep the roof from caving in while the rain poured with little relent.

---

[5] Bien, 'Offices, Corps, and a System of State Credit', p. 94.

These findings vindicate prior analyses that have stressed the political successes of French chartered companies over their commercial failures, and encourage further studies of the companies' stakeholders, thereby eschewing an anachronistic focus on shareholder primacy. It is only by understanding these companies as means to a diversity of ends, rather than as ends in themselves, that we can fully appreciate why they were such significant tools of French commercial policy. Members of the Company may well have lost their investment by the end of the century – in the absence of the institution's financial records, we cannot say for sure – but even if this was the case, those who were able to exploit the privileges the institution offered may still have regarded their investment as worthwhile.

From the outset, the Company was supported through its monopoly privileges in Paris. Boiteux bemoaned these privileges as an artificial restraint on the market. Yet the inescapable reality is that there was no insurance market in Paris to speak of before the Chamber, and the state had been unable to create a successful market through the latter. Private underwriting in the Chamber could have been salvaged after 1673 if not for its institutional deficiencies; as it was, its reputation was irreparably tarnished, limiting business and deterring any prospective underwriters from swelling the ranks of the post-1672 rump. The Company was thus created in the absence of private underwriters in Paris, not at their expense.

Following his father's example, Seignelay helped the Company to overcome the natural impediments it faced in gathering information on maritime affairs. Neatly but cautiously summarising a longstanding argument in the historiography, Robin Pearson notes that 'the low costs and information advantages developed by underwriters at Lloyd's of London and other centres of marine insurance usually gave them a competitive advantage over state corporations'.[6] Certainly, this was not the case with the Company: Seignelay supported Lagny in leveraging the state's global network of information gathering, drawing together the admiralties, overseas consulates, the colonies and notable merchants.

This network ensured that the Company had extraordinarily rich information resources at its disposal. Before the emergence of *Lloyd's List* or its precursor, the Company had access to extensive information on ship movements across Europe through Lagny's correspondence. Moreover, in 1686, Lagny oversaw the compilation of the *Rolle général des bastimens*, with the aim of recording shipping information on every vessel in France. This exercise came several decades before the emergence of *Lloyd's Register*. The

---

[6] R. Pearson, 'Escaping from the State? Historical Paths to Public and Private Insurance', *Enterprise & Society* (2020), p. 25.

Company's information resources thus matched, and arguably surpassed, those of Amsterdam and London.

Seignelay and Lagny were able to leverage this network to support the Company's activities in other ways. When circumstances required it, the Company's correspondents served as intermediaries. Furthermore, when business proved slow in the Company's early months, Seignelay and Lagny leveraged the state's information network to try to drum up business; when this did not have the impact they had hoped, Seignelay wrote to the Atlantic ports to issue a ban on foreign insurance. Merchants and ship-owners were henceforth instructed to turn to the Company when provincial markets could not meet the demand for coverage. This was a bold measure that nevertheless protected underwriting in the ports: the Company's *de facto* Atlantic monopoly was one that supported, rather than hindered, the French insurance industry.

This support allowed the Company to put together a global underwriting portfolio. Actors in La Rochelle, Dunkirk, Nantes, Saint-Malo, Rouen, Bordeaux, Le Havre and Dieppe all drew frequently on the Company's services. Through this business, the Company became a leading underwriter of France's Atlantic empire.

As a tool of commercial policy, the Company's privileges – including those for its members – came at a premium. These privileges were not bestowed to facilitate corporate profits: any profits were incidental to the institution's activities. Just as the Company's members had ambitions beyond the bottom line, so did the state: just like his father, Seignelay hoped through the Company to prevent the outflow of specie to Amsterdam and London. Yet he went further than his father in treating the Company explicitly as a tool of the public good, supporting the state in achieving its commercial ambitions at the expense of England and the Netherlands. Specifically, Seignelay intended for the Company to be a creditworthy institution that consistently made prompt payment on insurance claims. It was this obsession with creditworthiness that underpinned the Company's letters patent, requiring the institution to keep its funds in cash in its offices. This denied the Company the ability to make commercial investments, as London's insurance companies would do in the eighteenth century. Seignelay justified this liquidity requirement through the baseless logic that Dutch insurers could not be trusted to make payment on claims; the Company's liquidity thus functioned as a 'value-added' service that ostensibly distinguished it from its foreign competitors, ensuring any insurance claims would be paid promptly.

In this way, the Company left its mark as (to the best of my knowledge) the first chartered company in the history of marine insurance. The boom of incorporation in the marine insurance industry in eighteenth-century

Europe and North America was built on many of the same principles articulated by Seignelay and Lagny in justifying the Company and its privileges.

The Company left its mark in other ways too, as Seignelay relied on it to serve as a model insurance institution in selling the 1681 *Ordonnance de la marine* to the kingdom. This made the Company a valuable tool of state formation: the widespread reliance of Breton actors on the Company forced them to acknowledge the *Ordonnance* and, by extension, the state's claim to maritime jurisdiction. The Company therefore supported the state's quest to undermine Breton claims to an independent legal identity.

Seignelay's influence trickled down into the Company's portfolio itself. He coerced the institution into giving sea loans to support the state's whaling projects in 1688, thereby circumventing the Company's letters patent that promised the institution would never be subjected to forced loans. Similar practices followed after the outbreak of the Nine Years' War, with the Company becoming a vessel for the subvention of wartime commerce: it insured Caribbean voyages in the early part of the war when the state was unable to protect the colonies from English and Dutch attacks; it insured Irish voyages when the state tried, but failed, to restore James II to the thrones of his kingdoms; it insured neutral shipping extensively when the state was powerless to prevent the English and the Dutch from rejecting the rights of neutral shippers; and it insured privateer voyages to support the *guerre de course* when the navy was not living up to expectations. The Company's experience thus points to the value of chartered companies under Louis XIV as nuanced tools of power: their creation at the same time acknowledged, and attempted to overcome, French weakness in given markets, whether overseas or at home. In the Company's case, its establishment and its portfolio reflected the state's inability to protect shipping in times of crisis. The strength of the Company's information resources thus did not manifest in its portfolio: its *raison d'être* during the war was to support the riskiest voyages that served state interests and the needs of domestic and colonial commerce.

Where these information resources came into play was in the conflict resolution process. Unlike the Chamber, the Company externalised its dispute resolution, in line with its letters patent and the *Ordonnance*. Learning the lessons from the 1673 dispute crisis, the *Ordonnance* required insurance disputes to be resolved before external arbiters in the first instance. Arbitration judgments to which the Company was party were subsequently ratified by the Parisian admiralty court, whose primary role in insurance disputes after 1681 became that of a mediator. Nevertheless, the admiralty court took some insurance cases in the first instance at its own discretion later in the Nine Years' War.

Despite later claims to the contrary, the Company was not a vexatious disputant. Indeed, the extant evidence points strongly to the opposite being true: less than four in every hundred claims submitted to the Company up to 1692 resorted in action before arbiters, the admiralty court or both. This low incidence of conflict points to the Company's capacity to draw on its information resources to verify claims and to use informal tools of conflict resolution to reach compromises where any disagreements arose. As Seignelay had intended in its creation, the Company was an institution that could be trusted to meet its commitments.

Thus, when treated in the terms in which it was established, the Company was successful. The Company's competitive advantages did not translate into profits, because profits were not the goal: the institution was playing by the rules of a very different game compared to insurers in other markets, including those of London and Amsterdam.

The missing element in the insurance triangle was sufficient state support. If the political will had been there, new members could have recapitalised the Company and the cycle could have started all over again, as happened with the CIO and various other chartered companies. However, the Company had lost the state's crucial support. Pontchartrain *père* had proven indifferent to the Company's needs throughout the war, offering it no support when claims started to overwhelm the institution around 1695 and showing little interest in Lagny's offer to bring in new members and capital in 1698. Simply put, there was little motivation for him to salvage an institution that had been a pet project of the Colbert clan. His son, who succeeded him as secretary of state for maritime affairs, oversaw a propaganda campaign against the Company at the turn of the century. This coincided with the reignition of delicate debates on privilege in the commercial sphere, which took centre stage in the Council of Commerce after 1701. Here, within an institution that instantiates the perils of assuming common interests between French merchants, the Company became a political football: Noé Piécourt focused on a single dispute with the Company within a broader polemic against monopoly companies. Despite its limited engagement in proceedings before arbiters and the Parisian admiralty court, the propaganda campaign destroyed the Company's reputation. This, combined with the failure to recapitalise the institution, ensured its demise.

INSURANCE, PRIVILEGE AND POWER

Despite two state experiments, the Parisian insurance market did not succeed in challenging those of London and Amsterdam. The comparative framework I have proposed has helped us to understand why this was the case.

Reflecting on this framework, and its application to London, Amsterdam and Paris, there are some key conclusions to draw that develop prior findings. First, yes, institutions matter, but they matter in their plurality and their complementarity over space and time.⁷ As Regina Grafe and Oscar Gelderblom have noted, 'even within a given polity, merchants used multiple institutions to solve the fundamental problems of exchange'.⁸ Although the Amsterdam and London markets had quite different sets of institutions, both flourished. In creating the Chamber, Colbert combined the functions of the *Kamer van Assurantie* and the Amsterdam Exchange: the Chamber was an open-access space facilitating the circulation of information and conflict resolution. Nevertheless, it did not succeed in the long run. Thus, my findings support recent works in acknowledging that specific institutional structures in business were not silver bullets.⁹ Although the limited partnership was pioneered in Florence, the structure was rarely employed in the city throughout the late medieval and early modern periods; although the English EIC and Dutch VOC transformed the world as the first major joint-stock corporations, many other joint-stock corporations failed miserably, and the model would only be widely adopted in the Industrial Revolution.¹⁰ These institutional structures can only be understood within the broader political, legal and economic environment in which they were established.

This leads us into the second conclusion: that state and municipal authorities were essential to the fate of pre-modern insurance markets.¹¹ Pearson has identified four key roles the state has played historically in 'shaping the business and legal environment' for insurance: as 'gatekeeper', e.g. by 'prohibiting or authorising certain types of insurance'; as 'regulator', helping to overcome moral hazard and information asymmetries by compiling and enforcing clear rules and/or limiting the supply of insurance; as 'facilitator', again overcoming information asymmetries by gathering and supplying information where private resources alone could not do so effectively; and as 'participant', creating insurance corporations that directly competed in, or had a monopoly over, the market.¹² Through these roles, Pearson suggests that states have 'constricted, created, grown, and distorted markets',

---

[7] V. Bateman, *Markets and Growth in Early Modern Europe*, Abingdon: Routledge, 2016, pp. 174–7.
[8] R. Grafe and O. Gelderblom, 'The Rise and Fall of Merchant Guilds: Re-thinking the Comparative Study of Commercial Institutions in Premodern Europe', *Journal of Interdisciplinary History* 40 (2010), p. 478.
[9] This is also the finding of Acemoglu and Robinson, *Why Nations Fail*, pp. 446–7.
[10] F. Trivellato, 'Renaissance Florence and the Origins of Capitalism: A Business History Perspective', *Business History Review* 94 (2020), pp. 229–51; Harris, *Going the Distance*.
[11] This supports the broader findings of David Ormrod on the role of the state in English (and, later, British) economic development; Ormrod, *The Rise of Commercial Empires*.
[12] Pearson, 'Escaping from the State?', pp. 1–30.

with 'path-dependent effects' on them – and the institutional frameworks underpinning them – over time.[13]

We can see these roles playing out in the cases of Amsterdam, London and Paris. Neo-institutionalists have often valued the state as an actor in economic growth only to the extent that it guaranteed property rights: in Joel Mokyr's words, 'subjects want the state to enforce the rules of the game but not to accumulate so much power that the state can threaten those very rights it is asked to protect'.[14] In this way of thinking, as Hoffman, Postel-Vinay and Rosenthal suggest, the state is at risk of becoming 'a hollow shell devoid of its own motivations', valuable only to the extent that it willingly bound itself.[15]

The markets of London and Amsterdam make clear that the early modern state had a role to play in economic development beyond protecting property rights and then getting out of the way. State and municipal intervention helped to overcome natural market deficiencies pertaining to all types of transaction costs (namely, information, bargaining and enforcement). While a core of merchant-insurers might be able to 'self-regulate' to a large extent (and I use 'self-regulate' carefully here, as courts were key spaces of conflict resolution even in early markets), it was only when new players brought new capital into each market that Amsterdam and London took off. Yet new players, inevitably, sparked demand for one or multiple institutions to facilitate conflict resolution and the gathering and dissemination of information for assessing natural, anthropogenic and moral hazards.[16] While Paris was unique, insofar as Colbert and Seignelay were trying to build an insurance market essentially *ex nihilo*, the same principles held true. Whereas Amsterdam and London had all the elements necessary for their markets to take off, Paris did not: the insurance triangle was not consistently complete between 1664 and 1700. The state under Louis XIV emerges here not as an entirely 'vicious' economic actor, as Hoffman, Postel-Vinay and Rosenthal suggest, but one whose good intentions fell victim to self-sabotage. Indeed, the market was heavily reliant on the state to address its natural deficiencies: Colbert's efforts were valiant, but ultimately came up short; Seignelay's strategy was thwarted by his death and the hostility of his successors towards the Company and his policies more broadly.

---

[13] Ibid., pp. 3 and 8.
[14] J. Mokyr, 'The Institutional Origins of the Industrial Revolution', unpublished paper, p. 9. This said, the role of state provision of public services in modern economic growth is recognised in Acemoglu and Robinson, *Why Nations Fail*.
[15] Hoffman, Postel-Vinay and Rosenthal, *Priceless Markets*, p. 280.
[16] This is recognised in Leonard, 'Contingent Commitment', p. 71.

Without stronger, more consistent state support, the Parisian market could not achieve lift-off.[17]

The corollary to this is that we need to reflect on our understanding of the state as an agent in the economy. In the Introduction, we first encountered the North-Weingast and Harris formulations of the 'credible commitment' argument, both revolving around the Northian dichotomy between north-western and southern Europe. North and Weingast's hypotheses on the supposed stagnation of the French fiscal system under Louis XIV cannot withstand the weight of literature discussed throughout this book that has analysed the transformation of privileged corps into financial intermediaries towards the end of the seventeenth century. This transformation allowed the state to exploit the better credit of venal officeholders as collective entities, offering a means of circumventing the problems of credible commitment.[18] Moreover, *pace* the neo-institutionalists, the so-called Glorious Revolution did not disempower the English/British state to the benefit of the populace: it empowered the state to tax the populace (and maritime commerce) to a hitherto unprecedented level, which served as the basis for servicing the extraordinary public debt.[19] France underwent institutional change, but England/Britain triumphed in economic terms in the long run in large part thanks to 'successful mercantilism', as Patrick O'Brien puts it: Britain maintained a formidable, cost-effective Royal Navy and enforced a strong protectionist regime (through the Navigation Acts and related legislation) capable of sustaining maritime (and especially colonial) commerce that enriched Britain and the state alike.[20]

---

[17] Guillaume Lelièvre makes similar observations regarding the East India Companies; Lelièvre, *La préhistoire de la Compagnie des Indes orientales*, p. 301.

[18] The point is made explicitly in Potter, *Corps and Clienteles*, p. 21. For more on this, see Chapters 1 and 2.

[19] Here, besides the classic work of Brewer, *The Sinews of Power*, see J. Hoppit, *Britain's Political Economies: Parliament and Economic Life, 1660–1800*, Cambridge: Cambridge University Press, 2017, pp. 277–305, which highlights the role of imported goods in contributing to the lucrative excise (and thus sustaining naval spending to protect trade). A group of academics are exploring this further; E. Dal Bo, K. Hutkova, L. Leucht, and N. Yuchtman, 'International Trade, Domestic Production, and the Rise of the British Fiscal-Military State: New Evidence on the Sources of Fiscal Revenue, 1680–1820', seminar at the Institute of Historical Research, March 2022.

[20] Ormrod, *The Rise of Commercial Empires*, pp. 334–51; P. O'Brien, 'The Formation of a Mercantilist State and the Economic Growth of the United Kingdom 1453–1815', WIDER Research Paper, No. 2006/75; P. O'Brien, 'The Nature and Historical Evolution of an Exceptional Fiscal State and Its Possible Significance for the Precocious Commercialization and Industrialization of the British Economy from Cromwell to Nelson', *Economic History Review* 64 (2011), pp. 408–46; Leonard, *London Marine*

My findings from the 'southern' side of the Northian dichotomy have also undermined Harris' argument on the role of 'credible commitment' in the fate of Europe's early chartered companies. If his argument that the French state could not credibly commit to investors was pertinent to the ultimate success of the EIC and VOC over the CIO, the logical consequence would be that the French state's efforts to garner investment in its chartered companies would have failed. Yet the French state under Louis XIV proved able to attract investors for the multitude of chartered companies it established. Furthermore, these companies were never intended to be beholden to their shareholders. Understanding them, I have argued, requires us to abandon anachronistic assumptions on shareholder primacy and embrace a more nuanced understanding of why they were created and how they functioned. In this way, we can see how treating membership of Seignelay's companies as a form of quasi-venal office helps us to make a crucial step forward.

Insurance has offered a unique vantage point for this debate on corporations, and brings us back to the question of 'missed opportunities' in French history. The Company had been successfully deployed to subvent maritime commerce during the Nine Years' War, but a recapitalised Company could have achieved further success, especially if the monarchy had treated marine insurance as a complementary tool of the navy rather than as a substitute for it. This was the winning formula that brought the London market to supremacy in the eighteenth century: through successful convoy systems, the Royal Navy and Lloyd's were able to coordinate effectively to support each other's activities, ensuring the development of a market with secure foundations.[21]

Thus, while neo-institutionalism offers some helpful concepts for studying pre-modern insurance, market development in the seventeenth and eighteenth centuries provides no support for the Northian dichotomy. Consistent with Frederic Lane's argument on the state's capacity to serve as a 'protection provider', the French state under Louis XIV simply followed England and the Netherlands in recognising the need for intervention in the insurance industry, and took significant (but, in the end, inadequate) steps to support it.[22]

Insurance, pp. 16–17. Of course, maritime/colonial commerce alone does not explain British growth in the eighteenth century; for an analysis that also incorporates agricultural and industrial development (questioning the value of the term 'mercantilism' in the process), see Hoppit, *Britain's Political Economies*.

[21] Here, see the discussion in the Introduction and Chapter 5.

[22] The phrase is from Müller, *Consuls*, p. 31; on Lane's analysis on protection costs, see F. Lane, *Profits from Power. Readings in Protection Rent and Violence Controlling Enterprise*, Albany: State University of New York Press, 1979; M. Bullard, S. Epstein, B. Kohl, and S. Stuard, 'Where History and Theory Interact: Frederic C. Lane on the Emergence of Capitalism', *Speculum* 79 (2004), pp. 88–119.

This brings us back to the role of insurance in furthering the interests of the absolute monarchy. Over thirty leagues from the sea, *rue Quincampoix*'s gaze was global, reflecting the monarchy's interests across land and sea. Both the Chamber and the Company were products of a broader state push to integrate Paris into a countrywide capital market in service to maritime commerce and empire. The state conceived, justified and understood them as manifestations of royal protection against natural, anthropogenic and moral hazards in commerce within and beyond metropolitan France. The state put its infrastructure of information gathering at the institutions' disposal in support of this institutionalised approach to commercial reform. Yet these institutions were products of their time, speaking to the need for a framework for absolutism that can accommodate the shifts of the 1680s and 1690s.

The Company was one of several chartered companies that were an extension of the system of privilege at the heart of absolutism itself. Through this system, the state was able to mobilise private resources in support of its commercial and colonial policies, ensuring that the power of the absolute monarchy extended and radiated across the globe, over land and sea.[23] Yet these companies' precarious existences point to their role in operating at the very margins of absolutism: they pushed at the limits of royal power overseas, with very mixed results along the way.[24]

Through incorporating the chartered companies into the analysis of metropolitan institutions, I propose a new approach to understanding absolutism – an approach we might call 'absolutism as risk management'.[25] This posits that the absolute monarchy lacked the resources to sustain core functions – justice, war, exchange – without the support of its subjects. To be sure, relying on the resources of the populace is not at all unique in the history of state formation: to take only the key example, any state with a public debt draws on private capital to achieve set ends. Nevertheless, building on decades of work on patronage and privilege, this book suggests that the absolute monarchy set itself apart through its remarkable ability to leverage its monopoly on privilege to shift the risks of its own policies onto its subjects, thus binding the latter to the monarchy and its interests. The monarchy achieved this, Rowlands argues, thanks to the fundamental 'dynastic' values at the heart of the Old Regime: to secure or improve their own social standing and that of their successors, subjects across the social spectrum put their assets and their credit on the line in facilitating a

---

[23] For a similar argument, see Roulet, *La Compagnie des îles de l'Amérique*, p. 587.
[24] By considering these companies as global actors, I follow the lead of Pettigrew and Veevers, 'Introduction', p. 17.
[25] This builds on an argument I lay out in Wade, 'Royal Companies'.

given state objective on land and/or at sea.[26] Thus, while neo-institutionalists have viewed absolutism as an impediment to credible commitment, absolutism as I conceptualise it was the *solution* to the challenge of credible commitment: the state's monopoly on privilege incentivised subjects to invest in absolutist enterprises, despite the risk of expropriation. As this book has made clear, absolutism under Louis XIV was not the manifestation of inertia, as North and others allege: transformations in how venal offices and chartered companies alike were deployed in service to state interests during the 1680s and 1690s bear witness to the institutional evolution that took place in these decades.

In saying this, I do not dispute Beik's conclusions on the fundamentally traditional nature of absolutism. Instead, it is my contention – following the lead of Rowlands – that traditional features of Old Regime society were remoulded in service to new interests and demands, both within and beyond France.[27] Thus, the risk inherent in the system of privilege on which absolutism was built – and on which family fortunes were made and lost – articulates the shortcomings of the social collaboration model. The system of privilege as it evolved under Louis XIV entrenched existing social hierarchies to an extent, but also offered avenues for the socially ambitious to advance. At every level, the absolute monarchy was built on the back of risks borne by those who hoped to enjoy its spoils, all the while recognising that, if the tide turned against them, they themselves would be wrecked on the rocks, while the French ship of state would sail on.

CODA: ABSOLUTISM AT ITS LIMITS

At the turn of the eighteenth century, the European world-economy was in a process of transformation. Amsterdam remained the leading insurance market; nevertheless, the 'centre of gravity' in the European world-economy was already shifting towards London. The Dutch economy had passed its prime, and the English state's mercantilist policies were transforming North Sea and Baltic trade by limiting England's reliance on Dutch carriers. Through these policies, London was becoming the central node in commercial networks connecting the Atlantic and Indian Ocean worlds to continental Europe.[28] Moreover, with the full weight of the state behind it, London would supplant Amsterdam as Europe's leading insurance market within decades.

By contrast, as Braudel remarks, France under Louis XIV proved unable to break out of the 'straitjacket' of dependency on Dutch services.[29] At

---

[26] Rowlands, *The Dynastic State*.
[27] Beik, *Absolutism and Society*; Rowlands, *The Dynastic State*.
[28] Ormrod, *The Rise of Commercial Empires*, pp. 334–51; for an analysis of the late seventeenth- and early eighteenth-century Dutch economy built on different foundations, see also de Vries and van der Woude, *The First Modern Economy*, pp. 409–504; see also Braudel, *Civilisation and Capitalism*, vol. III, pp. 175–276.
[29] Braudel, *Civilisation and Capitalism*, vol. III, p. 258.

the turn of the century, the demise of the Royal Insurance Company was underway and the Parisian capital market was stagnant, with a new war on the horizon that promised further economic disruption across France.[30] Provincial officeholders were exploited during this war, as they already had been during the Nine Years' War. This led them to turn their focus away from state patronage towards consolidating their standing within their local communities, thereby undermining state ties to the provinces.[31]

This all lay ahead, however, and nothing was inevitable. The system of privilege was assuredly approaching its limits, but throughout the Nine Years' War it had sustained an army of unprecedented scale in European history, alongside a navy which (despite its eminent shortcomings, necessitating the Royal Insurance Company's support) had held its own against the combined might of the world's greatest naval powers.[32] It had done this even during a trend of climatic cooling, which had resulted in harvest failures across France in 1693 and 1694 that impinged on tax revenues just as they were needed most.[33] Nevertheless, the introduction of taxes applicable even to privileged groups – namely, the *capitation* in 1695, followed by the *dixième* in 1710 – were manifestations of the financial difficulties the monarchy suffered through two gruelling wars.[34] While Colbert's immediate successors strove to develop the system of privilege to sustain the French military machine, it proved unable to meet the demands of the new century.[35]

By its nature, privilege was at a premium; it had become a prerogative of state alone, and the state lubricated the system of privilege at its prerogative in service to its own interests. Yet while this system enabled the state to fight its many wars, pushing it to its limits would ultimately come at a premium to the state itself.

---

[30] Hoffman, Postel-Vinay, and Rosenthal, *Priceless Markets*, pp. 50–68.

[31] Here, see the excellent discussion of several works on this matter in Breen, 'Law, Society, and the State', pp. 346–86; see also Hurt, *Louis XIV and the Parlements*. On the broader economic challenges of the War of the Spanish Succession, see as a starting point, J. Félix, '"The Most Difficult Financial Matter that has Ever Presented Itself": Paper Money and the Financing of Warfare under Louis XIV', *Financial History Review* 25 (2018), pp. 43–70; see also Rowlands, *The Financial Decline of a Great Power*.

[32] On the army, see Rowlands, *The Dynastic State*; on the navy, see Darnell, 'Naval Policy'; Symcox, *The Crisis of French Sea Power*.

[33] Degroot et al., 'Towards a Rigorous Understanding of Societal Responses to Climate Change', p. 546.

[34] Here, see McCollim, *Louis XIV's Assault on Privilege*; Rowlands, *The Financial Decline of a Great Power*, pp. 57–71.

[35] Rowlands, 'Royal Finances', p. 51; Rowlands, *The Financial Decline of a Great Power*; Rowlands, *Dangerous and Dishonest Men*.

BIBLIOGRAPHY

MANUSCRIPT AND ARCHIVAL COLLECTIONS

Archives de Dunkerque – Centre de la Mémoire Urbaine d'Agglomération
Rolle général des bastimens de mer (uncoded document).

Archives départementales de Loire-Atlantique, Nantes
C/760.

Archives nationales, Paris [AN]

AE/B/I/212-3.
AE/B/I/698.
AE/B/I/699.
AE/B/I/1070.
E//721/A.
MAR/B/7/55.
MAR/B/7/58-63.
MAR/B/7/491-6.
MAR/B/8/18.
MAR/C/7/15.
MAR/C/7/159.
MAR/G/229.
MC/ET/I/295.
MC/ET/CV/915.
O/1/30.
O/1/36.
T//1491/45.
Y//200.
Y//239.
Z/1d/30.
Z/1d/68-70.
Z/1d/73-88.
Z/1d/106-12.

Bibliothèque nationale de France, Paris [BNF]

Mélanges de Colbert 161.

Institute and Faculty of Actuaries Library, London

BYQ/517 pam prm3b.

The National Archives, Kew

SP 84/170/58.

PRINTED PRIMARY SOURCES

Boislisle, A., *Correspondance des contrôleurs généraux des finances avec les intendants des provinces*, vol. I, Paris: Imprimerie Nationale, 1874.
Bornier, P., *Conférences des ordonnances de Louis XIV. Roy de France et de Navarre: avec les anciennes ordonnances du Royaume, le droit écrit & les arrêts*, vol. II, Paris: Unknown, 1719.
Cleirac, É., *Les us et coutumes de la mer. Divisées en trois parties*, Rouen: Jean Berthelin, 1671.
Colbert, J. and Clément, P. (ed.), *Lettres, instructions, et mémoires de Colbert*, vol. II, book II, Paris: Imprimerie impériale, 1863.
―― *Lettres, instructions, et mémoires de Colbert*, vol. VII, Paris: Imprimerie impériale, 1873.
de la Porte, M., *La Science des Négocians et Teneurs de Livres, ou Instruction Générale Pour tout ce qui se pratique dans les Comptoirs des Négocians*, Amsterdam: Aux Dépens de la Compagnie, 1770.
Grotius, H. and van Deman Magoffin, R. (trans.), *The Freedom of the Seas – or the Right which belongs to the Dutch to Take Part in the East Indian Trade*, New York: Oxford University Press, 1916.
Henrat, P., *Répertoire général des Archives de la Marine, XVIe–XVIIIe siècles*, Paris: SPM, 2018.
Horace and C. Smart (trans.), *Horace Translated Literally into English Prose*, vol. I, Dublin: P. Wogan, 1793.
Irson, C., *Méthode pour bien dresser toutes sortes de comptes à parties doubles*, Paris: Claude Irson and Jean Cusson, 1678.
Mercure Galant dedié à Monsieur le Dauphin. Janvier 1701, Michel Brunet: Paris, 1701.
Peuchet, J., *Dictionnaire universel de la géographie commerçante*, vol. IV, Paris: Blanchon, 1798–99.
Plato and Griffith, T. (trans.), *The Republic*, Cambridge: Cambridge University Press, 2000.
Pouilloux, D., *Mémoires d'assurances. Recueil de sources françaises sur l'histoire des assurances du XVIème au XIXème siècle*, Paris: Seddita, 2011.
Sallé, J. (ed.), *L'esprit des ordonnances de Louis XIV*, vol. II, Paris: Chez Samson, 1758.

Savary des Bruslons, J., *Dictionnaire universel de commerce: contenant tout ce qui concerne le commerce qui se fait dans les quatre parties du monde*, vol. I, Paris: La Veuve Estienne, 1741.
—— *Dictionnaire universel de commerce: contenant tout ce qui concerne le commerce qui se fait dans les quatre parties du monde*, vol. V, Copenhagen: Claude Philibert, 1765.
Savary, J., *Le parfait négociant, ou Instruction générale pour ce qui regarde le commerce des marchandises de France et des pays étrangers*, vol. I, Paris: Frères Estienne, 1757.
—— *Le parfait négociant, ou Instruction générale pour ce qui regarde le commerce des marchandises de France et des pays étrangers*, vol. II, Paris: La Veuve Estienne, 1742.
Thoresby, R., *Ducatus Leodiensis, Or, The Topography of the Ancient and Populous Town and Parish of Leeds*, London: Maurice Atkins, 1715.
Toubeau, J., *Les institutes du droit consulaire, ou La jurisprudence des marchands*, vol. I, Paris: Nicolas Gosselin, 1700.
Valin, R., *Nouveau commentaire sur l'Ordonnance de la marine du mois d'août 1681*, vols I and II, La Rochelle: Jérôme Legier, 1766.

SECONDARY SOURCES

Acemoglu, D. and Robinson, J., *Why Nations Fail: The Origins of Power, Prosperity, and Poverty*, London: Profile Books, 2012.
Addobbati, A., 'L'assurance à Livourne au XVIIIe siècle, entre mutualisme et marché concurrentiel', in Nuñez, C. (ed.), *Insurance in Industrial Societies: Economic Role, Agents and Market from the Eighteenth Century to Today*, Seville: Universidad de Sevilla, 1998, pp. 13–30.
—— 'The Capture of the *Thetis*: A *cause célèbre* at the Madrid Council of War (1780–1788)', in Alimento, A. (ed.), *War, Trade and Neutrality: Europe and the Mediterranean in the Seventeenth and Eighteenth Centuries*, Milan: FrancoAngeli, 2011, pp. 146–59.
—— 'Italy 1500–1800: Cooperation and Competition', in Leonard, A. (ed.), *Marine Insurance: Origins and Institutions, 1300–1850*, Basingstoke: Palgrave Macmillan, 2016, pp. 47–77.
Akerlof, G., 'The Market for "Lemons": Quality Uncertainty and the Market Mechanism', *The Quarterly Journal of Economics* 84 (1970), pp. 488–500.
Alimento, A., 'Commercial Treaties and the Harmonisation of National Interests: The Anglo-French Case (1667–1713)', in Alimento, A. (ed.), *War, Trade and Neutrality: Europe and the Mediterranean in the Seventeenth and Eighteenth Centuries*, Milan: FrancoAngeli, 2011, pp. 107–28.
Allaire, B., 'Between Oléron and Colbert: The Evolution of French Maritime Law until the Seventeenth Century', in Fusaro, M., Allaire, B., Blakemore, R., and Vanneste, T. (eds), *Law, Labour and Empire: Comparative Perspectives on Seafarers, c. 1500–1800*, Basingstoke: Palgrave Macmillan, 2015, pp. 79–99.
Ames, G., *Colbert, Mercantilism, and the French Quest for Asian Trade*, DeKalb: Northern Illinois University Press, 1996.

Andriani, L. and Christoforou, A., 'Social Capital: A Roadmap of Theoretical and Empirical Contributions and Limitations', *Journal of Economic Issues* 50 (2016), pp. 4–22.

Antunes, C., 'Birthing Empire: The States General and the Chartering of the VOC and the WIC', in Koekkoek, R., Richard, A., and Weststeijn, A. (eds), *The Dutch Empire between Ideas and Practice, 1600–2000*, Cham: Springer, 2019, pp. 19–36.

Antunes, C. and Ekama, K., 'Mediterranean and Atlantic Maritime Conflict Resolution: Critical Insights into Geographies of Conflict in the Early Modern Period', in Sicking, L. and Wijffels, A. (eds), *Conflict Management in the Mediterranean and the Atlantic, 1000–1800: Actors, Institutions and Strategies of Dispute Settlement*, Leiden: Brill, 2020, pp. 267–83.

Antunes, C. and Sicking, L., 'Ports on the Border of the State, 1200–1800: An Introduction', *International Journal of Maritime History* 19 (2007), pp. 273–86.

Ashburner, W., *The Rhodian Sea Law*, Oxford: Clarendon Press, 1909.

Banks, K., 'Financiers, Factors, and French Proprietary Companies in West Africa, 1673–1713', in Roper, L. and Ruymbeke B. (eds), *Constructing Early Modern Empires: Proprietary Ventures in the Atlantic World, 1500–1750*, Leiden: Brill, 2007, pp. 79–116.

Barazzutti, R., 'La guerre de course hollandaise sous Louis XIV: essai de quantification', *Revue historique de Dunkerque et du littoral* 37 (2004), pp. 269–80.

—— 'Les Néerlandais du Centre-Ouest français au Canada: des relations particulières au XVIIe siècle', in Augeron, M., Péret, J., and Sauzeau, T. (eds), *Le golfe du Saint-Laurent et le Centre-Ouest français. Histoire d'une relation singulière (XVIIe–XIXe siècle)*, Rennes: Presses universitaires de Rennes, 2010, pp. 123–37.

Barbour, V., 'Marine Risks and Insurance in the Seventeenth Century', *Journal of Economic and Business History* 1 (1929), pp. 561–96.

Baskes, J., *Staying Afloat: Risk and Uncertainty in Spanish Atlantic World Trade, 1760–1820*, Stanford: Stanford University Press, 2013.

Bateman, V., *Markets and Growth in Early Modern Europe*, Abingdon: Routledge, 2016.

Baugh, D., 'Naval Power: What Gave the British Naval Superiority?', in Prados de la Escosura, L. (ed.), *Exceptionalism and Industrialisation: Britain and Its European Rivals, 1688–1815*, Cambridge: Cambridge University Press, 2004, pp. 235–57.

Béguin, K., *Financer la guerre au XVIIe siècle. La dette publique et les rentiers de l'absolutisme*, Seyssel: Champ Vallon, 2012.

Beik, W., *Absolutism and Society in Seventeenth-Century France*, Cambridge: Cambridge University Press, 1985.

—— 'The Absolutism of Louis XIV as Social Collaboration', *Past and Present* 188 (2005), pp. 195–224.

Bernard, L., *The Emerging City: Paris in the Age of Louis XIV*, Durham, NC: Duke University Press, 1970.

Bevilacqua, A. and Pfeifer, H., 'Turquerie: Culture in Motion, 1650–1750', *Past and Present* 221 (2013), pp. 75–118.

Bien, D., 'Offices, Corps, and a System of State Credit: The Uses of Privilege under the Ancien Régime', in Baker, K. (ed.), *The French Revolution and the Creation of Modern Political Culture*, vol. I, Oxford: Pergamon Press, 1987, pp. 89–114.

Blanquie, C., *Une enquête de Colbert en 1665. La généralité de Bordeaux dans l'enquête sur les offices*, Paris: L'Harmattan, 2012.

Blaufarb, R., *The Politics of Fiscal Privilege in Provence, 1530s–1830s*, Washington, DC: The Catholic University of America Press, 2012.
Bogatyreva, A., 'England 1660–1720: Corporate or Private?', in Leonard, A. (ed.), *Marine Insurance: Origins and Institutions, 1300–1850*, Basingstoke: Palgrave Macmillan, 2016, pp. 179–204.
Boissonnade, P. and Charliat, P., 'Colbert et la Compagnie de Commerce du Nord', *Revue d'histoire économique et sociale* 17 (1929), pp. 156–204.
Boiteux, L., *L'assurance maritime à Paris sous le règne de Louis XIV*, Paris: Éditions Roche d'Estrez, 1945.
—— 'Contributions de l'assurance à l'histoire de l'économie maritime en France', in Mollat, M. (ed.), *Les sources de l'histoire maritime en Europe, du moyen âge au XVIIIe siècle*, Paris: SEVPEN, 1962, pp. 447–63.
—— *La fortune de mer. Le besoin de sécurité et les débuts de l'assurance maritime*, Paris: École Pratique des Hautes Études, 1968.
Bosbach, F., 'The European Debate on Universal Monarchy', in Armitage, A. (ed.), *Theories of Empire, 1450–1800*, Aldershot: Ashgate, 1998, pp. 81–98.
Bosher, J., '*Chambres de justice* in the French Monarchy', in Bosher, J. (ed.), *French Government and Society 1500–1850: Essays in Memory of Alfred Cobban*, London: The Athlone Press of the University of London, 1973, pp. 19–40.
—— 'The Paris Business World and the Seaports under Louis XV: Speculators in Marine Insurance, Naval Finances and Trade', *Histoire Sociale* 12 (1979), pp. 281–97.
Boulaire, F., 'L'Irlande, la France et l'Europe en 1689–1690: les négociations de M. le Comte d'Avaux en Irlande', *Études irlandaises* 26 (2001), pp. 71–83.
Boulle, P., 'French Mercantilism, Commercial Companies and Colonial Profitability', in Blussé, L. and Gaastra, F. (eds), *Companies and Trade: Essays on Overseas Trading Companies during the Ancien Régime*, Leiden: Leiden University Press, 1981, pp. 97–117.
Braudel, F., *Civilisation and Capitalism 15th–18th Century*, vol. I, London: Collins, 1981.
—— *Civilisation and Capitalism 15th–18th Century*, vol. II, London: Collins, 1982.
—— *Civilisation and Capitalism 15th–18th Century*, vol. III, London: Collins, 1988.
—— *The Mediterranean and the Mediterranean World in the Age of Philip II*, vol. I, London: Collins, 1990.
—— *The Mediterranean and the Mediterranean World in the Age of Philip II*, vol. II, London: Collins, 1982.
Breen, M., *Law, City, and King: Legal Culture, Municipal Politics, and State Formation in Early Modern Dijon*, Woodbridge: Boydell & Brewer, 2007.
—— 'Law, Society, and the State in Early Modern France', *The Journal of Modern History* 83 (2011), pp. 346–86.
Brewer, J., *The Sinews of Power: War, Money and the English State, 1688–1783*, London: Unwin Hyman, 1989.
Brière, N., *La douceur du roi. Le gouvernement de Louis XIV et la fin des Frondes (1648–1661)*, Québec: Presses de l'Université Laval, 2011.
Briggs, R., *Early Modern France 1560–1715*, Oxford: Oxford University Press, 1998.
Bromley, J., *Corsairs and Navies 1660–1760*, London: The Hambledon Press, 1987.
Buffet, H., 'Lorient sous Louis XIV', *Annales de Bretagne* 44 (1937), pp. 58–99.

Bullard, M., Epstein, S., Kohl, B., and Stuard, S., 'Where History and Theory Interact: Frederic C. Lane on the Emergence of Capitalism', *Speculum* 79 (2004), pp. 88–119.
Burke, P., *The Fabrication of Louis XIV*, New Haven: Yale University Press, 1992.
Burset, C., 'Merchant Courts, Arbitration, and the Politics of Commercial Litigation in the Eighteenth-Century British Empire', *Law and History Review* 34 (2016), pp. 615–47.
Buti, G., 'Contrôles sanitaire et militaire dans les ports provençaux au XVIIIe siècle', in Moatti, C. and Kaiser, W. (eds), *Gens de passage en Méditerranée de l'Antiquité à l'époque moderne. Procédures de contrôle et d'identification*, Paris: Maisonneuve & Larose, 2007, pp. 155–80.
—— 'Flottes de commerce et de pêche en Languedoc au temps de Louis XIV', in Louvier, P. (ed.), *Le Languedoc et la mer (XVIe–XXIe siècle)*, Montpellier: Presses universitaires de la Méditerranée, 2012, pp. 133–61.
—— 'La "marine de Sète" au XVIIIe siècle: entre trafic de proximité et grand cabotage européen', in Dumond, L., Durand, S., and Thomas, J. (eds), *Les ports dans l'Europe méditerranéenne: trafics et circulation: images et représentations*, Montpellier: Presses universitaires de le Méditerranée, 2007, pp. 187–213.
Calafat, G., 'Jurisdictional Pluralism in a Litigious Sea (1590–1630): Hard Cases, Multi-Sited Trials and Legal Enforcement between North Africa and Italy', *Past and Present* Supplement 14 (2019), pp. 142–78.
—— 'Livourne et la Chambre de commerce de Marseille au XVIIe siècle. Consuls français, agents et perception du droit de *cottimo*', in Daumalin, X., Faget, D., and Raveux, O. (eds), *La mer en partage. Sociétés littorales et économies maritimes XVIe–XXe siècle*, Aix-en-Provence: Presses universitaires de Provence, 2016, pp. 209–26.
—— 'Ottoman North Africa and *ius publicum europaeum*: The Case of the Treaties of Peace and Trade (1600–1750)', in Alimento, A. (ed.), *War, Trade and Neutrality: Europe and the Mediterranean in the Seventeenth and Eighteenth Centuries*, Milan: FrancoAngeli, 2011, pp. 171–87.
Calafat, G. and Kaiser, W., 'Le laboratoire méditerranéen. Course et piraterie aux XVIe et XVIIe siècles', in Buti, G. and Hrodĕj, P. (eds), *Histoire des pirates et corsaires. De l'antiquité à nos jours*, Paris: CNRS Éditions, 2016, pp. 225–47.
Carlos, A. and Nicholas, S., '"Giants of an Earlier Capitalism": The Chartered Trading Companies as Modern Multinationals', *Business History Review* 62 (1988), pp. 398–419.
Ceccarelli, G., 'Risky Business: Theological and Canonical Thought on Insurance from the Thirteenth to the Seventeenth Century', *Journal of Medieval and Early Modern Studies* 31 (2001), pp. 601–58.
—— *Risky Markets: Marine Insurance in Renaissance Florence*, Leiden: Brill, 2020.
Chadelat, J., 'L'élaboration de l'Ordonnance de la marine d'août 1681' I, *Revue historique de droit français et étranger* 31 (1954), pp. 74–98.
—— 'L'élaboration de l'Ordonnance de la marine d'août 1681' II, *Revue historique de droit français et étranger* 31 (1954), pp. 228–53.
Chapman, S., *Private Ambition and Political Alliances: The Phélypeaux de Pontchartrain Family and Louis XIV's Government, 1650–1715*, Rochester, NY: University of Rochester Press, 2004.

Chaunu, D., 'Route des Indes ou îles esclavagistes? La "pénétration commerce de l'Amérique espagnole" à l'épreuve de la diplomatie des îles sous Louis XIV', in Schnakenbourg, É. and Ternat, F. (eds), *Une diplomatie des lointains. La France face à la mondialisation des rivalités internationales, XVIIe–XVIIIe siècles*, Rennes: Presses universitaires de Rennes, 2020, pp. 115–34.

Ciepley, D., 'The Anglo-American Misconception of Stockholders as "Owners" and "Members": Its Origins and Consequences', *Journal of Institutional Economics* 16 (2020), pp. 623–42.

Clark, G., *The Dutch Alliance and the War Against French Trade 1688–1697*, New York: Russell & Russell, 1971.

—— 'The Nine Years' War, 1688–1697', in Bromley, J. (ed.), *The New Cambridge Modern History*, vol. VI, Cambridge: Cambridge University Press, 1970, pp. 223–53.

Clark, H., *Compass of Society: Commerce and Absolutism in Old-Regime France*, Lanham: Lexington Books, 2007.

Clark, J., 'Marine Insurance in Eighteenth-Century La Rochelle', *French Historical Studies* 10 (1978), pp. 572–98.

Coedès, G., 'Siamese Documents of the Seventeenth Century', *Journal of the Siam Society* 14 (1921), pp. 7–30.

Cole, C., *Colbert and a Century of French Mercantilism*, vols I and II, New York: Columbia University Press, 1939.

—— *French Mercantilism, 1683–1700*, New York: Columbia University Press, 1943.

Collins, J., 'Les finances bretonnes du XVIIe siècle: un modèle pour la France?', in *L'administration des finances sous l'Ancien Régime*, Paris: Comité pour l'histoire économique et financière, 1997, pp. 307–15.

—— *The State in Early Modern France*, Cambridge: Cambridge University Press, 2009.

Cordes, A. and Höhn, P., 'Extra-Legal and Legal Conflict Management among Long-Distance Traders (1250–1650)', in Pihlajamäki, H., Dubber, M., and Godfrey, M. (eds), *The Oxford Handbook of European Legal History*, Oxford: Oxford University Press, 2018, pp. 509–27.

Cosandey F. and Descimon, R., *L'absolutisme en France. Histoire et historiographie*, Paris: Éditions du Seuil, 2002.

Cruz Barney, O., 'The Risk in Hispanic-Indies Trade. Sea Loans and Maritime Insurances (16th–19th Century)', in Brunori, L., Dauchy, S. Descaps, O., and Prévost, X. (eds), *Le Droit face à l'économie sans travail*, vol. II, Paris: Éditions Classiques Garnier, 2020, pp. 265–95.

Dal Bo, E., Hutkova, K., Leucht, L., and Yuchtman, N., 'International Trade, Domestic Production, and the Rise of the British Fiscal-Military State: New Evidence on the Sources of Fiscal Revenue, 1680–1820', seminar at the Institute of Historical Research, March 2022.

Dari-Mattiacci, G., Gelderblom, O., Jonker, J., and Perotti, E., 'The Emergence of the Corporate Form', *The Journal of Law, Economics, and Organization* 33 (2017), pp. 193–236.

Darnell, B., 'Naval Policy in an Age of Fiscal Overextension', in Prest, J. and Rowlands, G. (eds), *The Third Reign of Louis XIV, c. 1682–1715*, Abingdon: Routledge, 2017, pp. 68–81.

—— 'Reconsidering the Guerre de Course under Louis XIV: Naval Policy and Strategic Downsizing in an Era of Fiscal Overextension', in Rodger, N., Dancy, J.,

Darnell, B., and Wilson, E. (eds), *Strategy and the Sea: Essays in Honour of John B. Hattendorf*, Woodbridge: Boydell Press, 2016, pp. 37–48.

Darsel, J., 'L'Amirauté de Bretagne. Des origines à la Révolution', in Le Bouëdec, G. (ed.), *L'Amirauté en Bretagne. Des origines à la fin du XVIIIe siècle*, Rennes: Presses universitaires de Rennes, 2012, pp. 53–374.

Dawson, W., *Marine Underwriting at Rouen 1727–1742*, London: Lloyd's, 1931.

Dee, D., *Expansion and Crisis in Louis XIV's France: Franche-Comté and Absolute Monarchy, 1674–1715*, Rochester, NY: University of Rochester Press, 2009.

Degroot, D. et al., 'Towards a Rigorous Understanding of Societal Responses to Climate Change', *Nature* 591 (2021), pp. 539–50.

Delobette, É., 'Les mutations du commerce maritime du Havre, 1680–1730. Première partie', *Annales de Normandie* 51 année (2001), pp. 3–69.

Delumeau, J., 'Méthode mécanographique et trafic maritime: les terre-neuviers malouins à la fin du XVIIe siècle', *Annales. Economies, sociétés, civilisation* 16 année (1961), pp. 665–85.

Denière, M., *La juridiction consulaire de Paris, 1563–1792. Sa création, ses luttes, son administration intérieure, ses usages et ses mœurs*, Paris: Henri Plon, 1872.

de Pleijt, A. and van Zanden, J., 'Accounting for the "Little Divergence": What Drove Economic Growth in Pre-Industrial Europe, 1300–1800?', *European Review of Economic History* 20 (2016), pp. 387–409.

de Roover, F. Edler, 'Early Examples of Marine Insurance', *Journal of Economic History* 5 (1945), pp. 172–200.

De ruysscher, D., 'Antwerp 1490–1590: Insurance and Speculation', in Leonard, A. (ed.), *Marine Insurance: Origins and Institutions, 1300–1850*, Basingstoke: Palgrave Macmillan, 2016, pp. 79–105.

Dessert, D., *Argent, pouvoir et société au Grand Siècle*, Paris: Fayard, 1984.

—— *Le royaume de Monsieur Colbert*, Paris: Perrin, 2007.

Dessert, D. and Journet, J., 'Le lobby Colbert: un royaume ou une affaire de famille?', *Annales. Economies, sociétés, civilisations* 30 année (1975), pp. 1303–37.

de Vries, J. and van der Woude, A., *The First Modern Economy: Success, Failure, and Perseverance of the Dutch Economy, 1500–1815*, Cambridge: Cambridge University Press, 1997.

Dewald, J., 'Rethinking the 1 Percent: The Failure of the Nobility in Old Regime France', *The American Historical Review* 124 (2019), pp. 911–32.

de Zwart, P. and van Zanden, J., *The Origins of Globalization: World Trade in the Making of the Global Economy, 1500–1800*, Cambridge: Cambridge University Press, 2018.

Doyle, W., 'Colbert et les offices', *Histoire, économie et société* 19 année (2000), pp. 469–80.

Dreijer, G., 'Identity, Conflict and Commercial Law: Legal Strategies of Castilian Merchants in the Low Countries (15th–16th Centuries)', in De ruysscher, D., Cordes, A., Dauchy, S., Gialdroni, S., and Pihlajamäki, H. (eds), *Commerce, Citizenship, and Identity in Legal History*, Leiden: Brill, 2021, pp. 118–38.

Drelichman, M. and Voth, H., *Lending to the Borrower from Hell: Debt, Taxes and Default in the Age of Philip II*, Princeton: Princeton University Press, 2014.

Drévillon, H., *Le Roi absolu. Louis XIV et les Français (1661–1715)*, Paris: Éditions Belin, 2015.

Edwards, J. and Ogilvie, S., 'What Lessons for Economic Development Can We Draw from the Champagne Fairs?', *Explorations in Economic History* 49 (2012), pp. 131–48.

Epstein, S., *Freedom and Growth: The Rise of States and Markets in Europe, 1300–1750*, London: Routledge, 2000.

Farber, H., 'The Political Economy of Marine Insurance and the Making of the United States', *The William and Mary Quarterly* 77 (2020), pp. 581–612.

—— *Underwriters of the United States: How Insurance Shaped the American Founding*, Williamsburg, VA and Chapel Hill, NC: Omohundro Institute of Early American History and Culture and the University of North Carolina Press, 2021.

Félix, J., *Économie et finances sous l'ancien régime. Guide du chercheur, 1523–1789*, Vincennes: Institut de la gestion publique et du développement économique, Comité pour l'histoire économique et financière de la France, 1994.

—— '"The Most Difficult Financial Matter that has Ever Presented Itself": Paper Money and the Financing of Warfare under Louis XIV', *Financial History Review* 25 (2018), pp. 43–70.

Flynn, D. and Giráldez, A., 'Born with a "Silver Spoon": The Origin of World Trade in 1571', *Journal of World History* 6 (1995), pp. 201–21.

Frankot, E., *'Of Laws of Ships and Shipmen': Medieval Maritime Law and Its Practice in Urban Northern Europe*, Edinburgh: Edinburgh University Press, 2012.

Fusaro, M., 'Maritime History as Global History? The Methodological Challenges and a Future Research Agenda', in Fusaro, M. and Polonia, A. (eds), *Maritime History as Global History*, St. John's: IMEHA, 2011, pp. 267–82.

—— 'Politics of Justice/Politics of Trade: Foreign Merchants and the Administration of Justice from the Records of Venice's *Giudici del Forestier*', *Mélanges de l'École française de Rome* 126 (2014), pp. 139–60.

Fusaro, M., Addobbati, A., and Piccinno. L. (eds), *General Average and Risk Management in Medieval and Early Modern Maritime Business*, Basingstoke: Palgrave Macmillan, 2023.

Gelderblom, O., *Cities of Commerce: The Institutional Foundations of International Trade in the Low Countries, 1250–1650*, Princeton: Princeton University Press, 2013.

Gelderblom, O., de Jong, A., and Jonker, J., 'The Formative Years of the Modern Corporation: The Dutch East India Company VOC, 1602–1623', *Journal of Economic History* 73 (2013), pp. 1050–76.

Gindis, D., 'Conceptualizing the Business Corporation: Insights from History', *Journal of Institutional Economics* (2020), pp. 1–9.

Glenn Crothers, A., 'Commercial Risk and Capital Formation in Early America: Virginia Merchants and the Rise of American Marine Insurance, 1750–1815', *Business History Review* 78 (2004), pp. 607–33.

Go, S., 'Amsterdam 1585–1790: Emergence, Dominance, and Decline', in Leonard, A. (ed.), *Marine Insurance: Origins and Institutions, 1300–1850*, Basingstoke: Palgrave Macmillan, 2016, pp. 107–29.

—— 'The Amsterdam Chamber of Insurance and Average: A New Phase in Formal Contract Enforcement (Late Sixteenth and Seventeenth Centuries)', *Enterprise and Society* 14 (2013), pp. 511–43.

—— *Marine Insurance in the Netherlands 1600–1870: A Comparative Institutional Approach*, Amsterdam: Aksant, 2009.
Grafe, R. and Gelderblom, O., 'The Rise and Fall of Merchant Guilds: Re-thinking the Comparative Study of Commercial Institutions in Premodern Europe', *Journal of Interdisciplinary History* 40 (2010), pp. 477–511.
Grancher, R., 'Le tribunal de l'amirauté et les usages du métier. Une histoire "par en bas" du monde de la pêche (Dieppe, XVIIIe siècle)', *Revue d'histoire moderne & contemporaine* 65 (2018), pp. 33–58.
Greif, A., *Institutions and the Path to the Modern Economy: Lessons from Medieval Trade*, New York: Cambridge University Press, 2006.
Grinberg, M., *Écrire les coutumes. Les droits seigneuriaux en France*, Paris: Presses universitaires de France, 2006.
Hardwick, J., *Family Business: Litigation and the Political Economies of Daily Life in Early Modern France*, Oxford: Oxford University Press, 2009.
Harris, R., 'Could the Crown Credibly Commit to Respect Its Charters? England, 1558–1640', in Coffman, D., Leonard, A., and Neal, L. (eds), *Questioning Credible Commitment: Perspectives on the Rise of Financial Capitalism*, Cambridge: Cambridge University Press, 2013, pp. 21–47.
—— *Going the Distance: Eurasian Trade and the Rise of the Business Corporation, 1400–1700*, Princeton: Princeton University Press, 2020.
—— 'A New Understanding of the History of Limited Liability: An Invitation for Theoretical Reframing', *Journal of Institutional Economics* 16 (2020), pp. 643–64.
Haudrère, P., *Les Français dans l'océan Indien XVIIe–XIXe siècle*, Rennes: Presses universitaires de Rennes, 2014.
Hayhoe, J., *Enlightened Feudalism: Seigneurial Justice and Village Society in Eighteenth-Century Northern Burgundy*, Rochester, NY: University of Rochester Press, 2008.
Heijmans, E., *The Agency of Empire: Connections and Strategies in French Overseas Expansion (1686–1746)*, Leiden: Brill, 2019.
—— 'Investing in French Overseas Companies: A Bad Deal? The Liquidation Processes of Companies Operating on the West Coast of Africa and in India (1664–1719)', *Itinerario* 43 (2019), pp. 107–21.
Herzog, T., *A Short History of European Law: The Last Two and a Half Centuries*, London: Harvard University Press, 2018.
Higgs, E., *The Information State in England: The Central Collection of Information on Citizens since 1500*, Basingstoke: Palgrave Macmillan, 2004.
Hillmann, H., *The Corsairs of Saint-Malo: Network Organization of a Merchant Elite under the Ancien Régime*, New York: Columbia University Press, 2021.
Hirsch, J. and Minard, P., '"Laissez-nous faire et protégez-nous beaucoup": pour une histoire des pratiques institutionnelles dans l'industrie française (XVIIIe–XIXe siècle)', in Bergeron, L. and Bourdelais, P. (eds), *La France n'est-elle pas douée pour l'industrie?*, Paris: Belin, 1998, pp. 135–58.
Hoffman, P., 'Early Modern France, 1450–1700', in Hoffman, P. and Norberg, K. (eds), *Fiscal Crises, Liberty, and Representative Government, 1450–1789*, Stanford: Stanford University Press, 1994, pp. 226–52.
Hoffman, P., Postel-Vinay, G., and Rosenthal J., *Priceless Markets: The Political Economy of Credit in Paris, 1660–1870*, Chicago: University of Chicago Press, 2000.

Hoock, J., 'Le monde marchand face au défi colbertien. Le cas des marchands de Rouen', in Isenmann, M. (ed.), *Merkantilismus: Wiedeaufnahme einer Debatte*, Stuttgart: Franz Steiner Verlag, 2014, pp. 221–39.

Hoppit, J., *Britain's Political Economies: Parliament and Economic Life, 1660–1800*, Cambridge: Cambridge University Press, 2017.

Horn, J., *Economic Development in Early Modern France: The Privilege of Liberty, 1650–1820*, Cambridge: Cambridge University Press, 2015.

Hroděj, P., 'L'établissement laborieux du pouvoir royal à Saint-Domingue au temps des premiers gouveneurs', in Le Bouëdec, G., Chappé F., and Cérino, C. (eds), *Pouvoirs et littoraux du XVe au XXe siècle*, Rennes: Presses universitaires de Rennes, 2000, pp. 157–69.

Hurt, J., *Louis XIV and the Parlements: The Assertion of Royal Authority*, Manchester: Manchester University Press, 2002.

Isenmann, M., 'Égalité, réciprocité, souveraineté: The Role of Commercial Treaties in Colbert's Economic Policy', in Alimento, A. and Stapelbroek, K. (eds), *The Politics of Commercial Treaties in the Eighteenth Century: Balance of Power, Balance of Trade*, Basingstoke: Palgrave Macmillan, 2017, pp. 77–103.

—— '(Non-)Knowledge, Political Economy and Trade Policy in Seventeenth-Century France: The Problem of Trade Balances', in Zwierlein, C. (ed.), *The Dark Side of Knowledge: Histories of Ignorance, 1400 to 1800*, Leiden: Brill, 2016, pp. 139–55.

—— 'From Privilege to Economic Law: Vested Interests and the Origins of Free Trade Theory in France (1687–1701)', in Rössner, P. (ed.), *Economic Growth and the Origins of Modern Political Economy: Economic Reasons of State, 1500–2000*, London: Routledge, 2016, pp. 103–21.

Jackson, G., 'Marine Insurance Frauds in Scotland 1751–1821: Cases of Deliberate Shipwreck Tried in the Scottish Court of Admiralty', *The Mariner's Mirror* 57 (1971), pp. 307–22.

John, A., 'Insurance Investment and the London Money Market of the 18th Century', *Economica* 20 (1953), pp. 137–58.

John, R., 'After Managerial Capitalism', *Business History Review* 95 (2021), pp. 151–7.

Johnson, N., 'Banking on the King: The Evolution of the Royal Revenue Farms in Old Regime France', *Journal of Economic History* 66 (2006), pp. 963–91.

Kadens, E., 'The Myth of the Customary Law Merchant', *Texas Law Review* 90 (2012), pp. 1153–206.

Kaiser, W., 'Les "hommes de crédit" dans les rachats provençaux (XVIe–XVIIe siècles)', in Kaiser, W. (ed.), *Le commerce des captifs. Les intermédiaires dans l'échange et le rachat des prisonniers en Méditerranée, XVe–XVIIIe siècle*, Rome: École Française de Rome, 2008, pp. 291–319.

Kaiser, W. and Calafat, G., 'The Economy of Ransoming in the Early Modern Mediterranean: A Form of Cross-Cultural Trade between Southern Europe and the Maghreb (Sixteenth to Eighteenth Centuries)', in Trivellato, F., Halevi, L., and Antunes, C. (eds), *Religion and Trade: Cross-Cultural Exchanges in World History, 1000–1900*, Oxford: Oxford University Press, 2014, pp. 108–30.

Kaplan, S., 'Long Run Lamentations: Braudel on France', *The Journal of Modern History* 63 (1991), pp. 341–53.

Kessler, A., *A Revolution in Commerce: The Parisian Merchant Court and the Rise of Commercial Society in Eighteenth-Century France*, New Haven: Yale University Press, 2007.

Kettering, S., *Patrons, Brokers, and Clients in Seventeenth-Century France*, New York: Oxford University Press, 1986.

Khalilieh, H., *Islamic Maritime Law: An Introduction*, Leiden: Brill, 1998.

Kingston, C., 'America 1720–1820: War and Organisation', in Leonard, A. (ed.), *Marine Insurance: Origins and Institutions, 1300–1850*, Basingstoke: Palgrave Macmillan, 2016, pp. 205–28.

—— 'Governance and Institutional Change in Marine Insurance, 1350–1850', *European Review of Economic History* 18 (2013), pp. 1–18.

—— 'Marine Insurance in Britain and America, 1720–1844: A Comparative Institutional Analysis', *Journal of Economic History* 67 (2007), pp. 379–409.

Knight, R., *Convoys: The British Struggle Against Napoleonic Europe and America*, New Haven: Yale University Press, 2022.

Koskenniemi, M., *To the Uttermost Parts of the Earth: Legal Imagination and International Power 1300–1870*, Cambridge: Cambridge University Press, 2021.

Kwass, M., 'Court Capitalism, Illicit Markets, and Political Legitimacy in Eighteenth-Century France: The Salt and Tobacco Monopolies', in Coffman, D., Leonard, A., and Neal, L. (eds), *Questioning Credible Commitment: Perspectives on the Rise of Financial Capitalism*, Cambridge: Cambridge University Press, 2013, pp. 228–50.

Landry, N., 'Échanges entre une colonie et un port métropolitain: Plaisance (Terre-Neuve) et La Rochelle, 1688–1713', in Augeron, M., Péret, J., and Sauzeau, T., *Le golfe du Saint-Laurent et le Centre-Ouest français. Histoire d'une relation singulière (XVIIe–XIXe siècle)*, Rennes: Presses universitaires de Rennes, 2010, pp. 107–21.

Lane, F., *Profits from Power. Readings in Protection Rent and Violence Controlling Enterprise*, Albany: State University of New York Press, 1979.

Lazer, S., *State Formation in Early Modern Alsace, 1648–1789*, Rochester, NY: University of Rochester Press, 2019.

Legay, M., 'État, corps intermédiaires et crédit public: un modèle de gestion des finances à l'époque moderne?', in Meyzie, V. (ed.), *Crédit public, crédit privé et institutions intermédiaires. Monarchie française, monarchie hispanique, XVIe–XVIIIe siècles*, Limoges: Presses universitaires de Limoges, 2012, pp. 33–49.

Lelièvre, G., *La préhistoire de la Compagnie des Indes orientales, 1601–1622. Les Français dans la course aux épices*, Caen: Presses universitaires de Caen, 2021.

Leonard, A., 'Contingent Commitment: The Development of English Marine Insurance in the Context of New Institutional Economics, 1577–1720', in Coffman, D., Leonard, A., and Neal, L. (eds), *Questioning Credible Commitment: Perspectives on the Rise of Financial Capitalism*, Cambridge: Cambridge University Press, 2013, pp. 48–75.

—— 'From Local to Transatlantic: Insuring Trade in the Caribbean', in Leonard, A. and Pretel, D. (eds), *The Caribbean and the Atlantic World Economy: Circuits of Trade, Money and Knowledge, 1650–1914*, Basingstoke: Palgrave Macmillan, 2015, pp. 137–60.

—— 'Introduction: The Nature and Study of Marine Insurance', in Leonard, A. (ed.), *Marine Insurance: Origins and Institutions, 1300–1850*, Basingstoke: Palgrave Macmillan, 2016, pp. 3–22.

—— 'London 1462–1601: Marine Insurance and the Law Merchant', in Leonard, A. (ed.), *Marine Insurance: Origins and Institutions, 1300–1850*, Basingstoke: Palgrave Macmillan, 2016, pp. 151–78.

—— *London Marine Insurance 1438–1824: Risk, Trade, and the Early Modern State*, Woodbridge: Boydell & Brewer, 2022.

—— 'Underwriting Marine Warfare: Insurance and Conflict in the Eighteenth Century', *International Journal of Maritime History* 25 (2013), pp. 173–85.

Le Page, D., 'Les augmentations de gages à la Chambre des comptes de Bretagne sous le règne de Louis XIV', in Meyzie, V. (ed.), *Crédit public, crédit privé et institutions intermédiaires. Monarchie française, monarchie hispanique, XVIe–XVIIIe siècles*, Limoges: Presses universitaires de Limoges, 2012, pp. 51–92.

Lespagnol, A., *Messieurs de Saint-Malo. Une élite négociante au temps de Louis XIV*, vols I and II, Rennes: Presses universitaires de Rennes, 1997.

—— 'Les relations commerciales entre l'Irlande et la Bretagne aux temps modernes (XVe–XVIIIe siècles). Complémentarité ou concurrence?', in Laurent, C. and Davis, H. (eds), *Irlande et Bretagne. Vingt siècles d'histoire*, Rennes: Terre de Brume Éditions, 1994, pp. 169–77.

—— 'Saint-Malo, les Malouins et Marseille. Une relation particulière', in Daumalin, X., Faget, D., and Raveux, O. (eds), *La mer en partage. Sociétés littorales et économies maritimes XVIe–XXe siècle*, Aix-en-Provence: Presses universitaires de Provence, 2016, pp. 181–93.

Levillain, C., *Vaincre Louis XIV. Angleterre, Hollande, France: Histoire d'une relation triangulaire 1665–1688*, Seyssel: Champ Vallon, 2010.

Lobo-Guerrero, L., *Insuring War: Sovereignty, Security and Risk*, London: Routledge, 2012.

Lynn, J., *The Wars of Louis XIV 1667–1714*, London: Longman, 1999.

Malettke, K., 'Colbert devant les historiens (1683–1983)', in Mousnier, R. (ed.), *Un nouveau Colbert: actes du Colloque pour le tricentenaire de la mort de Colbert*, Paris: Editions SEDES/CDU, 1985, pp. 13–28.

Mandelblatt, B., 'How Feeding Slaves Shaped the French Atlantic: Mercantilism and the Crisis of Food Provisioning in the Franco-Caribbean during the Seventeenth and Eighteenth Centuries', in Reinert, S. and Røge, P. (eds), *The Political Economy of Empire in the Early Modern World*, Basingstoke: Palgrave Macmillan, 2013, pp. 192–220.

—— 'A Transatlantic Commodity: Irish Salt Beef in the French Atlantic World', *History Workshop Journal* 63 (2007), pp. 18–47.

Manning, S., 'Contrasting Colonisations: (Re)storying Newfoundland/Ktaqmkuk as Place', *Settler Colonial Studies* 8 (2017), pp. 314–31.

Martin, G., *La grande industrie sous le regne de Louis XIV (plus particulierement de 1660–1715)*, Paris: Librairie nouvelle de droit et de jurisprudence, 1898.

Martin, M. and Weiss, G., *The Sun King at Sea: Maritime Art and Galley Slavery in Louis XIV's France*, Los Angeles: Getty Publications, 2022.

Martin, S., 'La correspondance ministérielle du secrétariat d'État de la Marine avec les arsenaux: circulation de l'information et pratiques épistolaires des administrateurs de la Marine (XVIIe–XVIIIe siècles)', in Ulbert, J. and Llinares, S. (eds),

La liasse et la plume. Les bureaux du secrétariat d'État de la Marine (1669–1792), Rennes: Presses universitaires de Rennes, 2017, pp. 33–46.

Marzagalli, S., 'Was Warfare Necessary for the Functioning of Eighteenth-Century Colonial Systems? Some Reflections on the Necessity of Cross-Imperial and Foreign Trade in the French Case', in Antunes, C. and Polónia, A. (eds), *Beyond Empires: Global, Self-Organizing, Cross-Imperial Networks, 1500–1800*, Leiden: Brill, 2016, pp. 253–77.

McCollim, G., *Louis XIV's Assault on Privilege: Nicolas Desmaretz and the Tax on Wealth*, Rochester, NY: University of Rochester Press, 2012.

Ménard-Jacob, M., 'L'apprentissage de l'Inde par les Français de la première compagnie', in Le Bouëdec, G. (ed.), *L'Asie, la mer, le monde. Au temps des Compagnies des Indes*, Rennes: Presses universitaires de Rennes, 2014, pp. 159–75.

—— *La première compagnie des Indes. Apprentissages, échecs et héritage 1664–1704*, Rennes: Presses universitaires de Rennes, 2016.

Mettam, R., *Power and Faction in Louis XIV's France*, Oxford: Basil Blackwell, 1988.

Meyer, J., 'La France et l'Irlande pendant le règne de Louis XIV', in Laurent, C. and Davis, H. (eds), *Irlande et Bretagne. Vingt siècles d'histoire*, Rennes: Terre de Brume Éditions, 1994, pp. 139–51.

Meyer, W., 'English Privateering in the War of 1688 to 1697', *The Mariner's Mirror* 67 (1981), pp. 259–72.

Milgrom, P., North, D., and Weingast, B., 'The Role of Institutions in the Revival of Trade: The Law Merchant, Private Judges, and the Champagne Fairs', *Economics and Politics* 2 (1990), pp. 1–23.

Minard, P., *La fortune du colbertisme. État et industrie dans la France des Lumières*, Paris: Éditions Fayard, 1998.

Mokyr, J., 'The Institutional Origins of the Industrial Revolution', unpublished paper.

Morieux, R., *The Channel: England, France and the Construction of a Maritime Border in the Eighteenth Century*, Cambridge: Cambridge University Press, 2016.

Morineau, M., *Jauges et méthodes de jauge anciennes et modernes*, Paris: Librarie Armand Colin, 1966.

—— 'La marine française de commerce de Colbert à Seignelay', in Méchoulan, H. and Cornette, J. (eds), *L'état classique. Regards sur la pensée politique de la France dans le second XVIIe siècle*, Paris: Librairie Philosophique J. Vrin, 1996, pp. 239–55.

Moulin, M., 'Les rentes sur l'Hôtel de Ville de Paris sous Louis XIV', *Histoire, économie et société* 17 (1998), pp. 623–48.

Mousnier, R., *The Institutions of France under the Absolute Monarchy 1598–1789*, vol. II, Chicago: University of Chicago Press, 1984.

Muldrew, C., *The Economy of Obligation: The Culture of Credit and Social Relations in Early Modern England*, Basingstoke: Macmillan, 1998.

—— '"Hard Food for Midas": Cash and Its Social Value in Early Modern England', *Past and Present* 170 (2001), pp. 78–120.

Müller, L., *Consuls, Corsairs, and Commerce: The Swedish Consular Service and Long-Distance Shipping, 1720–1815*, Uppsala: Uppsala Universitet, 2004.

North, D., 'Institutions', *Journal of Economic Perspectives* 5 (1991), pp. 97–112.

—— *Institutions, Institutional Change and Economic Performance*, Cambridge: Cambridge University Press, 1990.

―― 'Institutions, Transaction Costs, and the Rise of Merchant Empires', in Tracy, J. (ed.), *The Political Economy of Merchant Empires*, Cambridge: Cambridge University Press, 1991, pp. 22–40.

North, D. and Weingast, B., 'Constitutions and Commitment: The Evolution of Institutions Governing Public Choice in Seventeenth-Century England', *Journal of Economic History* 49 (1989), pp. 803–32.

O'Brien, P., 'The Formation of a Mercantilist State and the Economic Growth of the United Kingdom 1453–1815', WIDER Research Paper, No. 2006/75.

―― 'The Formation of States and Transitions to Modern Economies: England, Europe, and Asia Compared', in Neal, L. and Williamson, J. (eds), *The Cambridge History of Capitalism*, vol. I, Cambridge: Cambridge University Press, 2014, pp. 357–402.

―― 'The Nature and Historical Evolution of an Exceptional Fiscal State and Its Possible Significance for the Precocious Commercialization and Industrialization of the British Economy from Cromwell to Nelson', *Economic History Review* 64 (2011), pp. 408–46.

Ó Ciosain, É., 'Les Irlandais en Bretagne 1603–1780: "invasion", accueil, intégration', in Laurent, C. and Davis, H. (eds), *Irlande et Bretagne. Vingt siècles d'histoire*, Rennes: Terre de Brume Éditions, 1994, pp. 153–66.

Ogilvie, S., *The European Guilds: An Economic Analysis*, Princeton: Princeton University Press, 2019.

―― '"Whatever Is, Is Right"? Economic Institutions in Pre-Industrial Europe', *Economic History Review* 60 (2007), pp. 649–84.

Olivier-Martin, F., *Histoire du droit français. Des origines à la Révolution*, Paris: CNRS Éditions, 2010.

Ormrod, D., *The Rise of Commercial Empires: England and the Netherlands in the Age of Mercantilism, 1650–1770*, Cambridge: Cambridge University Press, 2003.

Parvev, I., 'The War of 1683–1699 and the Beginning of the Eastern Question', in Heywood, C. and Parvev, I. (eds), *The Treaties of Carlowitz (1699)*, Leiden: Brill, 2020, pp. 73–87.

Pearson, R., 'Escaping from the State? Historical Paths to Public and Private Insurance', *Enterprise & Society* (2020), pp. 1–30.

Pettigrew, W. and Veevers, D., 'Introduction', in Pettigrew, W. and Veevers, D. (eds), *The Corporation as a Protagonist in Global History, c. 1550–1750*, Leiden: Brill, 2019, pp. 1–39.

Pfister-Langanay, C., 'Dunkerque sous Louis XIV: un port de commerce qui se cherche', in Piétri-Lévy, A., Barzman, J., and Barré, É. (eds), *Environnements portuaires. Port environments*, Mont-Saint-Aignan: Presses universitaires de Rouen et du Havre, 2003, pp. 261–71.

―― *Ports, navires et négociants à Dunkerque (1662–1792)*, Dunkirk: Société dunkerquoise, 1985.

Piant, H., *Une Justice ordinaire. Justice civile et criminelle dans la prévôté royale de Vaucouleurs sous l'Ancien Régime*, Rennes: Presses universitaires de Rennes, 2006.

Piccinno, L., 'Genoa, 1340–1620: Early Development of Marine Insurance', in Leonard, A. (ed.), *Marine Insurance: Origins and Institutions, 1300–1850*, Basingstoke: Palgrave Macmillan, 2016, pp. 25–46.

Pilgrim, D., 'The Colbert-Seignelay Naval Reforms and the Beginnings of the War of the League of Augsburg', *French Historical Studies* 9 (1975), pp. 235–62.

Potter, M., *Corps and Clienteles: Public Finance and Political Change in France, 1688–1715*, Aldershot: Ashgate, 2003.

Pourchasse, P., 'Les conflits permanents entre corsaires et neutres: L'exemple de la France et du Danemark au XVIIIe siècle', in Sicking, L. and Wijffels, A. (eds), *Conflict Management in the Mediterranean and the Atlantic, 1000–1800: Actors, Institutions and Strategies of Dispute Settlement*, Leiden: Brill, 2020, pp. 325–53.

Price, J., *France and the Chesapeake: A History of the French Tobacco Monopoly, 1684–1791, and of Its Relationship to the British and American Tobacco Trades*, vols I and II, Ann Arbor: Michigan University Press, 1973.

Pritchard, J., *In Search of Empire: The French in the Americas, 1670–1730*, Cambridge: Cambridge University Press, 2004.

Puttevils, J. and Deloof, M., 'Marketing and Pricing Risk in Marine Insurance in Sixteenth-Century Antwerp', *Journal of Economic History* 77 (2017), pp. 796–837.

Regourd, F., 'Capitale savante, capitale coloniale: sciences et savoirs coloniaux à Paris aux XVIIe et XVIIIe siècles', *Revue d'histoire moderne & contemporaine* 55 (2008), pp. 121–51.

Riello, G., 'With Great Pomp and Magnificence: Royal Gifts and the Embassies between Siam and France in the Late Seventeenth Century', in Biedermann, Z., Gerritsen, A., and Riello, G. (eds), *Global Gifts: The Material Culture of Diplomacy in Early Modern Eurasia*, New York: Cambridge University Press, 2008, pp. 249–50.

Rosolino, R., 'Vices tyranniques', *Annales. Histoire, Sciences Sociales* 68 année (2013), pp. 793–819.

Rossi, G., 'England 1523–1601: The Beginnings of Marine Insurance', in Leonard, A. (ed.), *Marine Insurance: Origins and Institutions, 1300–1850*, Basingstoke: Palgrave Macmillan, 2016, pp. 131–45.

—— *Insurance in Elizabethan England: The London Code*, Cambridge: Cambridge University Press, 2016.

—— 'The Liability of the Shipmaster in Early Modern Law: Comparative (and Practice-Oriented) Remarks', *Historia et ius* 12 (2017), pp. 1–47.

Rothkrug, L., *Opposition to Louis XIV: The Political and Social Origins of the French Enlightenment*, Princeton: Princeton University Press, 1965.

Roulet, É., *La Compagnie des îles de l'Amérique 1635–1651. Une enterprise colonial au XVIIe siècle*, Rennes: Presses universitaires de Rennes, 2017.

—— 'Les traités sur l'assurance maritime en France à l'époque moderne', in Borde, C. and Roulet, É. (eds), *L'assurance maritime XIVe–XXIe siècle*, Aachen: Shaker Verlag, 2017, pp. 125–41.

Rowlands, G., *Dangerous and Dishonest Men: The International Bankers of Louis XIV's France*, Basingstoke: Palgrave Macmillan, 2015.

—— *The Dynastic State and the Army under Louis XIV: Royal Service and Private Interest 1661–1701*, Cambridge: Cambridge University Press, 2002.

—— *The Financial Decline of a Great Power: War, Influence, and Money in Louis XIV's France*, Oxford: Oxford University Press, 2012.

—— 'Life After Death in Foreign Lands: Louis XIV and Anglo-American Historians', in Externbrink, S. and Levillain, C. (eds), *Penser l'après Louis XIV. Histoire, mémoire, representation (1715–2015)*, Paris: Honoré Champion, 2018, pp. 179–209.

—— 'Royal Finances in the Third Reign of Louis XIV', in Prest, J. and Rowlands, G. (eds), *The Third Reign of Louis XIV, c. 1682–1715*, Abingdon: Routledge, 2017, pp. 38–52.

Rowlands, G. and Prest, J., 'Introduction', in Prest, J. and Rowlands, G. (eds), *The Third Reign of Louis XIV, c. 1682–1715*, Abingdon: Routledge, 2017, pp. 1–23.

Ruffat, M., 'French Insurance from the *Ancien Régime* to 1946: Shifting Frontiers between State and Market', *Financial History Review* 10 (2003), pp. 185–200.

Rule, J. and Trotter, B., *A World of Paper: Louis XIV, Colbert de Torcy, and the Rise of the Information State*, Montreal: McGill-Queen's University Press, 2014.

Rupprecht, A., '"Inherent Vice": Marine Insurance, Slave Ship Rebellion and the Law', *Race and Class* 57 (2016), pp. 31–44.

Sahlins, P., 'Natural Frontiers Revisited: France's Boundaries since the Seventeenth Century', *The American Historical Review* 95 (1990), pp. 1423–51.

Schaeper, T., *The French Council of Commerce, 1700–1715: A Study of Mercantilism after Colbert*, Columbus: Ohio State University Press, 1983.

Schnakenbourg, É., *Entre la guerre et la paix. Neutralité et relations internationales, XVIIe–XVIIIe siècles*, Rennes: Presses universitaires de Rennes, 2013.

Schneider, Z., *The King's Bench: Bailiwick Magistrates and Local Governance in Normandy, 1670–1740*, Woodbridge: Boydell & Brewer, 2008.

Sempéré, J., 'La correspondance du consulat français de Barcelone (1679–1716). Informer comme un consul ou comme un marchand?', in Marzagalli, S. (ed.), *Les consuls en Méditerranée, agents d'information: XVIe–XXe siècle*, Paris: Éditions Classiques Garnier, 2015, pp. 121–40.

Shephard, J., 'The *Rôles d'Oléron*: A *lex mercatoria* of the Sea?', in Piergiovanni, V. (ed.), *From* lex mercatoria *to Commercial Law*, Berlin: Duncker & Humblot, 2005, pp. 207–53.

Shovlin, J., *The Political Economy of Virtue: Luxury, Patriotism, and the Origins of the French Revolution*, Ithaca, NY: Cornell University Press, 2006.

—— *Trading with the Enemy: Britain, France, and the 18th-Century Quest for a Peaceful World Order*, New Haven: Yale University Press, 2021.

Sicking, L. and Wijffels, A., 'Flotsam and Jetsam in the Historiography of Maritime Trade and Conflicts', in Sicking, L. and Wijffels, A. (eds), *Conflict Management in the Mediterranean and the Atlantic, 1000–1800. Actors, Institutions and Strategies of Dispute Settlement*, Leiden: Brill, 2020, pp. 1–18.

Smith, D., 'Structuring Politics in Early Eighteenth-Century France: The Political Innovations of the French Council of Commerce', *Journal of Modern History* 74 (2002), pp. 490–537.

Smith, W., 'The Function of Commercial Centers in the Modernization of European Capitalism: Amsterdam as an Information Exchange in the Seventeenth Century', *Journal of Economic History* 44 (1984), pp. 985–1005.

Snodgrass, M., *Coins and Currency: An Historical Encyclopedia*, Jefferson: McFarland & Company, 2019.

Soll, J., *The Information Master: Jean-Baptiste Colbert's Secret State Intelligence System*, Ann Arbor: University of Michigan Press, 2009.

Sonnino, P., 'Jean-Baptiste Colbert and the Origins of the Dutch War', *European Studies Review* 13 (1983), pp. 1–11.

—— *Louis XIV and the Origins of the Dutch War*, Cambridge: Cambridge University Press, 1988.

Spooner, F., *Risks at Sea: Amsterdam Insurance and Maritime Europe, 1766–1780*, Cambridge: Cambridge University Press, 1983.
Spufford, P., 'From Genoa to London: The Places of Insurance in Europe', in Leonard, A. (ed.), *Marine Insurance: Origins and Institutions, 1300–1850*, Basingstoke: Palgrave Macmillan, 2016, pp. 271–97.
Stapleton, J., 'The Blue-Water Dimension of King William's War: Amphibious Operations and Allied Strategy during the Nine Years' War, 1688–1697', in Trim, D. and Fissel, M. (eds), *Amphibious Warfare 1000–1700: Commerce, State Formation and European Expansion*, Leiden: Brill, 2005, pp. 315–56.
Steinberg, P., *The Social Construction of the Ocean*, Cambridge: Cambridge University Press, 2001.
Stern, P., 'Companies: Monopoly, Sovereignty, and the East Indies', in Stern, P. and Wennerlind, C. (eds), *Mercantilism Reimagined: Political Economy in Early Modern Britain and Its Empire*, Oxford: Oxford University Press, 2013, pp. 177–96.
—— *The Company-State: Corporate Sovereignty and the Early Modern Foundations of the British Empire in India*, Oxford: Oxford University Press, 2012.
Sternberg, G., *Status Interaction during the Reign of Louis XIV*, Oxford: Oxford University Press, 2014.
Symcox, G., *The Crisis of French Sea Power 1688–1697: From the* Guerre d'Escadre *to the* Guerre de Course, The Hague: Martinus Nijhoff, 1974.
Taillemitte, É., 'Colbert et la marine', in Mousnier, R. (ed.), *Un nouveau Colbert: actes du Colloque pour le tricentenaire de la mort de Colbert*, Paris: Editions SEDES/CDU, 1985, pp. 217–27.
Takeda, J., *Between Crown and Commerce: Marseille and the Early Modern Mediterranean*, Baltimore: Johns Hopkins University Press, 2011.
—— 'Silk, Calico and Immigration in Marseille. French Mercantilism and the Early Modern Mediterranean', in Isenmann, M. (ed.), *Merkantilismus: Wiedeaufnahme einer Debatte*, Stuttgart: Franz Steiner Verlag, 2014, pp. 241–63.
Talbott, S., *Conflict, Commerce and Franco-Scottish Relations, 1560–1713*, London: Pickering & Chatto, 2014.
—— '"Such Unjustifiable Practices"? Irish Trade, Settlement, and Society in France, 1688–1715', *Economic History Review* 67 (2014), pp. 556–77.
Tanguy, M., 'Un contrat nantais pour un voyage aux Antilles au XVIIe siècle', in Borde, C. and Roulet, É. (eds), *L'assurance maritime XIVe–XXIe siècle*, Aachen: Shaker Verlag, 2017.
Thomson, E., 'Commerce, Law, and Erudite Culture: The Mechanics of Théodore Godefroy's Service to Cardinal Richelieu', *Journal of the History of Ideas* 68 (2007), pp. 407–27.
Trivellato, F., '"Amphibious Power": The Law of Wreck, Maritime Customs, and Sovereignty in Richelieu's France', *Law and History Review* 33 (2015), pp. 915–44.
—— *The Promise and Peril of Credit: What a Forgotten Legend about Jews and Finance Tells Us about the Making of European Commercial Society*, Princeton: Princeton University Press, 2019.
—— 'Renaissance Florence and the Origins of Capitalism: A Business History Perspective', *Business History Review* 94 (2020), pp. 229–51.
—— '"Usages and Customs of the Sea": Étienne Cleirac and the Making of Maritime Law in Seventeenth-Century France', *The Legal History Review* 84 (2016), pp. 193–224.

Turgeon, L., 'Colbert et la pêche française à Terre Neuve', in Mousnier, R. (ed.), *Un nouveau Colbert: actes du Colloque pour le tricentenaire de la mort de Colbert*, Paris: Editions SEDES/CDU, 1985, pp. 255–68.
Ulbert, J., 'L'administration des consulats au sein du secrétariat d'État de la Marine (1669–1715)', in Ulbert, J. and Llinares, S. (eds), *La liasse et la plume. Les bureaux du secrétariat d'État de la Marine (1669–1792)*, Rennes: Presses universitaires de Rennes, 2017, pp. 73–86.
—— 'Les bureaux du secrétariat d'État de la Marine sous Louis XIV (1669–1715)', in Ulbert, J. and Llinares, S. (eds), *La liasse et la plume. Les bureaux du secrétariat d'État de la Marine (1669–1792)*, Rennes: Presses universitaires de Rennes, 2017, pp. 17–31.
—— 'La dépêche consulaire française et son acheminement en Méditerranée sous Louis XIV (1661–1715)', in Marzagalli, S. (ed.), *Les consuls en Méditerranée, agents d'information: XVIe–XXe siècle*, Paris: Éditions Classiques Garnier, 2015, pp. 31–57.
—— 'L'origine géographique des consuls français sous Louis XIV', *Cahiers de la Méditerranée* 98 (2019), pp. 11–27.
van der Cruysse, D., *Louis XIV et le Siam*, Paris: Fayard, 1991.
van Niekerk, J., *The Development of the Principles of Insurance Law in the Netherlands from 1500 to 1800*, vols I and II, Kenwyn: Juka & Co, 1998.
van Zanden, J., 'The "Revolt of the Early Modernists" and the "First Modern Economy": An Assessment', *Economic History Review* 55 (2002), pp. 619–41.
Vary, M., 'L'État et l'appropriation du littoral sous Louis XIV', in Le Bouëdec, G. (ed.), *L'Amirauté en Bretagne. Des origines à la fin du XVIIIe siècle*, Rennes: Presses universitaires de Rennes, 2012, pp. 377–88.
Venegoni, G., 'Creating a Caribbean Colony in the Long Seventeenth Century: Saint-Domingue and the Pirates', in Roper, L. (ed.), *The Torrid Zone: Caribbean Colonization and Cultural Interaction in the Long Seventeenth Century*, Columbia: University of South Carolina Press, 2018, pp. 132–46.
Verdier, N., 'Entre diffusion de la carte et affirmation des savoirs géographiques en France. Les paradoxes de la mise en place de la carte géographique au XVIIIe siècle', *L'Espace géographique* 44 (2015), pp. 38–56.
Vergé-Franceschi, M., *Colbert: La politique du bon sens*, Paris: Éditions Payot & Rivages, 2003.
Villiers, P., *Marine Royale, corsaires et trafic dans l'Atlantique de Louis XIV à Louis XVI*, Dunkirk: Société Dunkerquoise d'Histoire et d'Archéologie, 1991.
Waddell, B., 'The Economic Crisis of the 1690s in England', *The Historical Journal* (2022), pp. 1–22. doi:10.1017/S0018246X22000309
Wade, L., '"The Honour of Giving My Opinion": General Average, Insurance and the Compilation of the *Ordonnance de la marine* of 1681', in Fusaro, M., Addobbati, A., and Piccinno, L. (eds), *General Average and Risk Management in Medieval and Early Modern Maritime Business*, Basingstoke: Palgrave Macmillan, 2023, pp. 415–30.
—— 'Royal Companies, Risk Management and Sovereignty in Old Regime France', *English Historical Review*, (2023), pp. 1–32. doi:10.1093/ehr/cead107.
—— 'Underwriting Empire: Marine Insurance and Female Agency in the French Atlantic World', *Enterprise & Society* (2022), pp. 1–29. doi:10.1017/eso.2022.33

Wallerstein, I., 'Braudel on Capitalism, or Everything Upside Down', *The Journal of Modern History* 63 (1991), pp. 354–61.

Warlomont, R., 'Les sources néerlandaises de l'Ordonnance maritime de Colbert (1681)', *Revue belge de philologie et d'histoire* 33 (1955), pp. 333–44.

Weiss, G., *Captives and Corsairs: France and Slavery in the Early Modern Mediterranean*, Stanford: Stanford University Press, 2011.

Wennerlind, C., *Casualties of Credit: The English Financial Revolution, 1620–1720*, London: Harvard University Press, 2011.

—— 'Money: Hartlibian Political Economy and the New Culture of Credit', in Stern, P. and Wennerlind, C. (eds), *Mercantilism Reimagined: Political Economy in Early Modern Britain and Its Empire*, Oxford: Oxford University Press, 2013, pp. 74–93.

Wijffels, A., 'Introduction: Commercial Quarrels – and How (Not) to Handle Them', *Continuity and Change* 32 (2017), pp. 1–9.

Williamson, O., 'The Economics of Organization: The Transaction Cost Approach', *American Journal of Sociology* 87 (1981), pp. 548–77.

Wimmler, J., *The Sun King's Atlantic: Drugs, Demons and Dyestuffs in the Atlantic World, 1640–1730*, Leiden: Brill, 2017.

Wright, C. and Fayle, C., *A History of Lloyd's from the Founding of Lloyd's Coffee House to the Present Day*, London: Macmillan and Company, 1928.

Wright, R. and Kingston, C., 'Corporate Insurers in Antebellum America', *Business History Review* 86 (2012), pp. 447–76.

Wubs-Mrozewicz, J., 'Conflict Management and Interdisciplinary History: Presentation of a New Project and an Analytical Model', *The Low Countries Journal of Social and Economic History* 15 (2018), pp. 89–107.

Zanini, A., 'Financing and Risk in Genoese Maritime Trade during the Eighteenth Century: Strategies and Practices', in Fusaro, M., Addobbati, A., and Piccinno, L. (eds), *General Average and Risk Management in Medieval and Early Modern Maritime Business*, Basingstoke: Palgrave Macmillan, 2023, pp. 335–59.

Zwierlein, C., *Imperial Unknowns: The French and British in the Mediterranean, 1650–1750*, Cambridge: Cambridge University Press, 2016.

Zysberg, A., 'De Honfleur à Granville: bâtiments de commerce et de pêche au cours de la seconde moitié du XVIIe siècle', *Cahier des Annales de Normandie* 24 (1992), pp. 201–24.

—— 'Entre soumission et résistance: le système des classes et les levées des gens de mer en Provence et Languedoc pendant les guerres de Louis XIV (1672–1712)', in Daumalin, X., Faget, D., and Raveux, O. (eds), *La mer en partage. Sociétés littorales et économies maritimes XVIe–XXe siècle*, Aix-en-Provence: Presses universitaires de Provence, 2016, pp. 73–87.

—— 'La flotte de commerce et de pêche des ports normands en 1686 et 1786. Essai de comparaison', in Wauters, É. (ed.), *Les ports normands: un modèle?*, Mont-Saint-Aignan: Presses universitaires de Rouen et du Havre, 1999, pp. 97–116.

—— 'Les terre-neuvas honfleurs au temps du Roi-Soleil (1665–1685)', *Annales de Normandie* 68 année (2018), pp. 87–111.

UNPUBLISHED THESES

Dreijer, G., 'Maritime Averages and Normative Practice in the Southern Low Countries (15th–16th Centuries)', PhD thesis, University of Exeter/Vrije Universiteit Brussel (2021).
Heijmans, E., 'The Agency of Empire: Personal Connections and Individual Strategies in the Shaping of the French Early Modern Expansion (1686–1746)', PhD thesis, Leiden University (2018).
Hope, M., 'Underwriting Risk: Trade, War, Insurance, and Legal Institutions in Eighteenth-Century France and Its Empire', PhD thesis, Yale University (2023).

WEB-BASED SOURCES

Archives Monétaires.org [http://www.archivesmonetaires.org/inventaires/mp/F45.htm, accessed 1 October 2020].
Business Roundtable, 'Business Roundtable Redefines the Purpose of a Corporation to Promote "An Economy That Serves All Americans"' [https://www.business-roundtable.org/business-roundtable-redefines-the-purpose-of-a-corporation-to-promote-an-economy-that-serves-all-americans, accessed 21 May 2021].
CBG.fr, 'ASSURANCES La Chambre des assurances, Louis XIV 1671' [https://www.cgb.fr/assurances-la-chambre-des-assurances-louis-xiv-sup,v11_1114,a.html, accessed 1 March 2020].
iNumis, 'PARIS (VILLE DE), HENRY DE SANTEUL, PREMIER ÉCHEVIN, 1671' [https://www.inumis.com/shop/paris-ville-de-henry-de-santeul-premier-echevin-1671-1003786/, accessed 12 February 2020].
Jetons-Médailles Fréderic Boyer, 'Jeton Louis XIV chambre des assurances s.d.' [https://www.jetons-medailles.com/fr/louis-xiv/260-jeton-louis-xiv-chambre-des-assurances-sd.html, accessed 1 March 2020].

INDEX

NB places and names discussed in the main text are covered in this index; places and names given in tables alone are not (excepting the members of the Royal Insurance Company). A † indicates an individual/underwriting entity in the Royal Insurance Chamber whose portfolio is outlined in the online appendices.

Abbeville   137, 171, 294
absolutism
   as collaboration (and critique
      thereof)   11–15, 323
   as risk management   4, 26, 322–3
   as understood within
      neo-institutionalism (and
      critique thereof)   4–11, 322–3
Acadia   116
Aceré des Forges, Paul   258, 260–1, 264,
   266–8, 269–70, 273, 279
affaires extraordinaires   31
aides   31
Alaire du Beignon, M.   124
Aldán   253
Aleppo   114
Alexandria, Virginia   40–1
Alicante   137, 294
Altona   191–3
Amsterdam   2, 3, 15–19, 22, 23, 26, 29,
   38, 40, 41, 46, 80–1, 87, 90–1,
   111, 114, 120, 122, 127, 131, 137,
   149, 163–4, 176, 197–8, 212, 304,
   308, 309, 310, 311, 312, 314–15,
   317–18, 319, 323
   insurance law in   218–19, 234
   Kamer van Assurantie en Averij
      of   17–18, 81, 277, 312, 318
   Ordinancie of   218
   Schepenbank of   17
Anderson, Perry   11
Antwerp   3, 16, 17, 19, 80, 131–2, 137,
   145, 163, 212, 218–19, 221, 234

Apoil, Gabriel   181
arbitration
   versus litigation in legal
      scholarship   244
   see also Royal Insurance Chamber,
      Royal Insurance Company
Arnoul, M. (intendant in La Rochelle)   78
Arnoul, M. (intendant in Rochefort)   104
Arnoul, Pierre   94
assemblées de redaction   207–8
asymmetric bimetallic ratios   39–40
Aubert, Jean-Baptiste   112, 113, 114,
   119, 121
Aubry, Guillaume   52
augmentations de gages see under venal
   officeholding

Bar, Guillaume   51, 65, 68, 69, 70, 72,
   170
Barbados   144
Barbour, Violet   18, 22–3, 41 n.58, 277
Baroy, Mathurin   65, 72
Bart, Jean   192
Bastere, Pierre   137
Battle of Barfleur (1692)   196
Battle of Beachy Head (1690)   181, 187,
   189–90, 201
Battle of La Hougue (1692)   196
Battle of Solebay (1672)   147
Battle of the Boyne (1690)   187
Bayonne   78, 79, 81–2, 84, 108, 137, 143,
   148, 150, 154, 156, 175, 176, 209,
   253, 258, 261–4

347

Beguin, Charles 52
Beik, William 11, 13, 323
Bellavoine, Pierre 71
Bellinzani, Francesco† 30, 48, 50, 51, 53–4, 55, 57. 63, 87, 97–8, 100, 113, 124, 145–6, 217, 249, 278, 280, 311
Benson, Georges 51
Beothuk people 148–9
Bernard, Esteben 267
Bernier, M. 51
Bernier, Martin 268
Berthelot, François 155–6
Bie, Guillaume de† 51, 53, 159, 160–1
Bien, David 87
Bigot, Louis 258, 262, 268
Bilbao 111, 114, 143, 148, 169, 212, 295
Bogatyreva, Anastasia 34, 35
Boietet, Robert 51
Boirat, Simon† 51, 161 n. 64, 262, 269
Boiteux, Louis-Augustin 23, 35–6, 37 n.38, 41, 132, 138–9, 141, 164, 171, 200, 243, 245, 252, 257, 272, 277, 279, 312, 314
Bordeaux 78, 79, 108, 137, 138, 143, 148, 150, 154, 160, 169, 175, 176, 187, 209, 213, 254, 255, 258, 262, 264, 268, 298, 303, 315
   proposed insurance chamber in 57, 241
Boreel, Willem 41, 43
Bosher, J. F. 22, 32
bottomry *see under* sea loans (*prêts à la grosse aventure*)
Boullard, Pierre 268
Boulle, Pierre 10
Bourbon, Louis-Alexandre, comte de Toulouse 231–2
Braudel, Fernand 23 n.91, 29, 309, 323
Breen, Michael 12, 13, 245
Brest 171, 196
Bruges 17, 80, 138, 191
Bruneau, Mathurin, widow of 298
Brunet, Jean-Baptiste 155–6
Bruslé, M. 294
Bubble Act (1720) 20–1, 22
Buenos Aires 144, 160, 286
Business Roundtable 199

Cadelan, Pierre 52, 161 n.65, 255, 263, 269
Cádiz 40, 113, 131, 138, 143–4, 148, 156, 160, 169
Cagliari 264

Calais 82, 138, 192, 196, 212–13
Canary Islands 137
canon law 208
Cape of Good Hope 39, 110 n.93, 169, 198
Cape St Vincent 256
Cape Verde 169
capitation 75 n.76, 324
Cartagena 144, 256
Catalan, Pierre 111, 113
Catherinot, Nicolas 207
Caux, Charles de 192 n.94, 292, 293
Cayenne 116, 169, 180
Céberet du Boullay, Claude 66, 67, 68, 110
Chabert, Pierre 111, 114, 304
Chalmette, Jean-François 71
Chanlatte, Nicolas 51, 256
Charles V, king of France 210
Charles XI, king of Sweden 137
Charon, Charles 71
Charpentier, François 275
Charpentier, M. 93
Chaulnes, duc de 148
Chauvin, M. 65
Chauvin, Pierre 66, 70
chicanery 120, 241, 242 n.3, 276, 280, 287, 301
Christian V, king of Denmark 191
Ciboure 82, 84, 138, 150
cinq grosses fermes 60
Claessen, Nicolas 297
Clairambault, Nicolas 102–3, 106, 108, 111, 116, 117–18, 126
Clark, Henry 44
Clark, John 22
Cleirac, Étienne 37, 209, 210–11, 216
Clerville, Louis Nicolas de 35–46, 49, 299, 310
cod fishing 149
Code Napoléon (1804) 238
coffeehouses 20
Colbert, Jean-Baptiste 1–2, 3, 9, 10, 24, 25, 29–30, 32–5, 39–54, 56–7, 59, 60–2, 63–4, 69, 73, 75–6, 80, 84, 86–7, 94–100, 102, 105, 113, 115, 124, 137, 144, 145–6, 150, 155–6, 160–2, 163–5, 177, 188, 194, 211, 212, 215–16, 223, 231–2, 238–9, 241–2, 245, 246, 248, 258, 271, 274, 275–8, 279–80, 300, 301, 305, 307, 309–11, 312, 313, 318, 319, 324
   and bullionism 39–40, 46, 80

commercial policy of   10, 29–57, 59, 73, 76, 163, 211, 310
fiscal reforms of   30, 33–4
information network of   94–8
interest in/criticism of the Dutch of   29, 40–6
Testament Politique of   40
see also Royal Insurance Chamber, Monopoly company project (1664), proposed insurance chamber in *under* Bordeaux, proposed insurance chamber in *under* Marseille, *Ordonnance civile* (1667), *Ordonnance criminelle* (1670), *Ordonnance de la marine* (1681), *Ordonnance sur le commerce* (1673), *Ordonnance sur les eaux et forêts* (1669)
Colbert, Jean-Baptiste Antoine, marquis de Seignelay   3, 24, 30, 35, 57, 59, 62, 63, 64, 65–6, 68–9, 70, 73, 75, 76–84, 86–7, 100–6, 108, 109, 110 n.93, 111, 112, 113, 114, 116, 117–19, 120–1, 122–3, 124, 126, 169, 175–8, 181, 182, 186, 187, 189, 195, 197, 199, 200, 232, 241, 286–9, 298–9, 300, 307, 313, 314, 315–16, 317, 319, 321
  and bullionism   80
  and conflict with the Phélypeaux clan   126, 300, 317
  and naval policy   177–8, 181, 182, 187
  and privateering   195
  commercial policy of   10, 57, 59–87, 103, 168, 185, 199, 200, 288, 313–17
  criticism of the Dutch of   315
  see also Royal Insurance Company, French navy, French East India Company (*Compagnie des Indes orientales*, CIO), French Guinea Company (*Compagnie du Guinée*), French Mediterranean Compagnie (*Compagnie de la mer Méditerranée*)
Cole, Charles Woolsey   59, 144, 313
Collins, James   12, 13
commission agents (*commissionaires*)   50, 72, 93, 119, 163, 170–1, 213–14, 235, 265–6, 310
Common law   19, 22

Company of General Farmers†   155–8, 160, 161 n.65
consulates *see* administration of consulates *under* secretariat of state for maritime affairs (*secrétariat d'état de la marine*)
Copenhagen   17, 191
Cordes, Albrecht   266, 297
Cotolendy, François   98, 112, 113–14
Cotrugli, Benedetto   162
Council of Commerce (*Conseil de commerce*)   300–1, 305–6, 307, 317
Courten Association   6
Courtesia, Nicolas   51
Cousinet, Hierôme   65
Couvorden, M.   52
credible commitment
  as understood within neo-institutionalism   4–8, 199, 320–1
  solution to it through French system of privilege   321, 323
Crommelin, M.   161
Cromwell, Oliver   6–7
Crothers, A. Glenn   40–1
Crouzet, M.   51

d'Aubigné, Françoise, marquise de Maintenon   66
d'Avaux, comte   184
d'Oppède, M.   47
Darnell, Benjamin   194
Davenant, Charles   36
Day, Denis   51
Dee, Darryl   12–14
Defoe, Daniel   162
Dekessel, Jacques   52
Demeuves, Étienne   66, 67, 72, 191
Demoura, Antoine   295, 296
Demoura, Jacques Martins   295, 296
Denière, M.G.   71
Denis, Daniel   303–5
Denison, Pierre   51, 248
Deresne, M.   51
Desanteul, Henri†   46, 50, 51, 52, 55–6, 152, 154, 161 n.63, 256, 259–63, 264–5, 266, 267, 268, 273, 280, 312
Desanteul, Hugues   154
Desanteul, Nicolas   170, 297
Desanteul, Pierre†   51, 161 n.63, 259, 263, 264 n.80

Desjardins, Arthur 217
Desmaretz, Nicolas 61
Desmartins, Antoine 46, 50, 51
Dessert, Daniel 9
Desvieux, Louis 65, 68, 72
Desvieux, M. 52
Dhariet, Pierre 258, 261–2, 266
Dieppe 82, 124, 138, 169, 171, 194, 196, 254, 315
Dijon 12
dixième 324
Dolonne, Nicolas 254
Domaine d'Occident 66, 116
Dorigny, M.† 51, 217 n.65
droit de Committimus 71
droit de restorne 254, 293, 394
du Casse, Jean-Baptiste 116, 183
du Gué de Bagnols, M. 118
Dublin 138, 169, 186, 187
Ducamp, Jean 170–1
Dulivier, Leon 84, 85
Dulivier, Louis 84, 85
Dumont, Jean† 52, 161 n.64
Dunkirk 66, 77–9, 79–80, 83, 84, 120, 138, 169, 175–6, 194, 196, 254, 292–3, 300, 304, 306, 315
Dupré, Sieur 255
Durand, Pierre 303–4
Dusault, Denis (underwriter) 51
Dusault, Denis 189
Dutch East India Company (VOC) 5, 6, 7–8, 43, 145, 164, 199, 318, 321
Dutch War (1672–78) 23, 26, 34, 48, 61, 98, 100, 132, 145, 165, 194, 215, 238, 241, 257, 292
Dutch West India Company (WIC) 8

Émérigon, Balthazard-Marie 216–17
England/Britain
  and its economic divergence from rest of Europe 2, 323–4
  Board of Admiralty of 22
  Parliament of 4, 7, 197, 298
  Privy Council of 19
  see also London
English East India Company (EIC) 5–7, 8, 36, 199, 318, 321
English Muscovy Company 6
Eon de la Villebague, Julien 108, 109
Eon, Jean 42
European world-economy 2–3, 323–4
exclusive system (*exclusif*) 117, 144, 192 n.90, 285–9

Fabre, Joseph 108, 109, 110
Fabre, Louis-Marseille 112, 113
Fayle, C. Ernest 20–1, 197
financiers 25, 30–3, 56, 59, 60, 62, 63, 69, 76, 110, 115, 200, 301
  definition of 31
Flandrin, André 295–6
Flekkerøy 191, 192
Florence 131, 138, 318
Formont, Pierre† 52–3, 92, 161 n.64, 254–5
Forne, Jean-Baptiste 51, 161, 261, 263–4
Fouquet, Nicolas 32–3
Franche-Comté 12–13
Fredian, Jean Andre 224, 230
Frémont, Nicolas de 155
French *Compagnie du Bastion de France* 67, 110, 156
French East India Company (*Compagnie des Indes orientales*, CIO) 9, 13, 41, 43–6, 56, 63–4, 66, 67, 68, 72, 75, 86, 110, 164–5, 169, 198, 275, 307, 313, 317, 321
  and the *paulette* 45
  Royal Insurance Company membership as a path to directorship of 68–9
French exceptionalism 1–2, 42–3
French Guiana 169, 180, 183
French Guinea Company (*Compagnie du Guinée*) 63–4, 66, 67, 68, 86
French Mediterranean Compagnie (*Compagnie de la mer Méditerranée*) 66–7, 109, 110, 120, 224
French navy 95, 147, 177, 180–1, 182, 187, 190, 194–5, 196, 200, 308, 316, 321, 324
French Northern Company (*Compagnie du Nord*) 52, 53 n.111, 63, 66, 165
French Revolutionary Wars (1792–1802) 22
French Senegal Company (*Compagnie du Sénégal*) 63, 183
French Wars of Religion (1562–98) 1, 208
French West India Company (*Compagnie des Indes occidentales*) 45, 53, 63, 116–17, 156, 248 n.27,
Froment, Louis† 52, 92, 161 n.63
Frondes (1648–53) 1, 215, 238

gabelles 31
gages see under venal officeholding
Gaillard, Nicolas 65
Galway 138, 186, 187
Gaumont, Anthoine de 268
Gdansk 138, 191
Gelderblom, Oscar 318
Gellée, Jean 170-1
general average 17, 206, 217-22, 228, 237-8
   insurer liability for 206, 212, 221, 227 n.95
   Ordonnance de la marine's novel understanding of 226-9
   shipmaster liability in relation to 228 n.97
   see also jettison
general farmers 31, 66
   underwriting of *see* Company of General Farmers
Genoa 3, 113, 114, 119, 131, 137, 144
Gler, Jean, widow of 270
Glorious Revolution (1688) 4, 7, 8, 61, 184, 320
Glückstadt 191, 192
Goa 169
Go, Sabine 16-17, 18
Godefroy, Théodore 210-11, 216
Gomont, Antoine de 51
Goualt, Jean-Baptiste 69
Grafe, Regina 318
Grand Alliance (1686) 61
Granville 137, 196
Greenland 132, 136, 148, 150-1, 152, 156, 158, 160, 266, 311
Greif, Avner 15, 25
Grilleau, M. 108, 121
Grinberg, Martine 207
Grotius, Hugo 43
Guadeloupe 115, 145
Guernsey 182
guerre d'escadre 13, 194, 201
guerre de course 194, 316
Guidon de la mer 37, 206, 209-10, 212, 213, 214, 217, 218-19, 221, 224, 226, 227-8, 230, 234, 254, 293, 310
Guinea 169

Hallé, Guillaume† 52, 161 n.64, 259, 262
Hallé, Jean 71
Hamburg 17, 137, 191-2, 213

Hamilton, Thomas 137
Harris, Ron 5-8, 65, 199, 320-1
Haudrère, Philippe 9
Havana 144
Haveman, Peter 237
Haye, M. de la 164
Hazon, Louis Michel 170
Hébert, Guillaume André† 66, 67, 68, 69, 72, 161 n.65, 170
Heijmans, Elisabeth 9, 51, 67, 75, 86, 110
Hélissant, Elisabeth† 154-5, 161 n.64, 259, 261, 263, 264-5, 266, 268, 273
Hendaye 82
Henriquez, Juan 131, 132
Herbant, Jean 292, 293
Herinx, M. 51
Herlan, Henri 268
Héron, Pierre 66, 70, 72, 191
histoire totale 3
Hoffman, Philip 54, 162, 310, 319
Höhn, Philipp 266, 297
Honduras 144
Honfleur 137, 171, 182
Hope, Mallory 23 n.89, 131-2, 274 n.126
Horace 246
Horn, Jeff 10, 306
Hull 191
Hundred Years' War (1337-1453) 207
Hurt, John 12

Île-d'Yeu 181
Île-Tudy 295-6
information asymmetries 17, 89-93, 124, 162, 219, 241, 294, 310, 318
information state 92, 124
institutions
   and the insurance triangle *see* insurance triangle
   definition of 15
insurance policies
   disputes on *see* Royal Insurance Chamber, Royal Insurance Company, Paris
   risks covered by 223-31
   war augmentation clauses in 146-7
   see also marine insurance, Royal Insurance Chamber, Royal Insurance Company, Paris
insurance triangle 16, 17, 22, 24, 50, 309, 312, 317, 319

Inventaire général des vaisseaux (1664)   99
Irson, Claude   277–8, 307
Isenmann, Moritz   42, 306
Isles of Scilly   195
ius civile   207–9
ius commune   207
ius gentium   42, 46, 209

Jagault, Étienne   63, 64, 72, 233, 235–6, 297, 298 n.56
Jamaica   144
James II, king of England   61, 184, 185, 187, 200, 316
Jansen, Jean   224
jettison   206, 219 n.73, 225, 237, 255
John, Richard   199
Jouan, Isaac Pierre   161, 261, 263–4
Jousse, Anne†   161 n.63, 213, 214, 253, 259
Julien, M.   111, 114

Kaiser, Wolfgang   137
Kessler, Amalia   70, 162, 243, 271
Kingston, Christopher   21, 175
Kinsale   185, 186, 187
Kopervik   303, 304

La Rochelle   66, 78, 79, 105, 108, 114, 124, 131, 137, 143, 148, 150, 154, 169, 175, 176, 181, 192, 198, 262, 264, 297, 315
La Tremblade   212, 303
Lagny, Jean-Baptiste de   65, 66–7, 68, 70, 77, 81–2, 84, 100–14, 116–26, 175, 182–3, 185, 186, 190–1, 193, 198, 200, 223, 285–6, 299–300, 303, 305, 307, 314–15, 316, 317
  information resources of   100–18, 175
    involvement in compilation of the *Rolle général des bastimens*   103–8
  involvement in the establishment of the Royal Insurance Company   101–2
  responsibilities of   102–24, 185–7, 190–3
    involvement in administration of French East India Company   66–7, 110
    involvement in colonial governance   116–18

Lalive, Christophe   55, 63, 163, 252, 268–9, 275, 278, 280
Lallier, Alexandre   170, 292, 293, 298 n.56
Lane, Frederic   321
Lasson, Catherine de   262, 264, 273
'league-and-a-half per hour' rule   292–6
Lebrun, Charles   65, 70, 74
Lebrun, Claude   65
Le Couteux, M.   52
Leers, Jean Mathieu   190–1
Lefebvre, Elisabeth†   161 n.64, 261, 263
Lefebvre, François†   51, 161 n.63, 260–3, 268, 269, 270
Lefebvre, Phillippes   65, 68, 69
Legendre, Thomas   108, 109, 192–3, 298–9
legitimacy of prizes   188–9
Le Havre   138, 143, 148, 150, 154, 169, 181, 183, 192–3, 196, 212–13, 253, 293, 294, 315
Le Jariel, Mathurin   65
lemons problem   21, 91 n.12
Lenfant, Étienne†   52, 161 n.65
Le Noir, Pierre   71
Leonard, Adrian   21
Le Peletier, Claude   61
Le Roux, Jean   47, 95
Lescouteux, Antoine   170
Lescouteux, Jacques   170
Le Tellier, François-Michel, marquis de Louvois   10
Leval Le Fer, Sieur   77, 81
Le Vasseur, Charles   304
Levillain, Charles-Édouard   61
Levy, Claude-Frederic   305
Lhuillier de Creabé, Charles†   46, 50, 51, 161 n.63, 259–63, 268
Lillieroot, Nils   237–8
Limerick   169, 186, 187
Lisbon   112, 138, 143, 148, 169, 253, 255, 292
Lisle, Oudard Thomas de†   52, 65, 68, 161 n.65, 260–1
Livorno   98, 113–14, 148, 263–4
Lloyd's coffeehouse/Lloyd's of London
  and its arrangement with the Post Office   21
  and *Lloyd's List*   91, 127, 314
  and *Lloyd's Register*   108, 127, 314
  and the Royal Navy   21–2, 308, 321
  and the Smyrna convoy disaster (1693)   197, 201

information flows in 20–1, 90–1
origins of 20, 90–1
rise to supremacy of 20–2
loi de dérogeance 75–6
London
  Admiralty 19
  Aldermen's Court 19
  Chancery 19
  Court of Assurance 19
  Insurance code 19
  King's Bench 19
  Office of Assurances at the Royal Exchange 19
  Royal Exchange 19–20, 197 n.111
London Assurance 20
Londonderry 185, 186, 187
Loquette, Pierre 298
Louis XIII, king of France 1, 53, 208, 216, 246
Louis XIV, king of France 1, 2, 5, 10, 11, 12, 13, 14, 15, 25, 32, 34, 35, 42, 53, 59, 60–1, 66, 78–9, 80, 95, 96–7, 101, 145, 164, 181, 184, 190, 201, 205, 215, 238, 239, 246–8, 284, 307, 309, 313, 316, 319–21, 323
  and universal monarchy 42
  interests of 60–1, 145, 164, 184, 205, 239
  representation of 246–8, 284
  see also Royal Insurance Chamber, Royal Insurance Company, French navy, Colbert, Jean-Baptiste, Colbert, Jean-Baptiste Antoine, marquis de Seignelay, Lagny, Jean-Baptiste de
Louvois *see* Le Tellier, François-Michel, marquis de Louvois
Lubert, Louis de 65, 67, 68

Macé, M. 107
Madame de Maintenon *see* d'Aubigné, Françoise, marquise de Maintenon
Madame de Montespan *see* Rochechouart, Françoise-Athénaïs de, marquise de Montespan
Madeira 112, 137, 138, 255, 292
Magon de la Lande, Jean 84 n.112, 108, 109, 144, 186, 285–9, 307
Magon, Nicolas 298

Magy, Augustin 109, 110, 120–1, 168, 223–4, 230
Maillard, Florentin 71
Maillet, M. (consul to the French nation in Chania) 113
Maillet, M.† (member of the Chamber) 51, 161 n.65
Maillet, Nicolas† 51, 161 n.64, 260–1
Marcadé, Siméon 71
Marchand, M.† 52, 263
Marchand, Mathieu 262, 268
Marchand, Louis 262
Margas, Étienne† 52, 161 n.65
marine insurance
  anti-Semitic legend on the origins of 22–3, 242
  as a bellwether for economic transformation 2–3
  origins of 2–3
  over-insurance in 234
  see also insurance policies, *droit de restorne*, insurance triangle, Royal Insurance Chamber, Royal Insurance Company, Lloyd's coffeehouse/Lloyd's of London, 'league-and-a-half per hour' rule
Marre, Guillaume de la† 51, 161 n.64
Marseille 12, 79, 104–5, 107–8, 109, 110, 120–1, 131–2, 138, 148, 168, 171, 175, 224–5, 237, 254, 274 n.126
  chambre de commerce of 96 n.30, 100
  proposed insurance chamber in 47, 57
Martinique 115, 145, 169
Mary II, queen of England 61
Mathieu, Rémi 138
Maurice, Marguerite 74
Mayer, Joachin 303, 304
Mazarin, Jules 1, 53, 215
Ménard-Jacob, Marie 9
Mercier, Charles 237
Mi'kmaq people 148–9
Miannay, sieur de 294
Michael I, tsar of Russia 6
Michel, M. 114
Mignot, Gilles† 51, 152–5, 160, 161 n.63, 260–1, 268, 269, 311
Milgrom, Paul 244
Minard, Philippe 124
Mishra, Rupali 6
Mokyr, Joel 319
Mollien, Gerard 65, 170

Monbeton de Brouillon, Jacques-François de 181
monopoly company project (1664) 29, 34–46, 49, 56, 76, 122
Montesquieu *see* Secondat, Charles Louis de, baron de La Brède et de Montesquieu
Moral hazard 91, 214, 241, 294, 318–19, 322
Moreau, François Launay de 52, 258, 259–60, 264, 265–6, 267–8, 269, 273, 279, 285–6
Morel de Boistiroux, Marius-Basile 100–1
Moret, M. 51
Morineau, Michel 103–4
Morisse, Philippe 51

Nantes 78, 79, 107, 108, 109, 121, 138, 143, 150, 169, 175, 176, 190, 192, 194, 212, 232, 298, 315
Navigation Acts 145, 320
navy *see* French navy, Royal Navy
neo-institutionalism *see* as understood within neo-institutionalism *under* credible commitment, North, Douglas, Weingast, Barry, Greif, Avner
Netherlands
  and its economic divergence from rest of Europe 2
  Estates General of 7–8, 41, 43, 189
  see also Amsterdam
neutral shipping 188–93, 200–1, 316
Newfoundland 105–6, 107, 132, 136, 145, 148–51, 152, 154, 156, 158, 160, 169, 172, 180–2, 183, 198, 256, 266, 311
Niceron, Antoine 70–1
Nieuwpoort 191
Nine Years' War (1688–97) 5, 13, 23, 26, 61–2, 116, 168, 201, 236, 292, 300, 305, 316, 321, 324
Nogaret de La Valette, Jean-Louis, duc d'Épernon 209
North, Douglass 4–6, 10, 15, 25, 244, 320–1, 323
Nouel, M. 111, 114
Nzwani 169

O'Brien, Patrick 320
Ogilvie, Sheilagh 250
Olivier-Martin, François 222

Ordinances of Barcelona (1484) 19
Ordinancie of Amsterdam 218
Ordonnance civile (1667) 216, 271
Ordonnance criminelle (1670) 216
Ordonnance de la marine (1681) 26, 54, 64, 76, 77, 80, 82, 83, 105, 205–7, 214–40, 245, 252, 254, 274–5, 283, 289–90, 291, 292, 293, 297, 304, 307, 311, 316
  and averages *see* general average, particular average
  and handling of arbitration 274–5, 283, 289–90, 291, 292, 297
  and Royal Insurance Chamber's influence on 205–6, 214–22
  compilation of 214–22
  Royal Insurance Company's role in promotion of 205–6, 222–32
Ordonnance of Montils-les-Tours (1454) 207
Ordonnance sur le commerce (1673) 54, 216, 238
  jurisdictional crisis created by 258, 269–71, 279, 312
Ordonnance sur les eaux et forêts (1669) 216

Pages, Theodore 198
Paignon, Gilbert 65, 70
Parasol, Julien 253
Parat, Antoine 181
Paris
  admiralty court of *see* Parisian admiralty court
  merchant court of 69–72, 162, 243, 245, 248, 258, 265, 267, 268–70, 271, 279, 283, 312, 313
  merchant guilds of 70, 71
  parlement of 73, 101, 271, 291
Parisian admiralty court 24, 55, 72, 74, 139, 191, 245, 258–75, 277, 279–81, 283, 289–91, 296–8, 301–5, 307, 312, 316–17
  and its handling of disputes involving the Royal Insurance Company 296–8, 301–5, 316–17
  and jurisdictional conflict with merchant court (1673) 245, 258, 269–70, 279, 312
  and the transformation of its role post-1681 283, 289–90, 296–7, 306–7, 316

introduction of summary procedure (1673) in   245, 270–4, 279, 312
particular average   206, 227, 238, 255–7, 295–6
   shipmaster liability in relation to   228 n. 97
Pasaia   143, 148
Pasquier, Jean   65, 72
Patoulet, M.   77, 78, 79, 120
Pelletier, Antoine   65, 69, 72, 170
Perillié, M.   112, 114
Pertrus, Jeanne   298
Petit, André†   46, 50, 51, 152, 161 n.63, 259–63
Petit, Jacques†   51, 161 n.64
Phélypeaux, Jérôme, comte de Pontchartrain (Pontchartrain *fils*)   89–90, 91–2, 100, 125, 126, 300, 301, 303, 305, 307
   and conflict with the Colbert clan   126, 300, 317
   argument of regarding the Royal Insurance Company's information resources   89–90, 91–2, 100, 125, 126, 303
   role of in the smear campaign against the Royal Insurance Company   300, 301, 303, 305, 307
Phélypeaux, Louis, comte de Pontchartrain (Pontchartrain *père*)   89, 102, 117–18, 126, 182–3, 197, 200, 298–300, 307, 313, 317
   and conflict with the Colbert clan   126, 300, 317
   lack of support for the Royal Insurance Company of   298–300, 317
Piécourt, Noé   300–1, 303–6, 307, 317
Pilgrim, Donald   189
Placentia   148, 150, 181
Plessis, Armand Jean du, duke of Richelieu   1, 53, 209, 210–11, 214–15, 216

Plymouth   137, 182, 195
Pocquelin, M.   51, 270
Pocquelin, Philippe   151, 259
Pocquelin, Pierre   66, 68, 72
Pocquelin, Robert   51
Pollart, Jacques   155–6
Pondicherry   110
Pontchartrain *fils see* Phélypeaux, Jérôme, comte de Pontchartrain

Pontchartrain *père see* Phélypeaux, Louis, comte de Pontchartrain
Porte, Mathieu de la   231, 239
Postel-Vinay, Gilles   54, 162, 310, 319
Potier de Novion, Nicolas   101
Potter, Mark   74
public good (*bien public*)   36, 78, 80, 82–4, 86, 199–200, 299, 315

Québec   116, 169
Quimper   295–6

Rabier, Saluy
Ratier, Jacques   298
Rebillé, Bonnaventure†   52, 161 n.64, 259, 262
Regnault, M.   51, 83
Renard, Esteben de   267
rentes (perpétuelles) on the *Hôtel de Ville* of Paris   31, 33–4, 52, 54, 60, 61–2, 165, 170, 310
rentiers   30–2, 46, 53, 62
respondentia see under sea loans (*prêts à la grosse aventure*)
Revellois, Adrien   71
Rey, Jacques†   46, 50, 51, 152, 161 n.63, 256, 259–61
Rhodian Sea Law   209
Ricard, Jean-Pierre   80–1
Richard, Jacques†   51, 161 n.64, 259
Richelieu *see* Plessis, Armand Jean du, duke of Richelieu
Richome, M.   107
Rivoire, Henry de la   66
Robelot, Pierre   55, 72, 270, 278
Rochechouart, Françoise-Athénais de, marquise de Montespan   66
Roche, Pierre de la   151, 259
Rôles d'Oléron   209–10, 217, 218, 219, 221
Rolle general des bastimens (1686)   79 n.89, 103–8, 125, 127, 314
Roman law   19
Roscoff   171
Rosenthal, Jean-Laurent   54, 162, 310, 319
Rossi, Guido   16, 19
Rothkrug, Lionel   305
Rouen   34–8, 41, 43, 45, 46, 76, 78, 79, 108, 109, 121, 132, 138, 143, 148, 169, 171, 175, 176, 192–3, 210, 212–14, 226, 237, 295, 299, 310, 315

Rousseau, Denis† 52, 65, 68, 69, 70, 72, 161 n.63, 261, 263, 268
Roussel, Jean 52, 161 n.63, 261
Roux, Claude de, chevalier de Saint-Laurent 116
Rouxelin, Étienne† 54, 161 n.64, 260–2, 270
Rowlands, Guy 60, 322, 323
Royal Exchange Assurance 20
Royal Insurance Chamber (*Chambre générale des assurances et grosses aventures*, 1668–86)
  arbitration in 250–8, 264–8, 272–5, 277, 279–81, 312
  as attempt to institutionalise the Parisian capital market 57, 132, 163, 310–11
  by-laws (1671) of 47–8, 52, 93, 98–100, 145, 246, 248–52
  compulsory arbitration (1673) in 245–6, 271–5, 277, 280–1, 307, 312
  dispute crisis (1673) of 257–81, 296, 307, 312, 316
  establishment of 46–57
  general assembly of 54, 92–4, 97–100, 212–13, 217, 248, 251–2, 256–7, 268
  information resources of 92–100, 145–6
  membership of 50–4
  registration monopoly (1673) of 48–9, 275
  religious activities of 250
  representation of 241–81
  rooms of, as envisioned in the by-laws 248–50
Royal Insurance Company (*Compagnie générale des assurances et grosses aventures*, 1686–c.1710)
  and arbitration 283, 289–96, 301–8
  articles of association (1686) of 64–5, 75, 101, 120, 167, 223, 232, 284
  de facto Atlantic monopoly of 76–81, 86, 168, 175–7 197–8, 315
  establishment of 100–2
  information resources of *see under* Lagny, Jean-Baptiste de
  letters patent (1686) of 35, 59, 64–5, 69–71, 74–6, 81, 84, 101–2, 119, 199–200, 222–3, 290–1, 315–16
  liquidity of 76, 119, 121–2, 315
  membership of 64–76
  membership of as form of quasi-venal office 86, 307, 313, 321
  Parisian monopoly of 68–9, 81
  rate of conflict of 301–3
  representation of 283–308
  shareholder liability in 65
Royal Navy (England/Britain) 21–2, 182, 188, 201, 308, 320, 321
Ruffat, Michèle 35

Saavedra, Francisco de 40
Sadoc, Anthoine 51
Sahlins, Peter 14
Saint Kitts 115, 116, 145
Saint-Domingue 116, 145, 169, 180, 181, 183, 297
Saint-Jean-de-Luz 81–2, 84, 138, 150, 262, 264, 273
Saint-Malo 77–8, 79, 107, 109, 123, 138, 149, 169, 171, 175–6, 184, 186, 194, 196, 213, 232, 259–60, 264, 265, 285, 286–8, 315
Salé 106, 109, 112, 114, 253, 255
San Sebastián 92, 143
San Thomé 164
Sanson, Guillaume 292–3
Sanson, Robert† 51, 152, 161 n.64, 262
Santiago de Compostela 294
São Miguel 292–3
Savary, Jacques
  and *Le parfait négociant* 52–3, 89, 125
  endorsement of the Royal Insurance Chamber 275–80, 307, 312
  involvement in dispute in the Royal Insurance Chamber over the *Ordonnance sur le commerce* 54
  involvement with the Royal Insurance Chamber in the compilation of the *Ordonnance de la marine* 217
Schaeper, Thomas 305–6
School of Salamanca 242
Scottish East India Company 6
sea loans (*prêts à la grosse aventure*) 64, 68, 81–4, 85, 86, 87, 99, 124, 133, 135–6, 149, 151, 163, 167–8, 170, 171, 172, 174, 176, 178, 179, 184, 186, 188, 193, 194, 198, 199, 212, 233, 234, 235, 251, 258, 264, 266, 267, 310, 316
  bottomry 136
  respondentia 133, 136

Second Siege of Vienna (1683)   61
Secondat, Charles Louis de, baron de La Brède et de Montesquieu   89–90
secretariat of state for maritime affairs (*secrétariat d'état de la marine*)   24–6, 53, 89, 92, 96–7, 102–27, 145–6, 175, 181, 186, 300 *see also* Lagny, Jean-Baptiste de, Clairambault, Nicolas
Seignelay *see* Colbert, Jean-Baptiste Antoine, marquis de Seignelay
Sève, M. de   160, 241
Shephard, James   210
'ship of state' motif   247–8
Smyrna convoy, capture of (1693)   197, 201
Soaves, Simon   237–8
Soll, Jacob   94, 102
Sorindho, Louis   137
Soto, Domingo de   242
Soullet, M.   65
Soullet, Nicolas   65, 100–1
sous-ferme du Canada   66
South Sea Company   20
Spanish silver fleet   144
Spooner, Frank   16–18, 163–4, 287
St John's   148–9
Stelle, M.   114
Suplegeau, Étienne   51, 161 n.64, 269
Surat   110
Symcox, Geoffrey   194

Takeda, Junko   12–13, 14
Tardif, Thomas   66, 68, 71, 72, 170
Tarin de Cussy, Pierre-Paul   116, 181, 183
Teignmouth   190
Tétouan   114
Thirty Years' War (1618–48)   1
Tortuga   116, 181, 183
traites   31, 66
Tranchepain, François   65, 72
transaction costs   5, 15, 25, 56, 91, 96, 122, 244, 319
Treaty of Aix-la-Chapelle (1668)   143
Treaty of Dover (1670)   61, 145
Treaty of Karlowitz (1699)   61
Treaty of the Pyrenees (1659)   215
Trivellato, Francesca   22, 208–9, 242

Tunis   112, 114, 230
Turgeon, Laurier   107

Ulbert, Jörg   126
Ulpian   211
universal monarchy   42
Us et coustumes de la mer see under Cleirac, Étienne

Valenty, Romul   52, 253
Valin, René-Josué   216–17
van Vayemberg, M.   52
Vangangelt, Gaspart   52
Vankessel, Mme   52
Vanopstal, Jean-Anthoine†   52, 161 n.63, 253, 259
Vaux, Henri de†   52, 161 n.64–5, 260–1, 263, 267
venal officeholding
    and *augmentations de gages*   32, 45, 62, 73
    and *gages*   32–3, 60, 62
    and the *paulette*   30, 32, 45, 74
Venice   131, 138, 148, 151, 154, 259
Veracruz   144
Vigault, Joseph de   294
Villeneuve, Balthazard-François de   205
Villiers, Patrick   190
Vinx, Alexandre†   51, 161 n.63, 260–1, 263
Vitry-la-Ville, Hugues Mathé de   65, 67, 68, 69, 74
Vivien, François, sieur de la Vicomté   287–8
Vlissingen   144, 182
Voulges, Guillaume de†   161 n.65, 270

War of Devolution (1667–68)   61
War of the Réunions (1683–84)   61
War of the Spanish Succession (1701–14)   61, 308
Waterrecht   218
Weingast, Barry   4–5, 244, 320
Weytsen, Quentin   219
William III (of Orange), king of England   7, 61, 184, 187, 189
Wright, Charles   20–1, 197

Zysberg, André   104

www.ingramcontent.com/pod-product-compliance
Lightning Source LLC
Chambersburg PA
CBHW052056300426
44117CB00013B/2143